GENTLEMEN & Players

GARDENERS *of the* ENGLISH LANDSCAPE

TIMOTHY MOW

7/0228619

SUTTON PUBLISHING

First published in the United Kingdom in 2000 by
Sutton Publishing Limited · Phoenix Mill
Thrupp · Stroud · Gloucestershire · GL5 2BU

British Library Cataloguing in Publication Data
A catalogue record for this book is available from the British Library.

ISBN 0-7509-2342-5

Endpapers: front: A Thomas Robins *capriccio* of the landscape at Davenport House, Shropshire, 1755 (Private Collection; photograph Bristol City Library); *back*: A view of Ingestre Hall from Robert Plot's 1686 *The Natural History of Stafford-shire* suggests how few landowners could afford, or be bothered, to maintain all the intricate parterres of a formal garden. Grass, statues and twin Jacobean garden buildings survive to be viewed from a terrace. Only two simple beds in a separate enclosure appear to have been kept up. A new fashion in economical garden design would inevitably replace these empty shells (University of Bristol, Special Collections).

Typeset in 10/13 pt Bembo.
Typesetting and origination by
Sutton Publishing Limited.
Printed and bound in England by
J.H. Haynes & Co. Ltd, Sparkford.

CONTENTS

For

Eleanor and Jessica

LIST OF PLATES

Between pp. 110 and 111

1a. Octagonal Temple at Hunstanton Hall, Norfolk
1b. Amphitheatre Garden at Chilworth, Surrey

2a. General view of Westbury Court, Gloucestershire
2b. The Urn of the Four Seasons, Melbourne Hall, Derbyshire

3a. The Exedra at Chiswick
3b. Long horned cattle at Rousham, Oxfordshire

4a. The Chinese House at Shugborough, Staffordshire
4b. The Sham Castle at Hagley, Worcestershire

5a. The Ruined Abbey at Painshill, Surrey
5b. Arched Grotto at Croome Park, Worcestershire

6a. The Grotto at Hawkshead, Shropshire
6b. The landscape at Blenheim, Oxfordshire

7a. Downton Castle, Herefordshire, in its landscape
7b. Plan for coach roads, Blaise Castle Park, Bristol

8a and b. Endsleigh, Devon, before and after, from Repton's *Fragments*

ACKNOWLEDGEMENTS

Any writing on garden history has to be the sum total, not just of sources studied, but of gardens experienced and of the opinion of friends with whom they have been enjoyed. Without the enthusiastic support and generous help of David Lambert, Conservation Officer of the Garden History Society, this book would never have been written. I first met David on the committee of the Avon Gardens Trust where, together with Stewart Harding, we fought, among other battles, for the preservation of Thomas Wright's landscape at Stoke Park. Stewart also gave me a memorable introduction to Repton's work in Avon at Oldbury Court, Brentry and Blaise Castle. From my Avon Gardens Trust committee time Peggy Stembridge and the late Bob Savage gave me many insights into Thomas Goldney's garden and grotto.

My first interest in garden history, as an extension to my professional discipline of architectural history, came on a visit back in the early 1980s to the overgrown and decayed garden at Painswick House in the high Cotswolds. Roger White, then Secretary of the Georgian Group, was my guide and his fascination with garden buildings led us to explore the remains of the Rococo layout there, to publish subsequently an article on the site and then to act as advisers on the committee set up to restore the lost garden. John Harris, the man who rediscovered or reinvented the 'Rococo Garden', was another prime mover in it all and I have enjoyed his ebullient company on many occasions since; his writings on garden history have always been a source of inspiration. Other Painswick enthusiasts to thank are Lord and Lady Dickinson, Paul Moir, Linden Huddleston, Nigel Temple and Paul Edwards.

Speaking on the gardens of the Puritan Commonwealth at an international conference in Washington DC in May 1992, I met John Dixon Hunt, Michael Leslie, Tom Williamson, Stephen Bann, Christopher Ridgway and Robert Williams, all of whom have advised me in my new ventures within the field of garden history. Tom Williamson's *Polite Landscapes* has been a prime reference during the writing of this study.

Several of my fellow lecturers at Robert Williams and Christopher Ridgway's York conference on John Vanbrugh's landscape design in July 1999 were most helpful with information and advice. I would like to thank Peter Goodchild, whose article on John Beale and Backbury informed my earlier research on seventeenth-century gardens, David Jacques, whose *Georgian Gardens: The Reign of Nature* is required reading for all my students, Judith Roberts, with whom I swapped anecdotes on Switzer, and Michael Symes, who has interesting views on the Lanes of Tisbury and the chronology of their grottoes.

A book on Palladian bridges and another, which I was commissioned to write by Tim Graham of Millstream Books on garden walks near Bath, were catalysts for this present study, so too were the sections on the gardens at Strawberry Hill and Fonthill that formed parts of my recent biographies of Horace Walpole and William Beckford. Another stimulus has been my undergraduate teaching and my supervision of postgraduates in the History of Art department at

Bristol where, with Michael Liversidge, my Co-Director, we have launched an MA in Garden History.

Many other friends and colleagues have helped me during the research for this book: Patrick Howard, Andrew Ballantyne, Mark Horton, John Phibbs, Patrick Taylor, Elisabeth Whittle, Kate Harris, Dianne Barre, Susan Gordon, Patricia van Diest and Peter Mitchell, John and Michie Herbert.

Hannah Lowery and Michael Richardson of Bristol University Library's Special Collections have been not simply helpful with primary texts, but positive in their suggestions of sources I had never considered. That is how a University Library should work. I owe Michael in particular a debt of gratitude for the illustrations which he brought out from the apparently inexhaustible resources of the stacks. Anthony Beeson at Bristol Public Library, David Eveleigh at Blaise Castle Museum, Anthony Mitchell at Prior Park and Stourhead, Jeffrey Haworth and Tom Oliver at Croome, and Kate Feluś at Stowe have all provided insights and advice.

Jeremy Glanville helped with computer setting, Gordon Kelsey and Ann Pethers produced many of the photographs, Reg and Maureen Barton collated the text and Douglas Matthews has prepared a thorough index. Jaqueline Mitchell and Clare Bishop have been highly professional, efficient editors and my agent, Sara Menguc, has been encouraging as ever.

I should like to thank my friend and usual co-author, Brian Earnshaw, for help with many aspects of the research and for his sensitive editing of the manuscript. My father, my son Adam, and my wife Sarah have joined me on many garden expeditions in a spirit of positive appreciation. My only regret is that our two little girls, to whom this book is dedicated, will never see the gardens and landscapes that we have enjoyed.

Timothy Mowl
Bristol
Spring 2000

Picture Credits

The author and publisher would like to thank the following for permission to reproduce pictures (page numbers are given):

Basingstoke Library: 78; The Bodleian Library, University of Oxford: 72–3; Bristol City Council: 184, 185, Plate 7b; University of Bristol, Special Collections: xiii, 7 (top), 13, 14, 17, 19 (top), 26, 28, 35, 37, 46, 49, 54, 55, 57, 58, 66, 68, 70 (top), 71, 84, 85, 87, 93, 94, 96, 99, 102, 110, 112, 126, 127, 130, 132, 133, 146, 149, 166, 168, 174, 177, 179, 188, 189, Plates 8a/b; British Museum: 97, 143; Christ Church College, Oxford, & Evelyn Trustees: 39, 41, 43; Courtauld Institute: 6, 172, 173; *Country Life*: 158; Croome Estate Trustees: 155; Brian Earnshaw: 61, 88, 91, 141, Plates 1a, 2b; Flintshire Record Office: 90; Lambeth Archives Department: 118; Richard Mullane: Plate 5a; Courtesy of the National Portrait Gallery, London: 1, 62, 105; Norfolk Record Office: 115; Private Collection: 138, 139; The Walker Art Gallery, Liverpool: 32, 109; The Provost and Fellows of Worcester College, Oxford: 7 (bottom).

Author: xi, 19 (bottom), 30, 31, 40, 59, 70 (bottom), 75, 76, 77, 111, 120, 122, 123, 140, 145, 147, 152, 153, 156, 157, 176, Plates 1b, 2a, 3a/b, 4a/b, 5b, 6a/b, 7a.

INTRODUCTION

This book should be read as an attempt to do horticultural justice to the English upper classes. More prosaically it aims to assess the relative contributions of the patrons – the 'Gentlemen' – and the professional gardeners – the 'Players' – to the shaping of the Arcadian garden-parks of England during the last half of the seventeenth and the whole span of the eighteenth century. For the benefit of non-cricketers may I explain that until 1962 there was every year at Lords an MCC fixture of the Gentlemen against the Players, which seemed to assume that the players, who were paid a salary, could not be gentlemen like the unpaid amateurs. Political correctness, along with other forces, did away with these matches, but I have borrowed the terms to tune in to the existing divisions of the English class system.

That still leaves the precise limits of the book – 1620 to 1820 – requiring an explanation as those dates include the entire magisterial unfolding of the formal garden layouts of the later Stuarts. These can only be considered Arcadian, on the very rare occasions when they have survived, by their accidental overgrowth. England's unique contribution to garden design was not formal at all but the gradual evolution from formalism to an ideal landscape of trees, water and hill slopes set about with garden buildings, predominantly classical and templar. This has never been forgotten or lost its hold on the national imagination through the subsequent Victorian 'Gardenesque' or the Edwardian 'Architectural' gardens of Edwin Lutyens and Gertrude Jekyll. Whatever the aesthetic merit of the formal gardens of the last half of the seventeenth century they were mere copies of French and Dutch originals, an interlude, a delaying tactic, politically inspired, in the natural growth of the Arcadias. Inigo Jones, the first native professional of the period under study, returned from the Continent in 1614; Samuel Hartlib arrived from Prussia advocating Puritan utilitarianism in 1628. That offers a compromise date of 1620 which fits neatly enough with 1820, four years after the death of the last uncertain Arcadian, Humphry Repton, by which time the Gardenesque of John Claudius Loudon was becoming fashionable.

Arcadian gardens were artistically of the first importance because they compressed classicism, with its columned and domed buildings, into a Romantic framework by placing those evocative temples within carefully staged refinements of the real, picturesque Nature. Then they added the occasional Chinese bridge to the composition or pinnacled folly tower, not in any correct scholarly Gothic, but in a cheerfully unauthentic 'Gothick' of ogee arches and toy battlements. This created fantasy landscapes with evocative clashes of style, images to which the great Romantic poets of the next generation would eagerly respond. Wordsworth fancied that he saw the smoke of a hermit's fire above Tintern Abbey, though it was only the fumes of a cannon foundry. The river that 'sank in tumult to a lifeless ocean' in Coleridge's *Kubla Khan* was a memory, gloriously enhanced, of Samuel Emes's remarkable 'cup and saucer' waterfall which the poet had seen in the grounds of Erddig Park, Denbighshire. That cascade did in fact serve to pump water noisily up to the house, hence 'as if this earth in fast thick pants were breathing'. Keats made puns about 'Attic shapes' and 'fair attitudes'. Shelley's landscapes in *Alastor* and

Epipsychidion are only Richard Payne Knight's much painted Teme gorge dramatised. Byron would even sacrifice his fortune and his life to liberate the real Attica.

This is what makes the role of the gentlemen so intriguing. The English are perhaps too close to their lords, too tied to the comic stereotypes of innumerable plays and films to judge them accurately. As a class of hereditary politicians the lords have been not simply masterly but inspired and benign. British democracy has been created over the four hundred years since the Dissolution of the Monasteries by the long, but brilliantly executed, retreat of the House of Lords: an episode of political sophistication and good sense unparalleled in Europe. Power was passed over to an unlimited electorate with singularly little revolution, violence or loss of national institutions. The abolition of hunting with dogs raises strong feelings, the abolition of an hereditary legislative body raises so little feeling that, at the start of the twenty-first century, almost a hundred hereditary peers, as many as existed in Cromwell's time, are still securely in position, while a Socialist government continues to create hundreds, not of senators, deputies or people's representatives, but of 'lords' with their traditional territorial ties, as 'of Putney', 'of Handsworth' or 'of Penge'. The title is still seen as honourable by its class opposites.

Parallel with this political process the English landscape park was created not by any retreat of the lords and gentlemen, but by their brazen advance into the expertise of the professionals, or players. The following chapters will consider which party was conservative and which was daringly experimental, reaching out towards new visual perceptions of how the natural world might be reshaped. Often philistine where the fostering of native-born composers, sculptors and painters was concerned, the gentlemen were pre-eminent in politics, in sport, in architecture and in garden design. Consequently, there was an interchange between the patrons and the paid, a productive uncertainty and a pulling in two directions which is the province of this book.

In 1962 James Lees-Milne, very much a gentleman himself, though a salaried player to the National Trust, published an important book on this theme. His *Earls of Creation* dealt with the artistic contributions of the Earls of Pembroke, Bathurst, Oxford, Burlington and Leicester in the mid-eighteenth century. Concerned more with architecture than with gardens, the book did not try to measure up the innovations of the gentlemen against those of the players and by its structure it left gaps. I have, for instance, an uneasy, probably unsustainable, suspicion that the greatest and most innovative gardener of the entire century was Richard Temple, 1st Lord Cobham, who unfortunately did not leave behind the memoirs that could support the claim. Lees-Milne may well have left him out because he was a mere viscount.

So much for the upper classes and their claims for consideration. A secondary but perfectly serious motivation for writing has been green wellies. I never wear them myself, preferring to scrape thick mud off my heavy shoes and occasionally to suffer wet socks. But Wellington boots symbolise the walking approach to garden study, and in each chapter I have tried to walk the reader around at least one garden that survives.

Valuable studies of English gardens can be, and often are, written from library desks on the other side of the Atlantic, using the wealth of rare source books, memorabilia, illustrative material and journals which affluence has accumulated in American universities. In the past we valued the Elgin Marbles and bought them. Americans have had the wit in our time to value our records of a great artistic movement and buy them as they came on the market. Good luck to them. But there is still no substitute for the green wellies approach, for walking the grounds, not once but often and in every revealing season. The garden walks in each chapter are both a substitute for real experiences and an inducement to tempt readers into repeating them.

Other English Arcadias of the eighteenth century tend to be compared with Henry Hoare's supremely satisfying achievement at Stourhead, Wiltshire. There all the elements of the eclectic garden, some of them – the Pantheon, the Gothic Cottage and the Palladian Bridge – visible in this view, unite in an ideal evocation of the classical past. It is a Claude Lorrain painting realised with garden buildings set against mature woodland around a lakeside walking circuit punctuated with references to Virgil's Aeneid.

The rewards can be golden. I remember the lake at Enville, Staffordshire, one bitter January day when the stone sea-horses were riding a glimmering sheet of hard ice, Robin Hood's Temple at Halswell, Somerset, in its last sad decay above the ploughed fields of a one-time park, and Hackfall in the North Riding of Yorkshire where a wild garden of rocks above an angry river may have lost half its original intentions in thick undergrowth yet still seemed a proper place for wolves to howl in. Only when a terrain has been walked can the imaginative effort behind it be evaluated. Exegesis of obscure poetry is no substitute. The three Arcadian greats are Studley Royal, Stourhead and Stowe; but how could Studley Royal go wrong once the Aislabies had decided to impose a French forest garden on a steep-sided Yorkshire dale already endowed with a fast stream and a cathedral-sized ruin? Stourhead demanded rather more effort as its springs had to be gathered together, but its hillsides were ready waiting to provide a flattering backdrop. Only Lord Cobham's Stowe began with no advantages beyond the level fields of Buckinghamshire and yet was still made great. Their ranking order can be appreciated only by walking all three, not by unravelling source books and commentaries. Measured not on beauty but on effort, innovation and ingenuity Stowe has to be the ultimate Arcadia and it exemplifies the Englishness, the serendipitous topographical misunderstanding, behind the whole ambitious concept of reconstructing an ideal classical past. When James Thomson, in the 'Autumn' canto of his poem

The Seasons, hailed the newly laid out grounds of Stowe as a place where 'gay Fancy then/ Will tread in thought the groves of Attic land', he was writing with no conception of the blue distances and harsh rocky landscapes of Greece. As the poet of a wet, green, Atlantic island it was enough for him to be happily deceived. If the imitation was not very close to its model then it was at least equally valuable and encouragingly easy to copy.

Stowe landscape was one stage in the experimental process of a national obsession, and a stage which was evolving even as Thomson penned that addition to his poem in 1744. A gentleman, Lord Cobham, initiated the garden with some unresolved idea of trees and temples. Then the players, the professionals – Charles Bridgeman, John Vanbrugh, William Kent and Lancelot Brown – turned the idea into an idyll, and the idyll became a tourist trap for the intelligentsia of a landed élite. Yet so unstable was the creative process that, when Brown had done what he could, lacking a dam and a lake, for the Grecian Valley which his player predecessors had begun, he immediately moved on to let sporting fashions and the economies of estate management refine and ultimately weaken the entire Arcadian concept.

That is how it had been from the beginning with an interchange of interests – commercial acquisitiveness and aristocratic vision – three steps backwards and four steps forwards, ever since Inigo Jones's return to London. And this was how the evolution of the English Landscape Garden would continue until, by the time of Humphry Repton's death in 1816, commercial pressures towards maximum consumption had killed off the Arcadian ideal with the sentimental complexities – rockeries, bog-gardens, lily ponds, pergolas, bird-baths and regimented floral displays – of the 'Gardenesque'.

The English Landscape Garden depended upon the bringing together in conscious union of the icons of both Classicism and Romanticism: the Homeric, Virgilian and Horatian associations of the one, with the wild woods of the other. With inspired direction and a better informed patronage the two might have come together much earlier than they did. Inigo Jones and John Beale, two near contemporaries, had each grasped the significance of one of those two vital elements of the Arcadian pastoral garden. In the 1630s, while Beale was still a fellow of King's College, Cambridge, grappling with Plato and eastern mysticism, Jones, the favoured architect of the Stuart court, had built a pair of scholarly domed temples on the high south wall of Covent Garden, half urban ornaments, half garden buildings. Then in the 1640s Beale, by that time a refugee from the tensions of the Civil War, had noticed that, in a particular fold of wooded hill country, at Backbury on the middle reaches of the Wye in Herefordshire, Nature had produced a garden superior in many respects to any man-made creation. He had taken mental comfort and inspiration from a hill and seen landscape as a revelation of the divine. If he had been able to publish this addition to the received Christian canon then Inigo Jones's temples could have found a natural setting, as in the paintings of two other contemporaries – Claude Lorrain and Nicholas Poussin.

It was not to be. Neither artist was yet sufficiently represented in English collections for their visuals to be current. Instead two counter-forces, Puritan utilitarianism and the formal garden fashions of French politics, intervened. John Evelyn had been perfectly placed to become the patron of garden Arcadias. His American-born cousin George had even built a temple-fronted grotto in his brother's garden at Wotton in Surrey, but Evelyn, fixated on science and utility and jealous of his cousin's master-stroke, spent the rest of his horticultural career urging the planting of trees in geometrical, money-making ranks, never bringing them together with temples. Consequently, for fifty years, from 1660 to 1710, the professionals, the paid gardeners and the nurserymen, ruled, expressing the political theory of the divine right of kings and an orderly

'View of a Portico by the Side of a River, with Herdsmen and Cattle' from John Boydell's 1777 edition of Claude Lorrain's Liber Veritatis. Already by the middle of the seventeenth century artists like Claude (1600–82) and Nicholas Poussin (1594–1665) were anticipating the Romantic potential of classical temple architecture set against a background of wild Nature. It would take eighty years before English garden designers would realise the painter's vision.

authoritarian state, by plants bedded out in regiments of disciplined, axial unity. It was only in the second and third decades of the new century that reaction set in and an inspired knot of influences, amateur and gentlemanly for the most part, brought lakes, lawns, temples and woods together to create an English pastoral Arcadia.

This book sets out to convey the way in which the professionals and the amateurs opposed and sometimes complemented each other. It was not all conflict; in 1761 Lord Dacre described the easy accord between him and Capability Brown in a letter to Sanderson Miller of Radway. Speaking of his own estate, Belhus in Essex, Dacre wrote:

> the truth is that I never ride that way without longing to do something there; as I know that that coarse meadow and moory sided canal might be converted into a very pleasing scene: And Brown is of the same opinion: we have now another Scheme for it of much less (tho' still a good deal) of Expence; it is to make it in the River Stile instead of the Lake.[1]

In this way the players offered the practicalities to satisfy the aspirations of the gentlemen: Brown's drainage pipes to create Dacre's pastoral idyll. The texts in each chapter have been chosen to illustrate such practicalities.

It should be stressed that not every player-professional was destructive of the Arcadian theme and that not all gardeners fit easily into one category or the other. Vanbrugh could always pass as a clubable gentleman, though he was a clear case of a well-paid player. Stephen Switzer was almost tearfully aware that he had fallen from an original genteel status. If William Kent was a brilliant paid hack, where does that leave his master, the Earl of Burlington, who certainly played the part of an active garden adviser? The supreme professional, Lancelot Brown, ended up as a country gentleman and an adviser to a king and a prime minister; even more ambivalent, as his chapter will expose, was his role in the Arcady saga – villain or hero? Another puzzle, which may relate to the relative status of architects and gardeners, was why, if a second division sculptor and architect like Robert Taylor (1714–88) was knighted, did not Brown, who changed the rural face of Britain, receive the same honour? Both men were elected Sheriff, Taylor for London, Brown for Huntingdonshire. Were the Arthurian implications of a second 'Sir Lancelot' riding purposefully about a revived Lyonesse more than even George III could stomach?

At the end of the great garden century came the ironic twist. With the triumph of the 'wild men' of the Picturesque movement and of full-blown Romanticism, the future of the English Landscape Garden, of templed and hermitage-strewn woodlands, artfully disposed, should have been secure. But in the garden world the dominant factor in those turn-of-the-century years was the effete and oleaginous figure of Humphry Repton, the would-be gentleman but arch-professional. His quite brief career (1789–1816) marked the abandonment of Brown's etiolated Arcadia and the yoking of the Picturesque to a Gardenesque, which was in essence no more than the garden styling of upper-middle-class suburbia.

CHAPTER ONE

INIGO JONES –
THE STAGE DESIGNER
AS GARDENER

Inigo Jones (1573–1652) never expressed any feeling for flowers in the copious marginal annotations of his architectural books. His only recorded comment on gardens was the grudging and mistrustful sidelong thrust that 'in gardens loggias stucco or ornaments of chimney peeces or in the inner parts of houses thes compositiones are of necessety to be yoused'.[1] The 'compositiones' to which he referred so cautiously were the decorative devices of Mannerist classicism. This explains his unease. On his second visit to Italy in 1613–14 Jones noted with critical relish every detail of the classical orders on surviving remains of ancient Rome, but he recorded no reaction to the astonishing Mannerist gardens of contemporary Italy which he and his patron-companions, the Earl and Countess of Arundel, could hardly have failed to visit on their leisurely travels about the peninsular. Other Elizabethan and Jacobean English travellers to Florence and Rome had come back full of the marvellous grottoes, stone giants, automata and waterworks of the key villas – the Aldobrandini at Frascati, the

Inigo Jones envisaged gardens in terms of the stage designs which he prepared for masques at the Caroline court. These were disciplined axial responses to the symmetrical classical façades overlooking them – Italy as interpreted by Bourbon France.

Villas d'Este at Tivoli, Lante and Bomarzo near Viterbo and, above all others, the gardens at Pratolino, seven miles outside Florence. There, between 1569 and 1584, Bernado Buontalenti had created prodigies of hydraulic engineering for Francesco, the Medici Grand Duke of Tuscany.

Jones, it seems, was not impressed. The overriding interests of his long life appear to have been the revival and imposition on his native country of the forms of antique Roman and sixteenth-century Venetian classicism, the efficient co-ordination of teams of artists in works to support royal prestige, and the keeping up of a close association with the aristocracy. Gardens came nowhere; and yet it seems that he was responsible for the two most celebrated and influential gardens of his time, one in the fashionable heart of the capital, poised above the south side of his Piazza for the 4th Earl of Bedford at Covent Garden, the other, of royal dimensions, for the 4th Earl of Pembroke at Wilton House near Salisbury in Wiltshire. Neither has survived. Seventy years after they were laid out the garden of Bedford House had been covered by streets and houses, while at Wilton only a scatter of re-sited statues and the fragments of a grotto house remain in later schemes of planting. Both have, however, left potent ghosts to haunt subsequent planners and designers.

In any attempt to summarise Inigo Jones's character the words 'formidable' and 'competitive' come more readily to mind than either 'likeable' or 'loyal'.[2] Notes which he scribbled on the flyleaf and margins of his copy of Palladio's *Quattro Libri* indicate that he was an obsessive hypochondriac given to fits of depression. Under the heading, 'Against Mellancoly', he noted:

> Buglas leaves or the rootes are good to be yoused in meates and drinkes, to stirr and move moderately. Copulation must be utterly eschewed for that thearby, the best blood of a man is wasted and naturall strength infeebled [he never married]. To kimb the head often, to sing, youse musike. To sleepe somewhat longer than ordinary. The opening of the piles is commended.[3]

Nevertheless, all his life he rose instinctively and, one suspects, ruthlessly to the top. He loved a lord, any lord with influence; he walked with kings but spurned the common touch. Born the son of a London Welsh cloth maker, according to Sir Christopher Wren he was apprenticed in his youth to a joiner in St Paul's churchyard. By unknown steps he scraped up an acquaintance with an aristocrat, possibly Francis Manners, a brother of the 5th Earl of Rutland, who took him to Italy in the last decade of the old century. By 1603 he was being described as 'a picture maker' and was accompanying the Earl of Rutland to Denmark to invest King Christian IV with the Garter. As a natural consequence he was soon back in England designing stage sets for Christian's sister, Queen Anne, the Italophile wife of James I. In 1605 he staged *The Masque of Blackness* which had been written by Ben Jonson and marked the beginning of a long and sour relationship between the two men; Jones ended the victor when Jonson retired from Court authorship.

In these years Salomon de Caus (*c.* 1577–1626) was the Court's principal designer of gardens. De Caus was a distinguished hydraulics engineer of Franco-Dutch origin, de Caus or Caux being the French version of the common Dutch surname de Kock.[4] He specialised in large artificial rock fountains, notably one created about 1611 for the garden of Somerset House in imitation of the 'Parnasus' rock at Pratolino, and he had a talent for publicity, shared in a lesser degree by his relative Isaac de Caus. Salomon's handsomely illustrated book, *Les Raisons des Forces Mouvantes* was published in 1615 and again in 1624. It made the construction of devices like musical statues, twittering birds and automata nymphs pursued by automata satyrs seem as easy as powering a saw mill by water or raising a boat by a canal lock, all parts of the same scientific continuum.

If Inigo Jones ever had any inclination towards grotto design or the construction of stone giants then he missed his chance when he and Salomon de Caus were both serving the arrogant and secretive Henry, Prince of Wales. In 1611 the Prince passed over them both, turning to a Tuscan designer, Constantino de Servi, for work on his gardens at Richmond. These were in no way Franco-Italian, but old-fashioned Italian Mannerist with irregular pools, islands and grotto-giants in the sixteenth-century style.[5] Lacking a setting of steep, rocky hills they will have looked gauche, a cabinet of curiosities. The Prince died in 1612, Salomon left to work in Germany and Jones took his sabbatical year off to tour Italy with the Arundels. He came back informed and confident enough to make a resounding success of his appointment in 1615 as Surveyor of the King's Works. Architectural triumphs like his new Banqueting House at Whitehall followed in 1619.

Commissions for work in gardens during the 1620s were few and far between. Jones was called in to design a small, apsed banqueting house in the grounds of Theobalds; there was work, usually in timber and plaster, on hunting lodges at Bagshot and in Hyde Park, and he is likely to have given assistance on a conventionally designed terraced garden and loggia, both statue crammed, at Lord Arundel's town house on the Thames.[6] Nevertheless Jones was able to design, as it were by proxy, any number of ambitious gardens and garden buildings in these years – all of them stage sets for the backdrops and sliding shutters of the elaborate royal masques staged every winter at Whitehall Palace. It was these which must have given Jones a critical awareness of contemporary English garden design and an alert feeling for the best formal Franco-Italian garden design, particularly after the new King Charles's marriage in 1628 to Henrietta Maria, sister of Louis XIII of France and daughter of the great King Henry IV.

Excellent bird's-eye views of the garden works by Claude Mollet and the Francini brothers were readily available, and it is clear from Jones's set designs that he was an avid collector of any prints. For Jones plagiarism was an honourable trade. His 'Vale of Tempe' for *Tempe Restored* of 1632 is taken from Giulio Parigi's stage set for *The Garden of Calypso* of 1608, only one of many borrowings from Parigi's works as published in Remigio Cantagallina's book of engravings. Jones's Greek temple for the masque *Florimene* is very close to a drawing of Nôtre Dame de la Rotunde at Rouanne by Jacques Androuet du Cerceau. Only with his many drawings of trees for the side wings of his stage sets are the branches so convincingly interlaced, the slender trunks so natural, that here at least it seems possible that he may have looked out from his own window and drawn from life.

One result of drawing so many garden scenes for stage sets was that he developed a compositional bias towards tunnel vision. Trees and rocks on the left are almost always matched symmetrically by trees and rocks on the right, even his rustic villages tend to the mirror image. When he came to design Wilton Garden, quite apart from his borrowings from Jacques Callot and Parigi, the layout has this feeling of a narrow view framed by an imaginary proscenium arch.

When Jones's garden opportunities came in the 1630s he reacted predictably as an architect determined to discipline nature within a geometrical frame, to set up naked statues of gods and goddesses and to make solid stone garden buildings the focus. He knew what features he would have to retain. Grottoes were as popular as ever. Isaac de Caus had remained in England and designed for the Whitehall Banqueting House in 1623 'a Rocke or grotto where the King did regale himself privately'.[7] This was not free-standing but, like most such grottoes in England, a *sala terrena* occupying part of the basement to the Banqueting House. Anyone inclined to treat such rooms as merely 'grotesque' garden jokes should visit the grotto constructed at Woburn for Lucy, Countess of Bedford before 1627.[8] For all its riot of decoration, rib vaults of sea shells, friezes of wild sea creatures and niches of rocaille work, it has a cool elegance, more Caroline than Jacobean in feeling. Lacking documentary evidence it is usually attributed to Isaac de Caus, and on that non-evidence and a later Bedford connection he is sometimes also credited with the garden at Bedford House on the south side of the Covent Garden Piazza.[9]

This is most unlikely. Inigo Jones is known to have designed the other three sides of the Piazza for Lord Bedford: two terraces of handsome houses set above continuous round-arched arcades to east and north and on the west side, St Paul's church, severely Tuscan, an appropriately rustic order for a garden space, flanked symmetrically by classical gateways and matching houses. But the prodigy was the fourth, the south side, a stroke of imaginative planning. Instead of houses there was a high garden terrace with a semicircular viewing bastion and the ultimate in gazebos, two elegantly domed pavilions with projecting porticoes. Poised one at each end, they were uniquely Roman additions to London's streetscape. For England this concept of garden and city intertwined was an absolute innovation. There was nothing in Paris's Place Royal or Place Dauphine to equal it. The garden behind that superb terrace was a conventional quartered rectangle with a 'wilderness' of densely planted trees to its east and a Banqueting House, semi-circular in plan behind two columns *in antis*, on its west side. A grotto was built under the 'evidence' house where the estate papers were kept. Isaac de Caus probably designed that, but again there appear to be no surviving records.

What is apparent from these enclosed areas with their terraces and high garden houses is that patrons sought safe enclosure and at the same time wanted to look outwards, as if resenting the imprisoning walls. At Wilton, Jones was given the opportunity to resolve that neurosis. He broke conventional garden design ruthlessly out from its confinement, imposing upon the natural landscape of a flat river valley and the wooded Wiltshire hills a 1,000 foot long, 400 foot wide, three-part garden. Its sections he pulled together by a broad axial walk striding across the River Nadder as if it were an insignificant ditch. As he had reached out at Bedford House towards the urban aesthetics of Clementine Rome, so here at Wilton Inigo Jones almost anticipated the Baroque formal gardens of Le Nôtre: a new Versailles before its time.

The 4th Earl of Pembroke had inherited from his brother, William the 3rd Earl, an emblem-infested Jacobean garden crammed with Trinitarian devices, and by 1632 he was beginning to consider a replacement, so Lord Pembroke would have considered it expedient to make a lavish French gesture. The King apparently 'did love Wilton above all places', visiting it regularly every summer. To confirm the royal favour Pembroke agreed to use Jones, who was as close a friend of the Earl as a commoner could expect to be, to design a huge twenty-one bay garden front to the existing courtyard house.[10] It was, like Hatfield, to have one wing for the King and one for the Queen and naturally a French queen should be honoured with a royal French garden. Wilton was up against stiff French competition. At Rueil, just outside Paris, Cardinal Richelieu was spending 780,000 livres on the waterworks of the garden, designed in 1633 by Jacques Lemercier. John Evelyn's 1644 account of this 'Paradise' gives somes impression of what a royal minister and favourite was expected to produce.[11]

But for Inigo Jones the garden at St Germain-en-Laye, laid out in the second decade of the seventeenth century for Henrietta Maria's father, Henry IV, was the obvious model.

At this point, unfortunately, the unreliable Wiltshire antiquary and gossip, John Aubrey, takes up the narrative:

> that did put Philip . . . Earle of Pembroke upon making this magnificent garden and grotto, and to build that side of the house that fronts the garden, with two stately pavilions at each end, all *al Italiano*. His Majesty intended to have had it all designed by his own architect, Mr Inigo Jones, who being at that time, about 1633, engaged in his Majesties buildings at Greenwich, could not attend to it; but he recommended it to an ingeniouse architect, Monsieur Solomon de Caus, a Gascoigne, who performed it very well; but not without the advice and approbation of Mr Jones.[12]

The Gardens about it are so magnificent, as I much doubt whither Italy have any exceeding it for all varietyes of Pleasure: That which is neerest the Pavillion is a Parterre, having in the middst divers noble brasse statues perpetually spouting Water into an ample Bassin, with other figures of the same metall: But that which is most admirable is the vast enclosure and variety of ground in the larger garden, as containing Vineyards, Corne fields, Meadows, Groves, whereoff one is of Perennial Greenes; and Walkes of vast lengthes, so accurately kept & cultivated that nothing can be more agreable and tempting: In one of these Walkes within a square of tall trees, or rather a Grove, is a basilisc of copper, which as it is managed by the Fontaniere, casts Water neere 60 foote in height, and will of it selfe moove round so swiftly, that it is almost impossible to escape wetting: This leads to the Citroniere where there is a very noble conserve of all those rarities, and at the end of it the Arco of Constantine painted in Oyle on a Wall, as big as is the real one at Rome, so don to the life, that a man very well skilld in Painting may mistake it for stone, & sculpture; and indeed it is so rarely perform'd that it is almost impossible to believe it Paynting, but to be a Worke of solid stone: The skie, and hills which seeme to be betweene the Arches, are so naturall, that swallows & other birds, thinking to fly through, have dash'd themselves to pieces against the Walls: I was infinitely taken with this agreable cheate: At the farther part of this Walke is that plentifull, though artificial Cascad of Water, which rolles downe a very steepe declivity, and over the marble degrees, & basins, with an astonishing noyse and fury, Each basin hath a jetto in it & flowing like sheetes of transparent glasse; especially that which rises over the greate shell of lead, from whenc it glides silently downe a Channell, through the middle of a most spacious gravell Walke, that terminates in a Grotto, resembling the Yawning mouth of hell: Here are also fountaines that cast Water of an exceeding height; and Piscinas very large, in which two of them have Ilands for fowle, of which here is store . . . Hence we were brought to a large & very rare Grotto of shell-worke, artificially stuck on in the shapes of Satyres & other wild fansys: In the middle stands a table of Marble, on which a fountaine playes in divers formes of glasses, cupps, crosses, fanns, crownes &c. Then the Fountaniere represented a showre of raine from the topp, which was mett with the slender pissers from beneath; at the going out, two extravagant Musqueteeres shot us with a streame of water comming out very fiercely from their musket barilles.

John Evelyn, Rueil, 27 February 1644

The accuracy of this account must be judged by the fact that Salomon de Caus had died six years earlier in 1626 and the de Caus family came not from Gascony but from Dieppe and, before that, from Holland.

The true design process which resulted in the Wilton garden was plagiaristic and complex but predictable, given Inigo Jones's past record. He was not primarily a garden designer, indeed it is possible to suggest that what he imposed upon Wilton was both grossly labour intensive and an insensitive response to the site. But he was an enabler, a team leader with the ability to bring artists and artisans together, tied to fixed contracts, to work on the dramatic and innovative projects which he himself had conceived. When Jones was designing in 1631 a backdrop for a new Court masque, *The Shepherd's Paradise*, he had copied very closely, even down to the patterns of the topiary work, an etching 'Parterre du Palais de Nancy', drawn in 1625 by the celebrated French engraver Jacques Callot. It was French, it was dedicated to the wife of the reigning Duke of Lorraine, so it was perfectly appropriate. Jones proceeded to use the front and rear portions of Callot's garden for his new plan for Wilton. To provide a middle section for Wilton and also a royal compliment he simply took the middle portion of the garden at St Germain-en-Laye, a grove of small trees cut by paths in diagonal crosses meeting in circular clearings. He used the sector of the St Germain garden nearest to the palace as a model for the oval orchard area which was planned to lie next to the Grotto at the far end of Wilton Garden. To bind the three disparate parts of the garden together the broad axial walk was projected. The garden was, of course, designed expressly to lie in axis with the enormous royal south range to Wilton House which Jones had already conceived but which, as events turned out, was never built. The wildly

Inigo Jones's strictly axial garden backdrop for his 1631 masque The Shepherd's Paradise. *Such sinuous French parterre de broderie designs would soon replace the simpler English knot gardens.*

ambitious garden, 400 feet wide, was begun to front the proposed 400 foot long new range. Work was to continue on the garden until 1636 when the Grotto was finished. Only then was the present, dramatically cut down, south front begun.

The scheme aroused such interest that, for the first time in English garden history, a book was planned to celebrate its construction. There were to be English and French editions with the alternative titles, *Wilton Garden* and *Le Jardin de Vuilton*, and it was to be lavishly illustrated. But as soon as the enormous palace was abandoned the publication faltered. Nine copies of a rough, undated compilation, cannibalised from the wreck by an enterprising stationer, have survived.[13] We depend for most of our knowledge of the layout of the garden upon three illustrations of it prepared for this aborted book. Two of these perspectives are drawn from the north, looking south towards the Grotto. The other looks north towards an elevation of the massive royal range. The finely drawn perspectives appear to have been drawn for printing by Jacques Callot before his death in 1636. Two are peopled by his inimitable miniature figures. With Hubert le Sueur casting the statue of a bronze gladiator, Nicholas Stone carving nude marble goddesses and Isaac de Caus in charge of the hydraulics, Jones must have thought it tactful to bring into the team the expensive French illustrator Callot to lend equal distinction to the book, always with an eye to the favour of Queen Henrietta Maria. Unfortunately, as soon as the proposed palace was given up the

The 'Parterre du Palais de Nancy', drawn in 1625 by Jacques Callot, was copied by Inigo Jones to make a back shutter for The Shepherd's Paradise. Wilton House, as it existed before the fire of 1647, had twin viewing towers similar to those of the palace.

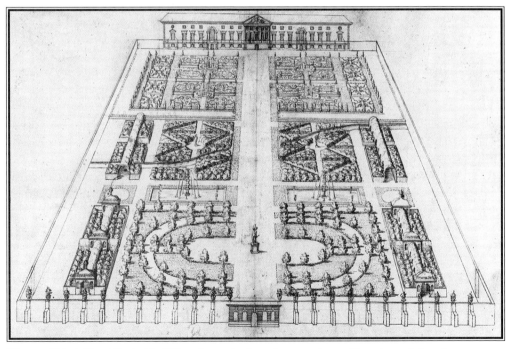

The unpublished 'Grand Design' for Wilton shows why the garden was twice as wide as the south front that was eventually built. Jones copied the three stages of the French royal garden at St Germain-en-Laye but, to conceal the River Nadder winding through the grounds, put the Wilderness section in the middle instead of at the end of the layout.

publication of the book faltered and only a lame version of it, with Isaac de Caus's illustrations, came out undated during the chaos of the Civil War. A tour of the garden in its prime can, however, be reconstructed by combining the brief description printed in *Wilton Garden* with a bluff and cheerful account of a visit made before the Grotto was finished by Lieutenant Hammond in 1635.[14] There is also the faintly disapproving commentary on the garden by Celia Fiennes written in the 1680s when the Grotto was functioning all too efficiently.[15]

Entry was from the basement of the south front; there was no initial viewing terrace alongside the house. To gain an overall impression of the whole garden a visitor would have had to climb one of the two flanking towers of the south front of the house which Jones added for structural as well as aesthetic reasons. The leads of the flat roof would also have afforded a commanding viewpoint. The garden at St Germain-en-Laye on which Wilton was based was steeply terraced so this flattened-out version laid across level river meadows did not work well visually.

The 'curious broad Alley' carried the eye compellingly towards the Grotto, 1,000 feet distant; and it is interesting that Hammond marched straight for this and only observed the other garden features on his return journey. For most visitors the Grotto was the garden. But first came four great squares, each subdivided into quarters, and all filled, not with flowers, but with the clipped topiary patterns of *parterres de broderie*. Each of the four squares was centred on a pool of fountains around the nude statue of a woman. 'In one is Venus with her sonne Cupid in her Armes; in another Diana with her bathing sheet; in a third is Susanna pulling a thorne out of her Foote; and in the 4th Cleopatra with the Serpent'. Hammond noted gleefully that 'with the turning of Cockes' there was 'washing and dashing the Eyes and Thighs of faire Venus and Diana'. At the side of these parterres and between them and the next division of the garden – the Grove – was a low raised terrace to enable visitors to look down on the parterres and the eight flower beds ranged between them and the side walls.

The most unsatisfactory element in the garden design, and one that suggests it may well have been illustrated by someone unfamiliar with the site, was its treatment of the Nadder. This is a clear trout stream, about 40 feet wide, which could easily, as John Evelyn complained when he was there in 1654, have been 'cleansed and raised' to make a fine reach of ornamental water. Yet in an age devoted to such 'ponds of pleasure', as Sir Henry Wotton called them, the Nadder was ignored and left to wind like some irrelevant thread through the rigid geometry of the Grove. In a conventional Italian three-part garden the Grove would have occupied the last section. Because Wilton was directly based on St Germain-en-Laye its Grove was placed dysfunctionally at the heart of the garden.

The 'two Arbours of 300 ffoote long' which should have flanked the Grove never materialised. Identical features appear on the upper terrace in the Palais de Nancy engraving and they were a favourite garden feature in Jones's stage sets. He drew replicas of them in 1634 for a scene of a 'Garden and a Princely Villa', for Thomas Carew's masque *Coelum Britannicum*;[16] but apparently his provision of shade for Wilton was considered excessive in an English climate. In this second section of the layout the Grove itself was actually planted, though its trees were never allowed to grow to any great height as they would have hidden half the garden from the house. In the two central clearings of its strict geometry stood statues of Bacchus and Flora carved by Nicholas Stone; but visitors attempting to approach them down their avenues from certain directions would have found the Nadder blocking their path, another sign that this hugely influential garden, far from responding to its natural site, actually defied it.

Beyond the Grove were two rectangular pools with dramatic waterworks. In each pool stood a tall blocked column topped with a crown which could be made, in what, considering the fate of

Charles I, was a most unfortunate allegory, to spin wildly in jets of water spurting from each side of the pool. These were followed by 'a Compartment of greene with diverse walkes planted with cherrie trees and in the middle is a great Ovall with the Gladiator of brass the most famous Statue of all that Antiquity hath left'. Flanking this formal cherry orchard on either side there were complex covered arbours including little green pavilions, but no visitors mention them. With the statue of the Gladiator the iconography of the garden was complete: Love in the first section, Fertility in the second and Military Prowess in the third.

Then at last came 'the fayre House of Freestone' on which the fame of the garden would rest for the remainder of the century. This, designed by Inigo Jones, was a loggia with a front of blocked pilasters and marble statues, its three arches leading into the Grotto chambers. Lieutenant Hammond had to take it on trust that the waterworks would eventually offer 'the Singing and Chirping of Birdes, and other strange rarities'. He was shown round by Isaac de Caus in person, describing him unflatteringly as 'the fat Dutch keeper thereof, a rare Artist' and 'this outlandish Engineer'.[17] De Caus never seems to have been able to construct the moving automata promised in both Salomon's *Raisons des Forces* and the plagiaristic reprint of Salomon's book which Isaac was to publish in 1644 under a new title, *Nouvelle Invention de lever l'eau plus hault que sa source*. When de Caus died in Paris in 1648, the secret of how to operate one of the garden's optical devices to create three rainbows died with him.

Celia Fiennes, who obviously got very wet on her visit fifty years later, experienced the 'strange rarities' which Hammond only heard about. She passed briskly over 'many gravel walkes with grass squaires', the statues were still in place but the topiary work had gone. There were 'dwarfe trees of all sorts and a fine flower garden'. Then came the 'Grottoe'. Just inside the door 'a sluce spoutts water up to wett the Strangers'. Next came a central room with a stone table from which a pipe spouted water up into 'the hollow carving of the rooff' to descend 'in a shower of raine all about the roome'. Figures in the niches could all 'weep water on the beholders'. Her trials had not ended. From one of the side rooms she heard 'the melody of Nightingerlls and all sorts of birds which engaged the curiosity of the Strangers to go in to see but at the entrance off each room, is a line of pipes that appear not till by a sluce moved it washes the spectators, designed for diversion'. Her disapproval is almost tangible.

In the wooded hillside beyond the Grotto, and to the right of the garden's main axis, there was an amphitheatre of three terraces emphasised by cypress trees and linked by a flight of moon steps. It was illustrated in *Wilton Garden* but whether it was an 'Echo', an acoustic 'marvel' like the one drawn in John Evelyn's 'Elysium Britannicum', or merely a place from which tired visitors could look back and appreciate the scale and detail of the garden, is not known.[18]

So Jones the team leader had brought together the suave French presentation of Callot, the sculpture of Stone and le Sueur and the amusing Italian prodigies of de Caus in a pan-European garden, axial and united. He envisaged garden projects as team work based on binding contracts. Wilton records relating to this garden are scant, but in the same years Jones was working with almost the same team on the gardens at Somerset House and there the accounts survive to illustrate his methods.[19] He drew the Diana Fountain himself, in a rather shaky perspective, which may explain why he had entrusted the far more complex Wilton garden perspectives to Jacques Callot. That ensured his overall control. Then it was drawn up that for the brass statue of the goddess Hubert le Sueur should be 'paid according with severall Bargaines made with him by Inigoe Jones'. Similarly for the 'Marble worke and workemanshipp' Nicholas Stone was to be paid 'according to a bargaine made with him by the said surveyor'. From Wilton there is only a late, 1636, record relating to 'ye new kitchen garden which Garden Mr De Caux is to lay out in fitt proportions, walks & Quarters to bee planted with fruits, hearbes & rootes by Dominick Pile who is to have ye Custody thereof'.[20]

It would be valuable to have some personal record of Jones's real reaction to the celebrated Grotto House at Wilton because there is no evidence that he would have automatically disapproved of such scientific toys. At some time in the 1630s he seems to have built an even larger grotto, or possibly it was only a grand banqueting house, at Albury, the Earl of Arundel's favourite Surrey retreat. One of Wenceslaus Hollar's 1645 illustrations of the estate shows it as a two-storey, columned, classical building with a portico at either end, the whole engaging structure tucked into a hillside covered with vines and overlooking a lakeside walk. Another of the Hollar engravings shows a group of gentry strolling with apparent appreciative pleasure through the park's natural-seeming landscape of lake and clumped trees. There is not a statue, clipped bush or straight ruled line in sight; yet Albury was Lord Arundel's favourite retreat: 'I desire that Daniel House give me a particular accounte howe my water & all thinges are at Albury, & that he will have greate care that agaynest the Gallery & House, store of Roses Cherimine wodbines & ye like sweetes be plantes'.[21] In a letter to John Evelyn sent from Padua in 1646 Arundel writes of 'the poore Cottage at Alleberrye where I hope to be ere long & ende my dayes'.[22] Simplicity and homely pleasures were becoming the taste of the sophisticated.

So there were alternative contemporary ways of approaching garden design in addition to the one arbitrarily chosen by Jones in an act of sycophancy to a foreign queen. Perhaps only an architect could have devised the Wilton Garden. In matters of architectural style Jones had always been deeply influenced by that infinitely aristocratic ambassador and, in his last days, superior Provost of Eton, Sir Henry Wotton. But curiously, in matters of garden design, he chose to go in the opposite direction to that which Sir Henry had advised in his influential *The Elements of Architecture* of 1624.[23] Sir Henry, the gentleman, was suggesting an informal garden; Jones, the player, was designing a formal one. Professional gardeners naturally inclined to designs which involved maximum expenditure.

The *Elements* anticipates to a remarkable degree the artfully casual garden manner of much later Edwardians like Gertrude Jekyll and Edwin Lutyens. Wotton writes: 'Gardens should bee *irregular* or at least cast into a very wilde *Regularitie*', they should be viewed 'rather in a delightfull confusion, then with any plaine distinction of the pieces'. He urges that a visitor should be able to pass 'by severall *mountings* and *valings*, to various entertainments of his *sent* and *sight*', presented with sudden diversities 'as if hee had beene *Magically* transported into a new Garden'. Wotton seems to have been hankering after the walled and enclosed gardens of his youth but arranged in some informal unity. Finally, with all the precious sensitivity of a Vita Sackville-West, he praised his old friend Sir Henry Fanshawe who, in his garden at Ware Park in Hertfordshire, 'did so precisely examine the *tinctures*, and seasons of his *flowers*, that in their *setting* the *inwardest* of those which were to come up at the same time, should be alwayes a little *darker* than the *outmost*, and so serve them for a kinde of gentle *shadow*, like a piece not of *Nature*, but of *Arte*'.

This strain of appreciation for a more 'natural' Nature was latent among sensitive souls like Wotton and Arundel in the 1620s and 1630s. It ran parallel to the other two themes: disciplined order and utilitarian horticultural science. When the English monarchy was overthrown and the aristocracy was subdued in the 1640s there would come a brief interlude when all three strains of garden design could flourish together.

CHAPTER TWO

SAMUEL HARTLIB AND THE GARDENS OF PANSOPHIC REASON

Inigo Jones was an example of the gardener as player, not as gentleman. A well-travelled, professional civil servant, he had offered garden design on the side for a fee to noble patrons, never designing a garden for himself to reveal his own tastes. His schemes for the grounds of a great house were intended to give an outward show of wealth and Franco-Italian sophistication: expressions of solidarity with western Europe's Renaissance culture. If England had continued to follow the same political sequence as her continental neighbours, then Jones's Wilton Garden would have led in seamless progress to the Franco-Dutch formal gardens of post-1660.

That was not to be. Instead there came the Civil War of 1642–6, the regicide of 1649, which deeply disturbed the national psyche, and then a brief Presbyterian republic of the 'Saints', as the religious élite of the sect liked to describe themselves, until 1652 when the Commonwealth of 1652–9 was imposed by Oliver Cromwell as Lord Protector and leader of the Puritans' New Model Army. In every sense of the term it was a revolutionary period. For a conservative, insular society to judicially murder its anointed monarch raised general expectations that the world must be coming to an end: King Jesus must succeed the lost King Charles and there would be an absolute social change. They were years wild with conflicting constitutional theories and experiments. The aristocracy was in nervous retirement; the Church of England was dis-established and had gone virtually underground. Such intellectual ferment resulted naturally in radical new notions on agriculture and gardening. Contrary to conventional biblical exegesis it was believed that the Second Coming of Christ required, as a precondition, a perfect society of prosperity and plenty, so that had to be achieved.

At the heart of this horticultural rethink, leading the self-styled 'Hortulan Saints', the devout Protestant garden experts, was Samuel Hartlib (died 1662) writing like some earnest literary spider at the centre of a web of correspondence, publications and idealistic projects. Hartlib is still a relatively obscure figure, barely noticed in histories of English garden design. Neither precisely a player nor a gentleman he was not, in the usual sense of the term, a gardener. Yet almost single-handed he coaxed into life an agricultural revolution of new crops, new ways of rearing livestock and a new landscape of enclosed private fields, hedged and bounded, that would change the face of the countryside more radically than the creations of any subsequent gardener or park designer, even including Capability Brown. Hartlib's vast correspondence is treasured at Sheffield University where it has been edited and put on CD ROMs.[1] Conferences are held on both sides of the Atlantic to consider his influence, but true posthumous recognition still eludes him. This may be because, as a pensioner of Parliament, awarded £100 a year in 1646, he is still associated with regicide. But the ideas which he projected so successfully in the 1650s were earthy and practical, aimed at a national prosperity, not the aesthetic arrangement of aristocratic demesnes. This does not catch the popular imagination of garden enthusiasts. Gardening in Hartlib's prime years was essentially a time of technical advance and scientific innovations, of new plants and new ways of growing them rather than new ways of arranging them; and in that time, as Parliament's £100 pension acknowledged, Hartlib was the leader.

His father was a Protestant German merchant who had fled from Jesuit persecution in Lithuania to Prussia. There he married, as his third wife and Samuel's mother, the daughter of an English merchant trading from Dantzig. Born at Elbing and educated in Germany, Samuel Hartlib not only absorbed his father's Protestant faith but one particular brand of ardent, *bien pensant*, Protestantism, the Pansophism preached by the Moravian Jan Komenski (1592–1620), known across Europe by the Latin form of his name: Comenius. Pansophism was a form of Christian rationalism akin to the Pelagian heresy of the fifth century. It urged that perfection was attainable in this world and could be achieved by the universal sharing of every scientific advance, generously and without reserve, between all nations. Education was at the heart of Comenius's system and agriculture was the most obvious science by which hunger and want could be banished and a foundation laid for human happiness, though always within a strict Christian framework. No one hoping for a return to Eden, man's supposed primal state, would forget that Eden had been a garden.

When Hartlib settled in England in 1628 he saw his Pansophist mission as being, not to the poor and needy, but to the élite and the intelligentsia. He believed that it would be by the gentry's conversion to new economic realities that the poor would eventually be rescued from their poverty. Hartlib should never be seen in nineteenth-century terms as a Christian socialist. He aimed for the hearts and minds of the upper classes and was soon remarkably successful. Bishop Williams of Lincoln, later Archbishop of York, lent him a small episcopal palace to use as a school for the education of sons of the gentry. Among his circle of correspondents were influential lawyer-politicians like Oliver St John, later to be Cromwell's Lord Chief Justice and virtual deputy, Sir Henry Wotton, soon to be Provost of Eton and himself a garden fancier, the poet John Milton, John Evelyn and that coterie of scientists, antiquaries and eccentrics which would, in 1660, cohere to form the Royal Society. Ironically Hartlib would never be proposed for membership though he had a better claim than most. His ties with the Commonwealth establishment had been far too close.

What never comes over from Hartlib's writings is any feeling of charm to account for a proselytising foreigner's instant success in Caroline society. By 1641 he had achieved sufficient funds and backing to be able to bring his hero, Comenius, over to England for a prolonged visit, rather as twentieth-century American evangelists are flown in to arouse the faithful. Hartlib appears to have been earnest, enthusiastic and methodical, conducting what he described as 'a general news agency'. Sincerity exudes from his texts. The secret of his influence may have been the appeal to individual greed as well as to general prosperity behind his activities, that and his generosity, not only to poor scholars, but in fair attributions of credit to other men for the 'secrets' and discoveries which Hartlib publicised. It is the eighteenth century which is always described as the 'Age of Reason', but Samuel Hartlib was reason incarnate. If the farmers of Brabant had evolved a new rotation of crops which meant that a third of all fields would no longer have to remain fallow for a year, then reason directed that all England should know about it in practical detail, try the system out and advance towards prosperity.

'Yea, happy is that people whose God is the Lord. Psalm 4, 6–7', he wrote as the epigraph to his *Enlargement of the Discourse on HUSBANDRY* of 1652. But in his Prologue added the eminently down-to-earth:

If any desire to have the great Clover of Flaunders, or the best sorts of Hemp and Flax-seeds of those parts, or Saint Foine, La Lucerne, Canary-seeds or any sorts of Seeds of this kinde: Let them enquire at Mr James Long's shop at the Barge on Billingsgate; and they shall upon timely notice have them procured new and very good from France and Flaunders at reasonable Rates.[2]

His was a capitalist Christianity, pan-European in inspiration, and a list of only a selection of his publications in the 1650s shows how well he deserved that £100 a year from Parliament. *A Discourse of Husbandrie used in Brabant and Flanders, shewing the Wonderfull Improvement of Land there* (1650); *Samuel Hartlib his Legacie or an Enlargement of the Discourse on HUSBANDRY used in Brabant and Flaunders* (1652) *Cornu Copia, a Miscellaneum of Luciferous and most Fructiferous Experiments, Observations, and Discoveries immethodically distributed* (1652); *The Reformed Spirituall Husbandman* (1652); *Discourse of the whole Art of Husbandry, both Foreign and Domestick* (1659).

In 1653 he published *A Discoverie for Division or Setting out of Land as to the best Form*. This was intended for the 'Direction and More Advantage and profit of the Adventures and Planters in the

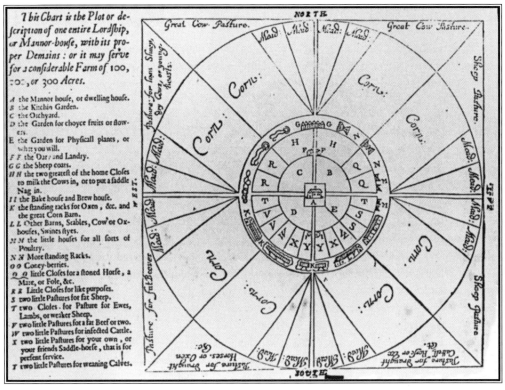

The ultimate spider's web of harsh Commonwealth utility. Samuel Hartlib and Cressy Dymock's plan of 1653 for the ideal country estate, or 'entire Lordship', with the manor house at the precise centre of radiating quadrants of gardens, arable fields and pasture land.

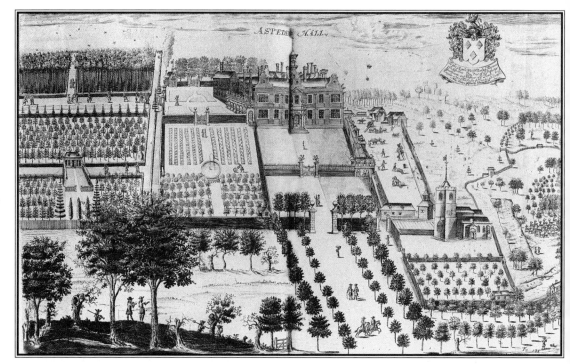

The unimaginative geometry and insistent utility of the average mid-seventeenth-century provincial estate is exemplified in this view of Aspenden Hall from Sir Henry Chauncy's 1700 The Historical Antiquities of Hertfordshire. *The farmyard with its manure heaps is on one side of the formal axis; vegetable gardens, an orchard and a tree nursery are on the other. This is the English estate trapped in its Artisan Mannerist stage of evolution.*

Fens and other Waste and undisposed Places in England and Ireland'.[3] Written jointly with one of his agricultural correspondents, Cressy Dymock, this contained a large, fold-out plan of chilling utilitarian rationalism to illustrate 'an entire Lordship or Mannor-house'. This ideal estate is drawn as a large circle of lands, swept clear of any peasant clutter. In the smallest circle at its centre is the house with four equal quadrants of garden around it. Behind the house are quadrants B, a 'Kitchin Garden', and C, 'the Orchard'. To the front are quadrants D, 'the Garden for choyce fruits and flowers', and E, 'the Garden for Physical plants'. Flanking the north and south entry roads to this abstract perfection Hartlib has set the conventional twin pavilions which usually offered the gentry pleasure and privacy away from a servant-crowded house, but Hartlib labels them as 'the Bake house' and 'Brew house' in the front, with another pair, 'the Dare' (dairy) and 'Landry' (laundry) behind.

There follow, in ever widening circles, an area for milking cows, tending sick animals and keeping saddle-horses, a circle of cattle sheds and stables, a wide circle for corn and, lastly, four outer areas for pasture. The cattle were to be kept, deliberately but with no thought for the practical convenience of labourers or of the farmer himself, at some distance from the house to avoid 'offensive sights and smells'. 'Finally', the text ran:

here your house stands in the middle of all your little world enclosed with the Gardens and Orchards, refreshed with the beauty and odour of the blossomes, fruits and flowers, and the sweet melody of the chirping birds; that again encompast with little Closes, that all young, weak, or sick Cattle may be fostered under your own eye . . . and all bound together as with a girdle (and surely never had the old proverb, 'ungirt, unblest', a fitter or fuller sense of application) and all that covered again, as with a fair large cloak of Meadow and Tillage.[4]

There was, then, some poetry behind this vision of geometrical gardens and farmlands, but Hartlib never went into further detail over his 'choyce flowers'. In one of his earlier books he had made it clear that John Parkinson's *Paradisi in Sole, Paradisus Terrestris* (a Latin pun on 'Park in the Sun') published in the same year, 1628, that Hartlib settled in England, was the ultimate in flower encyclopaedias and a book which he, Hartlib, would never attempt to rival. He saw his function, correctly, as the co-ordinator of an existing but undirected national movement, not as its prime initiator. Simplistic historical texts often give the impression that the agricultural revolution was a purely British advance made in the first decade of the eighteenth century by aristocrats like 'Turnip' Townshend based in East Anglia. The truth, unflattering to the national ego, is that most of the important new crops, turnips included, and the new systems of crop rotation and the restoration of fertility to worn out soils, were pioneered in the seventeenth century by France and the Low Countries. The same goes for horticulture; the English gentry were beginning to catch the contagion of flower mania from Holland, the rival Protestant economy. To satisfy this genteel hobby and to inform open minded landowners, scholarly and provocative books were coming on to the market. Parkinson's *Paradisi* had exposed Gerard's *Herbal* of 1597 for the plagiaristic and inaccurate work which it was. Gervase Markham's *Farewell to Husbandry* (1631) for 'the enriching of all sorts of Barren and Sterile grounds in our Kingdome, to be as fruitful in all manner of Graine, Pulse, and Grasse as the best grounds whatsoever',[5] showed that there was a national eagerness for exactly those improvements by new crops and new rotations of fields that Hartlib, with his continental experience, would soon be offering. All he needed to do was to co-ordinate and publish these methods, create a market for seeds from France and Flanders, effect introductions and encourage an informed body of gardeners, farmers and landlords. It would be Pansophism realised.

These were exciting years for plant men. John Tradescant the elder, trained by Robert Cecil at Hatfield to be a gardener of vision and ambition, had been travelling Europe and the Mediterranean for almost twenty years to collect plants and bulbs, the latter by the thousand from Dutch nurseries. As Hartlib noted approvingly, 'many things might I add of this kind, but for brevities sake I refer you to Master John Tradescant, who hath taken great pains herein, and daily raiseth new and curious things'.[6] It was about 1629 that Tradescant set up his 'Ark' in South Lambeth, a combined botanical and nursery garden. He and Jean Robin, head gardener at the Louvre, regularly exchanged new species brought back from Canada and Virginia.

There was no need for Hartlib to specify those 'choyce flowers' in his quadrant garden. They would have been a selection of the ones that Parkinson listed in his eighth chapter as 'Out-landish' flowers: to twentieth-century eyes it is a modest and unremarkable list which would have left flower beds bare for sometimes whole months together, but to seventeenth-century gardeners they were 'choice'. In roughly their flowering sequence Parkinson offered:

Aconitum (Winter wolves bane), Hepatica, Laurestinous or Wilde Bay Tree, Dog-tooth Violet, Safron-cross, Double Daffodil, Garden Poppy, Oriental Nicenthus, Crowne Imperiall, Tulips, French Cowslips, Fritillaria, Auricula (Bears Ears), Grape Flower,

Flowerdeluce, Honeysuckles, Day Lilies, Crowfoot, Martagons, Gladiolus, Double Yellow Rose, Syringa, Iasmines, Balsame, Larkes-spures, Mountain Crocusa, Cyclamen, Purple Marigold, Blew Bell-Flower, Meadow Saffron, Black hellebore or Christmas Flower.[7]

Hartlib's abstract geometry of a circular garden and estate may appear remote from reality, the aristocratic geometry of Wilton Garden applied to the farmyard, but in practice it set in train a national movement away from the peasant farming of the old open field system towards enclosures. He realised that it would involve social upheaval and hardships, but there would be the rewards of increased production. 'I have observed', he noted severely: 'in all places in England the great inconveniences that come by want of Enclosure both to private & publicke . . . unremediable intanglements or intermixture of Interest of several Persons in the same Common, in the same field, in the same Close, nay sometimes in the same acre'.[8] To disentangle those 'intanglements' would, over the next two hundred years, destroy a historic rural economy. Indifferent to such consequences, rather than unaware of them, Hartlib played on both the greed and the piety of his readers with equal skill. He concluded his *Discourse of Husbandrie used in Brabant and Flanders* with a naked appeal to capitalist instincts:

Thus I have plainly shewed what I promised in my Preface, that was, how an industrious man in Brabant and Flanders would convert five hundred Acres of barren and heathie Land from little value in five years to be worth above seven thousand pound a year. You may continue this yearlie profit of seven thousand eight hundred a year upon this five thousand Acres. If you will by *Liming, dunging,* or *marling* and *devonshiring* [burning the turf] again the first hundred Acres, laid down with *Clover grass,* and sowing it with *Flax* and *Turnips* as before.[9]

With all his enthusiasm and proseletizing zeal Hartlib had no talents for visual preception. That circular estate in his *Discoverie for Division* looked a most unseductive proposition, but his ideas were soon being picked up by livelier writers with a warmer sympathy for their readers. Walter Blith's *The English Improver Improved* of 1652 made a direct appeal to Cromwellian veterans newly settled on landed estates. Its frontispiece is headed 'Vive la Republick', a foreshadowing of 1789, and features, below scenes of battle, the latest ploughs, farming implements and surveying apparatus. In the centre of all this is set a promise of 'Improveableness' in yields of farm land: 'Some to be under a double and Treble others under a Five or Six Fould. And many under a Tennfould, yea some under a Twenty fould Improvement'. In addition to the usual advocacy of clover and sainfoin, Blith offered wealth from the planting of 'Welde, Woade, and Madder, three rich commodities for Dyars', 'Hops, Saffron and Liquorish, with their Advance' and 'Rape, Cole-seed, Hemp, & Flax, and the profit thereof'.

Blith was a Republican, writing just before Cromwell imposed his order on the New Saints, but Blith's spirit and his visual assault would survive the Commonwealth years. John Worlidge's *Systema Agriculturae* of 1669 repeats Blith's promises in rhyming couplets with an even more engaging frontispiece to capture Royalist sensibilities.

Realising perhaps that his little pamphlet – books were amateurish in a competitive publishing world – Hartlib tried to revive that college for the sons of fellow Puritan improvers which he had run briefly under the wing of the Bishop of Lincoln in the 1630s. But when he proposed in 1651 'the Erecting of a Colledge of Husbandry', his appeal was one of devout idealism:

The frontispiece to Walter Blith's The English Improver Improved *(1652) catches the country in its brief republican phase. Idealism and utility come together in this persuasive propaganda for enclosures and 'improvements'; the Agricultural Revolution has begun.*

I find by Experience, that it is nothing but the Narrowness of our Spirits that makes us miserable; for if our Hearts were enlarged beyond ourselves, and opened to lay hold of the Advantages wich God doth offer, whereby we may become joyntly serviceable unto one another in Publicke Concernments; we could not be without Luciferous Employments for ourselves; nor Unfruitful to our neighbours.[10]

Yet entry to this godly college would have required 'a payment of fifty pound' and would have been open only to a man with £250, 'as a stock to set up for himself'. He would have, more-

First cast your eye upon a Rustick Seat,
Built strong and plain, yet well contriv'd, and neat,
And scituated on a healthy soyl,
Yielding much Wealth with little cost, or toyl.
Near by it stand the Barns fram'd to contain
Enriching stores of Hay, Pulse, Corn and Grain;
With Bartons large, and places where to feed
Your Oxen, Cows, Swine, Poultrey, with their breed,
On th'other side hard by the House, you see
The Api'ary for th'industrious Bee.
Walk on a little farther, and behold
A pleasant Garden from high Windes and Cold
Defended (by a spreading, fruitful Wall
With Rows of Lime, and Fir-trees streight and tall,)
Full fraught with necessary Flow'res and Fruits,
And Natures choicest sorts of Plants, and Roots.
Beyond the same are Crops of Beans and Pease,
Saffron, and Liquorice, or such as these;
Then Orchards so enrich'd with fruitful store,
Nature could give (nor they receive) no more,
Each Tree stands bending with the weight it bears
Of Cherries some, of Apples, Plums and Pears:

Not far from thence see other Walks and Rows
Of Cyder-fruits, near unto which there flows
A Gliding Stream; the next place you discover
Is where St. Foyn, La Lucern, Hops and Clover
Are propogated: Near unto those Fields,
Stands a large Wood, Mast, Fewel, Timber yields,
In yonder Vale hard by the River stands
A Water-Engine, which the Winde commands
To fertilize the Meads, on th'other side
A Persian Wheel is plac't both large and wide
Toth' same intent; Then do the Fields appear
Cloathed with Corn, and Grain, for th'ensuing Year.
The Pastures stockt with Beasts, the Downs with Sheep,
The Cart, the Plough, and all, good order keep;
Plenty unto the Husbandman, and Gains
Are his Rewards for's Industry and Pains.

'The Explanation of the Frontispiece'
from John Worlidge's *Systema Agriculturae*, 1669

over, to be 'a single man; and if he shall at any time marry, he is from thenceforth to be accompted dead to the Society'.[11] Such were the tensions of the Puritan spirit. There is, however, no doubt that this dual appeal to base and noble instincts was effective. In 1638 England was still a corn importing country. By 1660, despite the ravages of civil war, she had become a substantial corn exporting economy. That was perhaps Hartlib's most notable memorial; but there were others and more tangible in stone and earth.

Despite its apparent abstract impracticality his suggestions for a house at the centre of a geometrically conceived area were taken up at the highest level by both Royalists and Parliamentarians, albeit with a modification from circles to rectangles, a geometry closer to that of the very Pansophic Physic Garden at Oxford, opened in 1632. The enclosure with which Sir John Harrison, a wealthy royal tax farmer, or licensed tax collector, surrounded his heavily magnificent house at Balls Park, Hertford, has gone now, but as recorded in prints and a faded mural within the house it was originally Hartlibian.[12] High walls surrounded the four equal-sized gardens around the house, and at each corner was a two-storeyed garden house. Whether Sir John Harrison used these as Hartlib directs for brew-house, bake-house, dairy and laundry is not known, but the stable ranges and utilities were all kept at a distance from the house on the perimeter wall, thus avoiding those 'offensive sights and smells'.

To experience today the realities of one of Hartlib's gardens of reason it is only necessary to visit the seat which Lord Chief Justice, Oliver St John, raised in the years of his power: Thorpe Hall, a mile outside Peterborough. It remains a country house experience like no other in the tight relationship between the gardens and the house. As *Discoverie for Division* rightly claimed 'here your house stands in the middle of all your little world enclosed'.[13] A high walled rectangle cuts off the composition completely from the flat fields around. There is no park to ease the link between gardens and ordinary countryside, but handsome sitting niches are set in pairs at intervals on the outside of the grey stone walls, as if to make up for this harsh separation. There

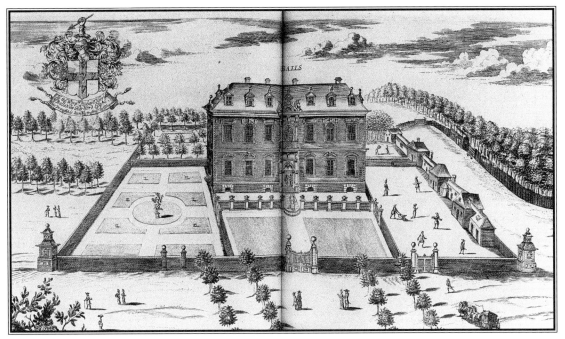

Samuel Hartlib was influential for more than ten years before the Civil War and the grounds of Balls Park, Hertford, were laid out in about 1640 for the royal tax farmer, Sir John Harrison, in a foreshadowing of Hartlib's approved geometry.

Cromwell's Lord Chief Justice, Oliver St John, was so devoted to his tightly enclosed formal garden that he had six great viewing bays constructed on the garden front of his otherwise severely plain Thorpe Hall, near Peterborough.

are entry fronts to north and south, approached between massive gate piers with only a brief, unimpressive lawn between the gates and the front doors; the broad main gardens, those of pleasure to the east, orchard and kitchen gardens to the west, are hidden away, private worlds for the owner. All the architectural emphasis of Thorpe is concentrated on the east where six great projecting bays of 'Ipswich-style' windows overlook, on the left, what was Hartlib's garden E, 'for Physical plants', and on the right, D, 'the Garden for choyce fruits and flowers'. St John's garden designer, probably John Stone, has followed Hartlib's ordering exactly. These two gardens can be viewed easily from the house, indeed Thorpe has been created virtually to enforce such viewing by the windows; but to actually reach the gardens requires an exit from the south front. Here a choice of inspection patterns opens up.

To the left a raised viewing walk allows a visitor to overlook the choice flowers in the eastern gardens. But in the true spirit of Hartlib's husbandry the entrance to the kitchen garden on the right is the more ceremonial. The way runs through a pedimented arch at the end of the stable range which, against Hartlib's advice, is built contiguous to the main house. Beyond, in Hartlib's area B, is the kitchen garden, now modernised, and there are still orchard trees growing in what would have been C on Hartlib's idealised plan. If the left-hand turn had been taken then the raised walk would offer the only partial escape from Thorpe's claustrophobia with an uninteresting vista over the containing walls to the fields beyond. At the end of the walk and obviously intended as an excursion point for the ladies is a heavy, three-bay garden house of blocked Doric columns. In keeping with the whole concept this only provides views back into the gardens, none to the outside world. The original layout of the flower beds is not known.

Much is made in garden histories of a move, effected around 1610, from English knots to French parterres. In fact, of the nine ground plots for knots illustrated in William Lawson's *New Orchard and Garden* of 1623, three, the 'Cinkfoyle', 'Flowerdeluce' and 'Trefoyle', could all pass as delicate and complex enough to be called parterres. Plant fanciers would choose knots rather than parterre designs because knots left spaces for flowers. Poor gardeners would take the parterre because then all the intricate interstices could be filled with coloured gravel. At Thorpe there appears to have been no directional emphasis towards what would have been the herb garden, that for 'Physical plants' in the north-east corner. The orchard in the north-west, on the other hand, was once furnished with another garden pavilion.

While full of interest, Thorpe's 'little world enclosed' gives the impression of being in nervous retreat from the surrounding estate which it should dominate. It has neither natural graces nor any sense of sequence. A final verdict has to be that reason does not make a garden, but it would be unfair to dismiss Hartlib's designs on one instance carried out for an owner who would have been far too busy in the state to give his grounds any feeling of practical humanity. Snitterton Hall, outside Matlock in Derbyshire, another rare survival of the Commonwealth years, is more likely to represent Pansophism as applied to a challenging terrain and modified by functional compromises.

The house, built in what would by the late 1640s have been a very old-fashioned Tudor vernacular, was the home of a Royalist colonel, John Milward who had made his peace after 1646 with his parliamentarian neighbours. Snitterton clings to steep sheep pastures among the rough, deeply quarried and mined hills of the Derwent valley. Here, unlike Thorpe, Nature can only be excluded and ordered with an effort, and yet that effort has been made. Stone walls and strong confinements abound, but the small scale and the headlong slopes humanise it all.

The way to the house is up a steep mountain lane which climbs with a confusion of trees, hedges and sandstone walls rising on its right, but even when the lane reaches house level

A relic of Hartlibian geometry at Snitterton Hall in Derbyshire. Retired from the Civil War, the Royalist Colonel John Milward created four square enclosures around his house, copies of the four quadrants of the 'entire Lordship'. This would have been the 'Garden for choyce fruits or flowers' with its viewing terrace and a two-storey 'elaboratorie' or garden house.

Snitterton still hides away behind a rough stone wall. At one end of this wall stands a two-storey pavilion; its twin at the other end has gone, leaving only the quoining. Here it seems at least possible that Hartlib's prescriptions of utility may have been followed, for the pavilion which survives does not look like a 'banquet house' or resort of pleasure. It has a substantial chimney on one outer wall. Only one small mullioned window on its upper floor looks out onto the road. All its generously large windows face in towards the 'choyce flower' half of the rectangular front garden. From its upper floor a door leads out onto a very high viewing terrace. Rather than a bake or brew house, it could well have been John Milward's 'elaboratorie', a grand potting shed and place for experiments with seeds and cuttings. The other lost pavilion may have been a 'herbal'.

Over the front porch is no Milward heraldry. Instead there are carvings of the olive, oak, rose and mulberry tree taken from the pages of the *Great Herbal* of 1530 to symbolise not only peace, strength, fidelity and prosperity, but Milward's own commitment to plant lore and husbandry. Out of sight, behind the wall of that viewing terrace but lying cheek-by-jowl with the main house, are the extensive but unpretentious buildings of the estate farm with its barns, byres and stables. To the other side, in the falling ground behind the lost herbal pavilion, three walled terraces descend the hill. The uppermost was a butts for archery, the lowest was the 'Pleasure Orchard'. These deviate from Hartlib's ideal and were the modifications to Pansophist orthodoxy that could be expected from a Royalist gentleman.

Behind the house, overlooking a wide valley of broken land, is the kitchen garden in its proper Hartlibian place (B) with a large stone privy for manure. A high peach wall props up this area from the hillslope. At one end is a sheltered alcove, at the other a raised platform, the only sign that anyone in these enclosed spaces was interested in the wild hills that surround Snitterton. Colonel Milward was related to Izaak Walton and Charles Cotton, and it seems almost inevitable that the initials of the author of *The Compleat Angler* should have been carved deep into the wall next to J.M. Below the peach wall is the 'Great Orchard' and the 'Cherry Piece'. Last of all is an angled fishpond with a ruined fishing house at its central angle. The short, shallow reach was for breeding the fish, the long, deep reach was where the fish matured and were netted. So the manor, its farm and its garden were a complete, self-supporting world of their own, a model of husbandry under a ghost of abstract geometry.

Samuel Hartlib survived the Restoration of 1660, as indeed did Oliver St John, while Colonel Milward became an active MP in the Cavalier Parliament of the new reign. Hartlib even petitioned for his £100 pension to be restored but that was more than royal benevolence could stomach. His verdict on the causes of the Civil War, printed in 1652 in his *Spirituall Husband-man,* may have been recalled: 'The venemous humours did proceed from the Mystery of Iniquity, which hath been set awork amongst us by the Popish and Prelaticall parties countenanced by Royal Authority'.[14] Now the 'Prelaticall' party was back in power again. But that Royal Society, for which his name was not put forward, was in many ways the natural successor to the informal society of the intelligentsia which he had built up with such good will and good intentions over the past two decades. If the immediate future for garden design after 1660 was to be one of ornate formal layouts, long power-vistas of clipped box, urns, greenery, statues and rigidly disciplined plants, then at least Hartlib had led his Hortulan Saints through a decade of utility, enquiry and applied science: an episode of earthy common sense that could never be quite forgotten.

Already in the 1650s he had begun to sense the tide turning against him. Foreign innovators can hardly expect to be popular. Hartlib wrote:

> For many years I have continued in the midst of some difficulties, and all our Changes, and have spent my self thereupon as upon a necessary duty, yet I have found no great Encouragement thereunto . . . nevertheless I hope I shall not faint. For I hope the Lord will continue me in the Apostle's minde, that I may say from my heart, 2 Cor. 12, 15, 16, 'That I will very gladly spend and be spent for the good of others', although for the most part it proves thankless office, and the more abundantly one is found to love the Publicke; the less he is loved. Yet let it be so with me, to minde the Publicke, and do good one to another, as servants of each other through love, for herein is the Law of Jesus Christ fulfilled, and his Kingdome advanced among us.[15]

There would never be another to approach the problems and challenges of gardening and agriculture in quite this selfless and dedicated spirit. Hartlib's name and serious presence will always be associated with a fascinating interlude of English garden history when, for a short time, gardens were not aesthetic markers to power or places of pleasure but resources for prosperity and a means to expedite the Second Coming. At the same time as Hartlib and his followers were making their ruthless, utilitarian, but largely logical proposals for landed estates and farms, classical architecture in London was being reduced, in a parallel process, to the puritan minimalist forms which would become standard when the city was rebuilt after the Great Fire of 1666. There was, however, in this remarkable republican interlude, a time when for twelve years it was possible to think the unthinkable and follow an entirely opposite strain of aesthetic idealism which the next chapter will consider.

CHAPTER THREE

JOHN BEALE AND A PURITAN VISION OF LANDSCAPE GARDENS

O n account of that £100 a year pension from Parliament and his failure ever to lay out a garden of his own, Samuel Hartlib must be ranked, like Inigo Jones, among the players. John Beale (1608–83) just scrapes by as a gentleman on the strength of his connections: Eton and King's College, Cambridge, the favour of the Duke of Buckingham, a father who was a Herefordshire squire and a mother, Joanna, who came from a family of courtiers. Against these, Beale was only a seventh child, ended up as the vicar of Yeovil, and only perceived, rather than planted, a natural garden where no one had ever noticed one before. He merits a chapter among English gardeners for his vision not his activity. It took a visually sensitive Puritan, writing during the Commonwealth with a devout sense of God's superiority to feeble men, to scorn formal gardens and anticipate by almost a hundred years the landscape ideals of William Kent and Capability Brown. While royalty were in exile and the aristocracy were lying low Beale, in his proposal for a book on 'Antique Gardens', could formulate confidently that, however much money and art might be spent on a plot of ground, a garden would come:

> noe where to perfection, without a reall and lofty hill, prominent or neighbouring over a river, and kind Vale, with parkes and lawnes, fayre boscage, or forrest. These appendances are necessary, and cannot be supplied by those Vepreta [hedges], and poore mimicall though sometimes chargeable mounts and wildernesses wch are enforced.[1]

It was a revolutionary breakthrough in the aesthetic analysis of gardens, parks and landscapes; but a breakthrough before its time. If Cromwell had left his Commonwealth in the hands of an able successor, instead of his weak son Richard, a republican regime of Puritan simplicities might just possibly have taken a permanent hold on English social life and thinking. In that case the idea of formal gardens in the Wilton manner: broad geometrical carpets of artifice with clipped hedges, fountains, patterned flower beds and mounts or viewing terraces for their appreciation might never have become generally fashionable. They were grossly expensive to lay out and keep up, a style of maximum capital expense, designed to make nursery gardeners rich and aristocratic gardeners impoverished. Instead, Beale's concept of Nature discreetly improved, a landscape of hills, woods and water, such as became general around English country houses in the mid-eighteenth century, could have become the mode among a Puritan ruling class from 1660 onwards.

But this is mere speculation. Beale failed to communicate his vision, the political climate changed and his opportunity to become a famous innovator never matured. It remains fascinating that such an advanced concept of landscape gardening could have been formulated so early, and it could hardly be a coincidence that it was Beale's country which would eventually perfect and popularise across Europe the 'English Garden' of natural topographical features gently improved rather than concealed and disciplined. In some fashion the Puritan reverence for the divine handiwork would survive and ultimately flourish in that sensitive appreciation of landscape which was to characterise the Picturesque movement of the later eighteenth century and flower at last into full-blown Wordsworthian Romanticism.

To the twentieth-century mind such enjoyment of natural features as hills, lakes and well-groomed meadows is so obvious a response that it is difficult to understand the apparent lack of such responses in an earlier society. To complicate the problem it is obvious from fifteenth-century religious paintings, both Italian and Flemish, that artists found it perfectly appropriate to insert well-composed landscapes of fantastic rock formations and consciously picturesque views of hills and rivers as backgrounds to paintings of saints, the Holy Family and donors. So at what point did an eye for such landscapes in paintings become open to their potential for garden design? Was it a continental taste which, in the absence of any impressive English school of painting in the fifteenth century, never crossed the Channel? If landscape was so current an artistic coin on the Continent then why were most gardens of the period in France an attack upon Nature rather than an appreciative response to it?

Elizabethan and Jacobean gardens were compounds of artifice, but what was developing in those reigns was an awareness of Arcadia, a feeling for the shepherd landscapes suggested by Theocritus and Virgil in their eclogues. No one would claim that Shakespeare was an accurate observer of real scenery on the strength of his 'Heaven kissing hill' or 'Night's candles are burnt out, and jocund day/Stands tiptoe on the misty mountain tops'. These are stylised images and Spenser's 'Bower of Bliss' is as intense a concentration of fruits, flowers and crystal fountains as any pleasaunce in Nonsuch or Hatfield House. But Shakespeare, notably in *As You Like It* and *The Winter's Tale*, does show, like Spenser, Marlowe and Sir Philip Sidney in their writings, an appreciation of the simple shepherd life and the hills and forests where such bucolic joys were best sited. Sidney's *Arcadia* in particular was generally valued and read. All its romantic, delicately mannered improbabilities take place in a pastoral land of rural lodges where the gentry retire to savour simple pleasures and privacy.

Arcadia, an idealised Greece, green and leafy as the real geographical Arcadia never was, seems, therefore, to have become the level of landscape appreciation which the nation's élite in Charles I's reign was coming to accept, and it was John Beale's good fortune to have been born in that most Arcadian of English counties, Herefordshire. With its abrupt but never threatening hills, its orchards, its consistent level of peasant prosperity and, above all, its apples and cider, Herefordshire was the county where the landscape of the shepherd eclogues of Classical literature was most satisfyingly realised. Beale was born in the heart of it all at Yarkhill on the river Frome, two miles north of the Wye and Backbury Hill where he was to have his vision of God as the ultimate gardener. It is an idyllic countryside of winding rivers and wooded hills where the Malverns edge down gently to the fertile plains around Hereford. This must explain why it was Beale who was able to make the move from Arcadia to landscape gardening.

There were other influences shaping his education. A natural scholar with a photographic memory, he went from Worcester Cathedral School to Eton in 1622 and in 1624 Sir Henry Wotton became Provost of Eton. Beale had been recommended to his care by the Duke of Buckingham through the influence of Beale's courtier uncles; and in his *Elements of Architecture* of 1624 Wotton had anticipated a more natural and relaxed style of gardening. The key sentence noted earlier is actually quoted by Beale in his synopsis of 'A Garden of Pleasure': 'as Fabriques should bee *regular*, soe Gardens should bee *irregular*, or at least caste into a very wilde *Regularite*.[2] So he must be seen as Wotton's first disciple, pressing on to a more extreme theoretical point than his teacher:

> For there is a kind of beauty, and a sure refreshment in a wildernesse, at least it is a good soyl if appendant to a pleasure garden. And it may be better, more kind, and more fruitfull, most certainly more fit for variety, and for all change of seasons by inequality, than by equality.[3]

From Eton, Beale went on to King's College, Cambridge where he became in 1632 a fellow. Between 1636 and 1638 he travelled as tutor to his cousin Robert Pye in France and Switzerland, but not in Italy. In 1637 he took holy orders but was showing a deep and exotic interest in eastern mysticism, Egyptology and the interpretation of dreams, not in the conventional forms of seventeenth-century religiosity. He did, however, share the current millennarian obsessions of the period, writing 'in very truth, and well-grounded Theology, we have no reason to conceive it to be long now, before the world shall be changed or consumed by the last fire'.[4] As a result of marrying the daughter of a local Herefordshire squire he lost his fellowship and retreated to Herefordshire where the tensions of loyalty caused by the Civil War seem to have precipitated him into some kind of nervous breakdown.

It was during his recovery from this that he fell under the influence of a local hermit and mystic, Henry Hereford, a relative of his wife and a one-time fellow of St John's College, Oxford. This hermit lived in a small cottage under the wooded lee of Backbury Hill and it was to a small sheltered meadow, enclosed by prehistoric or, as he thought, Roman earthworks at the top of Backbury, that Beale had got into the habit of retreating, at all seasons of the year, to study and recover his mental balance. This time of mental stress, slowly resolved in protective natural surroundings, would have given someone of Beale's intense religiosity a strong association between regeneration and a wooded hillside, a rough natural terrain and God's garden of peace.

At a more mundane level Beale was a devotee of cider, a connoisseur of the many cider-apple varieties and the vintage combinations that could be contrived by blending them with pears and crab apples. He would dismiss one as 'a more sullen crab, green about the end of Autumn', its liquors a mere 'Scythian wine, fit to quicken the palat of a sturdy hinde'.[5] Others would evoke from him all the raptures and finesse that a modern wine buff can extract from a sauvignon grape. Unexpectedly, this homely enthusiasm brought him into contact with Samuel Hartlib, a fellow Puritan and otherwise a strict utilitarian where gardens were concerned. But Hartlib loved orchards. He had noticed that only about four counties in England specialised in them and he was anxious for this easy bounty of Nature to be made more generally available.

Beale became caught up in Hartlib's web of correspondents and soon Hartlib had persuaded him to write and publish the Pansophist tract *Herefordshire Orchards a Pattern for all England Written in an Epistolary Address to Samuel Hartlib Esq. By I.B. 1657*. The original letters had been written in the previous year, 1656. It was dedicated gratefully to Hartlib 'the sedulous advancer of Ingenious Arts and Profitable Sciences', but those modestly anonymous initials 'I.B.' were a sign of Beale's shrinking disposition. If he had had the confidence a little later to publish 'Antique Gardens' with all his innovative theories under his own name he would have made his mark nationally. As it was he entrusted his best writing to John Evelyn to publish when Evelyn, a stylistic weathercock, had only half understood his theories and was preparing to trim his own garden notions to fit in with the royal Restoration of 1660. Consequently Beale's 'Antique Gardens' was never published.

In his Herefordshire Orchards, a Pattern for all England *of 1657, John Beale gave Hartlib's utilitarianism a smiling, pastoral face, a reaching towards Arcadia in an English guise. This frontispiece to John Worlidge's* Systema Agriculturae *of 1669 captures something of that cidrous Arcadian ideal.*

It is not certain whether Hartlib introduced Beale to Evelyn or whether Evelyn made his own contact, attracted by the poetic style and persuasive charm of *Herefordshire Orchards*. In general tone the book, though occasionally practical, is lyrical and often verges upon the notion that the natural growth of trees is as one with gardens:

Our Poets, new and old, and all best judgements do highly commend the pleasure of a Grove, *scriptorum chorus omnes amat Nemus, et fugit urbes*. We do commonly devise a shadowy walk from our Gardens through our Orchards (which is the richest, sweetest and most embellish'd grove) into our Coppice-woods or timber woods. Thus we approach the resemblance of Paradise, which God with his own perfect hand had appropriated for the delight of his innocent masterpiece.[6]

Even more significantly he approaches the idea that an irregularity like a hill is an advantage to be valued:

If the ground be very unequal, 'tis a great charge, and a very great vanity to levell it. For there is a kind of beauty, and a sure refreshment in a wilderness; at least it is a good sight if appendant to a pleasant garden: And it may be better, more kind, and more fruitfull, most certainly more fit for variety, and for all change of seasons by inequality, than by equality.[7]

If he had chosen a clearer word than 'unequal' this passage could be read as a timid declaration for the Picturesque, but Beale still clings to Hartlibian utility even in his most Arcadian encomiums:

I need not tell you how all our villages, and generally all our highways are in spring-time sweetened, and beautyfied with the bloomed trees, which continue their changeable varietyes of Ornament till (in the end of Autumn) they fill our Garners with pleasant fruit, and our cellars with rich and winey liquors.[8]

Orchards, he claimed, had given Herefordshire farmers long lives by their perfumes, shelter from storms and shade in summer. Their aesthetic advantage he left to the end of his eulogy: 'and (if I may acknowledge gratefull trifles) for that they harbour a constant aviary of sweet singers'.[9]

It was only in his slightly later correspondence (30 September 1659) with John Evelyn that Beale grew confident enough, not to lay down an express doctrine on informality in gardens, but to send Evelyn a long, precise description of the topography of the land around Backbury Hill, with a clear statement that such scenery was superior to man-made gardens and also, a Hartlibian touch, came much cheaper: 'the Mount is of a vaste height, millions of men and money could not easily rayse such a Mount'. Evelyn was a great list maker and loved to rank gardens in order of superiority but, Beale insisted, 'for one hundred pound, I would make it a fayrer Garden than many of those Princely Modern Gardens that are in yr liste'. He would cut out all the architectural garden features and plants that Evelyn valued so highly in his 'Elysium' manuscript. Beale was confident that trees were the making of a garden: 'Viridaria [plantations], Vireta [greensward], Walkes, Mounds, Groves and Prospects, bee the Principall, or ought to be soe, and the flowery area but the trimmings'.[10] Eighteenth-century landscape gardeners would have agreed with him but his claim, made in an age obsessed with new varieties of flowers, was close to heresy. The Commonwealth years were not so much a time of gardens as a whole but of flowers as singular specimens, eagerly collected, delicately nurtured. In his 1659 *Garden Book*, Sir Thomas Hanmer, Beale's almost exact contemporary, directed that tulips should be grown in a compounded earth of a little sand, some dry black mould and the rest willow earth, cyclamens and anemones in sifted dung and black mould, gilliflowers [carnations, not wallflowers] in rotted leaves or dung with some sand.

John Beale and Claude Lorrain were contemporaries. This 'Scene of Water and a Mill, with a Herdsman and Cattle' from Claude's Liber Veritatis *suggests that the two men shared, without knowing it, the same ideal of a peasant life in a tranquil shepherd's Arcadia.*

While Beale was satisfied with a few wild flowers and the Spring showing of apple blossom, Sir Thomas, a baronet of a distinguished Welsh border family, spent a lifetime of research and scientific gardening at his seat, Bettisfield in Flintshire. There he would coax new varieties of flowers into existence, exchange specimen bulbs with fellow enthusiasts in England and the Continent and pounce eagerly upon any plant or withered root brought back by sea captains from across the Atlantic. Beale's aesthetic preference was Claudeian, for a rugged, dramatic landscape with fine trees and a scatter of cottages, and it is worth remembering that while Beale was writing in the 1650s, Claude Lorrain was actually at the height of his powers, painting in Rome. Hanmer's aesthetic was for the individual flower, a rare white streak on a purple Brabancons tulip, the civet scent on a Muske Moly, the 'flesh colour'd flowers markt with a deeper red'[11] of the Male Royall Satyrium orchid. His book should be read to experience the horticultural excitement of the time and as a counterweight to Beale's advocacy of Nature wild and unadorned.

At this time the inconstant Evelyn, ready to blow with every wind of politics, was still in his Commonwealth phase – a Hortulan Saint – feeling his way, via pastoral Arcadias, towards informality. In 1654 his diary had recorded his grudging praise for Wilton Garden, 'heretofore esteem'd the noblest in all England'. It had, he allowed, 'a flower Garden not inelegant. But after all, that which to me renders the Seate delightfull, is its being so neere the downes & noble

I shall describe some of these strangers, and begin with one I had from the Barbadoes in the year 1655, which had a longish reasonable grey roote, which being planted in a pott in the Spring 1656, that May it put forth a great greene smooth hollow stalke, about 2 foote high, without any leafe on it, on the top whereof came two flowers shap't like Lillyes, of a fine shining red colour, betweixt an Orenge and a Pinke. In the end of June the flowers were gone, but the stalke continued till after the greene leaves were up, which was in the end of September. They were three in number, of the bignes of ye largest Daffodill leaves, which the frosts of that next wynter kill'd betimes, otherwise they would, I thinke, have continued till Spring.

Three rootes of this kind bore that yeare in three severall gardens in and neere London, but never since, though some of them are yet living, anno 1659, but different from what they did the first yeare, they did put their greene leaves forth of the earth in May, and kept them all the sommer, but no signe of stalke or flowers. I guess this to bee an Autumnall bulbe, which bore with us out of its season upon its transportation from the West Indyes hither, being out of the earth when the leaves should have come forth, and it is usuall for bulbes that come from remote parts to beare the first yeare and not afterwards, thought the rootes live still, as I have seene

often the experience of the flower of Garnsey, as wee call it. Tyme will enforme us better of the reason of these things. Some take this for Narcissus JACOBEUS, but I find severall differences in the descriptions, and till I am more assur'd shall call it Narcissus Barbadicus.

The Sphaericall Indian Narcissus, called also the great Indian Moly, and the Indian Ornithogalum is of great beauty, and rare in England, though it hath beene in France and Italy these twenty yeares. It hath on the top of a high stalke many branches, like those of a brancht candlesticke, the ends whereof turn upwards, and have on each a flower like a lilly, consisting of five leaves, some whereof have their leaves turning downe, and some the contrary, with six chives, and a long middle pointell crooked at the top. The color of the flower is red, like Martagon Pomponium. It flowers in September, and the greene leaves appear not till November, but if it beare not that yeare then in October, and live till the end of May, if frosts nip them not.

Sir Thomas Hanmer on what he believed were exotic Narcissi, from his *Garden Book* of 1659

plaines about the Country & contiguous to it'. On the next day he crossed those 'downes' and declared them 'for evennesse, extent, Verdure, innumerable flocks, to be one of the most delightfull prospects in nature and put me in mind of the pleasant lives of the Shepherds we reade of in *Romances* & truer stories'.[12] So he was conscious of his debt to writers like Sidney and, if not yet quite capable of digesting aesthetically the wilder wooded hills along the Wye, at least moving that way, coaxed on by the wealth which the flocks represented.

Evelyn was so impressed in 1659 by Beale's account of Backbury, yet so curiously incapable of writing his own account of the Surrey hills around Wotton, his birthplace, that he included Beale's description, without naming Beale, in his proposed 'Elysium Britannicum'. The point he was trying to make was a direct quotation from Beale's 'A Garden of Pleasure': that a garden designer should never impose his plan 'to any particular phantsy, but to apply unto it the best shape that will agree with the nature of ye place',[13] in itself a revolutionary notion and one that would have pleased Humphry Repton in the early nineteenth century. Unfortunately Evelyn could not resist a chance to insert his own pedantic scholarship into Beale's account of his Herefordshire scenery:

This Mount is of a vast and prodigious height, the ascent is by severall wayes some more oblique, some by more gentle degrees, windings and meanders (not unresembling that renowned persil Garden of Semiramis neere Chaona in Media described in chap. 7 lib. 3 of our Elysium) and there are likewise frequent rests, or if one desires it ascents, more direct, or one may take a gentle round, or walk up the hill by plaine and smooth passage without bush thickett, or any obstacle, or by more than semicircling Trenches, which are yet perfectly drie and carpeted with so short a mossy grasse, as cannot bedew the feet in any tyme of winter;

The relatively unchanged view out from the lower slopes of Backbury Hill, Herefordshire, over John Beale's 'Vale of Misery full of poore and wilde Cottages'. Beale and Wordsworth both sensed 'The still sad music of humanity' in such peasant small-holdings.

not withstanding which, those avenues are so deepe and the extreames so fenced, that our friend has there followed his studies most part of the Winter, sheltered and protected from all winds and importunity of weather: For the brims of those trenches are all along skreened with goodly Oakes, forming a natural close walk or Gallery: Upon the sumite of the Hill (the aire seeming allways serene and pleasant) is an ample greene plaine of a square figure, and every way crowned with thicketts of Oakes, the bordures whereoff are all winter long decked with a frieze of primeroses, violets and some other lively and odorant plants.[14]

On Backbury today it is still possible to follow Beale's various routes to the summit. Field paths across open slopes, grassy tracks and paved lanes through low oak woods offer alternative ways, and by some trick of the strata the tracks and lanes appear to run on terraces, Evelyn's 'Trenches', mounting in easy gradients as if contrived by deliberate design. But it is from the prehistoric, Iron Age, camp at the top that Beale's natural study and sudden surprise vistas can be most impressively re-experienced. Evelyn's version concludes:

At a furlong distance from this sweete and naturall Garden breakes a most horrid and deep precipice, fitted for Solitary Grotts and Caverns and upon the Top of this is a prospect over a most desolate Country, called the Vale of Misery, full of poore and wild Cottages seated on many lesser hills, nemorous and perruked with woods, and other vast objects of rocks, caves, mountaines and stupendous solitudes fitting to dispose the beholder to pious ecstacies, silent and profound contemplation. Whilst all the other views from the garden are of quite different prospects from this and indeed from each other, as into most rich vales and other ravishing varieties.[15]

This is the passage which so exactly previews (with devout Puritan undertones) the Picturesque evocations of William Gilpin, Uvedale Price and Payne Knight. Significantly, the last two were both Herefordshire residents and reared in much the same Arcadian surroundings as Beale. The description, with its 'most horrid and deep precipice' might seem over-written

'At a furlong distance from this sweete and naturall Garden breakes a most horrid and deep precipice fitted for Solitary Grotts and Caverns' – a natural landslip on the east side of Backbury. Beale's sensibility was poised midway between the Italianate grottoes of his English contemporaries and a Claudeian feeling for wild Nature.

'Landscape with Hermit' by Salvator Rosa (1615–73). The painter and John Beale were contemporaries and Beale anticipated the eighteenth-century fashion for mock hermits and fake hermitages in parks by making a real Herefordshire hermit his guide in matters spiritual and topographical.

but the 'Solitary Grotts and Caverns' were not fantasy. They can still be explored, a minor fugue in a Salvator Rosa vein. The 'square figure' of the earthworks is unchanged, but what was in Beale's time a 'sweete and naturall Garden' is choked with brambles and dwarf conifers. On the eastern rim of the square a sudden and completely unexpected chasm breaks open, an ancient landslip which has created a long winding 'Solitary Grott' of rock some 15 feet deep, overhung with trees, frightening in an acceptable measure and opening to command the 'Vale of Misery'. The 'poore and wild Cottages', one of them the hermit Henry Hereford's own, are still there, now smartened up as retirement homes but still half submerged in orchards. 'Misery' hints at the hermit's influence and almost suggests a sense of that 'still sad music of humanity' which Wordsworth experienced in a very similar setting a few miles further down the same river Wye.

Beale envisaged the whole hillside as the park or garden to Old Sufton, a middling sized manor house set in the mouth of a miniature valley where the waters from Backbury find their way into the river meadows of the Wye: 'At the foote of this Hill stands the Mansion, and from the side of it gushes forth a rich and pure fountaine of excellent water which (being apt to be improved to advantages of pleasure for the Garden) conveys itself through the house in a natural streame'.[16] The stream now bypasses Old Sufton and has not been 'improved to advantages of pleasure', only a hedge of old roses and a pigeon-house 'improve' the grounds. Evelyn would have been disappointed, Beale would have been pleased.

The account tails off into Hartlibian proposals for a profusion of 'Medicinal Simples' and tree-man's jargon of 'the shelter of Daphones [laurels], Cupresseta [groves of cypresses], Myrteta [myrtles] and other thickets, Vepreta of pereniall greenes'.[17] But these are more Evelyn than Beale. The perceptive vision was beginning to slip away. How were those Viridaria to be clumped? Was the stream to be widened into a lake? Was the woodland to be thinned? Beale has had a glimpse of the land's 'capabilities' but he was no Lancelot Brown. Evelyn characteristically leaped in to urge that 'it were capable of being made one of the most august and magnificent Gardens in the World as far exceeding those of Italy and France',[18] but only by standard seventeenth-century devices:

> it might have likewise the addition of walls, Architecture, porticos, Terraces, stands, obelisks, potts, Cascades, Fountaines, Basons, pavilions, Aviaries, Coronary Gardens, Vineyards, walks and other artificial decorations in their true and genuin places all which may be introduced without excesse of charge because Nature has already bin as we may say so Artificial.[19]

He had completely missed the point which Beale had made so forcibly and recently in his letter to Evelyn of 30 September 1659:

> I except [avoid] the charges of Architecture, conteining Walls, Statues, Summer Houses, Cesternes etc. (wch may bee of vaste charge) and I except the charge of Plants, and workemanship in setting the Plantes; and I would take upon my owne charge the forming of all the bankes, walkes, squares, and other figures for flowers, vineyards, Myrteta, Laureta, Vepreta, Cupresseta hedges of all sorts, for fruite, fragrancy etc. Judge nowe howe much by the mere situation I am assisted.[20]

Beale had no feeling for all the enchanting garden toys that cram the pages of Evelyn's 'Elysium Britannicum' – echo-exedras, trick fountains, crystal caves, pits to observe the stars by daylight – all he needed for his ideal garden was 'the mere situation'. To some extent he was of his age; in no way was he precisely anticipating Capability Brown's landscapes of bare elegance. If anything his vision seems to have been closer to that of Philip Southcote's *ferme ornée* of the mid-1730s, a composed woodland with a fringe of farmland and a trimming of flowering trees. But his Backbury featured a grander natural landscape, one more Claudeian, than Southcote could offer at Wooburn in Surrey.[21] Gardening at Sayes Court in Deptford, which was almost a London suburb, Evelyn could only reach out with difficulty to a real countryman's aesthetic, though he sensed that he was in touch with a superior concept, one with the far stronger religious underpinning of the original gardener.

Modest to a fault, Beale abandoned his plan of writing a book on 'Antique Gardens' under the impression that he had converted Evelyn to his vision and that Evelyn would include his ideas in his 'Elysium Britannicum', while this has only been published in the late twentieth century.

A year later there was a Stuart on the throne again and Beale became, in July 1660, the vicar of Yeovil where he remained until his death in 1683. Unlike his friend and mentor, Samuel Hartlib, he was made a Fellow of the Royal Society and in 1664 contributed, anonymously, a long chapter on the cultivation and culture of the apple, 'Pomona', to Evelyn's encyclopaedic *Sylva, or a Discourse of Forest-Trees*. A moment for advance had been lost, a vision had not been communicated because the time had not been ripe. A later generation of landscape fanciers would appear, less interested in the supposed contours of the Garden of Eden and the gardens of Semiramis, more concerned with the potential of Woodstock park, the observable outlines of Helvellyn, Snowdon and Snaefell. Beale's had been a vision too far. Where he and John Evelyn had more accurately anticipated the gardens of the immediate future was in their obsession with the science of trees and tree planting.

CHAPTER FOUR

THE GARDENS OF THE EVELYNS – GEORGE, JOHN AND CAPTAIN GEORGE

Geeorge Evelyn was born in 1617 and his brother John, the diarist, in 1620, the sons of the wealthy squire of Wotton in the hilly south of Surrey. Their paternal uncle Robert had emigrated to America in 1610 and it was there that their cousin, another George, was born. He was known later as 'Captain' George, the kinsman whom John mockingly called 'the great Travellor' who 'had a large mind, but overbuilt everything'.[1] John's relations with his 'dear Brother George' were equally competitive and best described as tense but close.

In an autobiographical sketch, *De Vita Propria*, written retrospectively about 1697, John Evelyn claimed that his good wet-nurse had lived 'in a most sweete place, towards the hills, flanked with wood and refreshed with streames, the affection to which kind of solitude I sucked in with my very milke'.[2] The comment explains his response to John Beale's claims for the sympathetic effects of natural scenery on a troubled mind; but his own lame description of his beloved Wotton as being,

A Cavalier courtier with the heart and mind of a Puritan scientist, John Evelyn was Hartlib's real successor. With the many editions of his Sylva (1664) he converted all England to the utility of tree planting but, unlike Beale, never grasped the potential Arcadian poetry of that process.

in a Valley, yet realy upon a greate rising; being joynd to one of the most eminent hills in England . . . a noble Seate; for Mounts, Cascades & Fountaines . . . wanting neither Fountaines, Grots, and other amoenitys of Ponds; to which might be added Canales of considerable length[3]

proves that he had none of Beale's lyrical appreciation of natural landscape, only an eye for how that landscape could be artificially reshaped.

Until he was sixteen Evelyn was brought up by his grandmother in Lewes, in virtual exile from an ailing mother and remote father, acquiring a reserved and critical detachment of manner from which he never escaped. An intense and sincere Christian religiosity turned him into that curious hybrid, a Puritan High Church man, desperately moral on sexual matters and consequently an uneasy presence in the relaxed, not to say debauched, atmosphere of the Court of Charles II. That moral righteousness did not, however, lead him to avoid the seats of power. His description of himself as 'a man of the Shade, and one who had convers'd more amongst Plants and Books than in the Circles of Court',[4] was not far removed from downright humbug.

Oxford influenced Evelyn very little; he had no time for his tutors and no disposition towards youthful high spirits. A four month visit to the Low Countries in the summer of 1641, ostensibly to give him some experience of military campaigning, left him with a profound respect for the cleanliness and order of Dutch towns and an enduring admiration for the Dutch practice of planting long regular rows of lime trees everywhere: 'a stately row of Limes on the Ramparts' of Wilhelmstadt, 'Streetes so exactly straite . . . being so frequently planted and shaded with the beautiful lime trees, which are set in rowes before every mans house, affording a ravishing prospect' in Amsterdam, and 'a faire Garden and Parke, curiously planted with Limes' at Honselaarsdijk, the Prince of Orange's palace outside The Hague.[5] Trees planted in rows were no absolute novelty in English gardens before Evelyn began to write and publish; but it was he who first used and popularised the term 'avenue', and it would be his *Sylva* of 1664, with three further editions before 1706, which helped to turn the English gentry from an infatuation with flowers to a far more profitable interest in tree planting. Those months in the sober, tree-lined streets of Holland and Flanders would have far more impact on John Evelyn's garden-thinking than his subsequent three years in Italy.

He returned in October 1641 to an England torn between loyalties to King and Parliament. As a devout Anglican, John was committed to the royal cause but his father had died in 1640. Brother George now ruled at Wotton, and the county of Surrey was Parliament territory. Any open declaration for the King would result in ruin for the Evelyns. Forced to pose as a political neutral, John fell into a depression and, writing in his autobiography, records how he turned for therapy to gardening in the soft sandy soil of well-watered Wotton: 'I made (by my Bro: permission) the stews & receptacles for Fish, and built a little study over a Cascade, to passe my Melancholy houres, shaded there with Trees, & silent Enough.[6]

Later in his diary Evelyn gives a different account of this retreat to Wotton:

> I built (by my Brothers permission,) a study, made a fishpond, Iland and some other solitudes & retirements at Wotton, which gave the first occasion of improving them to those Water-Workes and Gardens, which afterwards succeeded them, and became the most famous of England at that tyme.[7]

He further describes this alfresco water feature as: 'a triangular Pond or little stew, with an artificial rock'.[8] Melancholy or 'Accidie' was a fashionable psychic disorder for the post-*Hamlet* generations of the early seventeenth century and fishing was a thoroughly respectable response to it. Sir Henry Wotton, when Provost of Eton, often relaxed with a fishing rod, and while Evelyn was actually creating his little triangular island study Izaak Walton was preparing his classic appreciation of the sport, his *Compleat Angler*. As noted in chapter two, Snitterton Hall had its own 'little retiring place' in the angle of its fishpond. This mid-century fashion for angling from a comfortable pavilion would, like the tree planting craze, broaden the gentry's concept of the bounds between Nature wild and Nature tamed as they extended their

Chauncy's illustrator was John Drapentier so this drawing may represent a Dutchman's mocking view of English whimsicality and the lack of logical order in an English estate, exemplified in this engaging tree house at Pishiobury. Notice the picnic tree, the raised cattle grid and the three gentlemen apparently shooting sheep.

gardens to link up with lakeside pleasaunces. In his diary entry for 22 July 1654 Evelyn captured the charm and convenience of a well-stocked park and fishing lodge as a fast-food outlet:

> We departed & dined at a ferme of my *U. Hungerfords* cald *Darneford magna*, situate in a Vally under the Plaine, most sweetly water'd, abounding in Trowts and all things else requisite, provisions exceeding cheape: They catch the Trouts by Speare in the night, whilst they come wondring at a light set in the sterne: There were Pigeons, Conys, and foule in aboundance, & so we had an excellent dinner at an houres warning.[9]

In October 1644 Evelyn left George at Wotton and escaped the Civil War to travel in France and Italy. He would study law at Pavia, cultivate the friendship of the dying Earl of Arundel, Inigo Jones's old patron, and not return to England until 1647. His 'Kalendarium' for this period presents problems. It was not a real diary but an account deliberately composed much later from notes and jottings. It is full of the various hydraulic curiosities which he had seen in the famous sixteenth-century villa gardens of Italy: 'a monster which makes a terrible roaring with a horn', 'hydraulic organs and all sorts of singing birds moving', and 'a copper ball that continually daunces about 3 foote above the pavement by virtue of a Wind conveyed seacretly to a hole beneath it'.[10] But almost all these details are second-hand, taken from travel writings by Pflaumem, Raymond, Monconys or, in the instance of Tivoli, Sir Henry Wotton. The question has to be asked whether Evelyn was really interested in these old-fashioned prodigies which had amused the Jacobean Court or whether he merely thought that he should be interested as a self-appointed scientist whose role was, as he put it, 'intelligent and taciturn observation'.

There seems to have been far more personal feeling in his delighted response to the sheer social utility of contemporary French tree planting in Paris. While the Italians were caught in the notion of a garden as a circuit of shade set at intervals with ingenious mechanical marvels, the French were moving away from the medieval concept of a garden as one or several private enclosures towards the idea of a park as a social meeting place. In Paris, for his 6 February 1644 entry, Evelyn wrote, using this time his own words and not those of an earlier traveller:

> I this day finish'd with a Walke in the greate Garden of the Thuilleres, which is rarely contriv'd for Privacy, shade, company, by Groves, Plantations of tall trees, especially that in the middle being of Elmes, the other of Mulberys; & that Labyrinth of Cypresse; not omitting the noble hedges of Pome-granads, the fountaines, Piscianas, Aviary, but above all the artificial Echo, redoubling the words so distinctly, and as it is never without some faire Nymph singing to its gratefull returnes: standing at one of the focus's, which is under a tree or little Cabinet of hedges, the Voyce seemes to descend from the Clowds; and at another, as if it were under grownd.[11]

'Privacy', 'shade' and 'company' are the key words here, and in a sense they contradict each other. Evelyn had a strong feeling for privacy and enclosure, for green shades where he could hide away and indulge his melancholy. Also Evelyn, the scientist savant, a future correspondent of Samuel Hartlib and a man who would be a founder Fellow of the Royal Society, had an interest in a scientific curiosity like an 'Echo', a terraced concave where a lovely girl could sing to herself. But on the other side there was the intoxicating, up-to-date openness of it all, life on the wheel: 'the middle Circle being Capable to contain an hundred Coaches to turne commodiously, & the larger of the Plantations for 5 or 6 Coaches a breast'.[12] This was the garden expanding into the park and reaching out to embrace the modern world. Evelyn never finally resolved these conflicting tensions. That was his limitation as a garden designer, but at least he was aware of them and tried out solutions.

While in Paris on his return journey Evelyn, aged twenty-six, married the twelve-year-old daughter of Sir Richard Browne, the King's ambassador to the French court. Politically this was an unfortunate move as he came back to an England where the King was a prisoner in Hampton Court and would soon be executed. Brother George had made his peace with Parliament and even witnessed the King's execution. Captain George was now in England, but in whose army he had served as Captain was never made clear. John found the atmosphere in the country oppressive and retreated to his father-in-law's house in Paris. It was at this point that the two George Evelyns totally reshaped the garden at Wotton. John took this as a moral defeat, seeing himself as the family's horticultural expert. He tried to suggest that his advice had been asked for and followed, but it is quite clear that the major works all took place while he was in Paris in 1651 and that he had virtually no say in the design of Captain George's innovative and extremely important Doric temple-portico grotto. Nor did he suggest its dramatic siting in the middle of a three-terraced Italian-style hill garden.

Between them the two George Evelyns, working in the depth of Samuel Hartlib's utilitarian winter of garden design, had produced something significant and original. If only it were possible to describe their new hill at Wotton as a dramatic natural feature then, with its scholarly Tuscan Doric portico, Captain George's bold gesture could be described as Claudeian, a Claude landscape of great trees and a classical temple. In harsh reality, however, that angular heap of terraces looked, as John Evelyn's sketches prove, anything but natural when it was first carved out, more like a ziggurat decorated with poplars. Nevertheless the columned temple gesture, complete with Doric frieze, had been made for the first time in England as a garden feature. Captain George, an American, much travelled in Italy, had persuaded his cousin George to take an imaginative step forward which John Evelyn, for all his experience of Italian gardens and Roman temple remains, was never able to follow up.

Today the garden of the two Georges has become truly Claudeian at last by natural decay, a secret and private place, almost claustrophobic, reached only through the house. The steep narrow valley of the Tilling Bourne closes in across the lawn which Captain George's excavations created by removing 'a mountaine that [was] overgrowne with huge trees and thickett, with a moate, within ten yards of the very house', done 'without greate Cost' by flinging the sandy soil into the rapid stream.[13] Even now the terraces, softened by landslip, are oppressively close to the drawing room windows and George's fountain. The stone wall which held up the lowest terrace has gone and with it the two little

The three-part Italian-style terraced garden cut out of the hillside at Wotton Place, Surrey, in 1651 by Evelyn's elder brother George. Their American-born cousin, also George, designed the Doric temple front to the Grotto of Venus, visible here at the centre of the lowest terrace.

Cousin George Evelyn had travelled in Italy, which explains the confidence of this dramatic building. John Evelyn was ungenerous in his criticism of 'greate faults in the Colonade'. By setting a Doric temple façade on an English hillside, George Evelyn was making giant strides towards Claude's picturesque deployment of classical remains.

flanking porticoes guarding paths up to the topmost terrace. But the main Temple-Grotto with its four columns, grand in scale and solemn in impact, survives, a convincing home for the Greek mysteries. Originally the dark interior of vermiculated rustication was lightened by a fresco of Venus riding a dolphin. Would the devout John have disapproved? He noted 'nakeds' in Italy but his own garden at Sayes Court would feature neither 'nakeds' nor temple columns and it seems likely that his Puritan disposition set him against such evocations of a pagan world. John was irritated by his brother's transformation scene. He claimed that the Captain 'was mistaken in the Architecture of the Portico, which tho' making a magnificent shew, has greate faults in the *Colonade*, both as to the Order, which should have ben *Corinthian* & the Ornaments, the rest is very tollerable'.[14] There is something about the classical orders which brings out the pedantic worst in architectural critics.

Very soon after Wotton's reshaping John bought his father-in-law's estate, Sayes Court, on the banks of the tidal Thames only half a mile from the naval dockyard at Deptford, and by 1652 had planned out a new garden complex around the dilapidated Elizabethan manor house and home farm. It was an odd place to settle in: level fields with none of Wotton's wooded hillsides, industry almost on his doorstep. But he bought it at a fair price; London with all his friends was only a short boat trip up the river. What has also to be remembered is that, setting aside the two dreadful facts that it had murdered his king and disestablished his church, by disposition John Evelyn was a natural Commonwealth supporter. He was moral, inclined to religious introspection, keen on science and scientific improvements, a perfect prey for Hartlib's great web of *bien pensant* letter writers. This paradox explains his confusing behaviour during the remainder of the 1650s. He was laying out a garden which was the very opposite of Brother George's at Wotton: not at all Italian, partly French, partly Dutch, full of horticultural improvements and in some respects very Hartlibian in its mix of utility and pleasure. Yet at the same time he was writing his 'Elysium Britannicum', intended to set up a model for future English gardens, its fluttering, interleaved pages crowded with Italian devices and curiosities: speaking statues, hydraulic organs, cool air machines, grottoes, formulae for artificial rocks, open-air echo chambers and water-animated figures. All these were frivolities which had singularly little place in the garden which he was planting as he wrote. This is the contradiction of the complex times in which he was working and of which he is a very fair reflection, these frivolities were scientific, they would have met with Hartlib's approval. We might

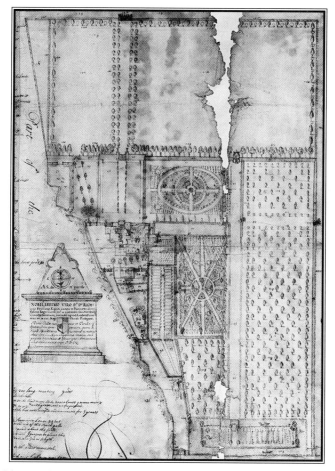

The cheerful chaos of the grounds of Sayes Court, John Evelyn's house at Deptford, has been obliterated by later building and left no trace beyond this detailed plan. At least half its acreage was planted with trees; the remainder was a jumble of formal enclosures, a fair reflection of Evelyn's mind.

see them now as largely inappropriate to a garden situation, but it was in this decade that the antiquaries, natural scientists, astronomers and all-purpose thinkers like Evelyn were gathering together, forming a scientific community that would, immediately the next reign gave them their chance, result in the Royal Society, in Newton, Boyle and Wren. Those toys of the 'Elysium Britannicum' were symptoms of their time, of a free-thinking if Puritanical-seeming decade.

Nothing remains of Evelyn's garden at Sayes Court. But so detailed is his plan of its layout and his accounts of it with a key of more than a hundred items to its various parts, that it is still possible to walk around it in the imagination. In this way all its contradictions can be enjoyed as they existed in its prime of the 1660s, when King, lords and ministers came there to absorb its lessons, to see the garden of the famous author of, not the 'Elysium Britannicum', for that was never to be published in his lifetime, but the far more practical *Sylva* and *Kalendarium Hortense* which he cannibalised from the wreck of the earlier project.

Unless they were arriving by boat, the visitors' first impression would have been very Franco-Dutch: a grand, even slightly pompous avenue of lime trees, double planted on each side of an arrow-straight drive aligned from Butt Lane onto the central bay of the Court. Before reaching the house this drive came to a line of palings planted with ash trees which it passed through by a gate between urn-topped stone piers. Then the mood turned homely Elizabethan, with twin bowling greens, one on each side of a drive lined by cypresses, up to the front door. To the right of the visitors at this point, over a wall with espaliers for fruit trees, was a purely Hartlibian whimsy, a milking green with walnut trees to provide, not only nuts, but thoughtful shelter for the milkmaids, all this immediately under the windows of the house. On the visitors' left, away from this home-farm wing of the establishment, was 'my Morine garden'. Pierre Morin had made a fortune by importing 'Alaternus' bushes (our lowly suburban privet) from the south of France to Paris where Evelyn had admired his town garden, an oval of clipped cypresses set within a rectangle, 'The Tulips, Anemonies, Ranunculus's and Crocus's &c being of the most exquisite'. Competitive as ever, Evelyn told his father-in-law that his 'Morine' garden at Sayes 'if God prosper us, will as far exceede that both for designe & other accomodations'.[15]

Immediately north of the Morine oval of flowers was one of those dominant barrier divisions which were such a feature of the garden, despite Evelyn's professed dislike of walls. This was a triple line of the huge Holly Hedge, the Tarras Mount and the Berbery Hedge. Beyond these was Evelyn's other great pride, the real centre of his confused maze of enclosures, around which all the others roughly circled: the Grove. In other gardens of the period this would be called a Wilderness, and what the Morine oval and the Grove had in common was sets of open-air 'Cabinetts', little private nooks of bushes or trees, four in the Morine, fourteen in the Grove, places where Evelyn could read and contemplate in privacy. The Grove's 'Union Jack' cross of walks was lined with privet hedges and into its triangles were crammed 1,300 walnut, service, sweet chestnut, ash, elm, beech and oak trees.

To the visitors' left of both Morine and Grove was what appears on the plan to have been Sayes's grandest and most nearly axial feature, the Long Promenade, 'being 526 foot long, 21 broad'.[16] But here Evelyn's whimsicality was evident. The Promenade's trees were only fruit trees, 'codlins' and 'pearemaines', a peasant touch which Beale would have appreciated and Hartlib approved. They connected one children's playground with another: a little gabled banqueting house and an enchanting treasure island of raspberry canes, asparagus and a mulberry tree set within a rectangular pond for swans, ducks and carp. This children's paradise could be reached either by a drawbridge at the end of the Long Promenade or by a little boat. Even further beyond the Promenade was the Great Orchard.

Walking back from the rectangular pond towards the house a mood of Hartlibian utility set in with more orchards and a long kitchen garden of ranked vegetable beds, farm buildings and an impressive lilac hedge, yet another of the garden's massive dividing units. Finally came the Private Garden and there for the first and last time there was a mild incidence of those 'Curiosities' with which Evelyn was filling the pages of his 'Elysium': an aviary for captive skylarks, robins and thrushes and one glass-fronted beehive, presented to Evelyn and his wife on their visit to Oxford in 1654, by Dr Wilkins, Master of Wadham College, Oxford and son-in-law to Oliver Cromwell. Two curiosities was not an impressive total, but it was expressly to see the beehive that Charles II visited Sayes Court with the Duke of Richmond and Lords Arlington and Lauderdale: half the ruling establishment, in 1663. Though they are unlikely to have escaped the Grove, the Morine and the island raspberry garden on the same day, it was the beehive, 'built like Castles and Palaces . . . adorn'd with variety of Dials, little Statues, Vases etc: very ornamental'[17] which Evelyn said the King had enjoyed. Set in one corner overlooking this walled garden for choice flowers was Evelyn's 'Elaboratorie, with a Portico of 20 foot long upon Pillars open towards the Private Garden'.[18] This, perhaps little more than a potting shed and place of retreat, had over it the pigeon loft to lend the murmurous sound of birds to Evelyn's meditations.

At a first glance the map of the Sayes Court gardens, dedicated incidentally to the Duke of Richmond and therefore intended to be noticed, appears a confusion. And so, in the sense of mood, it was a confusion of Franco-Dutch formalism, Parisian town house garden, children's playground, self-supporting farm and sylviculturalist's show piece. But what John Evelyn had created was what most good gardeners aim at, an enjoyable area full of surprises and sudden vistas, points of interest, changes of direction, in essence a series of enclosed gardens. Humour and earthy practicality show through the minor pomps and scientific earnestness.

What is unexpectedly absent, and this is a real failing in the sensibility of a man who had spent years of his youth in Italy and known Lord Arundel well, is any feeling for the

A drawing for a 'Transparent Bee-hive', intended as an illustration for Evelyn's never-published collection of garden curiosities, his 'Elysium Britannicum'. King Charles II visited Sayes Court one morning expressly to examine Evelyn's scientific garden toys, one of which was a bee-hive, 'transparent' in that it had a movable lid.

classical past. Classical sculpture was a subject on which Evelyn chose to remain blind; there was also the under-representation of 'Curiosities' at Sayes.

This last is more easily explained. Evelyn's curiosity-crammed 'Elysium' was ill-conceived. He not only realised that for himself when a third of the way through it, but he was told roundly that it was inappropriate and even rather silly by an impressive team of garden experts, twelve Oxford men to whom he had shown the manuscript. Their report is enclosed with the 'Elysium' like some permanent reproach to his immaturity. It might, if published, they told the author severely, save the gentry the expense of travelling to France or Italy, otherwise,

Ventiducts, Waterworks for Musicall especially and other motions (to ye Vulgar stupendous) devices by various casting reflecting and breaking of lights and shadows . . . and other Italian gloryes pompous beautys may one day be brought as fare as ye temper of ye climate will give leave, into English gardens,[19]

but not yet, the implication was, and please, not in our lifetime. Abashed by their verdict, Evelyn must have rethought his position and his readership. A scrappy minor book on orchards, grafting, nursery gardens and the construction of frets, by Nicholas de Bonnefois had proved an unexpected success when Evelyn had translated it in 1658. It was to go through three more editions under his title of *The French Gardener*. Encouraged by this he made a publishing decision more in tune with the temper of his times, scrapped the curiosities and gathered all his accumulated facts together into *Sylva, or a discourse of Forest-Trees and the propagation of timber*, which went through four

Note that whilst the Gardener rolls or Mowes, the Weder is to sweepe & clense in the same method, and never to be taken from that work 'til she have finished: first the gravell walkes & flower-bordures; then the kitchin-gardens; to go over all this she is allowed One moneth every three-moneths with the Gardiners assistance of the haw, & rough digging; where curious hand-weeding is lesse necessary.

Every fortnight looke on Saturday to your seede and roote boxes, to aire & preserve them from mouldinesse & vermine.

Looke every moneth (the last day of it) & see in what state the Bee-hives are: and every day, about noone if the weather be warme, and the Bees hang out for swarmes; having yr hives prepar'd & ready dressed.

The Tooles are to be carried into the Toole-house, and all other instruments set in their places, every night when you leave work: & in wett weather you are to clense, sharpen, & repaire them.

The heapes of Dung, & Magazines of Mould &c: are to be stirred once every quarter, the first weeke.

In Aprill, Mid-August, clip Cypresse, Box, & generally most ever-greene hedges: & closes, as quick-setts.

Prune standard-fruit & Mural Trees the later end of July, & beginning of August for the second spring: Vines in January & exuberant branches that hinder the fruite ripning in June.

The Gardner, is every night to ask what Rootes, sallading, garnishing, &c will be used the next day, which he is accordingly to bring to the Cook in the morning; and therefore from time to time to informe her what garden provision & fruite is ripe and in season to be spent.

He is also to Gather, & bring in to the House-Keeper all such Fruit of Apples, peares, quinces, Cherrys, Grapes, peaches, Abricots, Mulberies, strawberry, Rasberies, Corinths, Cornelians, Nutts, Plums, & generally all sort of Fruite, as the seasone ripens them, gathering all the windfalls by themselves: That they may be immediately spent, or reserved in the Fruite & store-house.

He may not dispose of any the above said Fruite nor sell any Artichock, Cabbages, Asparagus, Melons, strawberries, Rasberies, Wall, or standard & dwarfe fruite, Roses, Violets, Cloves, or any Greenes, or other flowers or plants, without first asking, and having leave of his Master or Mistress; not till there be sufficient of all garden furniture for the Grounds stock and families use.

He is to give his Mistris notice when any Fruites, Rootes, Flowers, or plants under his care are fit to be spent, reserved, cutt, dried, & to be gathered for the still house and like uses, & to receive her directions.

He is, when any Tooles are broaken or worn out, to bring the Instrument so unserviceable to his Master and shew it before another be bought.

Let him for all these observations, continualy reade and consult my Gardiners Almanac & Discourse of Earth.

From John Evelyn's *Directions for The Gardiner at Says-Court*, post-1686

editions by 1706, and his even more wildly successful *Kalendarium Hortense*, a practical month by month guide to the care of fruit and flower gardens. This would go through a remarkable ten editions before the end of the century. The first, with its encyclopaedia of tree facts, its vague aesthetic guidance for park planting and its financial inducements for timber planting as an investment, literally changed the face of the great estates of England. The obviously recent tree planting shown in the bird's-eye views of English country seats in Leonard Knyff and John Kip's *Britannia Illustrata* of 1707, is John Evelyn's best testimonial. The second, the *Kalendarium*, was simply a well-constructed guide which hit the market at the right time to fill a need. No great stylist, Evelyn could still communicate directly and he had the knowledge to pass on.

He had, in addition, a garden readily accessible from London, which proved that he could practise what he preached. Samuel Pepys had visited Sayes Court gardens twice before he actually met their creator. As Roger North admitted after a visit:

above all, his Garden was exquisite, being most bocaresque, and, as it were, an Exemplar of his Book of Forest trees. They appear'd all so thriving and clean, that, in so much Variety, no one could be satiated in viewing. And to these were added Plenty of ingenious Discourses, which made the Time short.[20]

In his own mind and by his own activities Evelyn was moving estate design on from a dated enthusiasm for hydraulic toys to a layout of trees extending far beyond the mere bounds of a garden. He was, of course, responding also to French influences which had come flooding in with the new reign. Le Nôtre was now the name to drop in informed garden circles as in the previous reign it had been that of André Mollet. The originality of this new wave of French garden fashions can be over-stressed. When his *Sylva* readers were finally given a plan for tree planting, in the 1706 edition, the blunt triangles of the groves and the intersections of the rides were only replicas of those which Inigo Jones had laid out at in the Wilderness at Wilton in 1635. They, in their turn, were taken from the Wilderness section laid out at St Germain-en-Laye in the early 1600s. But these were relatively toy plantings; Evelyn's contribution was one of scale and major investments.

Between the first 1664 edition of *Sylva* and the fourth of 1706, Evelyn expanded his text deliberately to emphasise the substantial financial reward from planting extensive woodlands and to impress on his readers how many leading aristocrats had already followed his advice. As a direct result of his writings, his advice and his royal connections, the deer park, which had tended in the past to be a separate fenced enclosure, a larder of live meat a little apart from a main house, became a noble leisure area enclosing the house itself and tied to it visually by both mile-long avenues and large, geometrically laid out plantations to shelter the deer. Kip's view of Westwood Park in Worcestershire shows a hunt in full cry among the dark woodlands that reflect the star shape of Westwood House itself. In a diary entry for 10 September 1677 Evelyn reflected with satisfaction on the transformation effected at Euston in Suffolk by following his planting scheme. An area of sandy heath, unprofitable for agriculture, had been turned into an aristocrat's leisure centre while the house functioned like a modern country house hotel. Clearly the pattern of house parties and weekend entertaining, which was to be so influential socially and politically in England for the next two hundred years, was already established. Following an account of the 'Canale . . . full of Carpes & fowle', Evelyn passed over a skew bridge to

an ascending Walke of trees for a mile in length: as tis also on the front into the Park, of 4 rows of Ashes & reaches to the Parke Pale which is 9 miles in Compas, & the best for riding & meeting the game that ever I saw, There were now of red & fallow deere almost a thousand, with good Covert, but the soile barren & flying sand in which nothing will grow kindly: The Tufts of Firr & much of the other wood were planted by my direction some yeares before. In a word, this seate is admirably placed for field sports, hauking, hunting, racing: The mutton small, but sweete: The stables are capable of 30 horses & 4 Coaches. The out offices make two large quadrangles, so as never servants liv'd with more ease & convenience, never Master more Civil; strangers are attended and accomodated as at their home in pretty apartments furnish'd with all manner of Conveniences and privacy.[21]

Initially he had offered little practical advice on the best geometry for a forest garden, but once Moses Cook had published his *The Manner of Raising, Ordering, and Improving Forest and Fruit Trees* in 1676, which included 'Several Figures for Avenues and Walks', Evelyn also offered suggestions for figures such as 'the Square with three Avenues breaking out at the three Angles' or 'the Circle with a star of Walks radiating from it'.[22] Not until its fourth edition did *Sylva* provide actual plans for planting trees axially to a main house, and by that time Evelyn was dead. Moses Cook laid out the forest garden at Cassiobury in Hertfordshire for the Earl of Essex in about 1669, inspired clearly by *Sylva*, and then later, as a partner of George London, brought his

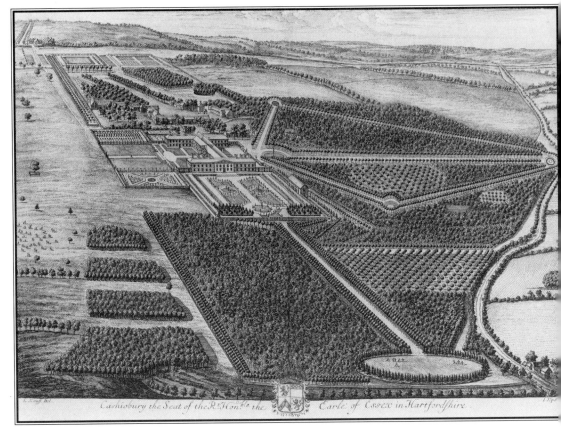

Moses Cook laid out this vast, French-style forest garden for the Earl of Essex at Cassiobury in Hertfordshire. In 1681 Cook became one of the founders of the Brompton Park Partnership, George London's new firm of nurserymen dedicated to projecting expensive formal garden designs. The tedium of these straight, tree-lined vistas leading from nothing to nowhere is here apparent, but they represented a profitable investment in timber, just as Evleyn had claimed in his Sylva.

expertise to the new Brompton Park Nursery: a neat example of gentleman–player interchange from ideas in print to roots in the ground. It should be remembered that John Beale supplied Evelyn anonymously with the whole section on orchards and cider making, 'Pomona', printed together with *Sylva* in all editions. Thus Hartlib's concern for husbandry was carried on in this way right through to the eighteenth century.

One most revealing entry in Evelyn's diary for 2 March 1671 indicates not only his status as the establishment's favourite savant, but the way in which the new gardens functioned socially, particularly those divisions of parts which were so prominent – hedges, walls and terraces – in Evelyn's own garden. He had just been trying to focus the King's wandering attention on the skills of Grinling Gibbons:

> I had a faire opportunity of talking to his *Majestie* about it, in the *Lobby* next the Queenes side, where I presented him with some Sheetes of my historie, & thence walked with him thro St *James's* Parke to the *Garden*, where I both saw and heard a very familiar discourse betweene [the King] and *Mrs. Nellie* as they cal'd an impudent Comedian, she looking out

of her Garden on a Tarrace at the top of the Wall, & [the King] standing on the greeene Walke under it: I was heartily sorry at this scene: Thence the King walked to the *Dutches of Cleavelands*, another Lady of Pleasure & curse of our nation.[23]

Behind the shocked puritanical disapproval Evelyn cannot quite conceal the enchanting casualness of a royal court where histories are discussed in walks across a park, laid out new in 1661; where saucy Nell Gwyn lies in wait on the top of her garden terrace, and the King chats back cheerfully to her from a green walk while standing several informal feet below.

Evelyn himself never constructed a true forest garden. What he did design for Henry Howard, later Duke of Norfolk, at Albury, his villa in Surrey a few miles from Wotton, suggests that he was still hoping to surpass the two George Evelyns' formal, engineered Italian garden at Wotton. John had cultivated the friendship of Inigo Jones's patron, the Earl of Arundel, as he lay dying in exile in Pavia, so he had a great respect for the Howard family and the younger Howards still favoured Italian rather than French garden models. Charles Howard, a younger son of Arundel and, like John Evelyn, a founder Fellow of the Royal Society, had carved a garden out of the Surrey hills which clearly impressed Evelyn while he was still in his Commonwealth phase. In August 1655 he had noted: 'I went to *Darking* to see Mr. Charles Howards Amphitheater Garden, or Solitarie recesse, being 15 Ackers, invirond by an hill: he shew'd us divers rare plants: Caves, an Elboratory',[24] and he visited this 'extraordinary Garden at Dip-den'[25] twice again in the next few years. So when Henry Howard asked Evelyn's advice on the garden which he had been constructing since 1655 at Albury, Evelyn eagerly 'designed for him the plat for his Canale & Garden, with a *Crypta* thro the hill &c'.[26] This was in September 1667, three years after *Sylva* and Evelyn's apparent conversion to French tree parks laid out longitudinally. But what he designed, or claimed to have designed, survives substantially at Albury today and is entirely lateral in its spread and Italian in its main feature, the Crypta, a tunnel 500 feet long cut through the sandy hillside in imitation of the famous grotto cut by the Romans at Posilippo, outside Naples.

It is easy to see why John had his eye on brother George's garden at Wotton. The sites were very similar with the house low down in a steep, wooded valley facing into a steep hillside rising only a few yards away from its garden front. The Howard house has been rebuilt but, on the sun-trap slope opposite, Evelyn's lateral terrace and the dry ditch of his canal still slice grandly along the contours with relics of the inevitable long yew hedge which followed them. The Crypta, however, remains a slightly sinister surprise, deep set within a later brick pavilion, only visible when the slope has been climbed and the great green terrace reached. Like Wotton it is a garden for backward views to the house rather than forward vistas from the house. It has a formality created by divisions rather than spaces. If Evelyn could have matched Captain George's Doric temple front the effect would have been more Claude Lorrain than Le Nôtre.

Though Evelyn continued busily writing and publishing, an authority on whatever caught his fancy: medals, navigation, naval warfare, the environment, salads and salad dressing, he never moved forward with the times on garden design, Albury being, if anything, a step backward. After the Glorious Revolution of 1688 he had retired completely from public life. He may have disapproved of the Stuart king's morality and Catholic faith but, like the dissenting bishops, he remained loyal to the monarch whom God rather than Parliament had appointed. This was a pity as in Dutch William, the new King, a fellow enthusiast for 'greens' and gardening generally, he might have found a kindred spirit. When William came to the throne in 1688 'greens' and formalism had still at least another thirty years of garden popularity ahead of them.

CHAPTER FIVE

GEORGE LONDON AND HENRY WISE – GARDEN DESIGN AS BIG BUSINESS

This is the most alien, un-English and disconnected chapter of the book. From Beale to Repton, chapter three to chapter fourteen, there is otherwise a logical sequence of ideas and experiments, as gardens and parks evolve. But the Franco-Dutch layouts, the formal gardens of the last half of the seventeenth and the first decade of the eighteenth century, those grounds which made such profits for nurserymen like George London and Henry Wise, were an imposition; they stand apart. Even as political icons they are unsatisfactory. Because Charles II introduced them deliberately in the first year of his reign they should be seen as clear symbols of royal power triumphant over a loyal and humbled Parliament. But when Lords and Commons united in the Glorious Revolution of 1688 to expel the Catholic Stuarts and bring in the Protestant William of Orange as a seal upon the liberties and rights of Parliament, they found that the new King William, being Dutch, was far more devoted to formal gardens, to an endless parade of choice 'greens' and disciplined parterres, to French fashions in horticulture, than King Charles had ever been. The appropriate classical gardens of republican liberty would have to wait for 1715 and Parliament's more apparent dominance over the Hanoverian kings.

From 1660 to 1715 garden design would develop around three themes: flowers, trees and axial formalism. The gentry's obsession with new and improved flowers dated back to the 1630s and it would be reactivated by John Rea, a Shropshire gentleman (died 1681), whose book *Flora séu, De Florum Cultura or, A Complete Florilege, Furnished with all Requisites belonging to a Florist* was published in 1665. Their more commercial interest in tree planting would be fired by John Evelyn's *Sylva, or a Discourse of Forest-Trees*, which came out a year earlier in 1664. The axial fixation which was to decide the layout of both flowers and trees for the next fifty years dates back even earlier, to 1661 and André Mollet's design innovations in St James's Park. Mollet (*c.* 1600–65) was a member of an influential dynasty of French garden designers. His father Claude claimed to have introduced the *parterre de broderie*, an innovation of doubtful aesthetic value, to France. André travelled widely, designing gardens in Holland for the Prince of Orange, in England for Charles I's Queen Henrietta Maria and in Sweden for Queen Christina. In 1651 he published the superbly illustrated *Le Jardin de Plaisir*, then, by obscure patronage, found a position of influence in Commonwealth England. So he was at hand when Charles II made his triumphant return to London. This could explain why the King, instead of putting some order into his ramshackle palace of Whitehall, commissioned Mollet to make St James's Park look impressively French.

The result was a grand *patte d'oie* radiating out from a quadruple semicircle of trees around the Horse Guards Parade ground. One long double avenue flanked a canal basin pointing to the

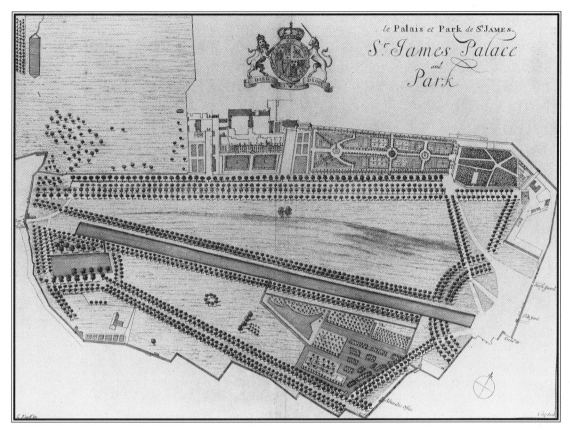

Charles II called André Mollet to lay out St James's Park to a bold, inexpensive design in 1661. A decoy pond for the water fowl which the king loved to feed and shoot is sited in the lower sector of the three-pronged patte d'oie. Above the quadruple avenues of The Mall lie the complex formal gardens of St James's Palace. These were to make way in the 1730s for William Kent's informal gardens at Carlton House. Every line of Mollet's layout is directed towards the future site of Buckingham Palace.

empty site of what is now Buckingham Palace. Two shorter arms stubbed off left and right, the left arm to ponds for water fowl, the right to a quadruple avenue on the line of the present Mall. By 1661 these avenues were planted and making an instant social impact. Poets praised the garden in verse, the new King walked there often, flirted among the groves with his mistresses and talked serious science with worthies like John Evelyn. An entire quarter of the modern capital was taking shape to French design. The ever serviceable Evelyn took the hint of royal direction, realised that trees were the current fashion and hastily produced his *Sylva*. On a relatively confined site Mollet had come very near to achieving the ideal French impression of focusing the eye upon apparent infinity. Pleased with the effect King Charles ordered an even grander *patte d'oie* with another central canal and flanking lime tree avenues to be laid out before the garden in front of his old Tudor palace at Hampton Court. It cost £1,466 and already by 1662 there were 758 limes in place, with Evelyn noting, 'The *Park* formerly a flat, naked piece of Ground, now planted with sweete rows of *lime-trees*, and the Canale for water now neere perfected'.[1] As at St James's, the arms of the *patte d'oie* sprang from a huge half-circle of limes, thereby creating the planning area which would later occupy the talents of London and Wise and the doubtfully authentic illustrated records of Leonard Knyff.

With these two resounding statements of royal taste the pattern was set; an aristocracy still reeling from Oliver Cromwell's abolition of the House of Lords showed its devotion to the restored monarchy by long avenues of trees and formal layouts up and down the country. As a direct result horticulture became big business. In 1681 George London (died 1714) signed a partnership with three other men – Roger Looker, Moses Cook and John Field – to set up an unusually ambitious nursery garden at Brompton, or as they called it, 'Brumpton' Park, on 100 acres of land north-west of the city of London, where the complex of the South Kensington museums now stands. All four men had impeccable gardening qualifications. Looker was gardener to the Queen at Somerset House, Field to the Earl of Bedford at Woburn. Cook had developed for the Earl of Essex an immense forest garden at Cassiobury in Hertfordshire. But George London outpointed them all in experience. He had served his apprenticeship under the King's gardener, John Rose (1622–77), at St James's Palace and been considered so promising that Rose had sent him to work and study in France, probably at Versailles with André le Nôtre. On his return he had been appointed head gardener to Henry Compton, Bishop of London at Fulham Palace and built up there, with the help of Church of England chaplains serving overseas, a renowned collection of exotics, shrubs and flowers.

Not one of these four men was by nature or experience an innovator. Their successful careers had been based upon their readiness to follow the current fashions in garden design and the particular preferences of their employers. By their training they were enablers, the facilitators of their patrons' various horticultural interests and when their Brompton Park partnership was commissioned in 1682 to plan and create a prodigiously expensive English Versailles for Viscount Weymouth at Longleat in Wiltshire their fortunes were made. The new grounds at Longleat alone would bring in £30,000 before they were finished.[2]

Roger Looker died in 1685, John Field in 1687. In 1689 Moses Cook sold his share to George London's young friend and assistant Henry Wise (1653–1738), thereafter until London's death in 1714, through the reigns of William and Mary and Queen Anne, their perfect partnership of complementary talents never looked back. Stephen Switzer (1682–1745) who worked for Brompton Park in the late 1690s, wrote a eulogy on George London which may read like flattery but which was no more than the plain truth:

> It will perhaps be hardly believed, in Time to come, that this one Person actually saw and gave Directions, once or twice a Year, in most of the Noblemens and Gentlemens Gardens in *England*. And since it was common for him to ride 50 or 60 Miles in a Day, he made his Northern Circuit in five or six Weeks, and sometimes less; and his Western in as little Time: As for the South and East, they were but three of four Days Work for him; most times twice a Year, visiting all the Country-Seats, conversing with Gentlemen, and forwarding the Business of *Gard'ning* in such a degree as is almost impossible to describe.[3]

While clearly very personable, a commercial traveller of the most superior kind, London was a man of obscure social origins, in no way a gentleman but a professional player in the garden game. Switzer tactfully disclaimed any knowledge of his parentage and since bastards and foundlings were often given as their surname the name of the town or village of their origin he could well have been an illegitimate Cockney. London never married, nor did Henry Wise until he was 42; but this was not remarkable in their profession as there was a peculiar prejudice among employers against married gardeners. Lord Weymouth rejected two men when he discovered they had wives. As with heads of Oxford and Cambridge colleges, gardening was considered a dedicated, full-time profession.

Apart from the prestige acquired by working in France, London's great advantage was his royal connection. When he moved to Brompton Park he kept up a friendly relationship with Bishop Compton and Compton was the brains and the manipulator behind the Glorious Revolution of 1688. In that dangerous week, when William of Orange had invaded and everything hung in the balance, it was essential for the Protestant Princess Anne to be separated from her Catholic father, King James. Compton and Marlborough's wife Sarah contrived to get the Princess out of Whitehall by the back stairs and then George London, as an entirely responsible and loyal Protestant, was made, together with the Earl of Dorset, her escort to Nottingham and the safety of her brother-in-law's Anglo-Dutch army. When William of Orange was safely on the throne he made his favourite, William Bentinck, Earl of Portland and appointed George London as Bentinck's deputy in the post of Superintendent of the Royal Gardens. London's talent for discreet friendships with important people was shown when Bentinck chose him as a companion to go on a tour of French gardens from January to June 1698. Together they caught up with the latest innovations, talked at length with Jean Baptiste de la Quintinie in his potager at Versailles and discussed garden design with André le Nôtre, who was by then a very old man. In 1699 London and Wise would publish a shortened translation of *The Compleat Gard'ner*, de la Quintinie's treatise on fruit trees.

Soon after, in an example of their teamwork, when London fell out of favour on the accession of Queen Anne in 1702 his partner Henry Wise moved smoothly into his place as the favoured royal gardener. The Queen associated London with extravagant expenditure, at Hampton Court in particular, and when Wise told Treasury officials that he could maintain the royal gardens for £1,600, when they had previously been costing £4,800 a year, he was appointed without more questions. Wise comes over initially as more of an administrator, a slick business man, than a gardener. When London went riding out to make contacts and offer advice Wise stayed at home in the large house on the Brompton Park site handling the day to day business of the nurseries. But once Anne was on the throne he proved himself every bit as energetic in the field as his partner and, in his relations with the Duke of Marlborough at Blenheim, as adept at handling patrons.

Wise's social origins are almost as obscure as London's but, unlike London the rough rider, he craved gentility. Late in life he sired a family of ten children, acquired a coat of arms crested by a lion holding a damask rose and entwined about with a serpent, then died leaving an astonishing fortune of some £100,000. To justify his heraldry he had claimed a Royalist grandfather Richard from Caddlestone or Cadiston in Warwickshire who was supposed to have lived to be 112; but no one has managed to trace either the village or the centenarian.[4] It is presumed that Wise, like London, served under John Rose at St James's Park and that would have been when both men absorbed French principles of design.

One significant feature of the many complex gardens laid out by London and Wise and their imitators in the last half of the seventeenth century is that, their upkeep being so expensive, they have almost all been destroyed, most of them within fifty years of their creation. Yet the gardens of no other period, even the most recent, have been more thoroughly recorded and made accessible to us. Jan Kip and Leonard Knyff's bird's-eye views of English country estates, published in the 1707, 1709 and 1715 editions of their *Britannia Illustrata*, capture that interplay of the three rival movements in garden design down to the last pavilion, parterre, orchard and potager.[5] On paper at least the achievements of the Brompton Park duo are immortal. What the views prove, apart from a fascinating diversity of taste and an often amazing reach of ambition, is how widely imitated André Mollet's avenues were. Many of the sixty-nine views have no elaborate waterworks; any number of the layouts have only a meagre show of parterres and no vestige of an axial plan. But there is hardly a single garden without an array of plantations and new avenues striding, sometimes miles out into the countryside, to symbolise the landowner's power and possessions and to lay up treasures for his heir when the trees had matured and become ready to harvest. Some great houses like Cassiobury, Bretby, Westwood and Richmond exist in a positive ocean of new planting, their woodlands starred, groved and arenaed with clearings. In others, like Badminton, the house sits at the spider centre of a web of between twenty and thirty avenues, lancing and criss-crossing out over the bare Cotswold plateau. It was the age of the tree and it was the sale of young limes and elms at various precisely stated stages of growth, of hornbeams to line alleyways through the taller trees and of every possible variety of orchard tree that made up a great percentage of Brompton Park's business.

During the last year of William's reign the relatively small Maestricht Garden, which London and Wise were creating in a loop of the Thames below Windsor Castle, absorbed '238 Large Spruce Firrs that are Clipt and Shapt into a Pyramid Forme and 8 or 9 foot high each in a Large Baskett with their Earth to them' and 41,150 'White Thorne', to hedge them round, all shipped up the river from Brompton Park.[6] In one month, November 1699, when London was roughing out a garden at Melbourne in Derbyshire, the Brompton Park nursery acres supplied 1,000 small Dutch elms at threepence each, 600 large limes at a shilling each and 2,000 hornbeams in addition to vast numbers of bulbs and bushes. The hornbeams were to hedge straight wilderness walks, the elms and limes filled in the resulting geometrical shapes between the walks.

As one of the more literate and loyal workers employed by the Brompton Park partnership wrote when the firm was riding high:

> If He who the first garden made
> Had put in Wise to keep it,
> Made Adam but a labourer there
> And Eve to weed and sweep it;
> Then men and plants had never died,
> Nor the first fruits been rotten;
> Brompton had never then been known
> Nor Eden e'er forgotten.[7]

It is easy to understand how Henry Wise managed to achieve what, in twentieth-century terms, would have been millionaire status before his death. French garden designs were devised to satisfy the maximum consumption demands of a Roi Soleil uncontrolled by any tax-cutting parliament. One quite small garden which London and Wise contrived at Kensington Palace, first for King William then Queen Anne, was requiring in 1696 a staff of seventy-two to service it, clipping its topiary work fortifications, tending its 'several Collections of hous'd Greens', its 'beautiful Hollow' and 'Garden of Dwarfs'.[8] Even the supposedly cost-cutting and money-grudging Queen Anne spent £26,000 on alterations there in the first four years of her reign. Under William and Mary and the last of the Stuarts, the aristocracy was still nervously grateful to the monarchs who had saved it from the menace of Roman Catholicism. As a result, London and Wise could flourish behind the example of royal extravagance. It was no coincidence that when the Hanoverians came to the throne garden design was soon simplified. The German kings were now in their turn nervously grateful to the lords in Parliament who had brought them over and appointed them to the seat royal. As a direct consequence expenditure on the royal gardens dropped sharply.

Tree planting to create garden features had two advantages. By their mere size trees outgrew gardens and directed designers eventually towards the laying out of parks. The other advantage was that they were an investment. Exactly the opposite was true of the parterres. To be enjoyed at their best they needed to be intimate in scale, but even so they were grossly expensive both to plant and then to tend, while making no financial return.

Parterres were essentially the product of France's delight in Mannerist decoration: intricate patterning where craftsmanship took precedence over beauty. The patriotic English alternative to the parterre was the 'fret' as championed by Rea in his *Flora*. This was a walled enclosure with fruit and roses grown alternately against the walls, and low plants like primroses and auriculas grown between these and the gravel path which ran around the whole. Next, enclosing a central rectangle of plain grass, came the actual fret itself, a low trellis fence some 3 feet high set in a 'carp back', a humped ridge of fine earth. Tall flowers like lilies and peonies were clumped at the corners of this 'carp back', and honeysuckles, clematis, jasmines and roses trained along the fret so that their perfume could be enjoyed from the path. Between the fret and the path were low growing flowers – anemones, narcissi, orchids, cyclamen, marigolds, lavender and the like.[9] The fret was simple and practical and a study of the Kip–Knyff illustrations, notably those of lesser gentry houses drawn for Robert Atkyns's *Glostershire* of 1712, will reveal them still thriving. Indeed the French-named plate-bandes around many of the more modish parterres are only frets by another name. London and Wise describe frets as 'plain compartments', but they were drawing their ideas, though not always their practice, from *Le Jardinier Solitaire* by the Sieur Louis Liger, a shortened and improved translation of which they published as *The Retir'd Gardener* in 1706. London and Wise never wrote their own guide for gardeners; they were essentially derivative.

The *Retir'd Gardener* divides parterres into eleven types, all permutations of three elements: 'Cut-work', 'Turfs' and 'Imbroidery'. 'Cut-work' consisted of interestingly shaped beds, 'cut' into either grass or gravel for the reception of plants or, as at Chatsworth, 'ye brightest Sand as is near that place'. 'Turfs' were shaped areas of grass on either soil or gravel. 'Imbroidery' has proved the most confusing for modern commentators, but it was, so their book claims, 'Draughts which represent in effect, those we have on our Cloaths'. These came in two kinds: '*Branch-work*', which was the leaves, and '*Flourishings*', which were the flowers. All these parterres represented a move from the bold, open designs in box or herbs of the old Tudor and Elizabethan knot gardens towards more sinuous, less practical shapes. But the real French *parterre de broderie* was so subject to destruction by rain and so ephemeral as to be very rare in this country. It was a Mannerist device and a case of craftsmanship outrunning art.[10]

True 'Imbroidery', *The Retir'd Gardener* explained, was created by laying 'such as powder'd Tile, which is red; beaten Charcoal and Iron-filing, which are black, and the yellowest Sand they can get, which coming all together, and being plac'd with Art, gives the Gardens the pleasantest Variety that can be'.[11] However, the text warns from experience, 'these sort of Fancies are only practis'd in middling Gardens, where there is not room to plant any thing of Consequence'.[12] They are not to be looked for, therefore, in royal palace gardens or in any quantity on the pages of *Britannia Illustrata*. The curvaceous garden rectangles in those pages were created by parterres of the kinds

One of the variants of a parterre offered in London and Wise's The Retir'd Gardener of 1706. In the centre is an area of 'Cut-work', grass beds on a gravel surround. This is surrounded by 'Branch-work' of curvaceous leaf forms. These could be executed with difficulty in flower beds but quite easily in powdered tile, charcoal and sand.

numbered III, V and VII in London and Wise's list of eleven, variations of cut-work and green turf. The four rectangles in front of Longleat for instance were III: 'The Form of a Parterre only of Green Turf' set against gravel. This type they described as looking 'well in spacious Gardens, where there's something else to please the Eye: For whoever in a small Garden should see nothing but a Grass-Plot without any other Ornament, his Eyes would receive but little Pleasure'.[13]

When they came to design a garden for the Duke of Marlborough's most celebrated captive, Marshal Tallard, living on parole at Newdigate House on Castle Gate in Nottingham, the duo had a space only 150 feet long by 140 wide to work in so there, true to their precepts, they laid an 'Imbroidery' of two sunflowers using in addition to the three quoted materials, 'Pit-coal fine beaten', 'Spar that comes from the Lead-Mines, or Cockleshell beaten very fine' and various gravels.[14] There was no place in such frail, fine work for box borders. Tallard, taken prisoner after Blenheim, returned to France in 1711. It would be interesting to know how long the coal dust survived the Nottingham rain.

Because of the partners' royal cachet the gates of every great country house were open to London, and, when he chose to stir himself as at Blenheim, also to Wise. They made their visits not to impose their ideas, but rather to offer their technical expertise, over fruit trees in particular, and to follow the whims and preferences of each individual lord. Turning the pages of *Britannia Illustrata* it is evident that variety rather than consistency was usual. Lord Radnor's Wimpole, Cambridgeshire was dazzlingly axial, receding in measured diminutions to the horizon. It had three enclosed parterres, two matching Wildernesses of yew with central pavilions and private cabinets,

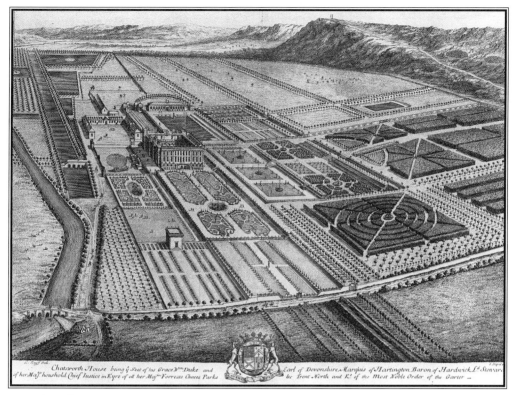

Kip and Knyff's staggering view from their Britannia Illustrata *(1707) of the grounds of Chatsworth, Derbyshire, as they were in their London and Wise prime. The complex of parterres, fountain gardens, canal, amphitheatre, maze and forest nurseries pays little or no attention to the topography of hill country. Celia Fiennes, visiting in 1697, commented on how 'the Gardens lyes one above another which makes the prospect very fine'.*

then an orchard, a bowling green, another orchard and an avenue dwindling to the skyline. Staunton Harold, Leicestershire, followed a water theme with a great canal and many fountains. Broome Hall, Suffolk kept the long potager to one side of the house and multiple parterres to the other. Dawley, Middlesex had an imposing orangery and exceptionally complex parterres. At Hampton Court in Herefordshire Lord Coningsby favoured ovals for his grand basin and his bowling green. He even risked two beds of the true *parterre de broderie* flanking one garden approach. At Chatsworth there was a complete reshaping of the grounds to match up with William Talman and Thomas Archer's new façades to the house. A bewildering number of enclosures, densely wooded wildernesses, long parterres, canals and lawns were laid out, all with no apparent relation to each other. As in so many of these *Britannia Illustrata* grounds there seems to have been no unifying concept of the whole. But from the account which Celia Fiennes gives in her turn of the century visits to these great houses it is apparent that she was not looking for any integrated plan in their gardens, only for a rare show of prodigies and marvels as in some aristocratic fairground.[15]

There had been enormous expenditure at Chatsworth and handsome profits for Brompton Park, but George London had no sense of how the gardens might have responded in poetic accord to a dramatic landscape of the river Derwent flowing through wooded hills.

The Duke's house lyes just at the foote of this steepe hill which is like a precipice just at the last, notwithstanding the Dukes house stands on a little riseing ground from the River Derwent which runs all along the front of the house and by a little fall made in the water which makes a pretty murmurring noise; before the gate there is a large Parke and severall fine Gardens one without another with gravell walkes and squairs of grass with stone statues in them and in the middle of each Garden is a large fountaine full of images of Sea Gods and Dolphins and Sea Horses which are full of pipes which spout out water in the bason and spouts all about the gardens; 3 Gardens just round the house; some have gravell walks and square like the other with Statues and Images in the bason, there is one bason in the middle of one Garden thats very large and by sluces besides the Images severall pipes plays out the water, about 30 large and small pipes altogether, some flush it up that it frothes like snow; there is one Garden full of stone and brass statues; so the Gardens lyes one above another which makes the prospect very fine; above these gardens is an ascent of 5 or 6 stepps up to a wilderness and close arbours and shady walks, on each end of one walke stands two piramidies full of pipes spouting water that runns down one of them, runns on brass hollow work which looks like rocks and hollow stones; the other is all flatts stands one above another like salvers so the water rebounds one from another, 5 or 6 one above the other;

there is another green walke and about the middle of it by the Grove stands a fine Willow tree, the leaves barke and all looks very naturall, the roote is full of rubbish or great stones to appearance, and all on a sudden by turning a sluce it raines from each leafe but in appearance is exactly like any Willow; beyond this is a bason in which are the branches of two Hartichocks Leaves which weeps at the end of each leafe into the bason which is placed at the foote of lead steps 30 in number; on a little banck stands blew balls 10 on a side, and between each ball are 4 pipes which by a sluce spouts out water across the stepps to each other like an arbour or arch; while you are thus amused suddenly there runs down a torrent of water out of 2 pitchers in the hands of two large Nimphs cut in stone that lyes in the upper step, which makes a pleaseing prospect, this is designed to be enlarged and steps made up to the top of the hill which is a vast ascent, but from the top of it now they are supply'd with water for all their pipes so it will be the easyer to have such a fall of water even from the top which will add to the Curiositye.

Celia Fiennes at Chatsworth, Derbyshire, 1697

The canal and water garden at Staunton Harold are a reminder of the influence of Holland, that second element in the Franco-Dutch garden which can often be overlooked. Fountains and water features are notoriously difficult to keep clean and wholesome from dead leaves and wind-blown rubbish. England, easily distracted by its hills and mountains, has never shared Holland's love-hate relationship with water and its control. But at Westbury Court in Gloucestershire, tucked away in a loop of the river Severn under the lea of the Forest of Dean, one formal water garden, far more Dutch than French, survived through the provincial conservatism of its owners, the Maynard Colchesters, far enough into the twentieth century for it to be rescued and restored by the National Trust to something like its original condition as recorded by Kip and Knyff for Sir Robert Atkyns's *The ancient and present state of Glostershire* (1712).

Two Maynard Colchesters, an uncle and his nephew, created the Westbury Garden between 1696 and 1740 with no help from London and Wise but advised, it seems, by their neighbour from Flaxley Abbey, Catherine Boevey, who was Amsterdam born.[16] To be enjoyed properly the garden should be played as its creators intended, and viewed first from the upstairs room of the Tall Pavilion, built in 1702–3 to a 'paterne' by a 'Mr. Pyke'.[17] Westbury is not a garden for secrets. From the long sash windows all its geometricity is laid out: its two 450-foot long canals, linked at their far ends by a fountain basin, its rectangular walk, brick-walled rectangular enclosure, straight hedges of dark clipped yews and, between the two canals, a rectangular parterre of what were vegetables in the Kip–Knyff illustration. The National Trust has played safe with flowers, but if the Trust's imaginative planting of authentic plum, pear and apple of the seventeenth century along the walls and walks is a sign, then equally authentic vegetables will

The Dutch-style water garden at Westbury-on-Severn, Gloucestershire, in its first condition, pre-1715, before a second canal was dug parallel to the first, making the vegetable garden a near-island. Ignoring Westbury Court, the axis of the garden works between a claire voie to the public road and the Tall Pavilion with its viewing parlour.

soon follow. For Westbury is a small-time squire's garden, bourgeois in its intimacy, almost the realisation of a Vermeer. It needs Queen Anne artichokes and Williamite beans.

Despite its modest dimensions Westbury is grand. The sheer, stone-edged precision of its canals and their great reflecting surfaces ensure that. A fountain sprays away at the far end, but the prevailing impression is one of calm discipline with all the sight-lines leading to the Tall Pavilion. The Maynard Colchesters' Elizabethan manor house was demolished long ago, but it was never relevant to the garden, being placed to the side. A rectangular stroll around the entire enclosure might look as if it would take only a few minutes, but such is the intensity of the planting, recreated in scholarly accuracy from the original accounts, that it will easily take up to an hour. That is the value of Westbury. With so few of these formal gardens surviving it is tempting to dismiss them as dull. But to anyone with a feeling for the scent of herbs, the dry, spicy flavours of seventeenth-century fruit, and the retiring beauty of old roses, weird auriculas and 'Persian' fritillaries it is a revelation of concentration.

Of all the many Brompton Park enterprises, laid out across England over a thirty-year period, only two gardens survive in anything like their original form and neither of them, not royal Hampton

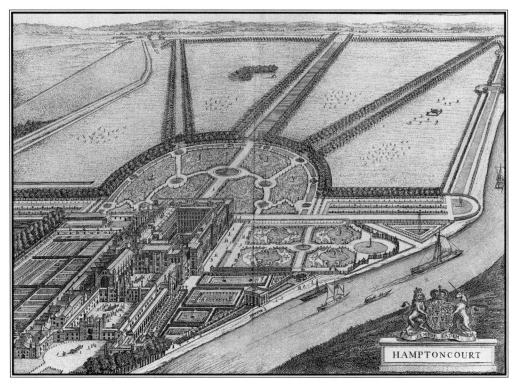

Hampton Court in an idealized view from Britannia Illustrata. *The great arms of the patte d'oie date back to 1662, before Wren's rebuilding. The complex parterres at its base were proposed for Queen Mary, partly achieved by King William and largely scrapped by Queen Anne, who hated the smell of clipped box. The Privy Garden in the right foreground was meticulously recreated in 1996 and its metalwork screens restored.*

Court for all its careful restoration, nor the gardens of Melbourne Hall, Derbyshire, offer the authentic seventeenth-century experience as immediately as Westbury does. The Privy Garden at Hampton Court still feels like a museum exhibit to be viewed but not touched, while the layout at Melbourne Hall has aged into a wonderful geriatric beauty which George London could never have anticipated.

Considering that they are in the grounds of a much chronicled and precisely costed royal palace, what was planned at Hampton Court and what was actually carried out is surprisingly obscure. London would have been active there until 1702, when Queen Anne succeeded to the throne, and Wise from 1699 onwards. They would both have been working as usual to the order and whim of their royal employers and within the existing framework of André Mollet's exedra and *patte d'oie* of 1661–2 which Wise completed and extended with further lime avenues to the bowling green in 1700–1. What is not in dispute is Wise's further planting of a grand, but little used, double avenue to the north through Bushy Park and his laying out of the Broad Walk before the east front of the palace. This ran north–south to Neptune overlooking the Thames and was intended to complement Sir Christopher Wren's new east façade, a less than authoritative composition of brick and stone, very much in need of a confident garden at its feet.

Only excavation and soil analysis will prove whether the enormous half-circle of parterres and thirteen fountains, which are shown in all Knyff's views, was ever laid out and planted in reality. Knyff was drawing and painting an intricate double arc of cut-work and turf beds outlined in box

This view across the replanted Privy Garden at Hampton Court demonstrates the essential conflict between geometry and plants. Already, only a few years after a scholarly reconstruction, with authentic bushes to punctuate the cut-work of grass and gravel and seventeenth-century flowers in the beds, the formal patterns are becoming lost as plants grow. Soon there will have to be a major replanting if the ideal image is to be retained.

in 1702, but already in 1699 Wise appears to have been laying the area with mere grass and gravel, while his plan shows only five fountains and no trace of a parterre, just four statues and borders of conical yews.[18] So it is possible that the whole complexity which Daniel Marot, a French Protestant designer based in the Hague, had designed back in 1689 was never realised, only projected. It would have lain under the Queen's apartments on the east wing and Mary had died in 1694. What is certain is that Wise made and remade the Privy Garden before Wren's south front in the period 1700–2, and here painstaking excavation and research has confirmed the exact accuracy of the Knyff views. So what we have there today after the replanting is an accurate recreation of a maturing formal garden by Wise. It is a sobering experience to look down on the site from one of the high flanking terraces. The *plates bandes* (planting strips of earth alongside the paths) of alternate yew and holly, cone and sphere, the green turf fleurs de lys and the crosses are laid out against golden gravel, looking just as Celia Fiennes saw them in 1712. On the terrace to the west Queen Mary's elm bower has been replanted with hornbeam. As a complement to the uncertain richness of Wren's architecture the effect is stunning, a confident geometry has been extended out as far as the riverbank and the repoussé work screens designed by the French metalworker, Jean Tijou.

London's work at Melbourne is a revelation of a different kind. He would have followed, as usual, the general instructions of the owner, Colonel Thomas Coke. But in 1698 London had just made his second visit to France and his head was stored with memories of French forest gardens like Pontchartrain, west of Paris.[19] Brompton Park sent Colonel Coke two alternative layouts and he chose the one 'to suit with Versailles'.[20] In 1712 John James brought out his *The Theory and Practice of Gardening*, a translation of A.J. Dézallier d'Argenville's definitive work on Le Nôtre's methods, *La théorie et la pratique du jardinage* (1709). By then London, Coke and his site manager, a local Derbyshire man, William Cooke, had between them created a near perfect, though small French garden, an anticipation of most of d'Argenville's prescriptions. Immediately in front of the house was a long, downward slope of parterres with a formal basin at its foot, backed by an exedra of trees. At that point the axial layout ended, all the Wilderness area lay away to the side. The parterres of Melbourne must have proved a gold mine for Brompton Park: 1,000 tulips, 1,000 narcissus, 2,050 crocus, 1,125 snowdrops, 500 hyacinths, 30 honeysuckle, 30 jasmine, 30 roses, 30 sweet briars were sent as a starter. Inevitably the parterres have gone to lawn, but all the Wilderness, hedges and woodlands at the foot of the parterres and to the right, have not simply survived but transformed themselves merely by growing old into an uncanny foreshadowing of the garden designs that would succeed them. They remain by the care and taste of the present owners in a magical suspension of maturity.

Simply by maturing over three centuries the grounds have become a quite different kind of garden. The criss-cross of straight formal alleys lined with hornbeam and yew, backed by tall beech and lime trees, became by mere growth an informal and profoundly romantic place full of surprise vistas. Simply to walk there is to experience the Metaphysical reality of Andrew Marvell's 'Annihilating all that's made/To a green Thought in a green Shade'.[21] Even the round water basins at the intersections are an exquisitely light green with delicate pond weed, while the grass of the paths (there is no gravel here) works on the feet as velvet works on the hand: soft, yielding but retentive. English pride in the native turf, its superiority to continental equivalents, suddenly becomes, not vainglorious boasting, but simple fact.

The part played by fountains in a London layout is another revelation. At each new crossing one, two and sometimes three fountains are visible, their frail silver jets, a mere 3 feet high, are the only colour relief against the omnipresent greens. Canopied wooden seat echoes canopied wooden seat, each painted green of course, and fountain replies to fountain. The antique yew hedges billow in miniature mountain ranges about Jan Van Nost's lead statuary, Andromeda's naked breasts are outlined against the green, Perseus in a fashionable hat jokingly averts his eyes from the Medusa's head which he holds at a disdainful distance, cherubs romp in pairs. And there the message comes over. This is an anticipation of the next stages of English garden design, not quite Arcadian – the statues have too much of Daniel Marot's French Mannerism about them – but approaching the light-hearted frivolity of the Rococo spirit of the 1740s.

From the point of view of garden history there are fascinating flaws in Melbourne's layout that prevent it from being a true woodland Arcadia or a Rococo garden. There are fine statues and urns to catch and surprise the eye but no garden building of stone. The Robert Bakewell 'Birdcage' is a jewel of ironwork and gilding, but as a centre-piece in the exedra of trees at the end of the long lawn and behind the Great Basin it is much too small to be an effective eye-catcher. The Urn of the Four Seasons, possibly a present from Queen Anne to Coke, one of her Vice-Chamberlains, and placed at a radiating point of avenues, is set on gibbering monkeys, an object of craftsmanship not taste. There is no considered theme to this or any of the other urns, cherubs and statuary. Thomas Coke was a Francophile but not a connoisseur of the Picturesque. What is most telling is the way Melbourne fails to include some prime local features of the

A view across the lower garden at Melbourne Hall, Derbyshire, makes two points. The jets of the fountains, silver against an all-pervading green, create a lively punctuation to emphasise the unity of the vista. But over the centuries the trees behind the yew and hornbeam hedges have grown wild and transformed a formal area into a romantic wilderness. Natural growth rather than intention has kept the garden abreast of changing fashions.

landscape. It turns resolutely away from the beautiful lake a stone's throw from the house, deliberately screening it off from view with a huge hedge. Directly behind the Birdcage and the exedra is an attractive hillside. Any garden designer of the mid-eighteenth century would have brought that into a vista and dramatised it with a temple or a Gothick tower. Coke cut it off with trees and it was a later owner who felled sufficient to allow a glimpse through the concealing belt of the field and slope beyond. Melbourne is essentially an enclosed world. No William Kent came in 1699 to leap the fence and find the whole landscape a garden. The surprise vistas of urn, statue and fountain are subdued surprises; the eclectic pleasures of Gothick arch, Greek temple and rustic cottage are still a few decades away. Perseus has a Rococo ripple to his armour and his hat but all the lines of the garden are straight; we still wait for the sinuous serpentine curve and the 'artinatural'.

CHAPTER SIX

SIR JOHN VANBRUGH, CHARLES BRIDGEMAN AND THE RISE OF THE TEMPLES

Sir John Vanbrugh never completely grasped the concept of a templed Arcadia, designing his garden buildings on too grand a scale to fit casually into a landscape. He thought in terms of formal axial vistas, as at Eastbury, Dorset, but was lured into a rewarding confusion of parts by Charles Bridgeman's boldly angular layout at Stowe in Buckinghamshire.

The problem with Vanbrugh (1664–1726) and Bridgeman (died 1738) is that Sir John was, like the houses he built, very much larger than life while, from a biographical point of view, Bridgeman was a virtual nonentity. When trying to assess the responsibility of one man or the other for any advance in garden design it is dangerously easy to assume that the flamboyant, extrovert Vanbrugh must have been the prime mover when there are often a number of factors suggesting the opposite. Another confusion arises from the times in which they lived. The last twenty-six years of Vanbrugh's life, from 1700 to 1726, was the period when the English garden was taking on an entirely new and influential direction, a time when that style of informal planting with groves and natural-seeming lakes beset with an eclectic range of garden buildings was evolving. In the last half of the century it would be recognised and imitated widely on the Continent as the *Jardin Anglais*, the first instance of such a two-way movement of design across the Channel. Vanbrugh and Bridgeman, both professionals, and by birth, players, were far from being the sole originators of this new, templed informality. Also involved were the gentlemen, aristocratic patrons, the Earl of Carlisle at Castle Howard, Lord Cobham at Stowe, Lord Burlington at Chiswick, the arch-amateur and advocate of change, Alexander Pope, and the professional designers, Stephen Switzer and William Kent. Even London and Wise, the old formal style gardeners, had an influence, if only because they lived on so inappropriately long into the new century, London until 1714, Wise dying as late as 1738 and still holding the post of King's Gardener up to 1728. Their firmness in keeping to the old Franco-Dutch rigidities of parterre and canal had its part to play by provoking a counter movement.

This rise then of a confident new casualness in garden design is not something to be dismissed in a single chapter. It came by unpredictable stages and often from chance collusions between patron and gardener. Vanbrugh and Bridgeman were both, for all their formal training, involved in the process, but the year 1700 and the turn of the century was a complex period when nothing should be taken for granted and many influences, publications, periodicals, political changes and military triumphs were all working together to produce a national self-confidence more assured than even that of the Elizabethan age. Elizabeth had been victorious on the sea; Queen Anne was victorious on land, and over the old enemy, the French.

A player on the garden scene like Vanbrugh was more influenced by the memory of military fortifications than by any vision of a classical Arcadia. Politicians like Lords Carlisle and Cobham, while alert to popular images of the Duke of Marlborough's campaigns, had other sources of inspiration. Their political party, the Whigs, looked to the past for its models from two different eras. Recent antiquarian studies had praised the Saxons as a Gothic, noble, if primitive, folk whose legal and executive institutions had guaranteed liberty to the people.[1] Rather more seductive to aristocrats with a classical education was the idea of a Republican Rome, when the senatorial and knightly classes had enjoyed the graces of Greek civilization while governing the state through a balanced constitution. The gardens of Castle Howard and Stowe represent a compromise between these three competing influences — military, Saxon and classical — with the classical proving the most visually accessible.

Charles Bridgeman, unlike Vanbrugh, began with no commitments to any of the three sources. His life profile is so low that even his birth date is unknown, but his father was probably a gardener to the Harley Earls of Oxford, hence Bridgeman's own connections with the 2nd Earl.[2] What is known is that he married Sarah Mist at Grays Inn Chapel, London on 2 May 1717, had seven children, four of whom survived him, and that he died leaving his wife in apparent poverty, desperate to realise money on her husband's tools, designs and reputation. He had been working as a surveyor for Henry Wise since at least as early as 1709; in 1726 he became Wise's partner in the Brompton Park nurseries and, jointly with Wise, 'Principall Gardiners' to George I.[3] Alexander Pope knew him, admired him and then characteristically insulted him in a clumsily turned couplet. They were never reconciled. After 1728 Wise retired and Bridgeman was formally appointed Royal Gardener. Through all these years he had been actively designing and laying out grounds up and down the country, so why his wife should have been poor, when he left in his will £2,000 to each of his daughters and two properties, the Bell Inn at Stilton and a London town house, to his son, is a mystery.

There are few mysteries associated with Vanbrugh; his life was a series of dramatic events.[4] It began with childhood in medieval walled Chester, a time in India as a servant of the East India Company at Surat,[5] a brief spell as an army officer and then a James Bond-like episode spying on France's coastal defences at Calais, which earned him two years as a prisoner in the Bastille. He still contrived to become familiar with the gardens and new buildings of Paris. Back in London in 1693 he made an instant name for himself as writer of witty, slightly heartless comedies, and became a clubbable man-about-town, easy with his social superiors and, from the tone of his letters, splendid company. Then, as a master-stroke of fortune, with no previous experience in architecture, he was commissioned in 1699 to design a great Baroque palace in Yorkshire – Castle Howard – for Charles Howard, 3rd Earl of Carlisle. Howard was a man five years his junior, a fellow member of the Kit-Kat Club, well travelled, sophisticated and soon to become First Lord of the Treasury.

It was while designing and building Castle Howard that Vanbrugh became involved with Wray Wood. For a stylistic movement as elusive of definitions, as charm-centred and inprovisatory as the English Garden of the eighteenth century, Wray Wood is as fair a starting point as any. It is always quoted in garden histories as a key innovation, and to win literary attention is more than half the battle. The wood lies literally only a stone's throw from the east wing of Castle Howard. There was nothing unusual in having a forest garden close to a post-1660 country house. They were a French fashion boosted by John Evelyn's *Sylva* of 1664. Bretby, Lord Chesterfield's Derbyshire seat, Lord Lindsey's Grimsthorpe, Lincolnshire, and the Earl of Essex's Cassiobury, Hertfordshire, mentioned in the preceding chapter, all had one. But these were all new, geometrically planted woods, cut through with straight avenues and trim circular clearings. Wray Wood was there already, a mature tract of handsome beech trees. Its importance was not that it was planted, but that it was preserved and appreciated. George London was expressly forbidden to impose a star of straight walks upon it and Stephen Switzer wrote about the stylistic originality of 'that beautiful Wood belonging to the Earl of *Carlisle*, at *Castle-Howard*, where Mr. *London* design'd a Star, which would have spoil'd the Wood . . . his Lordship's superlative Genius prevented it, and to the great Advancement of the Design, has given it that Labyrinth diverting Model we now see'.[6] The winding gravel paths were planned to twist around the trees to reveal statues, urns, seats and summer-houses. Works on the wood began in 1705–6 and by 1725 a visitor was describing:

> the wood, the beauty of this place, which for fine walks A fountain of a rock dropping water having a swan on it's top, Statues, Urns but especially Diana's statue with a stag, Gardens enclosed by a wall with sumerhouse, Cascade from a heap of stones, and other things agreable and very surprizing in a wood, may well be prefered to the finest Gardens.[7]

It is those last eight words: 'may well be preferred to the finest Gardens', which are so interesting as they appear to register a radical shift in the century's garden sensibility. But they were written twenty years after the first works began to wall and embellish the wood. The bastion-like wall and ha-ha ditch which enclose the trees have an air of Vanbrugh, the occasional soldier, spy and marine, but Lord Carlisle himself seems to have been responsible for the more casual interior graces of Wray Wood, so where had he picked up this new aesthetic?

Carlisle was a leading Whig politician and in December 1697 he visited the old philosopher statesman of his party, Sir William Temple, at his home, Moor Park, Surrey. Temple (1628–99) features in garden history, but for words rather than achievements, particularly for a passage in his 1685 essay *Upon the Gardens of Epicurus*. He had learnt, partly from intelligent observation of Chinese porcelain and lacquer work, but chiefly from his reading of travel books like Fernão Mendes Pinto's *Travels in the Kingdoms of Ethiopia, China, Tartaria* (1653), that the Chinese had a completely different aesthetic of garden design to that current in Europe. 'Among us', Temple wrote, 'the Beauty of Building and Planting is placed chiefly in some certain Proportions, Symmetries, or Uniformities; our Walks and our Trees ranged so, as to answer one another, and at exact Distances. The *Chinese* scorn this Way of Planting'.[8] Then, in two quite mildly phrased sentences, Temple undercut the entire notion of formal gardening:

But their greatest Reach of Imagination is employed in contriving Figures, where the Beauty shall be great, and strike the Eye, but without any Order or Disposition of Parts, that shall be commonly or easily observ'd. And though we have hardly any Notion of this Sort of Beauty, yet they have a particular Word to express it; and, where they find it hit their Eye at first Sight, they say the *Sharawadgi* is fine or is admirable.[9]

And so, in a few lines, he opened the way for painting to preside over garden design, for European landscape painters had manifestly long practised 'Sharawadgi'.

For seventeenth-century Europeans, still obsessed with their Augustan Roman past, any reports from China were like news from another planet. There, at the far end of the Silk Road, was this mysterious imperial twin to the Roman Empire, still intact, prestigious, ordered yet exotic. China was a source of artefacts of a superior technology and possessed of an undeniable beauty, but it obeyed a code of subtle aysmmetries, a complete reverse of the aesthetic coin. It is apparent from the tone of Temple's writing that this quality of '*Sharawadgi*' fascinated and frightened him: an art beyond his reach. Could he have impressed the much younger Lord Carlisle with its modish possibilities and urged a dramatic experiment in garden design to match an outstandingly dramatic house?

A few sinuous paths and natural waters had been ventured in parks before Wray Wood; Temple's own Moor Park had one such lake feature,[10] but none was ever accorded such trumpet blasts of printed praise. Writing in his 1718 *Ichnographia Rustica*, Stephen Switzer believed that a revolution, no less, had been achieved by Carlisle 'in his Wood at Castle Howard'. He had reached there,

the highest pitch that Natural and Polite Gard'ning can possibly arrive to: 'Tis There that Nature is truly imitated, if not excell'd, and from which the Ingenious may draw the best of their Schemes in Natural and Rural Gard'ning: 'Tis There that she is by a kind of fortuitous Conduct pursued through all her most intricate Mazes, and taught ever to exceed her own selfe in the Natura-Linear, and much more natural and Promiscous Disposition of all her Beauties.[11]

While Wray Wood could be admired as a 'Promiscuous' maze of serpentine paths, its Temple of Venus was not begun until after 1731 and only completed in 1735. The ideal perspective which Colen Campbell published in the 1725 third volume of *Vitruvius Britannicus* shows a 40-foot wide, four columned temple as a central point in the Parterre Garden on the south front, but neither Vanbrugh in his many letters to Lord Carlisle, nor any visitor mentions the feature although a similar layout of evergreen plantation and boundary walls with circular bastion turrets is shown on an estate map of 1727.[12] So all the important matter of precedence in temple building has still to be settled. It appears that Castle Howard had nothing like such a lead in that particular architectural race as might be supposed from Vanbrugh's reputation. Before his death in 1726 what Vanbrugh had persuaded Carlisle to achieve was not a classical templed Arcadia, but a garden of eclectic wonders.

First in 1705–6 came the military bastion walls around part of Wray Wood; but these were only exactly contemporary with the staggering hexagonal bastions, adequate to the defence of a sizeable Dutch town, which Vanbrugh had persuaded the Duke of Marlborough to let him build around the south parterre at Blenheim. Then in 1714, after a long interval at Castle Howard, came the great Obelisk and in 1719 the Pyramid Gate, two Egyptian-style markers on the entrance axis. The most bizarre of all Vanbrugh's garden features came in 1719–23: five-eighths of a mile of towered, medieval-style city walls, Chester's defences carried over into rural Yorkshire to act as a park boundary. At the same time (1721–5) the Parterre Garden or 'Architectural Parterre', a more classical

Vanbrugh's 'Architectural Parterre' with its profusion of obelisks on the south side of Castle Howard has disappeared, but this view of a contemporary obelisk garden at New Place from Chauncy's Hertfordshire *indicates what a dated, seventeenth-century curiosity it must have been, quite alien to any Arcadia.*

feature but one nightmarish in its scale, was set up before the south front. Last of Vanbrugh's additions was a lake, dug in 1723–4 and rectangular enough to have pleased George London, though not axially sited. The other Pyramid out in the grounds was raised by Nicholas Hawksmoor in 1728 and the Temple of the Four Winds, which Vanbrugh had most earnestly desired to see built, came, more or less to his designs, in 1728–31, though it was fitted up inside much later. While called a 'temple' it has the profile of a villa and bulks as such in the landscape. The Casino of Aurora, another large cruciform temple, set in the gardens of the Villa Ludovisi just outside Rome, was probably Vanbrugh's model for it rather than the often-quoted Villa Rotonda by Palladio. The Villa Ludovisi and layout were known from the detailed engravings in Giovanni Battista Falda's *Li giardini di Roma* of 1683.[13] But the Temple of the Four Winds again was constructed by Hawksmoor as was the Mausoleum (1727–38), much delayed and altered, the Carrmire Gate of 1728–30 on the south-west approach and the Temple of Venus (1731–5) on the edge of Wray Wood. By 1735, however, temples were becoming relatively common in great English parks.

The whole question of whether the garden buildings of an eighteenth-century park were intended to imply a subtle iconography, a hidden message, to the classically-informed visitor has become a favourite debating ground for garden historians with a literary bias. It is worth mentioning that the odd, eclectic mix of medieval wall, pyramid and temples which Lord Carlisle eventually achieved at Castle Howard does have a remarkable similarity to an illustration in Alexander Pope's 1716 translation of the *Iliad* showing the topography of Troy, the country around it and the Grecian camp, protected by a line of towers. If this is accepted Castle Howard itself would have been Troy.[14]

If the park at Castle Howard eventually took on some templed Arcadian airs it was by Vanbrugh's intention, but not by his actual achievement, and Blenheim Park, where he was working from 1705 to 1716, was never templed in his lifetime. Instead he presided over, rather than directed, an unsatisfactory compromise of a thoroughly old-fashioned formal axis – an arrow, barbed symmetrically at the sides with little plantations. This ran through the park to the north, the one direction from which visitors were unlikely to approach the palace, with a Grand Bridge, narrow, geometrical water features and the visually unrelated Bastion Garden or 'Woodwork' on the south side of the house. If, as seems probable, these uneasily linked garden episodes were the result of discussions between the Duke of Marlborough, the contractor, Henry Wise, and Vanbrugh, then the vast north avenue was probably Wise's contribution, the hexagonal bastion around the south parterre was built to make the Duke feel military in his garden, and only the actual scale of the walls and the ha-ha were to Vanbrugh's insistence.[15] The landscaping to the south of the house was a compromise: the plantations east of the Bastion Garden and next to the walled Kitchen Garden were planted in six or more formal star patterns; those across the River Glyme to the west were Wray Wood revived, a pleasant asymmetry of winding paths. By no interpretation could the grounds be described as Arcadian.

It was Bridgeman who mapped out these disconnected features in 1709, probably to Henry Wise's direction, with the north approach shown as cutting straight across the deep valley, almost a ravine, of the little Glyme. In a fit of vainglorious opportunism Vanbrugh determined to spend a fortune taking the relatively useless avenue over this valley in what was not so much a Roman bridge as an inhabited viaduct with thirty-two rooms in its arch. He had meant to top the whole unlikely structure with templar arcading, but the Duchess, who disliked and mistrusted his whims, put a stop to that extravagance.

There is no evidence that Vanbrugh had thought through the picturesque possibilities of a potentially superb site. What obsessed him at Blenheim and has earned him a reputation as a pioneer of Picturesque gardening, were the substantial remains, a whole courtyard and gatehouse, of the royal manor of Woodstock. The Woodstock Affair was a perfect instance of how reputations in this field can be built, not on deeds, but on the written word. The letters which passed between Vanbrugh and the Duchess on the subject of the old Woodstock Manor have afforded commentators an irresistible comic text. The remains of the Manor had become part of popular folk lore as the place where King Henry II hid his mistress, Fair Rosamond, from the jealous eyes of his Queen, supposedly in the heart of a maze. Discovered eventually by the Queen, Rosamond was forced to commit suicide. Popular plays were written on the story: one by John Bancroft in 1692, a second by Addison and Clayton in 1707. Always ready to live above his station and delighted by its historic and dramatic background, Vanbrugh found the empty building irresistible.

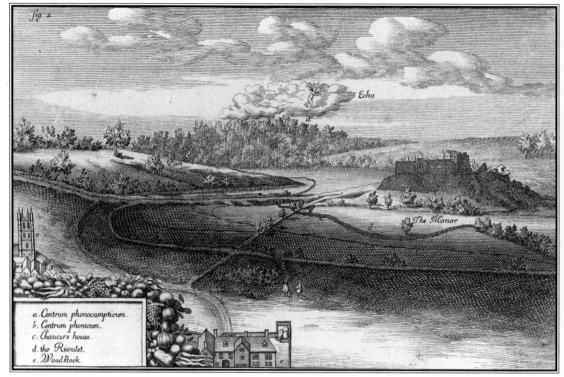

An illustration from Robert Plot's 1677 The Natural History of Oxford-shire, *made before Blenheim was built and the park reshaped, explains Vanbrugh's subsequent delight in the romantic power of Woodstock Manor, and his determined attempt, first to live in it, and then to preserve it as a picturesque ruin to be seen from the Palace.*

He patched it up, probably at Marlborough's expense, and lived there in Gothic grandeur from 1709 onwards, fighting a literary rearguard action with the the Duchess who was determined to have him out and the old Manor demolished as an eyesore from the windows of the new palace.

There is much to be said to support her apparent vandalism. The old building lay awkwardly at the very foot of the massive embankment leading to Vanbrugh's habitable viaduct. Coaches passing that way, if any ever did, would have been looking directly down on its roofs. But Vanbrugh would have none of this. He claimed that a 'Multitude of People' came daily to visit the remains and that it made, with other buildings and plantations, a 'Most Agreable Disposition' in the park. In a well-known piece of special pleading, which seems to anticipate the late eighteenth-century Picturesque theorists, William Gilpin, Uvedale Price and Richard Payne Knight, he urged in his usual hit-and-miss syntax that,

> were the inclosure filld with Trees (principally Fine Yews and Hollys) Promiscuously Set to grow up in a Wild Thicket. So that all the Building left, (which is only the Habitable Part and the Chappel) might Appear in Two Risings amongst 'em, it wou'd make One of the Most Agreable Objects that the best of Landskip Painters can invent.[16]

It was all to no avail. The Duchess had her reasonable way and Woodstock Manor was demolished. But Vanbrugh's idea for planting a Gothic relic around with dark evergreens has to be considered, whatever his real motivations were, as another aesthetic leap forward for the gardens of the new century: to that painterly approach to tree planting and building which William Kent would soon be perfecting at Stowe. What is rarely noticed is that, while Vanbrugh was failing to integrate an historic building into a new parkscape in 1716, forty-one years earlier, at the height of the fashion for formal gardens, a little known architect, William Samwell (1628–76) had persuaded Sir Thomas Grosvenor to align his new house, Eaton Hall, and all the impressive axis of its gardens, garden houses and seats to focus directly upon Beeston Castle.[17] The castle was a striking ruin perched upon a triangular crag like a Gibraltar in the middle of the rich, dull Cheshire Plain. This overt gesture towards the picturesque qualities of an historic relic was made in 1675 and the house and layout was completed in 1682, but because it provoked no controversy and resulted in no amusing exchange of letters, Samwell and the Grosvenors get no stylistic credit. The Grosvenors were to Chester rather as the Grimaldis are to Monaco, local princelings whose every action was observed and lauded. In 1675, living in Chester, two miles away from Eaton Hall, was the eleven-year-old John Vanbrugh, apparently an impressionable child, and a quick learner.

In 1716 Vanbrugh was sacked from his post at Blenheim, forbidden even to enter the palace grounds, and still he had achieved no templed Arcadia. He was, however, not short of commissions. In 1714 he had been knighted for the part he had played as Clarenceaux King of Arms in investing the future George II with the Garter, so profitable contacts came easily to him. His friendship with the Duke of Newcastle had brought him into garden planning partnership with Charles Bridgeman as the two men struggled to turn what had been Vanbrugh's own modest 'Castle Air' villa of Chargate at Esher into Claremont, a plausibly ducal seat for Newcastle. The gardens around the house give useful evidence as to the date when Vanbrugh moved from formal to informal ideas on design. A plan of about 1709, drawn when he was living at Chargate, is conventional.[18] A square Belvedere tower is to be sited on a hill behind the villa, otherwise the picturesque potential of the uneven grounds has been ignored. Two geometrically outlined waters are proposed on an axial line in the middle of a web of straight avenues intersecting at *ronds-points*. In the 'Survey of Claremont', published in the 1725 third volume of *Vitruvius Britannicus*, but probably dating from before 1717 and intended for volume two, a tangle of winding paths is shown climbing the steep wooded hillside, the Belvedere tower is now built in cruciform plan, bastions jut out at fierce angles, a mound and a round pond diversify the level areas and an enclosing ha-ha ditch has given the whole complex a fortified air. Soon Bridgeman's amphitheatre and moon steps will add another note of eclectic oddity. Yet here again there is no classical temple, no Arcadia, and the round-arched Belvedere proves that Vanbrugh's enthusiasm for castle-like structures never led him to look at any genuine medieval building through anything but Baroque-tinted spectacles.

In 1714 Bridgeman had begun working to transform the grounds of Stowe in Buckinghamshire for Lord Cobham, one of Marlborough's generals and a Whig political activist. Cobham was, like Lord Carlisle, a patron with ideas of his own and, when Vanbrugh came to Stowe in 1716 to advise on garden buildings, the very different templar pattern which began to develop suggests that Cobham the gentleman, rather than Vanbrugh the player, was the guiding influence. For that reason it is instructive to leave Stowe briefly and step ahead to Eastbury in Dorset. There, from 1718 onwards, Bridgeman and Vanbrugh had a much freer hand in designing an entire layout, almost from scratch, for George Doddington. Eastbury is, therefore, a demonstration of their mature garden style, uninfluenced, as they were to be at Stowe, by a strong-minded patron.

Judging from Bridgeman's detailed plans and illustrations of the garden buildings in the 1725 volume three of *Vitruvius Britannicus*, the gardens at Eastbury were a resounding first for temple

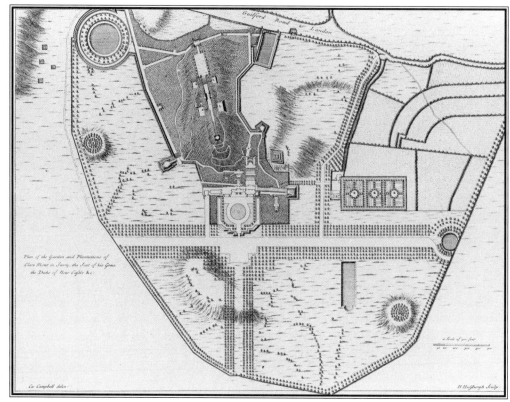

As he designed the gardens for this disastrously sprawling house at Claremont, Surrey, Vanbrugh was forced by the steep terrain into a dramatic, though still rigidly axial, forest garden poised on a hill-top and focused on a grim belvedere tower. He and Bridgeman defended the hill from a non-existent enemy with a military-style ha-ha and a great, bare amphitheatre.

Vanbrugh's Belvedere on the hill behind Claremont is castle-like in profile but has no Gothick detail, while the garden layout down to the Bowling Green which it commands is completely formal with its hedges and lawns. As usual the architect was caught between old and new garden styles.

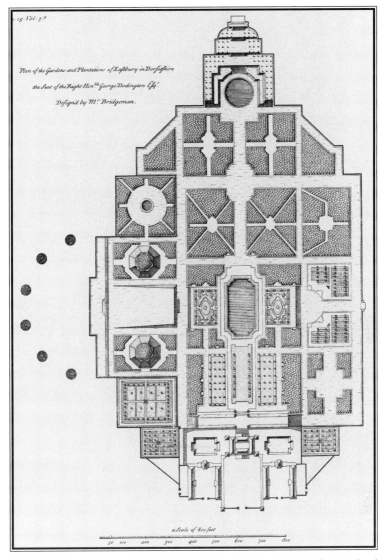

Plan of the Gardens and Plantations of Eastbury in Dorsetshire
the Seat of the Right Hon.ble George Dodington Esq.r
Designd by Mr. Bridgeman.

a Scale of 800 feet

When left in full control, after 1718, of the design of Eastbury House, Dorset, and its gardens, Vanbrugh and Bridgeman reverted to the formal geometry of the old-style London and Wise layouts with overscaled garden buildings. This indicates that Lord Cobham had been the inspiration behind the advances made at Stowe and Lord Carlisle behind those at Castle Howard: the gentlemen, not the players.

construction but a complete disappointment as far as any sign of movement towards an artfully asymmetrical Arcadia is concerned. Their layout was rigidly axial, a complex lozenge of largely symmetrical cypressed lawns and six geometrically sliced new woodlands. In the centre was a rectangular basin with a two-storeyed Ionic Bagnio or bathing pavilion, virtually a villa in its own right. At the far end, facing down towards the house, was a huge Corinthian temple, 56 foot square, the six columns of its portico 30 feet high, almost as tall as those of St Martin-in-the-Fields in Trafalgar Square. Outside the bounds of this disciplined and lozenged garden the park

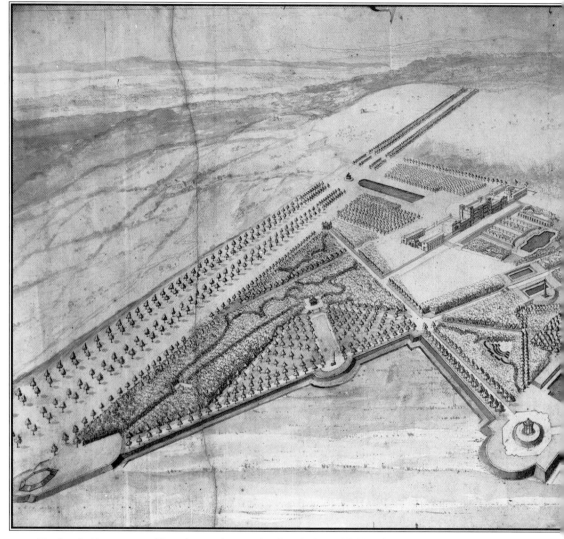

Urged on by his patron, an old war-horse with a nostalgia for redoubts and fields of fire, Charles Bridgeman had, by the early 1720s, enlarged the grounds of Stowe by this remarkable series of angular avenues and ha-has. Obliged to design his garden buildings on these angles, Vanbrugh was impelled away from axial formalism to an axial informality of

was even more geometrical. Three rows of square plantations led away at the sides and there was a curious double avenue of hillocks. Poetry and surprises were entirely absent.

Understandably when Earl Temple of Stowe inherited Eastbury he eventually blew the house up in 1775 and dismantled the gardens; only a kitchen range of the house, a chunky gateway and a few lines and mounds in the grass remain. Judging from what was eventually built in the grounds of Castle Howard after Vanbrugh's death, but largely to his prescribed dimensions, and from accounts of those two temples at Eastbury, it seems that his mistake in garden buildings was to design them too large. A large house can become an impressive palace, but a large garden building tends to stand too boldly among trees. Of their nature garden buildings should be, if

temples in unexpected conjunctions. His Rotunda, seen here in the near centre of Bridgeman's plan, is on the very edge of the pleasure grounds yet more the focus of walks and views than Stowe House itself. In the blank spaces beyond, the deliberate, rather than the involuntary, informality of Kent's Elysian Fields will evolve next.

not exactly toy-like, at least one dimensional step down from their parent house. The ideal Arcadia should be for humans to relax in, not for giants to oppress the earth. Stowe succeeded because its scale was correct, and it was Lord Cobham who was responsible for Vanbrugh and Bridgeman's success in the Buckinghamshire countryside. Stowe House was in existence before Vanbrugh's arrival and, though it was no beauty, it was not, like Eastbury, designed for a race of clumsy Brobdignagians. It set, in a sense, the tone of the grounds: grand but not impossibly vast.

Stowe's gardens were so successful, the most celebrated in the country, that they continued to develop and expand long after Vanbrugh, Bridgeman and even James Gibbs had gone. To understand the way in which Bridgeman's ingenious avenues on a limited and awkwardly shaped site, orchestrated Vanbrugh's temples and garden buildings into an exciting but geometrical asymmetry, the gardens must be walked through as they existed on Bridgeman's map deposited in the Bodleian Library, Oxford. This is dated to *c.* 1720 but it includes buildings which would not actually be built until later, but were there when Lord Perceval wrote his enthusiastic account of his visit in a letter of 14 August 1724:

The Gardens by reason of the good contrivance of the walks, seem to be three times as large as they are. They contain but 28 acres, yet took us up two hours. It is entirely new, and tho' begun but eleven years ago is now almost finished. From the lower end you ascend a multitude of steps (but at several distances) to the Parterre, and from thence several more to the house, which standing high comands a fine prospect. One way they can see 26 miles. It is impossible to give you an exact Idea of this garden, but we shall shortly have a graving of it. It consists of a great number of walks, terminated by Summer houses and heathen temples of different structure, and adorned with statues cast from the Anticks. Here you see the temple of Apollo, there a Triumphal Arch. The garden of Venus is delightfull; you see her standing in her Temple at the head of a noble bason of water, and opposite to her an Amphitheater, with statues of Gods and Godesses; this bason is sorounded with walks and groves, and overlook'd from a considerable height by a tall Column of the Composite Order, on which stands the statue of Pr. George in his Robes. At the end of the gravel walk leading from the house are two heathen Temples with a circle of water 2 acres and a quarter large, in the midst whereof is a Gulio or pyramid, at least 50 foot high, from the top of which it is designed that water shall fall, being by pipes convey'd thro' the heart of it. Half way up this walk is another fine bason with a pyramid in it 30 foot high, and nearer the house you meet a fountain that plays 40 foot. The Cross walks end in Vistos, arches and statues, and the private ones cut thro' groves are delightfull. You think twenty times you have no more to see, and of a sudden find yourself in some new garden or walk as finish'd and adorn'd as that you left. Nothing is more irregular in the whole, nothing more regular in the parts, which totally differ one from the other. This shews my Lords good tast, and his fondness to the place appears by the great expence he has been at. We all know how chargeable it is to make a garden with tast; to make one of a sudden is more so; but to erect so many Summer houses, Temples, Pillars, Piramids and Statues, most of fine hewn stone, the rest of guilded lead, would drain the richest purse, and I doubt not but much of his wifes great fortune has been sunk in it. The Pyramid at the End of one of the walks is a copy in mignature of the most famous one in Egypt, and the only thing of the kind I think in England. Bridgman laid out the ground and plan'd the whole which cannot fail of recomending him to business. What adds to the bewty of this garden is, that it is not bounded by Walls, but by a Ha-hah, which leaves you the sight of a bewtifull woody Country, and makes you ignorant how far the high planted walks extend.

Letter from John, Viscount Perceval to Daniel Dering, 14 August 1724

Lord Perceval summed up Bridgeman's design shrewdly with 'Nothing is more irregular in the whole, nothing more regular in the parts'. By a connection of four avenues Bridgeman created two interlocking triangles to the west side of the main axis of the house approached, as it was in Perceval's time, from the south. Down every straight vista there was a garden building and the pivot was not Stowe House itself but Vanbrugh's Rotunda, a temple of the gilded Venus from which one avenue led to the Octagon Lake and the spouting 'Gulio' (unfortunately it never spouted), a second to Nelson's Seat, and a third down a canal to a statued Amphitheatre and a tall column. Within each of the two triangles winding paths, entirely asymmetrical, led through thickly planted Wildernesses, in one triangle, to Vanbrugh's Temple of Sleep, and in the other his Temple of Bacchus. It was in these Wildernesses that Stowe was already, in 1720–4, coming very close to the ideal Arcadian templed garden which Kent would soon perfect on the other, eastern side of the central 'Abele' axis of tall poplars. When Kent had shown the way Lord Cobham's heir, Earl Temple, would set about Bridgeman's noble complex of avenues with an axe to trim the whole of Stowe's grounds, east and west, into one temple-crammed Arcadia of trees, clumped in an apparently natural disposition.

It cannot be a mere amusing coincidence that the surname of the family who first coaxed the templed Arcadia into mature existence was 'Temple'. The multiplication of such classical garden buildings was Cobham's pride and his joke. The motto of the Temples is taken from the Bible: 'Templa Quam Dilecta' – 'How beautiful are thy temples', and it was inscribed, along with Cobham's arms in shells and pebbles, on the Pebble Alcove. But what first made and still makes Stowe so memorable was not only the profusion of temples, but their individual quality. Vanbrugh's Rotunda is still authoritative, though altered. To see it in its original proportions with a much steeper dome it is necessary to visit Duncombe Park, North Yorkshire where there is a replica, possibly designed by him and, therefore, very early in date; *c.* 1719–20 has been suggested.[19] Of those pre-1724 garden buildings at Stowe easily the most perfect are the two Lake Pavilions which Vanbrugh designed to be lodges at what was then the main entrance on the avenue from Buckingham. They have a considered poise, a refined hesitancy in the rhythm of their Doric porticoes which proves that, even when he was constrained by Palladian disciplines in his old age, Vanbrugh could still make music out of stone.

Still perhaps slightly overscaled for Arcadia, the Rotunda at Stowe was actually achieved in Vanbrugh's lifetime. He designed it as a successful focal point pulling three of Bridgeman's bold side vistas together, away from the main house. Originally its dome had a steeper profile. Sited on the edge of the original ha-ha it commanded views out over Stowe's best south-westerly aspect.

From his co-operation with Bridgeman and Cobham, Vanbrugh had learnt one significant lesson in the early 1720s at Stowe. When his Rotunda was first built it was sited on the edge of the garden. It not only functioned as the focus to three axial avenues within the garden bounds, but it also looked out to the countryside beyond the limits. A temple could work outside a garden as well as inside it, make a visual leap over the fence, or more precisely, the sunken ditch. With this precedent in mind Vanbrugh was arguing strongly, late in 1723 and early in 1724, for a large garden building to be set on the edge of the confining ha-ha and bastion terrace around Wray Wood at Castle Howard. This, the Temple of the Four Winds with its four sizeable Ionic porticoes, would act as his Rotunda was acting at Stowe, projecting vistas out into the East Riding countryside as well as linking back obliquely to the south front of the house. Hawksmoor fought against him, urging a small, cheap Gothick turret, 'one Roome, (with a cellar and small waiting roome under it)'.[20] But Vanbrugh had appreciated the value of a firm visual marker, Italianate, therefore Arcadian rather than eclectic Gothick. 'Nothing of this plain or Gothick Sort will be determin'd on at last', he wrote to Carlisle on 11 February 1724.[21] Carlisle's son, Lord Morpeth, was ready to back him up having viewed all the designs Vanbrugh had sent and 'declar'd his thoughts utterly against anything but an Italian Building in that Place'.[22] In accordance with their wishes the timid Hawksmoor was obliged to construct his dead superior's four grand porticoes, a posthumous triumph for Arcadia and the visual leap.

After Vanbrugh's death in 1726 Cobham turned his Pyramid on the extreme western point of Stowe's park into an appropriately quirky monument 'Sacred to his Memory' and James Gibbs took over the role of temple designer in the park. An Arcadian pattern had been set which parks

Here, in one of the two Lake Pavilions, which acted as gate lodges to the old main approach to Stowe House from Buckingham, Vanbrugh hit at last on the perfect scale for an Arcadian park building and created a pair which might be ranked among the ten most beautiful templar structures in Britain.

and gardens all over the country would follow for the rest of the century and beyond. As Stowe had its Witch's House, its Hermitage, Gothic Temple, Saxon Altar and St Augustine's Cave – exotic structures among the pure classical temples – so that consciously eclectic pattern would be followed in other gardens as eagerly as the Arcadian. Variety and delight were the aims until the cold hand of the neo-classicists fell on English parks in the later decades of the century sweeping away so many Witch's Huts and Chinese Houses.

By the lucky chance of a century-long neglect, one almost complete garden by Bridgeman and Gibbs has survived in Hampshire: the Spring Wood at Hackwood Park. Laid out in existing woodland in 1725 for the 3rd Duke of Bolton, it makes a wry comment on Bridgeman's inability to learn and advance upon his experience at Stowe. He imposed upon Spring Wood precisely the predictable star geometry of rides that his old master George London had been prevented by Lord Carlisle from laying on Wray Wood twenty years earlier. So was Bridgeman at heart a Bourbon who had learnt nothing and forgotten nothing, a Brompton Park nursery man who only worked brilliantly at Stowe because he was designing alongside Vanbrugh and to the inspired direction of Lord Cobham? It seems likely.

Spring Wood is a hypnotic experience. In the centre of its avenues is a statue of Ceres. There, eight identical straight ways meet, each lined on both sides with glistening laurel hedges, the tall trees towering up behind them. It is a green nothingness in which all sense of direction is soon

The Temple of the Four Winds at Castle Howard looks more like an independent villa than a garden building. It is not Palladian in inspiration, but Vanbrugh's version of the Casino of Aurora in the grounds of the Villa Ludovisi in Rome. Nicholas Hawksmoor completed the structure in 1728–31 after Vanbrugh's death.

lost, one vista being exactly like the other. Bridgeman's original plans show that these straight rides should have been overlaid with a tangle of winding paths, as in those two triangles at Stowe, but the paths have gone.[23] Out on the southern edge of the wood is a line of three Bridgeman bastions, a last echo of Marlborough's wars and of an England where the army was the nation's heroic institution. These offer some relief from the basic tedium of a wood of geometrical rides while Bridgeman's deep, brick-walled ha-ha around the wood allows wide views out to the open countryside. Once there was a scatter of Gibbs's Doric temples down little side tracks and in hidden clearings. One, the Menagerie, survives, overlooking a small canal and a punctuation of grotesque urns, a welcome relief of classical incident in the monotony of green. For an Arcadia to succeed it needs to be articulated, there must be a sense of movement, of surprise vistas opening up, of columns and domes grouping unexpectedly among trees and above little lakes. By its happy survival Spring Wood only makes clear that Charles Bridgeman, left to his own devices by an absentee Duke, had not mastered that style or captured the spirit.

What Bridgeman had undeniably mastered were the avenue and the ha-ha. The avenue he inherited from London and Wise; the ha-ha he demonstrated more effectively at Stowe than it had ever been projected elsewhere in England. The ha-ha is one of the great legends of garden history, but one that needs to be taken with a little reservation. Certainly it allowed vistas within the garden to flow out easily into the surrounding fields and woods, but the ha-has of Stowe are

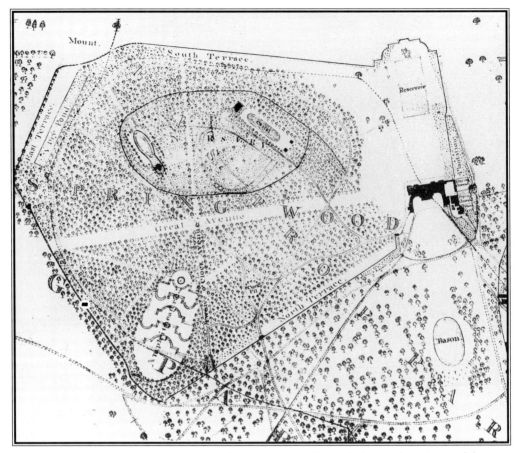

Left to his own inventions in 1725 at Hackwood Park in Hampshire, Bridgeman laid out on the Spring Wood the predictable spoked wheel of avenues which Lord Carlisle had prevented him from cutting into Wray Wood, Castle Howard, at the turn of the century. Subsequently, little events – a menagerie, an amphitheatre and a maison de plaisance – were added to give the wood diversity, and the trees grew into a romantic profusion behind their guardian hedges.

still formidable defensive works when approached from without and, as they were originally dug, their sides were as impregnable as a Celtic fortress in Caesar's *Gallic Wars*: they bristled with sharpened stakes. Cobham was an old soldier; at Stowe he obviously enjoyed the sense of living out a secure siege against non-existent armies. Did he think of Bridgeman's boldly aimed avenues as the equivalents of the sight-lines for canon from the ramparts of Vauban-style fortresses?

As for Vanbrugh, he would have been as pleased as Alexander Pope by the visual effect of all those straight avenues focused on temples and seats. It would be wrong to try and pre-read him into someone consciously striving towards the gently dispersed groves, natural-seeming lakes and columned temples of the later Arcadian garden. All the evidence suggests that he was of his time. He responded to garden geometry and confined the 'artinatural' winding path to obscure areas of wilderness. That letter of 1709 to the Duchess of Marlborough in which he proposed a 'promiscuous' planting of trees in varied shades of green to soften the remains of the old Manor at Woodstock was a remarkable artistic perception. There is, however, no evidence in his temples at Stowe – the Rotunda or the Lake Pavilions – that he ever made any attempt to put that perception into practice.

CHAPTER SEVEN

ADDISON, SWITZER AND 'THAT INEXPRESSIBLE SOMEWHAT'

Neither Joseph Addison (1672–1719), nor Stephen Switzer (1685–1745) could be described as great English gardeners. Only one Switzer-designed garden survives today in an unfashionable part of Wales and even that is far gone in romantic overgrowth and decay. As for Addison, he did once own a garden and make it the subject of several popular essays. But primarily the two men are significant as weather vanes to the direction in which the winds of garden design were blowing during that intriguing twenty-year interlude of visual myopia at the start of the new century; a time when Milton's poetry and the 3rd Earl of Shaftesbury's philosophy had set gardeners searching blindly for the ideal gardens of the printed page. Only the sheer philistine ignorance of the average upper-class Englishman of the period can explain why their garden designers were not immediately encouraged to study painters, paintings or, at the very least, prints, for direction. Dutch, French and contemporary Italian artists could so easily have come to the gardeners' rescue with the images of composition and colour for which they were groping. But at that period landscape painting had not yet become an English art form and most English art collections were limited to portraits, Dutch seascapes and religious subjects. Either that, or else the logical connections were simply not made.

Switzer, and immediately before him, Addison, could only imperfectly visualise the ideal gardens of Nature and Liberty about which they had been reading. This was 'that inexpressible somewhat', as Switzer put it in his clumsy, yearning prose, 'to be found in the Beauty of Nature, in a Rude Coppice or amidst the Irregular Turnings of a Wild Corn Field'.[1] That a writer and professional gardener could describe a cornfield as 'Wild' and possessed of 'Irregular Turnings' demonstrates in itself the visual naiveté of the time and suggests what a distance the aesthetes of the century had still to go. But at least it tells the direction in which they were travelling: towards Nature untamed and away from Nature disciplined. That, however, was a direction leading towards Wordsworth and the Romantic Picturesque of the Wye valley, the Lake District and the Highlands of Scotland. The templed Arcadia of the true eighteenth-century park would be a remarkable topographical hybrid – classical Greece as envisaged by garden designers who not only had never set foot in Greece, but had virtually no conceptions of its stony, sun-soaked reality. They interpreted it instead by extemporising on Claude and Poussin landscapes, using the lush lawns and bushy, deciduous treescapes of England, authenticating the resultant landscapes by tactfully sited temples of generally modest dimensions, token buildings, only rarely scholarly re-creations. Neither Addison nor Switzer could project that far. Their links were backwards towards the wholesome Puritan ideal of John Beale and Samuel Hartlib, to landscapes of husbandry, orchards and hedgerows. Consequently they both felt comfortable with the ideal Garden of Eden as described by a Puritan poet.

Milton was universally accepted at this time as the greatest poet of the nation: the Christians' laureate and England's Virgil of the Book of Genesis. If it seems odd that a poet, who had been a foreign secretary to Cromwell the regicide, should have secured this position in an apparently loyal and contented monarchy, the explanation is that the political ascendancy of the Whig party from 1688 onwards until the 1760s was more or less the delayed triumph of Cromwell's Commonwealth. If the Lord Protector had been able, in the 1650s, to invite George I's mother Sophia, a young girl at that time, over from Germany to preside as Queen over his newly reconstituted House of Lords, with Cromwell as First Minister, then the arrangement would probably have endured and the exile of the Stuarts would have been even more extended. As it was, during Charles II's reign, the 1st Earl of Shaftesbury could still pick up the political fragments of the Commonwealth, found the Whig party as an opposition to royal power and direct an aristocratic oligarchy towards the triumph of 1688 and the Glorious Revolution.

For any oligarchy to pull consistently together as a ruling team a watchword is required, and the Whig watchword was 'Liberty'. Not, of course, general democratic liberty, but the liberty of an élite to limit royal power and control the three kingdoms; and liberty needs a token philosophy. This was supplied by Shaftesbury's grandson, Anthony Ashley Cooper, the 3rd Earl. Naturally revered by the party for his lineage, he had been exiled to Naples by an asthmatic condition and there he wrote in 1709, *The Moralists: A Philosophic Rhapsody*. The most significant passages of this consist in a dialogue between Theocles, the teacher, and Philocles the disciple, and their exchange is written in what, from a generally laid-back and sophisticated aristocrat, was a remarkably intense poetic prose, memorable and persuasive.

Without ever being anti-Christian, Theocles bypasses revealed religion and urges Nature 'supremely Fair, and sovereignly Good! All-loving, All-divine!' as the guide and pattern for the moral, liberty-loving man to follow, God's image in this present world, 'Wise Substitute of *Providence*! Impower'd *Creatress*.'[2] The tone of the passage anticipates Wordsworth ninety years before that poet had printed a line:

YE Fields and Woods, my Refuge from the toilsom World of Business, receive me in your quiet Sanctuarys, and favour my Retreat and thoughtful Solitude. Ye verdant Plains, how gladly I salute ye! . . . Bless'd be ye chaste Abodes of happiest Mortals, who here in peaceful Innocence enjoy a Life unenvy'd, tho Divine.[3]

Informed so impressively that 'All Nature's Wonders serve to excite and perfect this Idea of their *Author*', Philocles is converted to this new religion and moves directly to underline its relevance to garden design. He discovers a 'Passion growing in me for Things of a *natural* kind' and landscapes in a '*primitive State*':

Even the rude *Rocks*, the mossy *Caves*, the irregular unwrought *Grotto's* and broken *Falls* of Waters, with all the horrid graces of the *Wilderness* it-self, as representing NATURE more, will be the more engaging, and appear with a Magnificence beyond the formal Mockery of Princely Gardens.[4]

This, from the reigning Whigs' exiled philosopher prince, could not fail to be influential. The problem was what, in English terms, were the 'horrid Graces of the *Wilderness*'? In Shaftesbury's words they sound suspiciously like a memory of the volcanic scenery around the Bay of Naples where he was writing. But the 'chaste Abodes of happiest Mortals', living in 'peaceful Innocence', suggests the Garden of Eden before the Fall, and for the topography of Eden the English reader already had one clear guide: Milton in *Paradise Lost*. Writing between 1760 and 1770 in his *History of the Modern Taste in Gardening*, Horace Walpole, a very sharp observer, was in no doubt whatever that Milton's description of Eden, written when the fashion for 'tiresome and returning uniformity' in garden design was at its height, had been formative in inspiring the relaxed Arcadian gardens of Walpole's eighteenth century.[5] 'The description of Eden', he wrote, 'is a warmer and more just picture of the present style than Claud Lorrain could have painted from Hagley or Stourhead'; and he went on to quote twenty-eight of Milton's lines to emphasise his point.[6]

Whether they prove it must be questioned, though Walpole's opinion has to be recorded and respected. Milton was blind and his great description of Eden, while inspiring and certainly informal, has qualities of visionary blindness. It has great patterns of sonorous word music that are only vaguely visual. Sometimes he imitates the jewelled scenery of Edmund Spenser's Bower of Bliss in Book 2 of the *Faerie Queene*:

> if Art could tell,
> How from that Saphire Fount the crisped Brooks
> Rowling on Orient Pearl and sands of Gold,
> With mazie error under pendant shades
> Ran Nectar.

But then in passages like:

> Sporting the Lion rampd, and in his paw
> Dandl'd the Kid; Bears, Tygers, Ounces, Pards
> Gambold before them, th'unwieldy Elephant
> To make them mirth us'd all his might, and wreathd
> His Lithe Proboscis

he seems to anticipate the jungle fantasies of a primitivist painter like Douanier Rousseau. How could an earnest Whig garden designer in Yorkshire match 'Groves whose rich Trees wept odorous Gumms and balme', or create a 'Saphire Fount' with waters 'Rowling on Orient Pearls' in Middlesex? Yet 'A happy rural seat of various views' was a tempting line, and Milton did give a useful direction by suggesting that classical temples, 'the Royal Towrs of great *Seleucia*, built by *Grecian* Kings' and Arcadian sites, 'that sweet Grove of *Daphne* by *Orontes*', while inferior to Eden, were at least roughly comparable and might be used as models.

The year 1714 and the smoothly handled accession of the Hanoverian George I to the throne marked the end of the Whig party's political uncertainties. Now the wilderness years were permanently behind them. They had a party philosopher in Shaftesbury and a party poet in Milton. The Revolution of 1688 had been confirmed, what was needed was a distinctive new architectural style and a new manner of gardening to signal that Revolution: something, if not exactly republican, then senatorial, both grand and simple, noble and yet relaxed. King George's

Guelph ancestors had hailed from the Veneto so the Palladian was a natural choice for a new house style. But logic dictated that there should be formal gardens for such formal Palladian façades, with straight avenues and disciplined flower beds. Here, however, the recent associations of such horticultural geometry were unfortunate. Formal gardens suggested Versailles, and France was the seat of royal tyranny from which the late Stuarts had drawn shameful pensions of French gold. Shaftesbury had pointed in a different direction. A party of Liberty should have gardens of natural freedom, in contrast to the 'formal Mockery of princely Gardens'. As a result a proudly insular nation would not simply go its own way stylistically, whilst the Continent obediently followed France into the Rococo, but go its own way in two diametrically opposed directions: formal Palladian houses, but with informal Arcadian gardens to surround them.

That was the difficulty which Addison and Switzer faced: how should that informality be shaped and directed in a country where London and Wise had profited so richly and for so long with their clipped yews, occasionally functioning fountains, hornbeam avenues and standard infilling of elms? As the inspiration for informality had been a literary one, the initial answer had to be equally literary: they should be the ideal gardens of the printed page. In the absence of artists it was a case of journalists to the fore.

As far as rankings in the gardening game go, Addison has to be classed as a gentleman, but only just. He was a son of the Church, educated at Charterhouse and Queen's College, Oxford. But to make the correct gentleman's Grand Tour of Italy, Switzerland and Germany, and to spend a year in France acquiring the language, he had needed a state pension of £300 a year from his political patron, Lord Halifax. For most of his life he was a hard-working Whig journalist, the archetypal armchair philosopher and populist, writing essays of apparently effortless stylistic clarity, cosy, friendly, even ingratiating. The essays came out between 1709 and 1716 in the *Tatler*, the *Spectator* and the *Guardian*, making him a national institution and his Sir Roger de Coverley character – benign, jovial and foolish – the model of the perfect English squire and paternalist land owner. In an age of literary pygmies, with Swift retired to Ireland, Addison passed as a giant. In 1716, near the end of his life, he contrived to marry the dowager Countess of Warwick and live in Holland House. Dr Johnson, uncharitable as ever, described the marriage as one of those arrangements by which a Sultan gives his difficult daughter a man to be her slave; and it is true that Addison did not long survive his new marital status. Pope, for one, was convinced he was a homosexual.[7]

While there was, so far as is known, never any social contact between Addison and Switzer, the intellectual closeness was strong. In his 1718 *Ichnographia Rustica*, Switzer quotes whole pages of Addison's essays word for word, enthusiastically acknowledging his inspiration. It is indeed difficult to find any ideas or novel approaches to gardens in Switzer which he has not drawn directly from Addison's light-hearted journalistic excursions. Addison throws off an idea; Switzer suggests its practical application. In that sense they were a team, but whether Addison would have been gratified to find himself described as a partner in such a duo is doubtful.

It was in his *Spectator* essay for 25 June 1712 that Addison picked up Sir William Temple's idea of 'Sharawadgi', the inspired asymmetry of the Chinese, and linked it ingeniously to the idea of treating a whole stretch of the English countryside as an interesting park-scape while continuing to use it as productive park land with aesthetics and economy happily united.[8] He began by denigrating 'the Beauties of the most stately Garden or Palace . . . the Imagination immediately runs them over, and requires something else to gratifie her', and he came very close to suggesting the use of paintings as models for free, natural landscapes: 'we find the Works of Nature still more pleasant, the more they resemble those of Art'.[9] But then he lost his way. He had recently been delighted by a double *camera obscura* where he had seen reflected trees moving in the wind on one wall and boats sailing on a river on another, all achieved by optical tricks with mirrors. Since the real countryside in reflection was so interesting why not retain farmland with all its activities and variety, both profitable and a pleasure to observe?

Why may not a whole Estate be thrown into a kind of Garden by frequent Plantations, that may turn as much to the Profit, as the Pleasure of the Owner? A Marsh overgrown with Willows, or a Mountain shaded with Oaks, are not only more beautiful, but more beneficial, than when they lie bare and unadorned. Fields of Corn make a pleasant Prospect, and if the Walks were a little taken care of that lie between them, if the natural Embroidery of the Meadows were helpt and improved by some small Additions of Art, and the several Rows of Hedges set off by Trees and Flowers, that the Soil was capable of receiving, a Man might make a pretty Landskip of his own Possessions.[10]

Addison, being a journalist and not a landowner, took this inspired notion no further. His next paragraph was an assault on tree clipping and Brompton Park commercialism. The illustrations in a contemporary county history like Sir Henry Chauncy's *Historical Antiquities of Hertfordshire* (1700) reveal how widespread the cult for absurd topiary-work had become. As Addison scornfully wrote:

Our Trees rise in Cones, Globes, and Pyramids. We see the Marks of the Scissars upon every Plant and Bush. I do not know whether I am singular in my Opinion, but, for my own part, I would rather look upon a Tree in all its Luxuriancy and Diffusion of Boughs and Branches, than when it is thus cut and trimmed into a Mathematical Figure.[11]

Not only was Addison following Shaftesbury's example: 'I sing of Nature's Order in created Beings, and celebrate the Beautys which resolve in Thee, the Source and Principle of all Beauty and Perfection',[12] but he was picking up that true line of Whig perception which John Beale had expressed and Samuel Hartlib had so much admired back in the Commonwealth years. It was a line which had been interrupted after 1660 by Franco-Dutch formalism, and then, but only blindly, formulated in Milton's Eden. In his 1657 *Herefordshire Orchards, a Pattern for all England*, Beale had described how 'all our highways are in spring-time sweetened and beautyfied with the bloomed trees, which continue their changeable varietyes of Ornament, till in the end of Autumn they fill our Garners with pleasant fruit and cellars with rich and winey liquours'.[13] Addison, his genteel intellectual heir, could not 'but fancy that an Orchard in Flower looks infinitely more delightful, than all the little Labyrinths of the most finished Parterre', adding a deliberate thrust at the commercialism of those nursery gardeners who 'contrive a Plan that may most turn to their own Profit, in taking off their Evergreens, and the like Moveable Plants, with which their Shops are plentifully stocked'.[14] A year later, in his *Guardian* essay of 1713, Pope's more fertile wit would deliver the final deadly quietus to the clipped yew tree.[15] It was no accident that after George London's death in 1714 the Brompton Park nurseries never flourished; journalism had rendered them unfashionable.

Switzer had neither Addison's urbane detachment nor Pope's wicked gift for ridicule, but after his employment in the Brompton Park nurseries he was ready enough to join in the assault on his old masters. Despite his foreign-sounding surname, Switzer was Hampshire born, from the village of East Stratton a few miles north of Winchester. He was not forthcoming about his education

This illustration from Chauncy's Hertfordshire *of a paddock in the grounds of Little Offley proves that Addison and Pope were not tilting at windmills when they satirised the general popularity of trees and bushes clipped into unnatural forms. Here crowns, balls and horsemen have been planted at random.*

even though he lost no opportunity in his writings to demonstrate a familiarity with the Latin classics. Mysteriously he claimed to have begun life as a gentleman who fell, 'by some small Revolutions and Meanness of Fortune' into what he described melodramatically as 'the greatest Slavery'.[16] This seems to have meant nothing worse than digging, scything and planting as a common labourer at London and Wise's Brompton Park nurseries, hence that account of George London's career quoted in Chapter Five. So, despite his flow of Latin tags, he must be classed firmly as a player. By several friendly relationships with aristocratic employers like the Earl of Orrery and Lord Bathurst he used his Brompton Park experience to good purpose. In 1718, the year of *Ichnographia*, he was based at Newbury and contracting to work for the Earl of Cadogan on his ambitious new layout for the grounds of Caversham Park on the Oxfordshire–Berkshire border, north of Reading. In the late 1720s he was working in Flintshire at Leeswood and possibly also at Rhewl. In the last twenty years of his life he kept a plant and seed stall in Westminster Hall while editing a monthly gardening periodical and publishing a series of specialist books on fruit growing, exotic kitchen vegetables, farming and hydraulics. A later edition of his *Ichnographia* came out in 1742 making claims which he would never have dared to make while Addison was alive, namely that he, Switzer, had been the original inventor of the *ferme ornée*.[17]

There was just a touch of truth in that assertion. Addison gloried in his amateur status. While strong on broad 'natural' principles, he was weak on practicalities, on his own admission 'very whimsical . . . I value my Garden more for being full of Blackbirds than Cherries'.[18] In his *Spectator* essay for 6 September 1712 he had described his several acres as 'a Confusion of Kitchin and Parterre, Orchard and Flower Garden', with flowers from 'under a common Hedge, in a Field, or in a Meadow, as some of the greatest Beauties of the Place'.[19] Like a second Theocles, but writing now of English, not Neapolitan gardens, Addison claimed to be 'more pleased to survey my Rows of Colworts and Cabbages, with a thousand nameless Pot-herbs, springing up in their full Fragrancy and Verdure, than to see the tender Plants of foreign Countries kept alive by artificial Heats'.[20] It was all very well to sneer at the fantastical bulb fanciers and collectors of exotic plants, the Sir Thomas Hanmers of the last century, but what was to take their place?

Switzer thought he had the answer. When his *Ichnographia Rustica* came out in 1718, Vanbrugh and Bridgeman had only just begun working together at Stowe. The Temple of the Four Winds was not yet even a notion at Castle Howard, the templed Arcadia was far from established as the ideal English park land, so the *ferme ornée*, as Switzer's book proposed it with a number of engaging illustrations, could easily have become the prevailing fashion rather than a mere novelty on a few eccentrically planted estates.

Switzer's problem was the constraint of market forces. In the very year when *Ichnographia Rustica* was published, scorning 'the beauty of the largest and finest of Regular Gardens',[21] he was contracting with Lord Cadogan to lay out at Caversham a particularly large, fine and 'Regular'

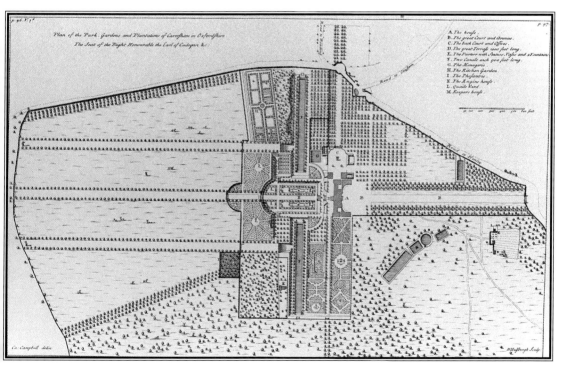

Stephen Switzer laid out the gardens and avenues of Caversham Park, Berkshire, for Lord Cardigan after 1718. This plan from Vitruvius Britannicus *proves how entirely formal and conventional his practice was when compared with his wild, visionary theories. There is one curving path through a wood but still no classical temples.*

garden himself. The contract survives,[22] a fascinating reminder of how long London and Wise's fashions endured after London's death and what lavish engineering operations were required to set up one of their gardens. Dated 20 April 1718, it stipulated that Switzer would have to complete the works by the end of next November. They would cost a carefully accounted £1,392 4*s* 9*d* with a massive £836 7*s* 11*d* contingency fund for extras. Between April and the end of July a workforce of up to 170 would be employed. Then, from 15 September onwards, after a break for gathering in the harvest, up to 80 men would be employed.

Everything was to be based on a rigidly cross-axial framework, far removed from Switzer's printed ideal of 'a little Regularitie' near the main house and thereafter 'many Twinings and Windings' and the 'mazie Error' of 'natural Avenues and Meanders'.[23] Caversham had three ruler-straight avenues running down to the Thames, star-shaped 'Woodworks' (wildernesses) and geometrical parterres. Lord Cadogan was to provide 'sufficient mules & horses to the full number of Twelve', and 'all such Flowers Edgings Greens Statues Vases & all other Ornaments'. Switzer's chief concern was in the earthworks and the fruit trees: 'five hundred Fruit Trees of the best kinds of Peach Apricock Plum Pear Cherry Vine & Apple' to be planted before their supporting walls and espaliers were built. 'The ground to be well dugg & manured in a method proper for its producing such Legume and other Kitchen Vegetables as shall be proper to crop it next year'.

In his writing Switzer lavishes airy poetical prose on 'the loose Tresses of a Tree or Plant, this is easily fann'd by every gentle Breeze or Air, and the natural tho' unpolish'd dress of a beautiful Field, Lawn or Meadow',[24] but then suddenly he panics and adds, within brackets, his reservations: '(a little trimm'd, and the exorbitant Luxury of their Branches retrencht, cut off and redress'd, and with their even clean Walks of Gravel, Sand, or any other material for Walls spread over)'.[25] Then, and only then, he felt it safe to claim superiority for his manicured wildness over 'the utmost exactitude of the most finish't Parterre and the curioused Interlacings of Box-Work and Embroidery'.[26]

He claimed to despise all parterres, 'but as the Opinion, and, indeed, the more solid Judgements of Persons, differ very much as to design', he included several elaborate pull-out designs for parterres in his *Ichnographia*, one a straight copy of that in the Hampton Court Privy Garden.[27] There are two large pull-out plans for his 'Natural and Rural way of Gardening', both impressively detailed and fascinating to study. The first, for 'The Manor of Paston',[28] is a compression of Vanbrugh and Wise's layout at Blenheim, which Switzer had personally worked on, a rigidly formal, hexagonal bastion work linked to an axial avenue. Only the flanking areas are, like the western woodland at Blenheim, a tangle of winding paths with ponds at their intersections. His suggestion that 'Lodges, Granges etc' might be built in the form of 'some antiquated place' reads like a memory of Vanbrugh's sojourn in the remains of Woodstock Manor.[29]

Switzer's second plan for the 'Natural and Rural'[30] is virtually Caversham but with its repeated cross-axial terraces and canals overlaid upon a bewildering maze of small farms, cornfields and sinuously curling streams with a patchwork of hedges and round ponds. The whole great lozenge of grounds (not unlike Vanbrugh and Bridgeman's Eastbury in its outline) is encircled by a perimeter walk, twisting and bending. 'For', wrote Switzer, the politically correct Whig, 'whatever some may think of Magnificence, there is an inexpressible Pleasure in these Natural Twinings and private Walks to a quiet, thoughtful studious mind'.[31] This was advice which would shortly be followed by Lord Burlington at Chiswick, though he would show no interest in Switzer's cornfields, as Switzer showed not the slightest interest in temples and eclectic garden buildings. That 'Natural and Rural way of Gardening' proposed by the *Ichnographia* was not the templed Arcadia of the future, nor was it the formal layout of the recent Stuart past. It hung suspended between the two, prevented, as much

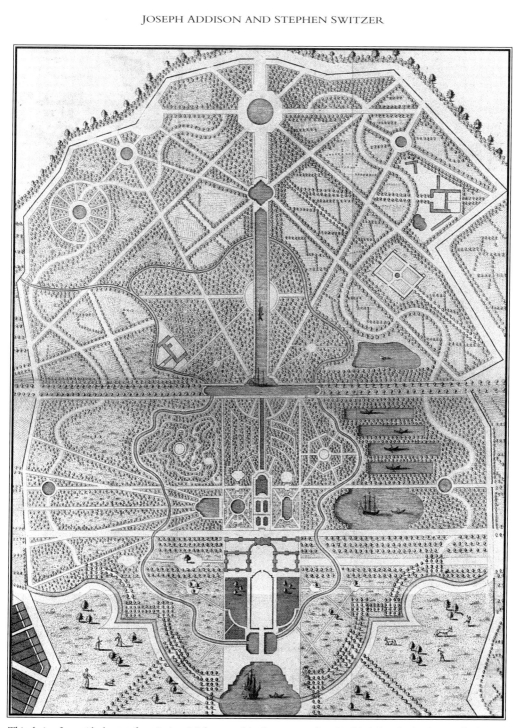

This design for an ideal estate from Switzer's Ichnographia *demonstrates how Beale's feeling for the charms of a fertile landscape, Sir William Temple's advocacy of 'sharawadgi' and Addison's urging that 'a whole estate be thrown into a kind of Garden', were influencing old-fashioned notions of formal gardening. Switzer retains, however, a grand formal axis behind his self-conscious curving paths.*

Between their twin neo-Classical sphinxes the White Gates at Leeswood, Flintshire, provide a claire voie of mixed Palladian and Rococo motifs to make travellers on the public road look up to Leeswood House rather than vice versa. Switzer disapproved of such ironwork, but his patron, George Wynne, overruled him.

by the natural conservatism of patrons as by Switzer's own ignorance of art, from making the logical advance to the classical and the eclectic. No book on gardening ever quoted as much poetry as the *Ichnographia*. There are whole pages of Pope's *Windsor Forest* and his *Essay on Criticism*, a long passage from the 'Seraphic' Cowley's translations of Horace, while Milton's description of Eden is reprinted by the yard. But there is never a mention of Claude or Poussin.

Leeswood, Switzer's last surviving garden, catches perfectly the irresolution and the compromises of his design career. It was laid out for a young Whig squire and would-be politician, George Wynne, who had suddenly become very rich, the sum of £300,000 is mentioned, when a vein of lead ore was discovered on one of his Flintshire mountains. Instead of rebuilding his dilapidated sixteenth-century manor house, Wynne moved half a mile sideways along the same steep line of pastoral hillside to a virgin site. There an architect, possibly Francis Smith of Warwick, was commissioned to raise a Baroque house on a Palladian ground plan, high on a north-west facing hillside. Wynne's staunch Whig affiliations in an otherwise Tory county may explain the clash of architectural styles.

As the grounds of the new Leeswood Hall lay entirely on an open slope, Switzer and Wynne decided that there should be a private forest garden at the east side of the house. This would be a French-style feature like Hackwood's Spring Wood. The rest of the park would act both as a natural frame for the Hall and, at the same time, a natural frame for the landscape as viewed from the Hall itself. Hence the astonishing White Gates.[32]

These are approached up a side lane from the main road to Mold. Up to that point there has been no hint of the Hall or the park. Then, out of a sylvan homeliness of hedge and farm, set back from the lane in a sweep of sophisticated richness that would be impressive even as a prelude to a royal palace in London, come the White Gates. They are not simple gates but a 100 foot reach of sophisticated ironwork screening, arguably superior to Tijou's work at Hampton Court and infinitely more dramatic in their bucolic setting. Elegant lead sphinxes look down disdainfully from the Doric side piers and four more piers of diamond fret openwork link eight grilles, each topped with a broken pediment, and double gates. The 17 foot overthrow of these with the Wynnes' dolphin *naiant* is more Rococo in feeling than Palladian, improbable as that may seem for a design of about 1726. 'The best of our Gardens', Switzer had written, 'discover the Slenderness of their View by a termination most Designers are fond of, I mean fine Iron Gates, a kind of Artifice not good, and a very great Expense in the Bargain'.[33] Now, eight years later, he was humouring Wynne with exactly that 'kind of Artifice'.

Perverse as the argument may sound the White Gates have to be seen as an alternative to the ha-ha. They do not open up the view from the house, so much as draw the visitor's attention to the Hall, far up the hill above a great open lawn fringed by an arc of trees. The White Gates were never intended to give a direct approach to the house, a driveway would have spoilt the lawn. Instead the Black Gates, fine but much less flamboyant, were set up immediately to the west of the house to allow a direct entry to the stable court from the lane. Seen from the Hall, the White Gates are only an incident, albeit a striking one, a good 100 feet below. They in no way 'discover' the view of farmland, domestic and yet also romantic, that 'inexpressible somewhat' of 'Wild' cornfields and 'Rude' coppices rising across the valley to wooded hills. So these grounds mark a clear advance on the avenue. Switzer loved rolled and tended grass as much as he despised the parterre; the White Gates frame the Hall in a proto-Picturesque landscape of trees and lawn. On the other side of the house this axial, yet open planning continued and is still traceable with another lawn, tree fringed again, rising to the skyline.

And at that point a question has to be put, if not for an answer, at least for honest consideration. Here is a house of the mid-1720s and it has never had any formal garden either to the front or to the rear. Switzer's beloved lawns have always swept up to its main façades. The earliest existing map and a drawing of about 1800 of the main front both confirm this.[34] Did he anticipate, possibly by accident but, if the text of his *Ichnographia* is examined, probably deliberately, those bare elegances of a house set unguarded on a landscape of rolling grass and trees that Capability Brown would make commonplace some twenty-five years later? Did he leap over the intermediate stage of the templed landscape to the one that Horace Walpole believed to be 'original by its elegant simplicity, and proud of no other art than that of softening nature's harshnesses and copying her graceful touch'?[35] If that was Switzer's intention then he framed it for the visitor, or the traveller on the road, with the extreme artifice of the White Gates. Their Palladian and Rococo motifs were once set between twin Doric temples, now removed to another entrance where they act as lodges. The golden limestone of their Baroque-style pediments are carved with the trophies of Music and War, a stylistic irresolution indeed, but as originally built these temple porticoes faced uphill to the Hall.

Immediately to the east of the house, behind a largely demolished service wing, are the walled kitchen garden and the forest garden. This last, on the evidence of *Ichnographia*, was a feature which Switzer considered indispensible to a superior garden layout.

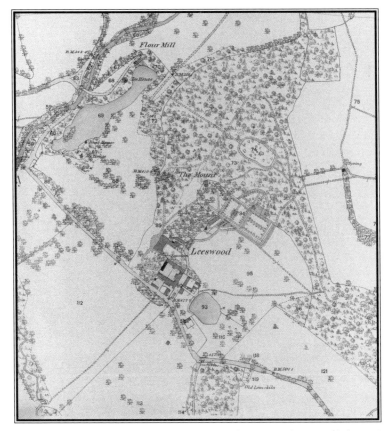

The Leeswood estate where relics of Switzer's layout still survive on a late nineteenth-century Ordnance Survey map. The forest garden, with its straight rides, Mound and Bowling Green, comes right up to the house as the chief recreational area. Towards the top left a funnel of casually planted trees sweeps downhill to the White Gates. Switzer's original lake was formal.

Even in its overgrown ruin, it still conveys a little of the poetry of such a shaded pleasure ground. At its entry two ways divide around a stone monument. One leads along a terrace walk entirely arched over by yew trees and, from a straight crossing of rides in the centre of the wood, by a right turning enters what was once the undulant oval of the Bowling Green. The second way leads to Switzer's Mound where the stone armchairs and stone table top, which he originally set at the top of the Bowling Green, have found a last home. In Switzer's day the Mound is more likely to have been topped with a 'Windsor Seat', a device he admired 'which is contriv'd to turn round any Way, either for the Advantage of the Prospect, or to avoid the Inconveniencies of Wind, Sun & Etc'.[36] Before the trees took over, the Mound, which bears no relation to the geometrical rides through the garden, would have commanded views back to the Hall and down to the White Gates. Switzer thought it 'entertaining' to be 'on the Precipice of a Hill' and believed it right 'if we have not such by Nature, to create them by Art, by digging a Hole in one place to make a Hill in another', and there were originally three circular ponds at the foot of the trees, now linked into one serpentine water.[37] No other 'rural Decorations', such as Switzer required for a wood 'desig'n chiefly for walking' have survived. But from the text it is apparent

But when the Wood is plac'd near the House, it is desig'n chiefly for walking, to be as private as is consistent with its own nature, as when it is naturally compos'd of several Levels, Hills, and Hollows. This is a Place desig'n by Nature, for the Exercise of a good Genius in Gardening.

'Tis in large Hollows and low grounds, and in the Middle or center of Woods, that we make our little Cabinets and Gardens, of which some are to be found in this Book, and others may be taken out of Mr. James's, besides an infinite Variety that may be contriv'd; but the Lines extended from them should not be carry'd out too far, for that will make one unavoidably split upon the former Error of Regularity.

If Water is to be had, one ought to look for convenient Places to make Heads at (at as little Expense as possible) and to frame such Figures as are most suitable to the Nature of that Hollow; so likewise of Hills.

If the Wood is thin, 'tis there one may clear it quite away, and make open Lawns. And if the Wood be an Eminence, then all the small Stuff on the Outside ought to be clear'd away, to open the distant Prospect, if it deserve it; but if it be an unsightly, barren Prospect, then let the Wood remain to blind it.

These, and such like Particulars as these, ought every Designer to observe, and then the regular Designer will not be so much blam'd for his Regularity, in as much as it is an open level Park, is not plac'd near his House, or is on the North Side, where Gardens and Walking-Places are not so absolutely requir'd, but his Design is for an open spacious Wood, where the Owner is to ride, hunt &c.

Neither will the natural Gardener be observ'd to have err'd, when he has fill'd all his little Eminencies and Hollows with little Gardens, Statues, and other rural Decorations; for his Wood is entirely for walking in; it lyes high, and he is not observ'd to have cut down any noble Trees, when, in Truth, the Nature of his Wood would not allow it; neither has he shewn himself fond of any Mathematical Figure, but has made his Design submit to Nature, and not Nature to his design. The Inside of his Wood is fill'd with Hares, Pheasants, the Statues of Rural and Sylvan Deities all cut out in Wood, while he contrives likewise that living Hares and Pheasants shall abound; by which Means, besides the couchant Furniture in Imitation, he has really a great deal that is alive and in Motion, darting themselves a-cross him where-ever he turns himself. He is often surpriz'd with little Gardens, with Caves, little natural Cascades and Grotts of Water, with Pieces of Grotesque Painting, Seats, and Arbors of Honeysuckles and Jessamine, and, in short, with all the varieties that Nature and Art can furnish him with.

Stephen Switzer, *Ichnographia Rustica*, 1718

that he was feeling his way with 'Statues of Rural and Sylvan Deities all cut out in Wood', wooden models of hares and pheasants, 'Pieces of Grotesque Painting, Seats, and Arbors of Honeysuckles and Jessamine' towards the circuits which the *ferme ornée* and eclectic gardens of the mid-century would soon elaborate and perfect.

There is one last footnote to be added. Switzer was clearly interested in the possibilities of the Picturesque, a fancier of views, of Addison's 'rough careless Strokes of Nature'.[38] The grounds of Leeswood show certain anticipatory signs of what Lancelot Brown would later perfect. But is there something more? It has always been a cliché, truer forty years ago than now after the plague of hedge-grubbing, that large areas of the English countryside are in themselves park-like: a cared-for landscape, artfully tree planted, neatly hedged and pictorial. Switzer's *Ichnographia* was a reasonably successful book;

One of the stone chairs, which Switzer set around the Bowling Green in the heart of the forest garden, now stands overgrown and commanding no views from the top of the Mound.

it went through a second edition long after the first, and Switzer's own carefully drawn plans are a pleasure to study. Some of the credit for that park-like quality of ordinary farmland should be given to him, the man who wrote that we should 'the UTILE harmoniously weave with the DULCI', and claimed,

> I believe I am not singular in my Opinion, if I afirm, that an even decent Walk carry'd thro' a Corn Field or Pasture, thro' little natural Thickets and Hedge Rows, is as pleasing, as the most finish'd Parterre that some Moderns have been so fond of.[39]

If he moved some way towards the templed Arcadia, was he also working towards an even more important development, the English countryside perceived as one large garden?

CHAPTER EIGHT

ALEXANDER POPE AND THE 'GENIUS OF THE PLACE'

Now that he has become, 250 years after his death, one of the great unread, recalled only for a few brilliant platitudes, it is not easy to appreciate what a towering celebrity Alexander Pope (1688–1744) was in his own time. When he moved, with his mother, in 1719 into the small Thames-side villa in Twickenham, which Lord Burlington had arranged for him and which James Gibbs was altering, he was already, though technically a Roman Catholic and a Tory, the cultural hero figure of the Protestant Whigs. He had published to critical acclaim his *Essay on Criticism*, *The Rape of the Lock*, *Windsor Forest* and *Eloisa to Abelard*, a commanding reach of the intellectual, the mock heroic, the pastoral landscape and tragic love. Most impressive of all, in that age obsessed with its own classical image, he had translated and published the first four books of Homer's *Iliad* in verses accepted by

Alexander Pope, drawn in 1747 after his death by Arthur Pond.

contemporaries as capturing the spirit of the great original. In a society determined to be Augustan and to reshape itself on the model of that Roman greatness before the martial simplicity of a senatorial aristocracy had been corrupted by the emperors, Pope seemed to offer the literary credentials of Greece on which that Roman nobility had, through Aeneas, been founded. 'I have great hopes', Robert Digby wrote to him, 'to see many old-fashioned virtues revive, since you have made our age in love with Homer'.[1] The Classics were the key; Pope held that key; he was the natural laureate of his times.

While he lived that image of genius would not be questioned. When he died in 1744 it was seen as perfectly appropriate that Francis Hayman's vignette should show Chaucer, Spenser and Milton in attendance at his death bed, while in 1751 Hubert Gravelot painted a dying Pope gathered to Apollo's bosom by the shade of Homer and all the Muses. Crippled and a member of a despised Christian sect, his very surname a social handicap, he was nevertheless eagerly cultivated as the guest of the rich and influential. Pope's letters reveal him struggling to fit his visits with Lord Harcourt, Lord Bathurst, Dean Swift, the Bishop of Rochester, Dr Arbuthnot and Lord Oxford

This view of the north bank of the Thames at Twickenham, a few yards up-river from Pope's Villa, illustrates not only the upper-class charm of the village, but the remarkable stylistic eclecticism of the riverine buildings – Chinese, Gothick, Indian, classical and Arabian. The grounds of Horace Walpole's Strawberry Hill lie behind the tree on the left.

into a crowded social calendar. Where garden design was concerned he was at a veritable cross-roads of influences, familiar with Bridgeman and Kent, hero-worshipped by Switzer, patronised by Lord Burlington, who was anxious to have him as a neighbour, and consulted at every point as Allen Bathurst laid out a five mile forest garden across the unrewarding Cotswolds at Cirencester.

All of which explains why, when Pope settled down to create his own garden at Twickenham, it was virtually bound to become significant and influential, as if Homer were evolving by way of Theocritus and Virgil's shepherd pastorals into Horace: the Roman poet who made his own small villa and estate immortal by his writing. There is no reason why a great poet should also be a highly original and inspired gardener, but that is exactly what, by an ingenious fusion of drama and compression, Pope became. Within grounds of less than five acres he devised a layout that offered an entertaining variety of incidents with a demonstration of the most advanced landscape effects of perspective and colour. It was a foretaste of the undulant line of the Rococo, an exquisite miniature version of what Princess Caroline was creating at the same time across the river in Richmond Park and a model for the garden which Kent would create in the early 1730s for the next Prince of Wales at Carlton House.

By 1722 all the elements of a setting for one of Antoine Watteau's *fêtes gallantes* were in place.[2] Pope seems from the start to have known exactly what he wanted and how to delight his admirers on a limited budget. Over the next twenty years his grotto would be doubled in size and enriched with a wealth of minerals, but the basic structure of the garden would not be altered and every visit was a controlled performance. Visitors who had entered the plain villa directly from the London to Hampton Court road would first be led out onto the small Thames-side square of lawn to take in views of the river. On one side was a smelly tanner's yard with a smoking chimney and on the other a public way down to a mooring; the cottages of Edwards the fisherman and Mrs Hathaway lay beyond that; Twickenham's charm was this social mix of the humble and the aristocratic. Just a little up-river from the Hathaway cottage was Lord Radnor's villa, half a mile downstream was Marble Hill, home of Prince George's discarded mistress, the Countess of Suffolk. Across the river on the Surrey side was the Duke of Newcastle's Claremont and soon Newcastle's brother, Henry Pelham, would be building Esher Place to William Kent's innovative Gothick designs.

By the end of his life Pope was filling this river lawn with messages of stone for the classically initiated. On the bank he proposed to set up statues of two river gods with inscriptions indicating Meles, the river of Homer's birth, and Virgil's slow-winding Mincius. To impress the point, busts of the two poets were enclosed within niches of the grove-work on each side of the lawn, together with those of Marcus Aurelius and Cicero. Pope, so the iconography ran, was the English Homer and Virgil who would restore classical literature and return England to strict Roman virtues. When they had absorbed the statuary, the river, its boats and neighbours, visitors would experience the theatrical stroke that everyone remembered and described. To reach his main garden on the other side of the road Pope had had a tunnel dug from his basement. This corridor and the two basement rooms overlooking the river became the Grotto, walled initially with rough stones, flints and fragments of reflecting glass.[3] Its ceiling was a star of looking glass subtly angled and the whole complex was designed so that someone sitting in the garden across the road could glimpse through the tunnel, as down a viewing glass, boats passing on the river. Pope's luck had been to tap a natural spring as the Grotto passage rose upwards towards the garden. This was fed back down the Grotto in a series of ingenious little falls and basins. As one delighted visitor from Newcastle described it in 1747:

> Here it gurgles in a gushing Rill thro' fractur'd Ores and Flints; there it drips from depending Moss and Shells; here again, washing Beds of Sand and Pebbles, it rolls in Silver Streamlets.[4]

Always fascinated by light effects and optical devices, Pope had contrived to double the impact of his streamlet. 'Cast your eyes upward', the same visitor declared, 'and you half shudder to see Cataracts of Water precipitating over your Head',[5] and that was only a start. Once the door to the river side was closed the looking glasses took over, 'it becomes on the instant, from a luminous Room, a *Camera Obscura*; on the Walls of which objects of the River, Hills, Woods, and Boats, are forming a moving picture in their visible Radiations'.[6] So Pope had recreated the double *camera obscura* effect which Addison had described in that *Spectator* article of 1712. What he had also evoked were the classical poets. Horace had his 'Fount of Bandusia in clearness crystalline' though not, it is true, in his cellar. Ovid's *Metamorphoses* had,

> In its most secret recess a well-shaded grotto, shaped by no artist's hand. But Nature had by her own skill copied art, for she had formed a natural arch of the living rock and crumbling tufa. A sparkling spring with its narrow stream trickled on one side.[7]

Impressed by all these effects of light and sound, and with Pope babbling and hobbling beside them, quoting his poets and pointing out his optical toys, the visitors would proceed through the

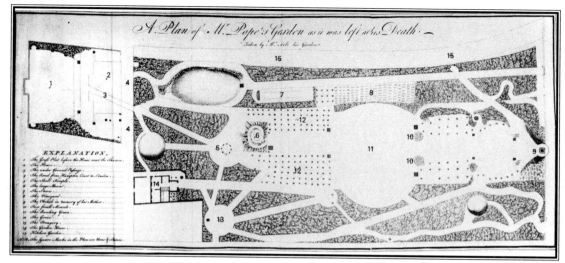

The plan of Pope's garden drawn in 1745 by his gardener John Searle to guide the visitors who flocked there after the poet's death. It was a brilliant demonstration to the bourgeoisie of how much 'variety' (Pope's obsession) might be contained within a limited space by ignoring symmetry yet including a sense of progression, from the mouth of the underground passage, between 4 and 4, to the Obelisk in Bridgeman's little amphitheatre at 9.

three chambers, the first well lit, the next two increasingly gloomy, to a corridor sloping steeply upwards to the daylight of the main garden. And it was at that point that Pope the Ovid imitator, impresario of darkness and maker of glittering toys, retired, and Pope the innovative genius of the new pastoral garden style took over. The corridor divided into three ways and it was up the middle and broadest path that Pope led his admirers. But for a while and to emphasise how little Pope had been influenced by Switzer, we will take the left-hand way, as Pope's housemaid, gardener and, on early morning inspections, the poet himself, would go.

This path mounted straight into the separate utilitarian section of the garden: first to an oval Drying Green for the washing, presided over by one stone urn, then to the Stove or Greenhouse where, on reeking hot-beds of horse manure, the devoted gardener, John Searle, coaxed into fruit the pineapples which Pope gave as presents to his benefactors, often in what he considered fair exchange for several tons of masonry shipped over long distances. After the Stove came the vineyard supported on the only wall in a garden otherwise surrounded by a thicket of trees 'which prevents all prying from without'.[8] Through a gap in this dense tree cover lay the long Kitchen Garden open to the western sun, but completely isolated from the pleasure grounds. It was just possible to find a way through to the main garden but the geometry of paths did not encourage it. Not for Pope the confusion of groves, cornfields, flower beds, farms and winding paths which Switzer was urging and which garden enthusiasts like Philip Southcote would soon be planting out.

To return to the exit from the Grotto again and to take Pope's ordained route for visitors, this broad middle way went up between bushes to the first carefully staged event on the sequence of the garden's central axis. 'Mr Pope used to say', Joseph Spence recorded in his *Observations*, 'that all the beauties of gardening might be comprehended in one word, "variety"',[9] and it was in this main axis that he exemplified that variety. Visitors would be confronted in a round open glade with the domed Shell Temple built on eight wooden columns entirely encrusted with shells. Kent made a detailed drawing of this enchantingly bizarre structure with its bow-legged, rusticated

Mavis Batey has demonstrated that the form of Pope's Shell Temple, drawn here by William Kent, was not wishful thinking, like its attendant nymphs, but a realised and enchanting Rococo structure. Not unexpectedly it fell down! The Rococo spirit was always trying to escape from the confinement of the Palladian in Kent's designs. Kent, the player, has his arm on Pope, the gentleman, and Pope's dog Bounce is present.

Corinthian columns and smoking central altar. But because he included a few attendant nymphs and tritons the building has been dismissed as an impossible, un-Palladian fantasy. Mavis Batey in her recent study of Pope has proved, by illustrating a similar undulant columned shell temple which Kent designed and built at Stowe, that his temple for Pope was no fantasy.[10] Kent and Pope were both by instinct more sympathetic to the relaxed, natural and fashionable style of the French *genre pittoresque* (early Rococo) than to Colen Campbell's rigid Palladianism or Lord Burlington's antique Roman revival. This dream-like Shell Temple (it collapsed in the 1740s and had to be rebuilt) struck a keynote of playful charm at the start of any visitor's tour of Pope's garden.

Immediately behind it rose 'the large Mound'.[11] An irregular spiral path climbed this 'rising as it were out of Clefts of Rocks, and Heaps of rugged and mossy Stones'[12] to a seat where three people could sit and look, in one direction, across the whole garden and, on the other, catch a sideways glimpse of the Thames and Richmond Hill. The Mound would have been the same size as the one which survives in the wood at Switzer's Leeswood. Once this had been enjoyed the visitors could enter the Grove between a regular quincunx of trees, a Bridgemanesque memento of London and Wise's formalism. This opened out between two urns into the Bowling Green bordered by two semi-circular sweeps of trees. On the far side of this pleasure ground were two smaller mounds and then the garden, punctuated by statues and urns, passed through two compartments sided by an undulant line of trees to the exedral ending. It was there, after her death, that Pope erected in 1735 an obelisk to his mother's memory, inscribed: 'Matrum Optima Mulierum Amantissima Vale' (Best of Mothers and most beloved Lady Farewell), a dutiful exercise, but an afterthought, not the garden's original conclusion. The exedral bank on which the obelisk would be sited had been a miniature Bridgemanesque amphitheatre. A team of Bridgeman's workers had raised and turfed this for Pope when Bridgeman himself was working in 1726 at Richmond for the Prince of Wales.

Pope had been as optically aware in his planting of the garden as in his decoration of the Grotto. 'You may distance things', he told his friend Spence, 'by darkening them and by narrowing the plantation more and more toward the end, in the same manner as they do in painting, and as 'tis executed in the little cypress walk to the obelisk'.[13] He explained further that 'the lights and shades in gardening are managed by disposing the thick grove-work, the thin, and the openings in a proper manner, of which the eye generally is the properest judge'.[14] In one sense both Pope and Kent were bad painters who used their training to devise, not a rigid, old-style forest garden, but an evocation of Pope's 1704–13 *Windsor Forest* where 'waving groves a chequer'd scene display,/And part admit, and part exclude the day'; its lines not geometric but curvaceous, where, 'interspers'd in lawns and opening glades,/Thin trees arise that shun each other's shades'.[15]

When this parade of the garden's main axis had been made there was an old-style forest section still waiting to offer more of that essential 'variety'. Here there was a whole tangle, a maze of paths to choose from, leading to two circular glades in the wood or, if the visitor was persistent, to the Orangery, another circular area where Pope's orange trees were set out in tubs when the season was fair. Finally, tucked away in the extreme right-hand rear corner of the grounds, was the Garden House, a two-storey cottage for alfresco meals, with a columned porch and an urn. Thence, by yet another round clearing, the refreshed visitors would descend to the right-hand fork of the original three and to the shades of the Grotto again. Pope urged gardeners to respect 'the Genius of the Place'[16] and that was what he had done. Faced with a dull, five-bay house opening straight onto a public road, he had made drama out of its unhappy site with his Grotto tunnel, and turned a few level acres on the other side of the road into a subtly shaded forest grove of incidents and surprises.

Horace Walpole, not always the most charitable judge of other men's gardens, commended Pope's design in a letter to Horace Mann as, 'a singular effort of art and taste, to impress so much variety and scenery on a spot of five acres'.[17] He was particularly pleased by 'two or three sweet little lawns opening and opening beyond one another . . . the whole surrounded with thick impenetrable woods'.[18] Lord Bathurst admired his friend's achievement so much that he suggested, 'I'll cut you off some little corner of my Park which you shall do what you will with'.[19] This indeed hints at a second influence of the Twickenham garden. Not only would it prove a model for the ambitious suburban or large city garden, like Prince Frederick's at Carlton House, but its miniature qualities were so engaging that soon major parks like that of Wentworth Woodhouse, would have to have a small-scale area – a Petit Trianon – for homely and more relaxed gatherings. In his travels across Britain in the 1750s Bishop Pococke would record them everywhere. Pope had pioneered the human scale; but he had done much more besides.

Whole books, or at least long chapters, have been written to count up Pope's debt to Antiquity in his garden design. These list the inspiration of Virgil's *Georgics*, Homer's garden of Alcinous and the Garden of Epicurus in the suburbs of Athens; but was that debt quite so heavy? For the poets, writers and rich villa owners of ancient Greece and Rome the term 'garden' was virtually synonymous with 'fruit orchard' and no one was more conscious of that than Pope. He

The Grove from John Ogilby's 1654 edition of The Works of Virgil. *Pope projected himself as the English Virgil and his friend and neighbour Lord Burlington modelled the 1716–17 Bagnio at Chiswick, sited at the end of one of his formal patte d'oie avenues, on this engraving. Few layouts of this period appear to have been planted with any awareness of how the young trees would look in their maturity. One gardener is using a roller to produce a velvety green sward.*

had personally translated Homer's account of Alcinous's plot and, initially, it is true that the Twickenham links appear convincing:

> Four Acre's was th'allotted Space of ground
> Fenc'd with a green Enclosure all around.[20]

But then follows the brimming fruit salad bowl of its contents, all tritely adjectival: the 'red'ning Apple', 'blue Fig', 'full Pomegranate', 'verdant Olive', 'dropping Pear' and 'order'd Vines'. Only the last item featured in the semi-public sector of Pope's grounds. There is no mention in Homer of a composition of ornamental trees or any formal feature, and since Alcinous lived in Greece a lawn could hardly feature in his gardens. Indeed the one element of native English gardens which virtually all writers of the period praise, the lush green grass of a rainy island, was bound to distinguish insular gardens from any on the Continent, ancient or modern, even those of France. The one major feature of Alcinous's garden was its water supply:

> Two plenteous Fountains the whole Prospect crown'd
> This thro' the Garden leads his Streams around.[21]

afterwards 'its current on the Town bestowing', hardly the equivalent of Pope's Grotto spring. Anyone who has had to translate Virgil's *Georgics* in his or her school days knows that this involves one long chase through the dictionary to look up the Latin names of Roman fruit, vegetables, agricultural implements and the technicalities of grafting branches onto trees. While Augustan English landowners did value these marks of bucolic simplicity in the lifestyle of the Roman aristocracy, there was no very close equivalent between English and Italian agricultural practices and even less with those of Greece.

Pliny's accounts, long and detailed, of the gardens at his two villas, one at Laurentum on the sea coast near Ostia and the other at Tifernum, up in the Tuscan hills, are a different case. They will be considered fully in the following chapter as they were more an obsession of Lord Burlington, who commissioned a translation of Pliny's relevant letters, than they were of Pope. However, since Switzer's *Ichnographia* had just been published with long quotations from Pope's poems, the poet will have known that Switzer believed the gardens he was projecting were based on those of Antiquity in general and of Pliny in particular. Switzer claimed in his preface that they were 'of the same kind as the gardens of Epicurus, a person (if Pliny speaks right) that first us'd this Extensive way of Gard'ning'.[22] But then, not content with Greek precedents, Switzer had continued, 'This may likewise be supposed was and is the manner of Gard'ning among the *Chinese*', adding for good measure that 'The *Romans* had doubtless the same Extensive kind of Gardens'.[23] Not persuaded by these unscholarly generalisations, Pope kept his Stove and Kitchen Garden out of sight behind high hedges.

What Switzer could not have realised when he published in 1718 was that he had inadvertently set Pope, his hero, a challenge which the poet could hardly fail to take up. Switzer's 'Extensive' gardens, a confusion of grove, garden and *ferme ornée*, were obviously out of Pope's reach for reasons of class and finance. More hurtfully Switzer had distinguished condescendingly between 'Town' gardens and 'Country' gardens, and his definition of the inferior 'Town' garden would fit Pope's five acres at Twickenham like a glove. 'Town Gardens' were those

> that are four, five, six or seven Miles out of Town, whither the Fatigues of Court and Senate often force the illustrious Patriots of their Country to retreat, and breathe the sweet and fragrant Air of Gardens; and these are generally too much pent up.[24]

Not only 'pent up' but inferior in their brief, seasonal prime. While 'Country' gardens included 'Woods, Coppices, Groves', 'Town Gardens' were 'first for Flowers' with their 'more trifling and fading Beauties'. These were 'over by the latter end of May [an interesting comment on the average eighteenth-century flower bed] and Borders are like Graves, and rather a Blemish than a Beauty to our finest Gardens'.[25]

Consciously or unconsciously Pope set out to refute this withering judgement with a 'Country' garden in miniature, no *ferme ornée* but one that relied almost entirely on the interplay of grass and trees. It was in part a compression of Lord Bathurst's Cirencester, with none of its tedious, vacant spaces, and in part a Lilliputian version of 'that incomparable Wood of my Lord Carlisle at Castle Howard' which Switzer had singled out for praise.[26] So, to that negative extent, Pope could have been influenced by his admirer. Because of Pope's literary reputation and skilful self-projection his garden would become almost a national shrine to his memory. That Newcastle gentleman who visited the place in 1747 had approached it 'with a kind of glowing Ardour, flutt'ring at my Heart';[27] and eventually Lady Howe, a later owner, became so tired of visiting pilgrims that she pulled the house down in 1805 and wrecked the garden.

A precise stylistic definition of Pope's garden is elusive, though Nikolaus Pevsner found no difficulty in decribing it as 'Rococo'.[28] The Grotto was richly walled with rocaille work – 'Flints, Spar, Ores, Shells' – and it debouched upon a rustic temple coated in shells. The term 'Rococo' would not be invented to describe that style until the nineteenth century, long after it had become unfashionable, but the term was devised from the linking of 'rocaille' and coquille', rocks and shells, these being the favoured decorative materials in Rococo buildings, which were otherwise distinguished by curvaceous, flowing, feathery forms. The central axis of Pope's garden, those little lawns which Walpole had admired, were a series of linked curvaceous forms, and from them ran a system of curving paths and round clearings. When Pope was laying out his grounds between 1719 and 1722 the Régence was in full swing in France and great Parisian town houses were being fitted up in glorious Rococo excess. The term 'Rococo Garden' has come, over the last thirty years, to be used to describe gardens characterised not only by winding paths and seemingly natural clumps of trees, but by a wealth of eclectic garden buildings, Chinese and Gothick as well as classical. Pope's garden had only room for one rustic shell temple, yet all its 'artinatural' curves, its rocaille and its coquille urge that it deserves the 'Rococo' description; in which case it would have been the earliest such garden in England.[29]

The matter of possible artistic influences on the poet naturally arises. If only he had not chosen, in 1714, his friend Charles Jervas to instruct him in the art of painting he might have made the full 'Rococo' leap. But Jervas was an early neo-classicist. Pope never once mentions Claude Lorrain in his letters and only admired Nicholas Poussin for solemn neo-classical paintings like 'The Death of Germanicus'. His Shell Temple owed everything to Kent's sense of fun and nothing to classical accuracy.

It would be interesting to be able to credit Pope, the poet of the intensely Gothic *Eloisa to Abelard*, with the first Gothick garden building of the century, King Alfred's Hall in Bathurst's Cirencester Park. Unfortunately the written evidence tells against Pope, the player, in favour of Lord Bathurst, the gentleman. Bathurst loved Pope dearly and always tried in his letters to suggest that he relied on the poet implicitly for advice on gardens and garden buildings. But hard fact proves that all the time Bathurst was building to his own inspired fancies.

The two men were creating a retreat for themselves, 'my Oakley Bower' as Pope called it, in the very early 1720s, at the far end of Bathurst's vast but disconnected park. In 1721 Bishop Atterbury wrote to Pope, 'may my Lord have as much satisfaction building the house in the wood and using it, as you have in designing it'. But then Bathurst began to rebuild it. In 1732 he was writing to Pope: 'I long to see you excessively for I have almost finished my hermitage in the wood, and it is better than you can imagine. Many things there are done that you can have no idea of.'[30] Then in 1733 Mrs Delany wrote to Swift:

Lord Bathurst has greatly improved the house in the wood, which you may remember but as a cottage. It is now a venerable castle and has been taken by an antiquarian for one of King Arthur's.[31]

Pope advised Bathurst on the original 'Oakley Bower' in Cirencester Park in 1721, but Bathurst soon pulled it down and, by 1732, he had completed this complex of banqueting hall and castellated towers alongside what appeared to be the ruins of a monastic foundation. Bathurst called it King Arthur's Castle until a local antiquary made a visit and took it for a genuine Saxon building; thereafter it was known as Alfred's Hall. It was one of the first Gothick garden buildings to be built in England and was constructed with stone retrieved from the nearby demolished Sapperton Manor.

This is the clearest evidence that Pope designed 'a cottage', and it was the ebullient Lord Bathurst, whose energy always left the poet feeling exhausted, who built the 'venerable castle', bringing Gothick structures, ruined arches and traceried windows for the first time into the eclectic range of English garden buildings.[32] It was at the same time, between 1730 and 1733, that William Kent was building a Gothick villa at Esher for Henry Pelham, the future Prime Minister. The Gothick at Cirencester and Esher was, therefore, a joint enterprise, of Bathurst and Pelham the gentlemen, and Kent the player, with Pope, the player-poet, nowhere.

Over the next twenty years, chiefly in his letters to Martha Blount, Pope would reveal his preferences in existing gardens with rapture over 'the prodigious Beauty . . . inexpressibly awful & solemn' of the terraced, ruin-strewn, cascade-threaded grounds of Sherborne Castle, Dorset: 'venerable broken walls' and 'disjointed stones'.[33] That was a Gothic response, but he was equally impressed by one of Bridgeman's angular Arcadias. In 1728 he would account Rousham 'the prettiest place for water-falls, jetts, ponds, inclos'd with beautiful scenes of green and hanging wood, that ever I saw'.[34] Rousham is often described as William Kent's finest, most subtle garden, yet Pope was praising it before Kent had even touched the grounds. It was all Bridgeman's work which he was enjoying. In these crowded years when great gardeners were treading on each other's heels it is a mistake to accord too much credit to any one man. The English gardens of the first half of the century were a composite achievement.

Later, between 1736 and 1742 Pope would offer advice to Ralph Allen of Prior Park, Bath, in the construction of a little garden in the woods to the west of the house. With a grotto house, a serpentine lake, a sham bridge, a cataract and Moses striking the rock it could be described as Protestant Rococo.[35] But Pope's only recorded wisdom on Allen's planting is a query in a letter of 1740 asking about the health of 'the Elms we planted on each side of the Lawn and of the little Wood-work to join one wood to the other below, which I hope you planted this Spring'.[36] This small upper grove was never anything but a distraction from the prospect valley below the house which Allen would later cross superbly with the Palladian Bridge, and on Lancelot Brown's direction, open up in a bold Arcadian spirit.

These apart, Pope's true service to the garden world was as a wit to flay humbug and as an aphorist to express memorably the truths about garden design which were emerging as friends, acquaintances and enemies experimented around him. Addison may have begun the attack on the topiary fanatics, but it was Pope's devastating mockery in a *Guardian* essay of 1713 that destroyed them and his *Epistle to Burlington* of 1731 that left any English landowner with a formal terraced and geometrical garden feeling miserably unfashionable.

I believe it is no wrong Observation, that Persons of Genius, and those who are most capable of Art, are always most fond of Nature, as such are chiefly sensible, that all Art consists in the Imitation and Study of Nature. On the contrary, People of the common Level of Understanding are principally delighted with the Little Niceties and Fantastical Operations of Art, and constantly think that *finest* which is least Natural. A Citizen is no sooner Proprietor of a couple of Yews, but he entertains Thoughts of erecting them into Giants, like those of *Guild-hall*. I know an eminent Cook, who beautified his Country Seat with a Coronation Dinner in Greens, where you see the Champion flourishing on Horseback at one end of the Table, and the Queen in perpetual Youth at the other.

FOR the benefit of all my loving Country-men of this curious Taste, I shall here publish a Catalogue of Greens to be disposed of by an eminent Town-Gardiner, who has lately applied to me upon his Head. He represents, that for the Advancement of a politer sort of Ornament in the Villa's and gardens adjacent to this great City, and in order to distinguish those Places from the meer barbarous Countries of gross Nature, the World stands much in need of a Virtuoso Gardiner who has a Turn to Sculpture, and is thereby capable of improving upon the Ancients of his Profession in the Imagery of Ever-greens, My Correspondent is arrived to such Perfection, that he cuts Family Pieces of Men, Women or Children. Any Ladies that please may have their own Effigies in Myrtle, or their Husbands in Horn beam. He is a Puritan Wag, and never fails, when he shows his Garden, to repeat that Passage in the Psalms, *Thy Wife shall be as the fruitful Vine, and thy Children as Olive Branches round thy Table.* I shall proceed to his Catalogue, as he sent it for my Recommendation.

ADAM and *Eve* in Yew; *Adam* a little shatter'd by the fall of the Tree of Knowledge in the great Storm; *Eve* and the Serpent very flourishing

THE Tower of *Babel*, not yet finished

St. GEORGE in Box; his Arm scarce long enough, but will be in a Condition to stick the Dragon by next *April*

A green *Dragon* of the same, with a tail of Ground-Ivy for the present

N.B. *These two not to be sold separately*

EDWARD the *Black Prince* in Cypress

A *Laurustine* Bear in Blossom, with a Juniper Hunter in Berries

A Pair of Giants, *stunted*, to be sold cheap

A Queen *Elizabeth* in Phylyraea, a little inclining to the Green Sickness, but of full growth

ANOTHER Queen *Elizabeth* in Myrtle, which was very forward, but Miscarried by being too near a Savine

AN old Maid of Honour in Wormwood

A topping *Ben Johnson* in Lawrel

DIVERS eminent Modern Poets in Bays, somewhat blighted, to be disposed of a Pennyworth

Alexander Pope, Essay from *The Guardian*, 1713

Pope's couplets could destroy the London and Wise manner:

> Lo, what huge heaps of littleness around!
> The whole, a labour'd Quarry above ground

and devalue the basic notion of symmetry in a garden with:

> Grove nods at grove, each alley has a brother,
> And half the platform just reflects the other.[37]

But it was Lord Cobham's Stowe which he set up as the model garden, not his patron Lord Burlington's more geometrical Chiswick. Significantly too he found Stowe improving with time as the trees grew up and a natural softness settled upon Vanbrugh's temples and Bridgeman's avenues. He wrote on 23 August 1731 to John Knight: 'if any thing under Paradise could set me beyond all Earthly Cogitations; Stowe might do it. It is much more beautiful this year than when I saw it before, & much enlarged, & with variety'.[38] Pope felt trapped by Palladian formalism; he roundly attacked Burlington:

> Yet shall (my Lord) your just, your noble rules
> Fill half the land with Imitating Fools;

and scorned builders who 'Turn Arcs of triumph to a Garden-gate', or,

> . . . . call the winds thro' long Arcades to roar
> Proud to catch cold at a Venetian door;
> Conscious they act a true Palladian part,
> And if they starve, they starve by rules of art.[39]

Whether he quite escaped from formal garden thinking himself must remain debatable. Bridgeman was his true contemporary and it is the Bridgemanesque garden – symmetry modified by art – that lies behind these lines:

> Consult the genius of the place in all:
> That tells the waters or to rise or fall;
> Or helps the ambitious hills the heavens to scale,
> Or scoops in circling theatres the vale;
> Calls in the country, catches opening glades,
> Joins willing woods, and varies shades from shades;
> Now breaks, or now directs, the intending lines;
> Paints, as you plant, and, as you work, designs.[40]

Pope was still thinking, with his theatrical, circling scoops and 'intending lines', in terms of Bridgeman's work of 1726 at Stowe: that favourite device of an amphitheatre and the direct geometry of straight, connecting avenues. As a young poet walking the open oak glades of Windsor Forest he had had perceptions of Theocritus and Virgil's shepherd Sicily, but conceived them in terms of England's green, deciduous woodlands because he had never made the Grand Tour. As a sophisticate, living through an unusual twenty years of peace with France, he, like Kent, was tempted by the superior charms of the *genre pittoresque*. His garden and his garden precepts were compromises shaped by those factors: Bridgeman, a pastoral ideal and the Rococo line.

CHAPTER NINE

LORD BURLINGTON, WILLIAM KENT AND AN ARCADIAN PICTURESQUE

The challenge and, it should be admitted, the fascination, of making any assessment of Lord Burlington and William Kent's contribution to garden design, lies in the difficulty of separating their real achievement from the golden haze of persuasive prose which Horace Walpole lavished on Kent in his *The History of the Modern Taste in Gardening* of 1771.[1] Historians from Macaulay in the nineteenth century, to Butterfield in the twentieth have warned their readers of the danger of taking Walpole's judgements on political and social history uncritically. Yet no one escapes the man's sheer readability, his contacts, his inside knowledge, his eye for the human frailties of the great and his gift for the memorable phrase. Under the seductive enchantments of his writing the dull, corrupt years of his father, Sir Robert's long premiership becomes a halcyon era of peace and prosperity, while the imperial successes of the two brothers, Henry Pelham and the Duke of Newcastle, as prime ministers are withered by convincing suggestions of treachery, dishonesty and, most tellingly, of buffoonery. By his memoirs of the reigns of

William Kent was celebrated by Horace Walpole as the genius behind the evolution of the templed Arcadia. His nine years training in Rococo Italy and several months in Paris will have left him impatient with the trite decorative forms of England's neo-Palladian style and the ill-informed neo-Classical aspirations of his patron and friend, Lord Burlington. Within those twin restrictions he designed inventively.

George II and George III, Walpole ensured that, in a consideration of the history of eighteenth-century Britain, no one would register the fact that under the two Pelham brothers a victorious world empire was raised and the north Atlantic became for a time virtually a British lake. The sin of the Pelhams had been to separate Walpole from the one love of his life, their nephew Henry

Fiennes Clinton, 9th Earl of Lincoln, marrying him off to his cousin Catherine. For that, a vengeful, able and single-minded homosexual blackened and ridiculed their reputations at every possible stage in his writings. Because his love was secret his viewpoint and bias has never been fully appreciated.[2] Political correctness is not yet an impartial force.

As with eighteenth-century politics, so with eighteenth-century garden history. Horace Walpole (1717–97) was fully informed on the part that Vanbrugh, Pope and Bridgeman had played in advancing garden design from the formal to the informal. In his *History* he gave both Bridgeman and Pope accurate credit. What he described as 'this simple enchantment' of the sunk fence (the ha-ha) allowed the garden 'to be set free from its prim regularity, that it might assort with the wilder country without'.[3] So far so accurate; but then his prose and his preference for a hero figure took over in the endlessly quoted and re-quoted passage:

> At that moment appeared Kent, painter enough to taste the charms of landscape, bold and opinionative enough to dare and dictate, and born with a genius to strike out a great system from the twilight of imperfect essays. He leaped the fence, and saw that all nature was a garden.[4]

And garden historians have been leaping that fence with him ever since. It hardly registers that Vanbrugh at Claremont and Bridgeman at Stowe had been fence-leaping with enormous ha-ha systems years before Kent. More important still the obvious fact that all Nature is not a garden is grossly underplayed. Large tracts of the English countryside are of unrelieved tedium. The northern bounds of Stowe are enclosed with a deep sunk ditch and walling, but only as a confinement to animals. All that side of the grounds was heavily planted with woods to conceal the level fields of Buckinghamshire. Only to the west and south-west, beyond the Temple of Venus, is there sufficient lilt and slope to the farmlands to justify including them within the gardenscape on the other side of the ha-ha. Walpole ignored such inconvenient realities, continuing his Kent encomium:

> He felt the delicious contrast of hill and valley changing imperceptibly into each other, tasted the beauty of the gentle swell, or concave scoop, and remarked how loose groves crowned an easy eminence with happy ornament, and while they called in the distant view between their graceful stems, removed and extended the perspective by delusive comparison.[5]

Thus the 'pencil of his imagination' bestowed all the arts of landscape on the scenes Kent handled. The great principles on which he worked were perspective, and light and shade; and so he was launched as a garden immortal on much truth, some exaggeration and some of the credit which rightly should have been given to other men.

Walpole's particular and conditioning experience was the grounds of his own Strawberry Hill at Twickenham.[6] There the 'leap' across the Thames to the heights of Richmond was absolutely essential to save his sloping field, fringed on one side with trees and scattered inconsequentially with flowering shrubs and acacias, from insipidity. It was anything but the 'enclosed enchanted little landscape' which he described it as being in a June 1753 letter to Sir Horace Mann.[7] All the enchantments he listed were outside it, beyond the leap:

> you see the town and church of Twickenham encircling a turn of the river, that looks exactly like a seaport in miniature. The opposite shore is a most delicious meadow, bounded

by Richmond Hill which loses itself in the noble woods of the park to the end of the prospect on the right, where is another turn of the river and the suburbs of Kingston as luckily placed as Twickenham on the left . . . Is not this a tolerable prospect?[8]

Tolerable indeed, but this is not so much garden design as an entire garden seen as a gazebo, 'perpetually enlivened by a navigation of boats and barges, and by a road below my terrace, with coaches, post-chaises, wagons and horsemen constantly in motion', hence Walpole's eager bias in favour of ha-has and leaps.

But how many of the really great eighteenth-century gardens require leaps or make any effort to escape enclosure? Pope's five acres and the nine acres of Kent's garden at Carlton House for the Prince of Wales depended completely upon privacy and confinement, on undulant lines of planting to please the eye of the owner and to frustrate the inquisitive neighbour. The two greatest, or at least best known, gardens of the period are Studley Royal, West Riding, created after 1720, and Stourhead, Wiltshire, begun after 1742. Both rely for their brilliant success upon the enclosed valley landscapes which they occupy: templed Arcadias, with a manicured corner of a village included at Stourhead and a vast ruined abbey at Studley Royal. They make the unkind point that without some serendipitous fold of land, rush of water or engaging variety of hillside, the most ingenious gardener will be hard put to achieve anything memorable. William Kent's finest garden building is undoubtedly the Worcester Lodge at Badminton, a Palladian structure more dramatic than anything Palladio himself ever designed. Yet it largely fails to make any mark on the vast park of Badminton and three miles distant from the house it is not even an eye-catcher. None of the other outstanding additions to the park, not Thomas Wright's Castle Barn, Hanseatic in its scale, his Hermitage or the poetic Swangrove House, a Sino-Gothick retreat for ducal mistresses can, for all their individual excellence, pull together or redeem the flat, dry Cotswold plateau on which the Beauforts unaccountably pitched their principal residence. If anyone had tried to leap the fences at Badminton they would only have seen flat fields, hedges and trees of unremarkable growth on the thin limestone soil.[9]

Rousham, General Dormer's Oxfordshire seat, is another instance of the problems of the leap. Walpole judged its grounds 'the most engaging of all Kent's works', and its internal prespectives are indeed most subtle.[10] But throughout its entire length, on one side only of the valley of the winding Cherwell, all its glades and small theatres are wide open to the unremarkable fields on the other bank. Ideally these should have been brought into the gardens and the whole made into one enclosure. Failing that, but conscious of the visual weakness, Kent had to add a Gothick trim to a cottage on the other side turning it into the 'Temple of the Mill', and then tried to enliven agricultural banality by a mock castle wall-cum-triumphal arch out in the fields, so ugly and unconvincing that some apologists credit it to an unknown builder, though it is plainly visible on Kent's drawn view from the gardens.[11] The whole garden is, therefore, flawed by just this leap to an ordinary landscape. Walpole makes no reservations; instead, in his dangerously lyrical prose, he describes, 'The whole is as elegant and antique as if the emperor Julian had selected the most pleasing solitude about Daphne to enjoy a philosophic retirement'.[12] His *History* remains essential reading for any garden historian, if only to discover how we have all subsequently been persuaded and distracted by romantic comparisons and fine writing.

With that caution it is safe to turn to the most celebrated partnership of gentleman and player in eighteenth-century garden history: that of Richard Boyle, 3rd Earl of Burlington and 4th Earl of Cork (1694–1753), Lord High Treasurer of Ireland and Lord Lieutenant of the West Riding, with

William Kent (1685–1748), ten years his senior, architect designer, painter and gardener. The improbable pair lived together happily in the same house or houses for almost thirty years, from 1719 to Kent's death in 1748, but without any hint of homosexual attachment. Burlington and his wife had three daughters, Kent in his will left most of his money to the actress Elizabeth Butler and to her children, George and Elizabeth, who are reasonably assumed to have been his children also. But the life spans of Kent and his friend, patron and employer Burlington, are misleading. Where their respective achievements in garden design are concerned, Kent, the elder, should be seen as the heir to the younger Burlington and to two other men, Alexander Pope and Charles Bridgeman. Kent was the artist who carried the innovations of the other three forward to their logical conclusion of the Arcadian Picturesque, as demonstrated chiefly in gardens at Chiswick, Carlton House (which alone was entirely to Kent's own design), Euston, Esher, Stowe, Claremont and Rousham. After 1748 the relatively pure Arcadian garden evolves naturally into the eclectic or Rococo garden, which indeed Kent cheerfully anticipated with his occasional Gothick or Chinese designs.

In 1716, when Burlington set vigorously about the transformation of the gardens at Chiswick, Kent was still far away in Rome, where he had been studying since 1709 to become a second Raphael, though with not the slightest chance of success. Because Kent began his career as a professional painter, it is assumed that he transposed his painting techniques and preferences more or less directly to his later garden designing. His most recent biographer, Michael Wilson, questions this facile line of thinking, but then has to admit that after Kent's death no fewer than thirty landscapes were found in his studio, including three Claudes, three Gaspard Poussins, four Orizontes, one Salvator Rosa and one landscape with a waterfall by Kent himself. This seems reasonably conclusive evidence of interchange and John Harris believes that a marked change in Kent's drawing style took place once he was able to study Claude's *Liber Veritatis* in the Devonshire House collections early in the 1720s.

Burlington had visited Rome on his standard Grand Tour of 1714–15, but for three of the four months which he spent in the city he was dangerously ill in bed. One of the several mysteries associated with the two men is whether they first met at this time, as their later meeting at Genoa in 1719 on Burlington's second Italian tour seems suspiciously contrived. Kent often earned money on the side as an amusing guide to young English aristocrats in the Holy City. But Burlington's attendant artist on his first tour was Pope's friend and art master, Charles Jervas, the neo-classicist, and Jervas's company could explain why Burlington, for all his superficial acquaintance with Rome, returned to England in 1715 with an unfocused and uninformed drive to build after the Antique.

Being as yet unmarried and lacking the wealth which was to come from his wife's dowry he could, at first, only experiment one at a time with relatively modest garden buildings after the Antique. The layout on which he displayed them was conventionally French, formal and unoriginal. Over the dim parterres and vegetable beds of the existing garden at Chiswick House he imposed a three-armed *patte d'oie*, its thick hedges backed by a growth of young trees. At the end of one arm, the *Grande Allée*, Burlington indulged himself with an Ionic domed and pedimented temple. This, sometimes called the Pantheon or the Pagan Building, was up in 1716, an early date for such an ambitious structure. Chiswick was already ahead of Castle Howard, where Vanbrugh's Temple of the Four Winds was still not built when he died in 1726, and Stowe, where there were no temples before 1719. James Gibbs was probably the architect of the Pantheon as Burlington had not yet fallen into the persuasive Palladian clutches of Colen Campbell. Not that Burlington, who did so much to swing the Whig aristocracy over to revived Palladianism, was

Kent trained in Rome, not as an architect or a garden designer, but as a painter. After his death, paintings by Claude, Poussin and Salvator Rosa were found in his studio, so this painting of Nicholas Poussin's 'The Ashes of Phocian collected by his Widow' is a reminder of the sources for Kent's templed Arcadias of natural lakes and casual tree plantings. By nature Kent was sympathetic to informal, yet contrived, Nature.

ever a pure Palladian in his own personal practice. For him Palladio was merely a route towards the authentic Antique Roman. Book 4 of Palladio's *Quattro Libri*, 'Antient Temples', was Burlington's bible, not Book 2 with its sixteenth-century villas of the Veneto. By the next year, 1717, however, Campbell had successfully targeted his new patron and it was then, with Campbell's help, that Burlington designed a three-storey bagnio or bathing house, in correct Palladian style at each level, yet looking overall like a classical pagoda; it was sited at the end of the westernmost arm of the *patte d'oie*, backing on to the as yet un-canalised Bollo Brook. A Rustic House, correct enough to have satisfied Inigo Jones, was built at the end of the third, eastern arm. So there was a most peculiar and irresolute garden, in place before Burlington set off for his quick second Italian visit, to pick up Kent in Genoa, send him ahead to Paris and continue on to Venice where he

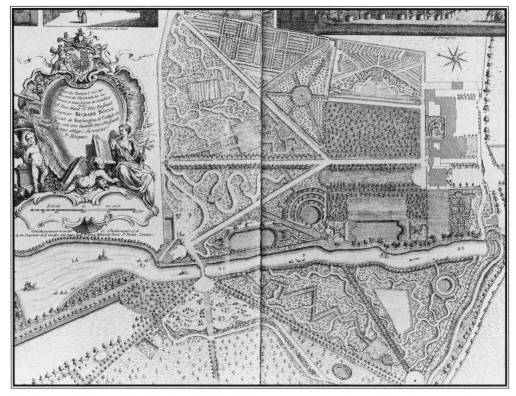

John Rocque's 1736 map of Lord Burlington's Chiswick layout demonstrates the three stylistic influences working to produce its confusion of oddly assorted features. First came the formal patte d'oie and the Bridgemanesque amphitheatre, then the apsidal hippodrome from Robert Castell's recreation of Pliny's gardens, lastly the sinuous 'artinatural' paths of a sub-Rococo. Kent had to make some kind of sense from all this.

bought some of Palladio's drawings. It had an old-fashioned *patte d'oie*, such as André Mollet had laid out in St James's Park in 1661, but each of its three arms was aligned on a classical temple or classical structures. These were Arcadian buildings but with no Arcadian planting.

One of the Burlington mysteries is whether he ever employed Bridgeman in those first ten years of garden works (1716–26) at Chiswick. Authorities on the place all become evasive on the question and refer their readers to Peter Willis's massive *Charles Bridgeman and the English Landscape* (1977). Willis, however, has suspicions but no confident proof, beyond a very late attribution in the 1801 edition of a book which Walpole had read over before his death. But in addition to the *patte d'oie* with its temples, perhaps four years earlier than Vanbrugh and Bridgeman's more innovative and landscape shaping avenues at Stowe, Chiswick had acquired a tiered grass Amphitheatre with an obelisk set in the middle of a small round pond and another domed temple, again architect unknown. The similarities to Bridgeman's Amphitheatre, round pond and obelisk at Claremont, with their equally unsubtle geometry, are impressive. If Bridgeman was employed here, then Chiswick can be added to Stowe, Claremont and Rousham as gardens where he laid down the geometry and Kent only came later to soften and diversify the planting. It was in these early years at Chiswick that the Quincunx, a large square grove of young trees, was planted near the base line of the *patte d'oie*. This, typical of Burlington's impetuous hit-or-miss gardening,

1a. The royalist Sir Hamon Le Strange built this octagonal temple at Hunstanton Hall, Norfolk, in the middle 1650s. It stands on an octagonal island in an octagonal lake at the centre of a star of avenues – a foretaste of Carolean formalism.

1b. An amphitheatre garden of the mid-seventeenth century at Chilworth, Surrey. It exemplifies the 'Solitarie recesse . . . invirond by a hill' that John Evelyn admired, and anticipates Bridgeman's amphitheatres.

2a. *When the scale of a late seventeenth-century formal garden is relatively modest it can survive the test of its upkeep, offering an intimate, satisfying world of Nature under control with the water of canals and fountains relieving the severity of dark, clipped yews. At Westbury-on-Severn, Gloucestershire, the National Trust has cleverly recaptured the utility as well as the beauty of the place by a rich planting of authentic Stuart apples, pears and soft fruit.*

2b. *Only around the Urn of the Four Seasons, a focal point in the lower garden at Melbourne Hall, Derbyshire, is it possible to experience the original scale and impact of the grounds as laid out after French models by Colonel Coke and his site manager, William Cooke, in the first ten years of the eighteenth century. Here the hornbeam hedges have recovered their directing function now that the trees growing behind them have been cut back. This has resulted in a loss of mystery and a gain in clarity.*

3a. The Exedra at Chiswick was the result of much discussion and probably of argument between William Kent and his patron-friend Lord Burlington. At one point Kent proposed to erect here the design eventually used for the Temple of British Worthies at Stowe. An unsightly grove sited too close to the Villa at Chiswick had to be cut back and this exedral shape was planted. It provided a setting for antique statues excavated from Hadrian's Villa at Tivoli, and suggested the gardens of Pliny at Tuscum as reconstructed by Robert Castell in his 1728 Villas of the Ancients.

3b. Long-horned cattle were first introduced into the paddock at Rousham, Oxfordshire, by General Dormer to impart the pastoral quality of a ferme ornée to the grounds. William Kent, who redesigned the garden in the late 1730s, would have approved; Charles Bridgeman, who first laid the same garden out on zig-zag axial avenues in 1725, might well have found the cows inappropriate.

4a. The Chinese House at Shugborough, Staffordshire, still retains a certain charm of saucy inauthenticity. It was the creation, in about 1745, of Thomas Anson, a gentleman amateur, and in its original state it was perched on an island between two bridges, with a boathouse on the opposite bank repeating the tilt of its roofline. Willow pattern plates are more likely to have been its inspiration rather than the experiences of Thomas's brother, George, Admiral Lord Anson, who called in at Canton in 1743.

4b. Hagley, the seat of the Lytteltons, was Bishop Pococke's favourite 'improved' park. Here Sanderson Miller's Sham Castle of 1747–8, which Horace Walpole memorably admired as presenting 'the true rust of the Barons' Wars', is seen as the Bishop recorded it – 'in a woody vale between hills which rise over it'. Like most such landmarks it is multi-sided to command separate views and contained a small park keeper's residence.

5a. *The grounds of Painshill, Surrey, laid out between 1738 and 1773 for the Hon. Charles Hamilton, depend more than most Rococo gardens upon the artifice of raised water, the dramatising of quite slight changes in contour by judicious tree planting, and the distraction of the visitor, every few hundred yards, by some eclectic building like the Ruined Abbey here set on the edge of the Vineyard by an arm of Painshill's subtly scaled lakes.*

5b. *Still partly in thrall to the scale of Rococo gardening, Lancelot Brown set this arched grotto, seen here before the recent restoration of the grounds at Croome Park, Worcestershire, on the banks of a little lake at the head of a river-like serpentine. The statue of Sabrina, goddess of the Severn, dates from the later expansion of the park which was contrived to include Picturesque views of that river.*

6a. *Arguably the most impressive of all such park features in England, the Grotto at Hawkstone, Shropshire, under construction in 1765, opens off this claustrophobic cleft in the sandstone hill. A steep, dark tunnel lit by occasional holes in the rock leads into the Labyrinth, a columned chamber which offers calculated glimpses of the park through rough oval apertures and then leads out onto a lofty viewing terrace.*

6b. *At Blenheim, Oxfordshire, a combination of Sir John Vanbrugh's extravagant over-building of 1705–16, and Lancelot Brown's inspired decision to flood Vanbrugh's habitable viaduct between 1764 and 1774, has resulted in a parkscape not so much Arcadian as Pastoral Imperial. A formal Baroque palace and garden building have been caught up into an improbable perfection by planting of an essentially informal character.*

7a. Seen with the bridge across the Teme, built to give access to the now severed wilderness walk, Downton Castle presents the irregular, Picturesque profile which Richard Payne Knight required. While looking Gothic it was in fact meant to recall a Roman border fortress, presiding over a rough, open sweep of wild Welsh frontier country.

7b. Repton's plan for two coach roads within the bounds of Blaise Castle Park, Bristol, was drawn in 1795. The orange route enters the grounds at the remotest possible point from the house, creating a sensational descent into and ascent from a dark, wooded valley. It ends with a sudden surprise view of the house. In contrast the green route was designed to offer an excursion within the park where vista after vista opens up through gaps in the trees, each giving the carriage-borne visitor glimpses across the Bristol Channel; its climax was the Gothic viewing tower. Brown paths were for walkers only and lead to sequences of mild, natural marvels – a Lover's Leap and a Hermit's Cave – in the limestone rocks.

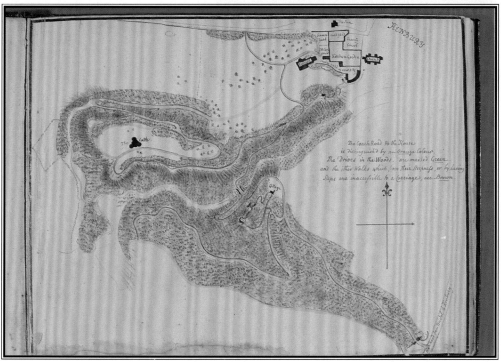

8a. Humphry Repton was called in by the Duke of Bedford to landscape the grounds of his sporting lodge at Endsleigh on the Tamar in Devon. This first view, before the suggested improvements, registers an unspoilt wooded valley with no mark of human occupation apart from the lodge. A grassy terrace leads the eye towards a classical temple away in the woods and a bank of rough earth is the only flaw on an otherwise perfect picture.

8b. With the overlay pulled back Repton has suggested a thorough Gardenesque treatment for the grass terrace, with trellis work, flower beds and a raised walk in front of a large trellis-framed greenhouse. The lawn will become a neat, rectangular extension to the domestic spaces of the house: a place where flowers can be picked without the effort of stooping, and where chairs are an invitation to polite conversation.

In the Orange Tree Garden at Chiswick, William Kent was required to transform a bare amphitheatre into a templed Arcadia. Given the precise geometry of the site he did his best, but the effect inevitably is one of an engaging toy rather than of romantic antiquity.

would soon block out all northern views from the new Villa which, between 1724 and 1729, would engage his attention and most of the money he had acquired from his wife's dowry.

It was during the 1720s, while Kent was still thinking of himself primarily as a painter and uninvolved, therefore, with garden design, that Burlington funded Robert Castell to translate and explain the younger Pliny's letters describing his two villas, Laurentinum and Tuscum (or Tifernum). Castell's *The Villas of the Ancients Illustrated* was published in 1728, the year when Burlington's celebrated Villa, immediately adjacent to the old Chiswick House, was just being fitted up. It would be reasonable then to suppose that Castell's book would throw some light on both the Villa and Burlington's garden improvements of these years. On the Villa it throws very little. Pliny's Laurentinum was an extraordinarily sophisticated complex; its single-storey rooms were adjusted, with no concern for any kind of symmetry, to take advantage of particular prevailing winds, sea views, full sunlight and cooling shades. It had rooms for virtually all seasons, amazingly twentieth-century in their sybaritic functionalism, more Lloyd Wright than Palladio. If the English gentry of this supposed Augustan period had paid any serious attention to authentic Roman villas like Laurentinum they would all have rushed off to the seaside and built asymmetrical bungalows so close to the cliff edge that they could not only enjoy the sound of the waves, but actually experience the spray bursting into their drawing rooms.

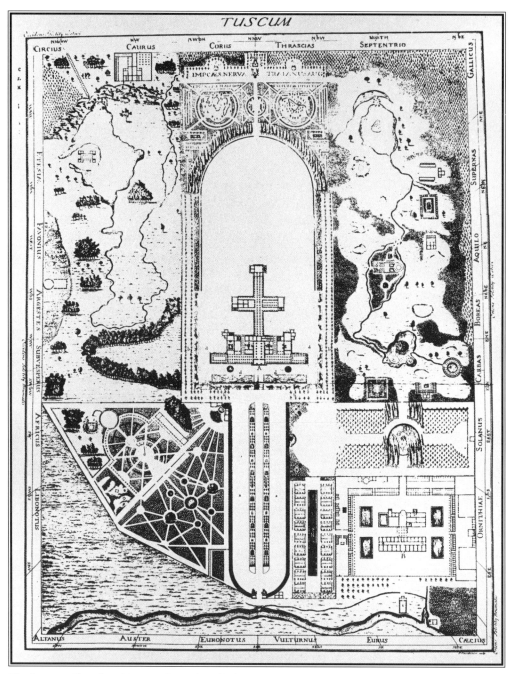

Pliny's account of his villa at Tuscum and its garden is hard to visualise, but this is how Castell, working to satisfy Burlington, construed its layout. Around the exedral central spaces three types of garden are grouped: on the top left, natural 'well watered Spots of Ground', at the bottom left, formal avenues, and at the top right, a contrived but 'agreeable Disorder' of artificial Nature, the Roman version of China's 'sharawadgi'. This last would give Kent his opening to recreate the Arcadias of Claude.

Pliny not only describes all this with apparent relish, he even stresses the Riviera-like charms of his Coenatio (private dining-room) 'which has a very wide Prospect of the Sea, with its most distant Coast, and several beautiful *Villas*. Besides this there is another *Turris*: containing a *Cubiculum* [bedroom suite], in which both the rising and setting Sun are beheld'.[13] Trapped in the inherited patterns of Renaissance thinking, Burlington clung to acceptable symmetries and a compact format for his Villa. Yet it is obvious that he still thought of his new structure as authentically Roman and not an inferior Palladian invention. His mind-set is hard to appreciate, but the effort has to be made. Colen Campbell had offered him a brilliantly improved version of Palladio's Villa Rotonda, but Burlington rejected it, leaving the design for the Earl of Westmorland to use when he built Mereworth Castle in Kent. What Burlington went on to raise at Chiswick was aesthetically inferior, but he must have believed that, with its clumsy mushroom dome – a cross between Vincenzo Scamozzi's Villa Pisani and his Villa Molini – he had come nearer to the true Roman than had Palladio.

Burlington was more open to Castell's persuasions on Pliny's garden at Tuscum in the Appenines than to his villa designs. In his translation from Pliny (Book 5, letter 6 to Domitus Apollinaris) there is a description of Tuscum's natural setting in 'a vast Amphitheatre' of 'Mountains: whose Tops are cover'd with lofty ancient Woods; which give opportunity to frequent and various sorts of Hunting'.[14] Then comes a detailed description of the gardens.

This Disposition, and Delightfulness of the House is far excelled by that of the *Hippodrome*: it is open in the Middle, and presents it self at once to the eyes of those that enter it: It is surrounded with Plane-Trees, which are cover'd with Ivy, and as the Tops are with their own, the Bottoms are green with foreign Leaves: the Ivy runs stragling over the Trunks and Branches, and in its Passage joyns together the neighbouring Plane-Trees: between which are Box-Trees; the outermost of which are encompassed with Lawrel, which assists the Plane-trees in causing a Shade. The straight Bounds of the *Hippodrome* at the further End being broken into a Semicircle, change their Form, and are shaded and surrounded with Cypress-Trees, which give a darker, and blacker Cast to the Place: yet in the innermost Circles (for there are several) it recieves a most clear Light, and is for that reason productive of Roses, so that the coolness of the Shade is agreeably mixt with the Pleasures of the Sun. Having finish'd this course by many and various Windings, it returns again to the straight Bounds of the *Hippodrome*, yet not the same way; for there are many Paths divided from one another by Rows of Box. In one Place is a little Meadow, in another the Box describes a thousand different Forms; sometimes in Letters which tell the name of the Master, sometimes that of the Artificer: in some Places they grow like Cones, and in other Globular: and after a most elegant Taste, a sudden Imitation of the Country seems accidentally introduced in the Middle, and is adorned on each Side with short Plane-Trees. Behind

these, is a Wall of the slippery winding *Acanthus*; and then more figures, and more Names. At the head of this is a *Stibadium* of white Marble, covered with Vines; which are supported by four Pillars of *Carystian* Marble. Out of the *Stibadium*, the water flows from several small Pipes, as if pressed out by the Weight of what lies on it, and is receiv'd and contained in a Bason, so artfully order'd, that tho full, does not run over . . . Over against the *Stibadium* is a Fountain that casts forth and receives Water, which being play'd up to a great height falls into it again, and runs off through Drains that are join'd to it. Opposite to the *Stibadium* is a *Cubiculum*, which returns as great Grace to the *Stibadium* as it receives from it. Splendid it is with Marble, its Folding-Doors jutt out and open into Places fill'd with Greens, and has different Prospects of other Greens both from upper and lower Windows: beyond this a *Zothecula* flies back, and is as it were the same *Cubiculum* with this as well as another, and has in it a Bed, and Windows on every Side, yet still has a dim Light occasion'd by the Shade: for a very beautiful Vine climbs up and covers the whole Building to the Top.

Robert Castell, Description of the Garden at Tuscum, from *Villas of the Ancients*, 1728

In addition to the usual water effects, fountains, cascades and marble seats cooled by rivulets, there are clear references to semi-circular enclosures, a 'Hippodrome' and 'a *Gestatio* in the form of a *Circus*, which encloses the many-shaped Box, and Dwarf-trees that are rendered so by Art'.[15] Castell's imaginative reconstruction of Tuscum's ground plan shows a vast and, inevitably from an eighteenth-century interpreter, symmetrical villa, surrounded at each corner by three different styles of garden design and one farmyard. Exedra-ended enclosures north and south of the villa are very prominent.

Ignoring the wider implications of the three gardens and Castell's challenging exegesis of the text in his 'Remarks on Tuscum', Burlington took an easy way out. While his Villa was being built he gave the garden some token Plinyesque features: two small rectangular basins with apsidal or semi-circular endings and exedras of clipped yew hedges. Alongside one basin a new templar garden house was built, a homely affair with a Tuscan portico. In the narrow space between the Villa and the gloomy Quincunx an iron railing in a further exedral shape was set up. But there was, as yet, nothing to match the long hippodromes of Tuscum and nothing to make even a gesture towards Castell's contentious three garden types. There was nothing either in Pliny's text to justify the three. But Castell, sensitive to garden fashions of the decade and a growing awareness of Picturesque nature, claimed that Roman villa builders had recognised these three garden types. The first was 'no more than select, well-water'd Spots of Ground, irregularly producing all sorts of Plants and Trees'.[16] Then came a second manner of conventional formal avenues. But the controversial manner was the third, the 'Imitatio Ruris'. In this Pliny, or so Castell wished to believe, hinted at a style

> where, under the Form of a beautiful Country, *Hills*, *Rocks*, *Cascades*, *Rivulets*, *Woods*, *Buildings*, &c. were possibly thrown into such an agreeable Disorder, as to have pleased the Eye from several Views, like so many beautiful Landskips; and at the same time have afforded at least all the Pleasure that could be enjoy'd in the most regular Gardens.[17]

Here then was proof of a kind that the gardens of the Ancients had sometimes been modelled on paintings.

By an ingenious leap in logic Castell, without actually quoting Sir William Temple, identified this third 'rough Manner' with 'Accounts we have of the present Manner of Designing in *China* . . . where, tho' the Parts are disposed with the greatest Art, the Irregularity is still preserved . . . an artful Confusion, where there is no Appearance of that Skill which is made use of, their *Rocks*, *Cascades*, and *Trees*, bearing their natural Forms'.[18] This was a most significant piece of writing as it meant that, for anyone thinking of designing an asymmetrical garden, to the exotic charm of distant Cathay could now be added the reassuring precedent of antique Roman gardening. Burlington would need Kent's artistic self-confidence to support him before venturing in that direction and even then he never went very far. The second manner of antique gardening, for 'those of a more regular and exact Taste', by implication old fogeys, was that of 'laying out the Ground and Plantations of Gardens by the Rule and Line', as in the designs of London and Wise, which would be seen as out of date, boring and predictable.[19] Castell could hardly press this point because Burlington's recent *patte d'oie* was old-fashioned even by London and Wise's standards.

If Burlington was reluctant to reshape his existing grounds completely to accord with Castell's reconstruction of Pliny's garden, the Countess of Suffolk, living just down the Thames at Marble Hill, may have committed her garden without reservation to the supposed 'Antique'. A survey of Marble Hill has been found recently showing an oval circus and a hippodrome leading down from the house to the river, with miniature essays in Castell's three garden types tucked away among the groves that surround those two main features.[20] No traces of this layout survive so it may never have been more than a Plinyian projection.

The Countess of Suffolk was near neighbour to Lord Burlington in Chiswick and there are signs on this estate map of her villa, Marble Hill, that she gave the gardens some features – the hippodrome, a natural and an 'Imitatio Ruris' contrived area – in imitation of Castell's plan of Pliny's Tuscum.

How closely, however, Castell's writing was in touch, not just with English, but with local Thames-side garden innovations, appears from *New Principles of Gardening*, a publication of the same year, 1728, written by Batty Langley, a Twickenham gardener soon to be famous for the designs of Gothick garden buildings which even Kent might have appreciated. Langley's book was nothing less than an aggressive defence of Castell's third manner of gardening – the Imitatio Ruris – expounded in great and convincing technical detail. So who was leading, the theorists or the working gardeners? Langley's introduction opens boldly with: 'Our gardens are much the worst of any in the World' and goes on to urge 'variety . . . a continued series of Harmonious Objects, that will present new and delightful Scenes to our View at every Step we take, which regular Gardens are incapable of doing. Nor is there any Thing more *shocking* than a *stiff regular Garden*'.[21]

That was only Langley's opening salvo. Being a nurseryman he was, of course, like London and Wise, anxious to sell plants: 'Honey Suckles, Sweet briars, white Jessamine, and the several Sorts of Roses'. But his insistence was upon the charm of irregularity: 'when we come to *copy* or to *imitate* Nature, we should trace her steps with the greatest Accuracy'.[22] There should be 'no three Trees together ranged in a strait line . . . *Parterres* are most beautiful when entirely irregular'.[23] Most telling were Langley's plates, drawn by his brother Thomas. Some unfolded generously to reveal four alternative garden plans, all with winding paths leading to 'varieties', a maze of charming pleasures with rule and line entirely abandoned. In others he hedged his bets, combining formal avenues with areas of Rococo paths. His claim: 'This Method of laying out Gardens, after the manner exhibited in the following plates, being *entirely New*, as well as most Grand and *Rural*',[24] was a little overstated, even gently absurd, but the book was expensively produced, well subscribed, revolutionary and yet practical. Twickenham was Pope's village, a mere four miles up-river from Burlington, Kent and Castell's Chiswick. Only five years later Kent, advanced by Burlington's patronage, would be planning his own more decorous but equally revolutionary garden of irregularities for the Prince of Wales. Who can say, at this distance, what lively human exchange of views, in Thames-side inns and over the sales counters of nursery gardens, were taking place between the patrons, talented hangers-on and enterprising nurserymen of these enchanted reaches of the Thames? The coincidence of the two like-minded books, Langley's and Castell's, both published in the same year, is suggestive. Langley seems to have been friendly with Pope's gardener, John Searle, as he had picked up Pope's optical trick of lengthening a prospect by darkening the most distant foliage.

Burlington, for all his rigid *patte d'oie*, had given Kent an example of a heavily templed garden. By 1730 there were two Deer Houses, an Orangery, a Doric Column and three statues as well as the five structures already mentioned. He had in addition given him practice in laying out exedras, which could be seen as a less helpful legacy, one very close to formalism. The garden's real blight was the Quincunx or Grove, separated from the new Villa only by a grudgingly limited exedra space. Kent's first task, after he took over an active direction in October 1733, was to cut a long Plinyesque hippodrome through the Grove, opening up vistas which should never have been closed. His sketches show how much thought went into this feature and its exedral finial.[25] At one stage a prototype for what would later become the Temple of British Worthies at Stowe was suggested. This was rejected for a topiary work with niches for four urns and the statues, said to have come from Hadrian's Villa, of Caesar, Pompey and Cicero. The sketches reveal Kent's delight in glimpses of other temples and the Doric column seen through a thin veil of young trees. It would be a mistake, while celebrating Kent's handling of the natural, undulating line of trees, to forget that his real love was architecture, the devising of almost free-form temples out of that most restricting of all classical disciplines in his time, the Palladian. Pope, so Joseph Spence recorded, believed that 'A tree is a nobler object than a prince in his coronation robes'.[26] Such sentiments were alien to Kent; to him a tree, usually ill-drawn, was a mere stage prop or back curtain, a crude mix of spruce with straggly, broad leafed specimens. Temples, cascades and shapely rocks were the staple of his best garden designs. He could turn out a grotto or a Gothick seat if he was pressed, but with his nine Roman years behind him he was by preference a romantic classicist. The garden at Carlton House, which established his reputation in England, had, however, only one temple, but any number of artfully dispersed trees, 15,200 if the accounts are to be believed.[27] Not a trace of it remains, but it was so influential, being royal, that a re-creation of its grounds is essential to an understanding of Kent's career.

Prince Frederick had bought Carlton House in 1732, the year when 'Our Trusty and Welbeloved William Kent Esqr: Our Architect' had concocted for the 25-year-old Prince that superb state barge which still survives at Greenwich.[28] With a garden design agreed, clearances began in September 1734 and planting on an intense scale ensued. The grounds were a special case as they were overlooked by raised mounds in the back gardens of all the houses in Pall Mall; so privacy was a priority. Inevitably the letter which that most curmudgeonly of English Palladians, Sir Thomas Robinson, wrote to his father-in-law Lord Carlisle on 23 December 1734, has to be quoted here because it proves the electric charge which Kent's Carlton House design was already sending through polite circles. Robinson was the man who later compromised the superb Baroque symmetries of Castle Howard and, later still, broke what would have been the finest sequence of Rococo state rooms in England at Claydon House, Buckinghamshire, by his malicious tale-bearing to Lord Verney. His own gardens at Rokeby Park, North Yorkshire, paid a sincere compliment to Castell's reconstruction of Tuscum with an exedral entrance court and an enormous exedral-ended lawn on the garden side of his twin-towered Palladian villa.[29] But, for all his own Roman formalism, he had the wit to recognise Kent's innovative achievement at Carlton House:

> There is a new taste in gardening just arisen, which has been practised with so great success at the Prince's garden in Town, that a general alteration of some of the most considerable gardens in the kingdom is begun, after Mr Kent's notion of gardening, viz., to lay them out, and work without either level or line. By this means I really think the 12 acres the Prince's garden consists of, is more diversified and of greater variety than anything of that compass I ever saw; and by this method gardening is the more agreeable, as when finished, it has the appearance of beautiful nature, without being told, one would imagine art had no part in the finishing, and is, according to what one hears of the Chinese, entirely after their models for works of this nature, where they never plant straight lines or make regular designs. The celebrated gardens of Claremont, Chiswick, and Stowe are now full of labourers, to modernize the expensive works finished in them, even since everyone's memory.[30]

Such it was, in a devoutly loyal country, to gain royal approval for an innovation in garden styling.

In its prime, Kent's garden was 1,250 feet long and roughly 300 feet wide, nine acres in all: five to Kent's landscape and four to the Wilderness which he left virtually untouched. The axis of the garden ran from the Wilderness next to Carlton House towards Marlborough House, its close neighbour. On leaving the house from its garden front a visitor would immediately lose all sense of London in a huge, largely semi-circular, lawn, undulant edged and surrounded by trees. On its base line and cut into an exedra of the Wilderness was the Bagnio, its one templar feature, a handsome domed octagon with a bath house on its ground floor and a 'Great Room' above, approached up twin flights of steps. This, the focal point of the garden, was for the Prince's convenience sited near the house and not, as might be expected, at the far end of the vista. The garden could be viewed best from its eastern extremity, looking back to the Bagnio with the house made invisble by the cunning planting. Behind the Bagnio was an irregular maze of dark rides cut through the Wilderness created from the old Spring Gardens.

After inspecting the Bagnio visitors would cross the lawn, an ample ground for the Prince's favourite sport of cricket, and then proceed down a widening funnel of lawns between trees. Winding paths led away, one on each side, to an alternative circuit route of the grounds. Then came the first surprise piece: exedral widenings to left and right, each with two crescents of shrubs and flowers backed by a trellised hedge with niches for statues and urns. Half-moon shaped pools, their banks made of rough stonework, were set within the first crescents of shrubs. Classical terms (human heads on pedestals) flanked them and the beds brimmed with lilacs, laburnums, honeysuckles, roses, jasmines, laurustinus and sweet briar, something for every season, and proof of the emptiness of Philip Southcote's claim to have been the first to have 'prevailed on Kent to resume flowers in the natural way of planting'.[31] Kent's gardens were never limited to the

Kent's drawing for the Bagnio in its setting at Carlton House differs in detail from the building shown on William Woollett's engraving of 1760. Where Kent has suggested a mix of angular conifers and a thin growth of small deciduous trees, Woollett illustrated a smooth planting of deciduous trees only.

austere Italian garden spectrum of broad leafed trees, evergreens and chiselled stonework. The Prince of Wales's account books for 1736 reveal purchases of Egyptian hollyhocks, narcissi, day lilies, pinks, carnations and tulips, which would have turned those six crescent beds into conventional cottage garden displays of bright blooms.

Now the funnel of lawns widened to a clearing with an irregular-sided, natural-seeming pool. The trees around it, a mix of elm, hornbeam, chestnuts, yews, firs, oaks and hollies, were enriched with tulip trees, mulberries and walnuts, all planted in imitation of Pope's undulant lines. Behind them, again as in Pope's Twickenham garden, there were winding ways leading to clearings. On the far side of the pool was an Aviary to give a focus to the walk. More woodland behind this concealed yet another sinuous route through the trees that concealed Marlborough House from the Prince's guests. When the vista back to the Bagnio had been enjoyed and the Aviary birds fed, the return journey could be made along any one of several paths through thick trees on either side of the grounds.

These five acres, an apparently simple *Rus* in the *Urbe* of the capital, confirmed Kent's reputation and, as the grovelling Robinson's letter makes clear, gave instant fashionable authority to the 'new taste in gardening'. The stylistic complexity of contemporary garden design will be appreciated if it is recalled that, while the Rococo was just being launched here in London, up in Yorkshire, at Studley Royal, French formal gardening in the seventeenth-century manner was coming to a romantic climax with a show of temples equal to that at Chiswick, far superior to the single Bagnio at Carlton House, and with all the advantage of the fast-flowing Skell for cascades and crescent mirror lakes.

The personality which brims over from Kent's drawings is memorable. One has Chatsworth's hillside transformed into a Tivoli of waterfalls, grottoes and pyramidal temples, while another has a man and his dog both pissing against one of the archways at Chiswick. In another, Hampton Court, Gothick Esher and a domed temple are all composed together in a capriccio while Triton spurs his horses across a lake. So it comes as a sobering thought to realise that no single garden laid out purely to his design has survived. Not only that, but very few such ever originally existed. Esher of about 1732–4 was entirely his, and apparently a Rococo paradise, 'Kentissime' in Horace Walpole's judgement. But it is all lost in suburbia, and the three exquisite Chinese temples which he designed for it were never built. So many of his best creations have gone. His Hermitage of 1730 for Queen Caroline at Richmond was a Rococo jewel, an octagon within a rustic shell and a reminder of those months Kent had spent in 1719 waiting for Burlington in Paris, observing the French scene. Merlin's Cave of 1735, for the same patron and the same park, was truly original: a top-lit Gothick complexity, vaulted, shadowy, Spenserian. That, together with his Esher Place of 1730–3, launched the Gothick revival: Merlin's Cave for the Queen, Esher for a prime minister, Henry Pelham.[32] Both were achieved and admired long before Horace Walpole began to work on Strawberry Hill.

Not all Kent's revisions of existing gardens were as successful as Richmond. At Claremont he enlarged Bridgeman's round pond into a natural-looking lake with an island temple; but that left Bridgeman's harshly geometrical Amphitheatre incongruously isolated on its north bank looking as it does today like some prehistoric earthwork strayed from Salisbury Plain. He went on to soften the planting of Vanbrugh's avenue and Bowling Green below the Belvedere, but in recent years the National Trust has returned the tree line to Vanbrugh's dramatic rigidity and the effect against the harsh, round-arched tower is admirable.

The park at Holkham, Norfolk, was a largely posthumous achievement, laid out slowly, from 1734 to 1756, using some of Kent's sketches for its stone bridge, obelisk, triumphal arch and other arches. Here, more than anywhere, it is evident that fine buildings will not make a great garden if the original topography is dull. East Anglia undulates slightly when it is not actually flat. At its best Holkham park has only an arid majesty. Much more should have been concentrated in a far smaller acreage. Euston has the same effect. With one of Kent's most satisfying temples, a broad, shallow dome resting easily upon a subtle triangle of pediment and supporting shoulders – it was his favourite, almost organic shape – Euston park still lacks an Arcadian air. Its shallow slopes need a heavier planting of trees; as Walpole noticed, there is little water and the clumps that Kent sketched to liven up the scene should be replanted. Clumps incidentally were never a Kentian innovation. In his 1728 *A Sure Method of Improving Estates*, Batty Langley advised, 'Ashes planted with Oaks, Chestnuts, &c. in Plumps, on the tops of little Hills in Parks &c. have a very good Effect'.[33]

The credit for the planting of trees in a relaxed and informal grove cannot often be given confidently to one man, and in any case all groves are, of their nature, transitory. Most of Stowe's trees of the 1730s and 1740s are blown down now or decayed and it is difficult to appreciate what precisely was carried out even to Kent's advice, certainly not to his exact direction. In the park during those years Bridgeman's straight avenues, which directed the eye firmly from one building to another, were felled or thinned. The new planting left the temples in an Arcadia rather than on the parade ground. But, in an essay by George Clarke,[34] Kent's personal touch has been questioned even in the Elysian Fields, that sector of Stowe's grounds immediately east of the central axis. While in no way doubting Kent's authorship of the temples, Clarke points out that there is no record of Kent having once visited Stowe in person. He urges that even the maturing of trees is a kind of destruction. As they have aged and towered above the pure Ionic rotunda of the Temple of Ancient

Lord Cobham's heavy-handed political iconography is carried effortlessly by the Arcadian convention of the Elysian Fields at Stowe where Capability Brown supervised the planting to Kent's basic design. From the exedra of British Worthies there is a clear symbolic view up to the Temple of Ancient Virtue. Unfortunately, the Temple of Modern Virtue, with a headless statue of Sir Robert Walpole, has disappeared.

Virtue and the formidable exedra-gallery of British Worthies, the Fields have acquired an antique, heavily burdened, Claudeian air which neither Kent nor Lord Cobham could ever have intended when the political squib of their allegory was planned. It raises a disturbing question. Should all our eighteenth-century landscapes be cut down every fifty years and replanted? If they were we would see them as the eighteenth century saw them, as in Jacques Rigaud's views of Stowe, with the stone temples rising proudly about thin, young growth. Much of what Burlington allowed Kent to do at Chiswick after 1730 was the thinning down of trees to allow one building to link visually with another, and the architecture therefore to become more prominent.

The whole matter of the natural line is arguable. Why should a garden, which is of its nature an artifice, be artificially made to look 'natural'? Burlington canalised the Bollo Brook at Chiswick and Kent, after many sketches, designed a classical cascade for its head: three romantic caverns of rugged stonework. But then he was allowed to go on, to soften the canal's straight banks and produce a sinuous natural-seeming lake. Was this an improvement? Would classical grotto mouths look better pouring their waters into a formal classical canal or into some ordinary pool? Walpole had his doubts on the question. After all his praise for the 'pencils of imagination' applied to deal 'in none but the colours of nature', he hesitates:

Though an avenue crossing a park or separating a lawn, and intercepting views from the seat to which it leads are capital faults, yet a great avenue cut through woods, perhaps before entering a park, has a noble air.[35]

Were Bridgeman's avenues 'capital faults'? Would the Elysian Fields at Stowe have gained by contrast if the rest of the park had been kept formal? Visitors could then have enjoyed the transition to the gentle curves and unfolding vistas of the Elysian lake, with the British Worthies looking up hill to the inspiration of Ancient Virtue, to Homer, Socrates, Epaminondas and Lycurgus, and the adjacent ruin of Modern Virtue with its headless statue of Sir Robert Walpole, all in an enclosed interlude of the apparently natural? Few would deny that Stowe gains enormously by the rigidity and symmetry of its central axis, from the house to the Corinthian Arch, with the Lake Pavilions symmetrically sited half way along.

In the end most accounts of Kent's gardening come down to the question whether an artist's technique in painting can be usefully transposed to garden design. So any argument must conclude with Rousham, where for once we can be in confident touch with the master's original intentions. Or can we? If Bridgeman's 1725 plan of Rousham's grounds is set alongside the 1738 plan of the same area, drawn by General Dormer's steward, William White, to illustrate what he and the gardener, John MacClary, were doing to Kent's directions, an evolution of garden styling from Bridgeman's firm angles to Kent's soft curves is obvious. When the steward's letters are read something else becomes equally clear.[36] All the sensitive decisions about the placing of the many hundreds of trees and flowering shrubs, which were being lavished on Rousham in the cause of Kent's 'new taste', were being made by White and MacClary, the men on the ground, not by Kent, who only visited the site once a year. The letters tell of poplars, alders, beech, oak, spruce, Scotch pine and laurel being planted, and replanted on a grand scale and to White and MacClary's personal judgement. So is that incessant chatter about painting with the pencil of the imagination, which is recorded over the next two decades from the group of gentleman gardeners like Shenstone, Southcote and Spence, anything more than pretentious aesthetics from the idle rich? Evergreens are dark, broad leaf trees are light, there is little more to the 'painting' than that. MacClary on his own initiative, not Kent, dug out tons of earth to improve the concave slope at the end of the Bowling Green and give the 'Seats' a better viewpoint.[37]

After 1725 Bridgeman left a characteristically jagged and dramatic garden shape, all sharp angles and straight lines to create sudden, direct vistas. He lined the garden-side bank of the river with piles and stone edging, making it ruler-straight at every switch of direction. At the end of the Bowling Green the concave slope was left clear for the view and a small but typical Bridgeman amphitheatre, also directed deliberately at the view, was cut next to it, a Claremont in miniature. Three basins of what would later become Venus's Vale were in place but all were exactly square, the largest with an exedral clearing to one side and a fountain garden at its foot. This opened on one side to the straight avenue of the Elm Walk, aligned at a temple on the site of the present statue of Apollo. Kent would move his Temple of Echo out of sight round a corner of woodland to gain a surprise effect. Bridgeman's woods were riddled with winding paths, far more than Kent would provide. These led to five geometrically shaped clearings, one a Pheasantry, and one the Cold Bath, neighboured by a Crescent Pond. Two lesser straight avenues offered vistas to the river.

Kent's transformation was primarily architectural. His Temple of Echo commanded an extension of the grounds to view Heyford Bridge, a genuine medieval structure, and his Praeneste arcade

At Rousham the statue of Apollo and the Townshend Temple of Echo both look out of the grounds to the medieval Heyford Bridge with the cheerful animation of 'Carriers Wagons, Gentlemen's Equipages, Women riding' and 'Men walking'. This was a case of the temple as gazebo.

The lights and shades of contrasted deciduous and coniferous trees are maintained around the vale of Venus at Rousham, but William Kent's original concept of open glades receding on each side of the grotto, with only a thin planting of trees, has been lost in the inevitable overgrowth.

gave, with its seven arches, seven framed pictures of the same view. He built the Pyramid Temple on a site below the Walled Garden, where Bridgeman had intended a grand exedra with terraces. The poetry of Kent's alterations is most evident in Venus's Vale. The basins remained geometric in shape but linked now by sloping lawns, dramatised by rustic arches and statuary, and the line of its woods softened by felling and planting. A new Grass Walk, serpentine and divided, like that around Carlton House garden, replaced Bridgeman's direct circuit route. His Amphitheatre was partly levelled and all the woods along the newly 'naturalised' river bank were thinned. A clump of elms was planted to half conceal the Heyford Bridge view in a typically artful device.

Statuary now directed the garden. This was one aspect of the reshaping which General Dormer, dying by inches in London, still controlled. White's letters are full of 'bustos' and 'colossi'. Today it is the savagery of Scheemakers' Lion attacking a Horse and his Dying Gladiator, the Terms and Apollo in his isolation that remain longest in the memory. Dormer's intended iconography has been so broken by the losses of time that it can only be reconstructed in a scholarly thesis, but virtually all Kent's visual treats have survived in an enchanted unfolding of ways. Rousham is a toy garden when compared with Stourhead and, as earlier criticisms may have suggested, it can be seen as flawed in the quality of the scene to the east which so many of its viewpoints command. In fairness here it has to be added that Mavis Batey and David Lambert in their 1990 *English Garden Tour* rate Rousham's vistas to the east highly, writing of 'well cultivated and wooded countryside', its views 'as important as those within the garden'.[38] The gardener John MacClary would have agreed, though from a different viewpoint. In a vain attempt to persuade General Dormer's heir, Sir Clement Cottrell, to take up residence at Rousham, he urged the delights of sitting in the Temple of Echo and watching the traffic over Heyford Bridge, 'sometimes twenty Droves of Cattle goes by in a Day' and Sir Clement might see 'Carriers Wagons, Gentlemen's Equipages, Women riding, men walking' and 'all the pretty natural turnings and windings of the River'.[39] Horace Walpole would echo MacClary with his description of the prospects from Strawberry Hill quoted earlier in this chapter. It was all a question of the function of a garden. Were they to be designed as private worlds offering a series of composed landscape pictures to be savoured within their grounds, or were they outward looking, merely a chain of viewpoints from which the eye was to be directed to the wider compositions of the country outside? Should one look out or in? If inwards, then the painter-gardener was in control; if outwards, then he had abandoned his role to the Creator, though minor adjustments could be made. To leap or not to leap was the question, one to which the next generation of gardeners would have to make their varying, individual responses.

Pan, the lustful, dangerous god of all Arcadias, presides at Rousham to emphasise the escapist, pleasure-seeking function of a garden where Venus is his co-patron. The propriety of such figures in a nominally Christian country was rarely challenged.

CHAPTER TEN

SOUTHCOTE, SHENSTONE, SPENCE AND THE ARCADIAN *FERME ORNÉE*

It was Dr Johnson who shrewdly bracketed the landscape gardening of his day as 'rather the sport than the business of human reason'. Philip Southcote (1699–1758), William Shenstone (1714–62) and Joseph Spence (1699–1768), were three typical sportsmen of that landscape game. They have left little behind them in the way of actual gardens, only a few traces in a Midlands golf course and the grounds of a Surrey seminary, but all three are useful as weather-vanes to indicate which way the winds of taste were blowing in the years after the innovations of Switzer, Vanbrugh, Pope and Kent. Southcote's Wooburn Farm, near Chertsey in Surrey, where the planting for the *ferme ornée*, by some accounts the first in England, began in 1734, and The Leasowes in north Worcestershire, which Shenstone took over in 1742, were both celebrated gardens much visited in their primes. Of the two, The Leasowes was probably the more imitated and influential because it did not attempt such a refined and essentially impermanent balance between flower garden, landscaped trees and farmland as did Wooburn. Those gardens on which Spence advised were much less known. His real contemporary fame came for *Polymetis* (1747) a popular treatise on Roman mythology, lavishly illustrated with classical nudes, a folio which for its visual appeal found its way onto most library shelves. Spence was the Boswell of the gardeners of his time and his influence has been most felt, not on the eighteenth-century public, but on twentieth-century garden historians. These have all found his posthumously published *Observations, Anecdotes, and Characters of Books and Men* (1820) essential reading to plunder for opinions and quotations on his fellow gardeners. He is our authority on Southcote's theories on tree planting and on the activities and innovations of that father figure of early eighteenth-century designers, Alexander Pope.

The *ferme ornée* was an ingenious attempt to satisfy two enthusiasms which had surfaced in society at roughly the same time. One was the craze for the world of Theocritus's nymphs and shepherds, 'natural' Arcadian or Elysian landscaping; the other was that scientific interest in stock breeding, crop rotation and forestry which we have since come to describe as the Agricultural Revolution. So there was the DULCI of the one and the UTILE of the other, both requiring expression. Addison had urged a compromise, Pope in his enclosed grounds had entirely ducked the challenge. His Tory friend Lord Bolingbroke had, in 1725, rechristened his house, Dawley in Surrey, 'Dawley Farm'. Pope wrote scornfully to Dean Swift on 28 June 1728: 'I overheard him yesterday agree with a Painter for 200*l.* to paint his country hall with trophies of Rakes, spades, prongs etc. and other ornaments merely to countenance his calling this place a Farm'.[1] Kent rejected the farm and opted for exquisitely artificial Elysiums that allowed fleeting and censored glimpses of the real world. Only Stephen Switzer had embraced the idea of union of the two, but with an embarrassing and impractical fervour, projecting entire estates where several farms were to be wound around with extended garden strips, streams and lakes with just one grand axial feature to re-assert gentry status.

Joseph Spence and the much travelled Bishop Pococke both claimed in their writings that Mr Southcote was 'the first that brought in the garden farm or *ferme ornée*'.[2] Spence wondered if Southcote might have picked up the idea from his continental travels, suggesting as a source, 'Fields going from Rome to Venice',[3] but both Spence and Pococke were ignoring a much earlier groundswell of garden fashion. In Spence's *Observations* there are up to thirty quotations from Southcote, a fellow gentleman, there is not one single reference to Batty Langley because, for all his influence, he was a player, a mere nursery gardener. So Spence ignored the clear directions in Langley's *New Principles of Gardening*, published in 1728, six years before Southcote had even bought Wooburn, that 'the several Parts of a beautiful Rural Garden' should include 'Vineyards, Hop-Gardens, Nurseries . . . Small Inclosures of Corn . . . Rude Coppices, Hay-Stacks, Wood-Piles, Rabbit and Hare-Warrens'. Langley's 'General Directions' anticipate virtually every element in Southcote's Wooburn and Shenstone's Leasowes.

XIX. That in those serpentine Meanders, be placed at proper Distances, large Openings, which you surprizingly come to; and in the first are entertain'd with a pretty Fruit-Garden, or Paradice-Stocks, with a curious Fountain; from which you are insensibly led through the pleasant Meanders of a shady delightful Plantation; first, into an open Plain environ'd with lofty Pines, in whose Center is a pleasant Fountain, adorn'd with *Neptune* and his Tritons, &c. secondly, into a Flower-Garden, enrich'd with the most fragrant Flowers and beautiful Statues; and from thence through small Inclosures of Corn, open Plains, or small Meadows, Hop-Gardens, Orangeries, Melon-Grounds, Vineyards, Orchards, Nurseries, Physick-Gardens, Warrens, Paddocks of Deer, Sheep, Cows, &c. with the rural Enrichments of Hay-stacks, Wood-Piles, &c.

Which endless are, with no fix'd Limits bound,
But fill in various Forms the spacious Round.
And endless Walks the pleas'd Spectator views,
At ev'ry Turn the verdant Scene renews.

These agreeable surprizing Entertainments in the pleasant Passage thro' a Wilderness, must, without doubt, create new Pleasures at every Turn: And more especially when the Whole is so happily situated, as to be bless'd with small Rivulets and purling Streams of clear Water, which generally admit of fine Canals, Fountains, Cascades, &c. which are the very Life of a delightful rural Garden.

And to add to the Pleasure of these delightful Meanders, I advise that the Hedge-Rows of the walks be intermix'd with Cherries, Plumbs, Apples, Pears, Bruxel Apricots, Figs, Gooseberries, Currants, Rasberries, &c. and the Borders planted with Strawberries, Violets &c.

The most beautiful Forest-trees for Hedges, are the *English* Elm, the *Dutch* Elm, the Lime-Tree, and the Hornbeam: And altho' I have advis'd the Mixing of these Hedges of Forest-Trees with the aforesaid Fruits, yet you must not forget a Place for those pleasant and delightful Flowering-Shrubs, the White Jessamine, Honey-Suckle, and Sweet-Brier.

XX. Observe, at proper Distances, to place publick and private Cabinets, which should (always) be encompass'd with a Hedge of Ever-Greens, and Flowering-Shrubs next behind them, before the Forest-Trees that are Standards.

XXI. Such Walks as must terminate within the Garden, are best finish'd with Mounts, Aviaries, Grotto's, Cascades, Rocks, Ruins, Niches, or Amphitheatres of Ever-Greens, variously mix'd, with circular Hedges ascending behind one another, which renders a very graceful Appearance. . . .

XXVIII. Distant Hills in Parks, &c. are beautiful Objects, when planted with little Woods; as also are Valleys, when intermix'd with Water, and large Plains; and a rude Coppice in the Middle of a fine Meadow, is a delightful Object.

XXIX. Little Walks by purling Streams in Meadows, and through Corn-Fields, Thickets, &c. are delightful Entertainments.

Some 'General Directions' from Batty Langley's *New Principles of Gardening*, 1728

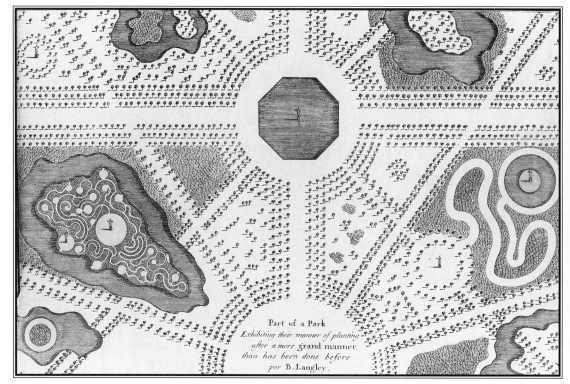

An illustration from Batty Langley's New Principles *of 1728 catches English garden design in its moment of indecision when the curves of the 'artinatural' Rococo are accommodated among the straight avenues of the old formalism. A nursery gardener's solution was to present both styles side by side but unco-ordinated.*

Unless Langley was blazing his own highly original trail in garden design, these directions prove that the homely features of a rustic farm were already becoming accepted points of interest to be included in a garden layout alongside the usual 'Plain Parterres, Avenues . . . Labyrinths . . . Grotto's . . . Ruins . . . Statues, Obelisks . . . Amphitheatres &c.'[4] Indeed the one item which is not found in this list is a temple, though later in life Langley would design many such as garden ornaments. The implication is that by 1728 large numbers of fashionable gardens had taken on board Switzer's idea of farm signifiers as aesthetic in their own right. But because Switzer had not appreciated the ornamental power of a classical or 'pagan' temple in a garden, Langley had still not absorbed the templar advances which Lord Burlington was making only a few miles away at Chiswick.

This suggests that, where garden buildings rather than the garden grounds were concerned, it was the gentlemen who were making the running, leaving professional gardeners like Batty Langley to trail along a few years behind them. An education in the Classics and wide reading of the latest travel books and histories would explain the exotic, eclectic direction taken by mid-century gardens. One aristocrat, the young Lord Petre (1713–42), a Roman Catholic familiar with French forest gardens, seems to have absorbed the enticing designs of Switzer's *Ichnographia* rather than Burlington's advances at Chiswick. In his brief lifetime Petre had begun to lay out two extraordinary estates, one on his own grounds at Thorndon Park in Essex, the other at Worksop, Nottinghamshire, for a fellow Catholic, the Duke of Norfolk. Designed by the

In a second illuminating confusion of the formal and the informal Batty Langley has made a notably uncouth Gothic ruin the focus of a straight double avenue of young trees. A classical cascade and a strangely untenanted island with tentative natural planting occupy the foreground in a study which might be entitled 'Waiting for William Kent'.

Frenchman, Bourgignon d'Anville, these two projects might, if they had been carried through to a conclusion, have put Switzer's ideas to the test of practicality.

Lord Petre was a tree-fancier growing 700 different specimens of tree, plant and bush, many of them rare American introductions, in his extensive Essex nurseries. Peter Collinson and Philip Southcote were his friends and collaborators in an enterprise that could have turned half a county into one great arboretum of preciously contrived tree clumping and bordering. Petre's own plans of 1738 for S-shaped clumps of carefully contrasted evergreen oaks, larch and silver fir against lower yew, holly and box are far more thoughtful and painterly than Kent's cruder but much better known efforts.[5] A letter by Collinson to Southcote suggests how exquisitely over-refined and self-conscious were the visual effects aimed at by garden designers and appreciated by garden tourists of the day:

> The effect must be Charming to see the Dark Green Elm with the Lighter Shades of the Lime and Beech – or the yellowish Green planes with the Silver Leafed Abele the Chestnut the oak and ash and the poplar the Acacia and Horse Chestnutt CUM MULTIS ALIIS, when Fann'd by the Gentle Breese then how Beautifully the Contrast, how delightfully the light and shades fall in to Diversifie the Sylvan Scene.[6]

Southcote was fourteen years Petre's senior, but proud to acknowledge himself the younger man's pupil. While Petre's ambitious plantings went virtually unnoticed in their time, Southcote's stroke of genius was to offer an informed London public grounds at Wooburn which they could comfortably walk around and easily absorb. With no fortune of his own, Southcote had married the seventy-year-old dowager Duchess of Cleveland in 1733 for a marriage settlement of £16,000, weathered the inevitable ridicule and promptly set about his clever simplification of Switzer and Petre.

In his 1770 *Observations on Modern Gardening*, Thomas Whately defined a *ferme ornée* as 'a walk, which, with its appendages, forms a broad belt round the grazing grounds and is continued, though on a more contracted scale, through the arable. This walk is properly a garden, all within it is farm.'[7] Walpole judged Wooburn, critically but accurately, observing that,

> The Profusion of flowers and the delicacy of *keeping* betray more wealthy expense than is consistent with the oeconomy of a Farmer, or the rusticity of labour. Wooburn farm is the habitation of such Nymphs and Shepherds as are represented in landscapes and novels, but do not exist in real life.[8]

Against this typically ungenerous dismissal should be set the very real pleasure and enthusiasm of an Irish gentleman farmer John Parnell (1744–1801) on his second visit to Wooburn in 1769:

> Here was at Mr Southcote's, beside all the lovely lawns of cattle and ornamental ground, a lovely field of wheat, a fine one of oats, of barley, and as fine clover as I ever beheld, ready to be cut and thrown over the ditch if they pleased into a crib in the pasture field where the horses were turned out.[9]

So, despite Walpole's dismissal, Wooburn was not merely an eccentric garden strip, it was a real farm run to the latest advances of farming practice. Parnell was as pleased by the 'beautiful spotted cows' and fields 'full of sheep', as by the Gothic hut, ruin and Chinese bridges.[10] Joseph Spence, on the other hand, was far more interested in Southcote's tree planting, his 'distancing' and 'attracting' or foreshortening of the surrounding landscape.[11] Southcote had explained his general aims to Spence who recorded them for posterity in his *Observations*:

> All my Design at first was to have a Garden on the middle high ground [this was a triangular area of pasture land and ornamental trees with, at its three corners, a ruined chapel, an octagonal temple and a Doric temple] and a walk all round my Farm; for the Convenience, as well as Pleasure. For from the Garden, I could see what was doing in the Grounds; and by the walk, could have a pleasing access to either of them where I might be wanted.[12]

Southcote was speaking in about 1752, by which time his more subtle effects of painting by planting, learnt from Lord Petre, were beginning to mature. His claim, mentioned in the previous chapter, to have 'prevailed on Kent to resume flowers in the natural way of gardening'[13] was vanity; his real contributions to mainstream English garden design were the optical subtleties of his tree planting, his 'distancing' and 'attracting', in an extension of Pope's practice. 'By attracting', Southcote explained:

> I intend to bring St Anne's Hill at least one third *nearer to me* (by planting in the middle, so as to hide the ground behind). The trees I plant, when grown up, will fall in with the trees near that hill and make but one slope of foliage, and so unite that part to my own as to the eye.[14]

'Distancing' on the other hand, was a trick learnt directly from Pope's confined grounds, making an object '*look three times as far off* as it is. This is done by narrowing the plantation gradually on each side, almost to a point at last'.[15] Southcote urged that woods should always be planted 'on the sloping side of a hill that you look up to from your house'; waters should be looked down upon from a height and 'there should be leading trees, or clumps of trees to help the eye to any more distant clump, building or view'.[16] Spence implies that Kent learnt much from Southcote's handling, the 'Temple' being 'the point in Mr Southcote's where Kent was most struck'.[17] This would have gratified Southcote as he recorded that, 'I believe I walked the ground above a hundred different times before I could fix the whole line of the walk from the Temple to the Octagon'.[18]

Some of Southcote's instructions verge on the over-fastidious:

We should prevent the rays of the sun from falling too strongly on the eyes by a proper interposition of shades, which when above, help the eye like a hat or umbrella (or on the sides, as one sees a picture much stronger when the sidelights are broken all round by a proper holding up of the hand).[19]

But this was an aspect of the sensibility of the age: an exquisite, wildly sentimental subtlety of response with kindred spirits joined in self-congratulation, as in Spence's claim that:

When I told Mr Southcote that the sight of his ground near his house was always apt to lead me into a pleasing smile and into a delicious sort of feeling at the heart, of which I had nothing when I was in his much nobler views along the brow of the hill, he said that Mr Pope had often spoke of the very same effect on him.[20]

Spence conveys the impression that Wooburn was a simple 125 acre estate with a garden belt of trees, bushes and flowers all around it. He gives a detailed sketch of the 'Order of Planting', with the trees – beeches, chestnuts and hornbeam – shading down through the bushes – lilac, laburnum, holly – to the flowers – roses, sweet william, primroses, jonquils.[21] In reality the perambulation of the Farm was more complex. It is evident that, as he laid it out, Southcote was working his way towards what would be Shenstone's solution in the 1740s, with a 'play' area of pasture dotted with eclectic pleasure buildings – Grecian, Gothick and Chinese – on one side of the grounds and a working farm of arable fields with only a few, lesser, pleasure buildings on the other. Wooburn's grounds were roughly rectangular, lying east–west with a road along the south side and a river, the Bourne, on the north. A higher middle ground, that triangular area in the centre, divided the pasture, with its concentration of park buildings, on the west side from the arable fields to the east. The perimeter belt of shrubs and flowers was by no means continuous but was, as Bishop Pococke noted, 'adorn'd . . . with spots and beds of flowering shrubs and other flowers to fill up angles'.[22]

Visitors entered by a Lodge at the south-east corner of the Farm and were escorted from one eclectic building to another by a gardener. While moving west they would have to cross the grounds twice at their mid-point, following two sides of the triangle, from the Ruined Chapel, via the avenue of the Long Walk, to the Octagon Temple, then back again to the Doric Temple, a copy of one by Lord Burlington at Chiswick, on the south side. Next came the western boundary of the Farm marked by the Menagerie Canal with Gothick buildings at each end, the Gothick Cottage being an ambitious structure with flanking pinnacles. A walk back east along the sluggish Bourne would bring them to the Octagon again. There they could either make their own way back to the Lodge, a course which Parnell advised,

Apollo crowns William Shenstone with the laurel wreath of poetry while the poet plays upon an organ – a wonderfully appropriate tribute to the effete bachelor bard from Dodsley's edition of The Works in Prose and Verse of William Shenstone *of 1764–9.*

or, if they were serious agriculturalists, press on through the arable fields, which he admitted were 'by no means so beautiful'.[23] So Wooburn Farm was, apparently, only partly successful in uniting the DULCI with the UTILE.

While there was a serious air of professional farming about the eastern two-thirds of Southcote's Wooburn, visitors made little mention of the agricultural elements of The Leasowes. William Shenstone, the poet-proprietor of the estate, devoted all his interest and his very modest income – £300 a year – to creating a continuous walk around his fields engineering cataracts and lakes, planting and thinning trees, setting up urns to the memory of dead friends and erecting flimsy, eclectic buildings. All was done to achieve that 'variety' which, from Pope onwards, mid-eighteenth-century gardeners were agreed was the essential quality of a truly improved estate.

Horace Walpole and his friend, the poet Thomas Gray, were not impressed. 'Poor man!' Walpole wrote, 'he wanted to have all the world talk of him for the pretty place he had made, and which he seems to have made only that it might be talked of.'[24] Gray added that Shenstone's 'whole philosophy consisted in living against his will in retirement, and in a place which his taste had adorned, but which he only enjoyed when people of note came to see and commend it.'[25] Their comments do usefully emphasise the extent to which gardening and a refined visual connoisseurship were the obsessions of the age. For a few decades the creation of a dramatically 'improved' area of ground was a sure route to literary and social celebrity. Without The Leasowes, Shenstone would never have achieved national fame as a poet, his verses being mediocre even by eighteenth-century standards.

In the twenty-odd years when he was improving his grounds Shenstone made no attempt to link the visually attractive sections of his visitors' route with his farm fields, and he was uneasy about Southcote's enthusiasm for floral touches. In a letter of 1749 he wrote that he had been planting flowers along the choicest section of the path 'till I almost begin to fear it looks too like a garden'.[26] This is a significant pointer to the way in which a garden and a park were dividing into two distinct concepts, with the park an essentially wild Arcadia, Claudeian and romantic, while the garden contracted into a formal show area of flowers. Thomas Whately praised The Leasowes for its Arcadian simplicity. 'It is', he wrote, 'literally a grazing farm lying round the house; and a walk as unaffected and as unadorned as a common field path is conducted through the several enclosures'.[27] Where Shenstone had profited by Southcote's example was in his appreciation of the need to lure visitors on from point to point, not merely by waterfalls and viewpoints, but by what were becoming the standard delights of a visitor-worthy estate: Gothick, Grecian and Chinese structures, wholly unauthentic and logically inappropriate to their site, fantasy buildings for those bored by the general sober rationality of their age.

Shenstone was quite unapologetic about this lack of authenticity. What mattered was a stimulus, however shallow, to the imagination: 'A ruin, for instance, may be neither new to us, nor majestick, nor beautiful, yet afford that pleasing melancholy which proceeds from a reflexion on decayed magnificence'.[28] He believed that flimsy little structures like his Gothick Screen, 'objects, perhaps not very striking, if they serve to connect ideas, that convey reflexions of the pleasing kind', were appropriate punctuations to a garden walk of vicarious experiences.[29] Hence the urns to the memory of dead friends and relations which he set up in shaded corners. For Shenstone's visitors, melancholy was a positive and enjoyable emotion. Shenstone saw the sequence of events on the garden circuit which he eventually developed as resembling 'an epic poem or dramatick poem' where 'the more striking scenes may succeed those which are less so'.[30] Edmund Spenser's *Faerie Queene* was probably in his mind.

It would be an error to take Shenstone's achievement at The Leasowes too seriously. It is true that for some thirty years it was one of the five best known and most visited gardens in England, but that was because it was lightweight, entertaining and unpretentious in an age of general leaden sobriety where the fanciful and the amusing – Ranelagh and Vauxhall Gardens in London for instance – were at a premium. Shenstone was unashamedly fey and, with the little rhymes which he stuck up on boards along his garden path, he was fey in the original sense of that word:

> Here in cool grott, or fringed Cell
> We rural Fauns & Fairies dwell;
> Tho' rarely seen by mortal Eye
> When ye pale Moon ascending high
> Darts thro' yon Limes her orient Beam;
> We frisk it near this crystal stream.[31]

This whimsicality and escapism is an aspect of eighteenth-century English culture not always given its due emphasis, but it lies behind all the enchanting eclecticism of the gardens subsumed in the next chapter under that useful portfolio term 'Rococo'.

Shenstone's education had been as superficial as his temperament: he had attended the local Halesowen Grammar School and Pembroke College, Oxford, but took no degree. His parents were very minor gentry in status and Shenstone, who had written his best poem, 'The Schoolmistress', by the time he was 23, subsided by gentle degrees into the role of poet poseur and part-time landowner. At some point between 1742 and 1744 he took over the running of The Leasowes, a property of 150 acres which his grandfather had bought and which Shenstone on his death would leave encumbered by debts from his own campaigns of improvement. The natural advantage of The Leasowes was the number of springs rising in the grounds to produce a chain of fishponds in attractive miniature valleys. As Wooburn was neighboured by Painshill, Oatlands and Claremont, all richly 'improved' and offering distant vistas for Southcote's techniques of 'attracting' and 'distancing', so The Leasowes had Hagley, the seat of the Lytteltons, Lord Dudley's grounds at Sedgely and the Earl of Stamford's Enville, all within vista range. There were strong tendencies at this period for improvements to proceed in clusters, a happy infection by gentry emulation. Hagley and Enville had two of the richest sequences of eclectic park buildings in England.

Even before he took up the reins of control at The Leasowes, Shenstone had, like the youthful John Evelyn before him, built himself a study, little more than a shack, on an islet of the existing Beech Water, north-east of the centrally sited main house. The gesture was characteristic, such poetic poses of

A view of The Leasowes with the Priory in the foreground. The woods around Virgil's Grove rise up on the left.
A party of ladies is walking the tourist circuit the wrong way round at point 8 on the plan illustrated opposite, while
a carriage is leaving near point 4. Visitors usually left their carriages at the house before walking the circuit.

romantic isolation came naturally to him. A plump man, negligent in his dress, wearing his own hair unpowdered, he took refuge behind attitudes. When the major poet, James Thomson, author of *The Seasons*, came to visit him Shenstone arranged to be caught 'reading a pamphlet in one of my niches'.[32] With engaging honesty he wrote at the start of his garden campaign in 1744 to his friend Richard Jago listing his assets and revealing a divided ambition: 'I have an alcove, six elegies, a seat, two epitaphs (one upon myself) three ballads, four songs and a serpentine river to show you when you come.'[33] What he had the eye to appreciate was that where that serpentine river ran through a little wooded dell, half-way down the west boundary of his estate, he had the potential landscape jewel of the grounds. By 1747, working with an occasional team of up to fifteen labourers, he had converted this into 'Virgil's Grove', soon to become an accepted pilgrimage place for lovers of the miniature Picturesque. It acquired an Obelisk inscribed to the Roman poet and two small waterfalls coaxed out of the prolific springs, one of them emerging dramatically from the mouth of a little artificial grotto-cavern.

Thomas Smith's painting of the Grove, later engraved by James Mason, presents a confusing image of multiple cascades tumbling through a thinly wooded valley and Thomas Hull's description of the place in his Shenstone's Walks of 1759 captures some of that confusion:

. . . look over your left Shoulder & you will see, thro' an intended Separation of the Boughs, a most glorious Cascade, in an Oval form, that falls with great rapidity – The Music of it, at this Distance, is very noble – By Degrees it comes nearer, we see it thro' several Chance Openings of the Trees, till it fills the romantic Valley beneath, &, among such a Number of rude Stones, seems to form Cascades of all Ages & Sizes.

Hull had claimed that, to achieve this effect, 'Nature is merely guided a little', but any number of conduits, channels and hidden pipes must have been involved. Hull insisted, however, that:

The Trees are all left to their own Growth, never a Leaf impair'd . . . On the Whole, You are to look on this sweet Spot (according to its glorious Master's own Description to *me*) merely as a Farm – Nature has been profusely kind & he treats her, as he does his Muse, with Warmth, Taste and Delicacy.[34]

Shenstone admitted that the dominant factor behind his planning was always financial constraint: 'I give my place the title of a *ferme ornée*; though if I had the money, I should hardly confine myself to such decoration as that name requires'.[35] James Thomson had given Virgil's Grove his

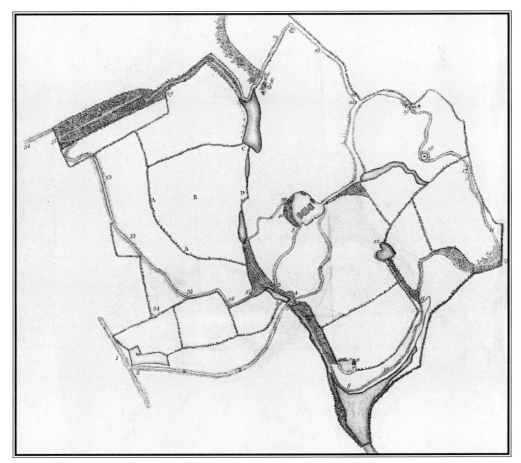

This plan of The Leasowes was published two years after Shenstone's death. Virgil's Grove lies between numbers 37 and 3, the Priory is no. 9, but only to be viewed at a distance, from 15 and 17, in order to secure its ideal composition. Many of the numbers represent gates leading to a dramatic change in the landscape. Lord Stamford's Root House is at no. 11 commanding a view of the Cascade descending from no. 12.

enthusiastic approval and the path which he urged to connect it with the Beech Water became the start of a perimeter trail, not gravelled or sanded, leading around the entire estate to 'furnish out a variety of scene in Proportion to its Length'. Shenstone believed in linear aesthetics: 'A garden strikes us most, where the grand and the pleasing succeed, not intermingle with each other'.[36] To that end, as funds became available, his picturesque circuit acquired, working anti-clockwise from the Grove, another cataract, a Ruined Priory (rented out to an old couple for £4 a year), a Root House below yet another cascade, an urn to the memory of a friend, a statue of Faunus, a Hermitage, a Gothick Building, an urn to Shenstone's cousin Maria, who had died of the smallpox and, out on an extension, a Lover's Walk. This had a Gothick Screen (which had been roughed out in two days by a local carpenter for £10) and a Temple to Pan. Returning again to the circuit, the tour ended with the Beech Water, another cascade and Virgil's Grove.

Marked on the route by wooden posts were select points where visitors were required to look in a certain direction and take in the 'landskip', exactly as if it were a painting. The part played by water in all this is evident. Those falls by the Root House were, so Hull claimed:

the noblest Cascade in the World; which appears from the Top of a Hill, & falls, as it were, by different *Steps*; now seen – now lost in the Shade of the Trees and Shrubs, & enlarges as it descends, till it becomes a rushing Torrent & most rapidly runs under your Feet as you sit in the Bower at the Bottom of the View.[37]

Another cascade below the Grove 'falls near twenty feet, amidst some broken rocks or fragments of Stone, into a deep hollow shaded with trees, which conducts it into the large expanse of water below the ruinated priory'.[38] There were five pools or small lakes on the circuit ensuring a constant flow of water, but the buildings, apart from the Priory, which had a Gothick parlour with antique paper, were insubstantial. Shenstone claimed that 'Ground should first be considered with an eye to it's [sic] peculiar character; whether it be the grand, the savage, the sprightly, the melancholy, the horrid, or the beautiful.' All that was needed then, when a sensitive landscaper had detected the essential tone, were a few 'suitable appendages – For instance, The lover's walk may have assignation seats, with proper mottoes – Urns to faithful lovers – Trophies, garlands etc. by means of art'.[39] Hence the several seats and urns to the memory of the dead, all accentuated a supposedly pre-existing melancholy and, as usual, Thomas Hull was in complete agreement. Such monuments carried, he wrote,

a degree of Religion . . . beyond what I feel in a Churchyard . . . a Worthy memory thus consecrated in such a sequester'd Spot, inspires, I think, a delicacy of sacred Sensation, not unlike that, which a good heart feels in doing a good Action, or bestowing a Charity or Bounty . . . in secret, rather than openly.[40]

As a theorist, Shenstone's *Unconnected Thoughts on Gardening*, published a year after his death, reveal him as the aesthetic magpie of his age. He toyed with Edmund Burke's ideas of the Sublime and the Beautiful and elaborated on Pope and Southcote's tricks of optical planting: 'To distance a building, plant as near as you can to it, two or three circles of different coloured greens . . . the imagination immediately allows a space betwixt these circles and another between the house and them.' He had no time for the true *ferme ornée* as Switzer had understood the term: 'Hedges, appearing as such, are universally bad. They discover art in nature's province.' But in reality 'art' infiltrated all his 'landskips'. He admitted, 'A rural scene to me is never perfect without the addition of some kind of building'; though in true Rococo sensibility he added, 'I have known a scar of rock-work, in great measure, supply the deficiency'. When quizzed by James Thomson as to his practice he was initially at a loss, but then decided that it was 'Collecting into a smaller compass, and then disposing without crowding, the several varieties of Nature'. More revealing was his later comment that 'in pursuance of our present taste in gardening, every good painter of landskip appears to me the most proper designer'.[41]

The significance of the circuit, a mere 35 acres of ornamental grounds out of a 150 acre estate, was its undeniable popularity. Walpole and Gray were correct in their malicious account of Shenstone's motivation: the place became a social honeytrap. 'My *ferme ornée* procures me interviews', the poet told his friend the writer Richard Graves, 'with persons whom it might otherwise be my wish rather than my good-fortune to see'.[42] There were the Lytteltons, Pitts and Luxboroughs, while he boasted that 'a Mr Bingley or Dingley? He seemed a Person of Fashion, came hither with his wife & a large Party to see my new Cascade by Moonlight'.[43] Prints of the grounds were published, Hull, Dodsley, Whately and Graves all wrote accounts of the place, Goldsmith, Gilpin, Parnell, Gray, Dr Johnson and John Wesley were among its many admirers.

Robert Dodsley, an ardent fan of Shenstone, persuaded Joseph Spence to visit The Leasowes in the summer of 1758, when Spence made a whole sheet of notes on the place. He did not, however, feel that they merited a place in his *Observations*, an interesting intellectual snub from a man who, with similarly limited means and an equal ambition, achieved in his own grounds at Byfleet very much less. Spence is the featherweight of these three weather-vane figures. Nothing survives of any of the trivial garden schemes on which he advised or which he carried through for his own amusement. None of his contemporaries praised his Byfleet garden or considered his planting there of any importance. Only his *Observations* have given him a place in garden history.

Spence was a friend and admirer of Pope, an Oxford Professor of Poetry, a clergyman and a lifelong bachelor, much in demand as the reliable tutor and guide for young noblemen making their Grand Tour of the Continent. The last of these young men, Henry Fiennes Clinton, 9th Earl of Lincoln, treated Spence as an amiable father substitute. Later, when he was happily married and living at Oatlands, near the Thames in Surrey, Lord Lincoln leased Spence, for a nominal sum, a small gentleman's house with a few acres of land at Byfleet. This was close enough to Oatlands for Spence to advise Lincoln on his own ambitious but unsubtle garden improvements, while pottering about pleasantly on the limited grounds of the Byfleet house. Spence never had the funds for garden buildings, but he seems genuinely not to have had any inclinations in that direction. His influence on the grounds at Oatlands was limited to advice on its orchards and on further tree planting. All his activities indeed concerned trees and those optical effects which he had heard about from Philip Southcote. So while it is just possible to see him as a feeble precursor of Picturesque theorists and gardeners like William Gilpin and Uvedale Price, it is more accurate to consider him as one of that numerous body of enlightened country gentlemen who, by their advice and their example, turned the bare fields of pre-enclosure England into a semi-parkland, the leafy 'grovettes' of Spence's choice. He was a recorder of the garden scene, never a potent director.

CHAPTER ELEVEN

GENTLEMEN IN CONTROL – THE 'ROCOCO' GARDEN

The creative but sometimes conflicting innovations in garden design which the last five chapters have traced resulted, by the mid-century, in what has come to be called the 'Rococo Garden', an eclectic free-for-all where classical garden buildings are joined by Chinese, Gothic and Mohammedan structures, all set in an asymmetrical fantasy against backgrounds of artfully placed trees and natural seeming lakes. The first tentative attempt to describe gardens as Rococo was made by Nikolaus Pevsner in 1944 when he was writing about garden style of the period 1700–20. He saw the wriggling paths threaded through formal settings illustrated in Switzer's *Ichnographia Rustica* as similar to contemporary French Rococo decoration.[1] But of more lasting influence on garden history were two articles of the 1970s by John and Eileen Harris who employed the term 'Rococo Garden' specifically to describe the delicate garden paintings of Thomas Robins the elder (active 1747–65) and the wild garden buildings of Thomas Wright (1711–86).[2] It was seen to fill a previously unperceived and wider vacancy and has come into general usage.

Squeezed between the Palladian and Robert Adam's boudoir version of neo-classicism the Rococo fits uneasily into Britain's progression of styles. It was only accepted as a standard decorative response in Dublin and Bristol,[3] but a Rococo mood, playful, experimental and graciously civilised, was felt more generally across the country and surfaced in garden buildings. These resulted in an extension of that Arcadia or Elysium to which Lord Burlington had been striving. Considered from a strictly English viewpoint a classical temple was already an eclectic exotic in a park of the home counties, and for someone with an open, experimental mind like William Kent it was only a small visual step to move on to the Chinese and the Gothick.[4] Indeed, since the English upper classes had been familiar with Chinese architectural forms from porcelain and lacquer work since, at the latest, 1670, the surprising thing is how slow they were to experiment with them. Thirty-six dramatic prints of the Imperial Chinese Palace gardens at Jehol, made by the Jesuit Father Matteo Ripa, had been in circulation since Ripa's return to London from China in 1724.[5] However, by their education system the English upper classes had studied Virgil and Horace, not Confucius, and the age was consciously Augustan.

Predictably it was the Temple family of Stowe who took the first recorded step towards China. In 1738 a frail, brightly painted Chinese House set on stilts had appeared on a pond in the grounds of Stowe (miraculously surviving two subsequent moves it has returned there but now stands disappointingly in a dry, weedy clearing). The eighteenth century invariably associated Chinese replicas with water because so many drank from willow-pattern china.[6] Three years later, and in Stowe yet again, an even bolder and more influential step forward was taken with James Gibbs's Temple of Liberty (1741–4), a triangular Gothick exotic, cupola crowned and pinnacled in thunderous orange ironstone. Batty Langley's hugely popular *Ancient Architecture* came out at the same time (1741–2), and Gothick eclecticism was well and truly launched.

The Chinoiserie equivalent of Gibbs's Temple of Liberty, one that offered a compelling and eminently copyable image for other gentry to follow, was devised in 1746–8 for the park of the Ansons, Shugborough in Staffordshire. Thomas Anson, the ruling squire of an unremarkable estate, had been short of money, but all that changed when his brother George returned in 1744 from circumnavigating the globe and capturing the treasure of the Manila galleon in the Pacific. George Anson had been obliged to spend several weeks in Canton, when he could have familiarised himself with Chinese forms. Whether that enforced stay or simple observation of a willow-pattern plate inspired his brother is not known, but the Chinese House that went up in the park on an island in the river Sow was intriguingly composed. Two delicate bridges sprang away from it and on the other side of the water a little boat-house mimicked the saucy tilt of its roof. The room inside, painted pink with a trellis pattern overall, had red lacquer work, mirror-pictures and a Rococo plasterwork ceiling. It was a perfect toy and must have been widely admired for in 1752 it was followed up, on another island in the same river, with a bold six-storey pagoda. But then, in a switch of images which was to be characteristic of the Rococo garden drive, Thomas Anson returned to his first enthusiasm, Greece. Between 1764 and 1771 James ('Athenian') Stuart built replicas of the Arch of Hadrian, the Tower of the Winds and the Lysicratic Monument together with a Doric temple and an 'Athenian' greenhouse. The effect of all these was rather that of a cabinet of curiosities than a coherent pleasure garden.[7]

How general such stylistic confusions became, not only in large landscaped parks like Shugborough, but in the more compact pleasure grounds of the prosperous middle classes, is shown by Thomas Robins's precisely detailed garden views. Benjamin Hyett, a Gloucester merchant who would go on to create the Rococo garden at Painswick, began in the 1740s with an even more eclectically curious layout on the grounds behind his Gloucester town house, Marybone House. Robins recorded it: a perfect compression of every garden fashion of the century's first fifty years. Immediately below the house was a playful Gothick pavilion. This was neighboured by formal parterres, still kept in labour-intensive perfection as in the days of London and Wise. But then, beyond this geometry and the surviving hulk of a genuine medieval monastic building, a four-storey Chinese pagoda flaunted its dragon wings above a small wilderness of writhing paths and a dead-straight terrace for promenades.

The proprietors of the two great London pleasure grounds – Vauxhall and Ranelagh – had been quick to copy the cheap, exotic wooden Chinese models. By 1751 Vauxhall had a semicircular arcade of Chinese-Gothic domed pavilions. Its rival Ranelagh had invested in a fragile Chinese island, all fretted patterns and abrupt angles, as a base for outdoor masquerades. Both the Prince of Wales and his brother the Duke of Cumberland frequented the gardens so eclectic pavilions would have gained a royal cachet and an association with sophisticated entertainments enjoyed in the open air.

Records of Chinoiserie in British gardens are patchy and unreliable, partly because wooden Chinese structures tended to be easily lost, partly because towards the end of the century park owners, caught up in the ice age of serious neo-classicism, would often pull down any park building which did not reflect Greece and Rome.[8] English parks of the 1770s would have been far more eclectic and richly 'Rococo' than they were fifty years later in 1820. Our best proof of their mid-century condition is to be found in the writings of Richard Pococke (1704–65), an English traveller and educationalist who became, by the patronage of Lord Chesterfield, Bishop of Ossory, an Irish diocese, but who would more justly be called the 'Rococo Bishop'.[9]

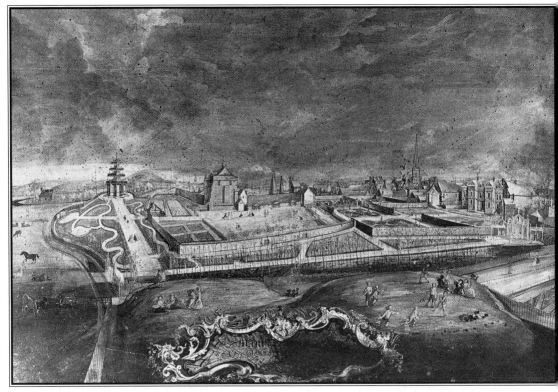

The eclectic confusion of a Rococo garden layout is evident in this Thomas Robins's view of Benjamin Hyett's house in the suburbs of Gloucester. A formal parterre, a Gothick screen, 'artinatural' paths, a Chinese pagoda and a genuine medieval monastic building all work together to achieve an epitome of Pope's 'variety'.

Pococke's earlier travels had been the perfect preparation for an eclectic aesthetic. He had gone up the Nile as far as Luxor where he noted the head of Ozymandias, visited Jerusalem, Baalbek and Damascus, sketched along the coasts of Turkey, stayed long enough in Constantinople to have his portrait painted 'à la Turque', then returned via Athens, Naples and the Alps. Back in the United Kingdom he continued to travel England, Wales, Ireland and, ultimately, Scotland; and everywhere he went he made a point of noting the park 'improvements', by which he meant the new serpentine waters, the various stylistically contrasted park buildings and the new plantations. These journeys were made in 1750, 1751, 1754, 1756 and 1757, so his notebooks (not published in edited form until 1888–9 by the Camden Society) give a generous cross-section survey of what was going on in the parks and gardens of the 1750s. Pococke was biased towards the exotic and culturally various by his own experience, but even so the whole of England and much of eastern Ireland was caught up in Rococo garden improvements. Prosperity appears to have opened up, for the gentry and the aristocracy, a new lifestyle of alfresco living, of escape from the confines of a main house to the privacy and picnic fun of menagerie houses, Chinese fishing temples, classical and Gothick banquet houses, all far out in the park away from the prying eyes of servants.

The larger the house the more determined the aristocratic owner appeared to be to escape from it. At the Marquis of Rockingham's gargantuan Wentworth Woodhouse for instance:

A wood to the south-west is the improvement of the marchioness. In it is an house with a large room, two smaller offices under, and here the family dine often in summer. There is a walk on the south and west with a little serpentine river and a bridge, several winding walks through the wood, and a view made by a moss hermitage. There is a skittle ground for the youth to divert themselves, not to omit a beautiful temple to Cloacina [a loo] with a portico around it, supported by columns made of the natural trunks of trees.[10]

At Wimborne St Giles in Dorset, Lord Shaftesbury had, in addition to the inevitable serpentine water, an island with a castle, a towered gateway, a thatched house, a round pavilion on a mount, 'Shake Spear's house, in which is a small statue of him, and his works in a glass case', a pavilion between 'both a Chinese and stone bridge', 'a duck which lays in rabbit's burrows' and 'a most beautiful grotto finished by Mr. Castles of Marybone; it consists of a winding walk and an anti-room. These are mostly made of rock spar, &c., adorn'd with moss'.[11]

Of all the garden layouts which Thomas Robins painted in precise detail, with borders of shells, flowers, birds and beasts, the one which has survived to prove the artist's accuracy and convey the mid-century Rococo mood with the most haunting, even sinister intensity, is Benjamin Hyett's second and more mature layout at Painswick in the high Cotswolds. Behind Painswick House, or

Robins's 1748 view of the grounds at 'Buenos Aires' (Painswick House) proves that curved lines were not an essential ingredient of a Rococo layout. Only one such path appears threading through a shrubbery; elsewhere small garden buildings and a mesh of conflicting axial lines create a garden for discoveries and privacy. Pan's statue stands roughly central above a cold bath for open-air frolics.

The Red House in the garden at Painswick is defiantly asymmetrical and angled so that its two disparate façades command two separate garden axes. It stands up at the extreme top right edge of Thomas Robins's view. It was usual in the Rococo period for garden buildings to be painted in cheerful colours.

Buenos Aires as Hyett styled it, lies a fan-shaped valley, private and secluded in feeling. Hyett had become a leading member of a local drinking club, dedicated to the worship, with appropriate mild orgies, of the Great God Pan.[12] While full-scale revelries took place in the purpose-built Pan's Lodge on an opposite hillside, Hyett held more intimate frolics in a cold bath down in his own valley garden, overlooked by a frighteningly real statue of Pan by Van Nost. This interactive nature of the garden was typically Rococo. Flowers are out for a few months, trees lose their leaves for half the year, but the true Rococo garden can offer active enjoyment of one kind or another at any time, and that explains their attraction. Painswick garden is open to the public and should be visited at snowdrop time if only to demonstrate how seductively alive a true Rococo garden can be at a dead season. It makes another point. In all the paths and alleys that link its multiple small temples and Gothic seats, in all its beds for flowers and vegetables there is only one curvaceous wriggling path of the kind usually described as typical of the Rococo. All the rest are straight. The English Rococo was more a time of the liberated spirit, of role playing than of stylistic tricks such as the S and C scrolls of the French Rococo.

Bishop Pococke was, however, as eager to notice twisted trees growing out of interestingly shaped rocks as he was to list serpentines, prehistoric avenues and root houses; so there was some measure of a Rococo air to these 'improvements', a feeling for bizarre silhouettes and charming grotesqueries. He divided 'improvements' into three kinds: 'the Wilderness way', which was easily the most common and implied a wood with garden buildings, 'the Farm way', a reminder of Southcote's venture at Wooburn, and 'the Park way', an anticipation of Capability Brown's reaction against Rococo layouts, with a move to broader, less cluttered parkscapes which could double as farm land elegantly clumped.

Rather surprisingly the Bishop classed the Hon. Charles Hamilton's grounds at Painshill in Surrey, evolved between 1738 and 1773, as a farm improvement, whereas today it appears an almost pure 'Wilderness way'. An exquisitely contrived two-mile circuit winds through heavily wooded grounds about a serpentine lake whose waters knot together at an island grotto of fretted rocks and multi-compartmented crystalline elegance. Perhaps an initial meadow of sheep led Pococke to classify it as a farm, but after that field Painshill's eclectic circus was continuous. A statued ampitheatre, vineyard, ruined abbey, Gothick rotunda, Roman arch and hermitage punctuate a route which afforded frequent cross vistas over quiet waters to rising woodland, then climaxed in an Alpine valley with a tall Gothick viewing tower at its head. The way back had a Turkish tent, a Temple of Bacchus and

This illustrates just one façade of the large grotto at Painshill, Surrey. The artifice eaves have been placed at the union of two lakes and serve as a bridge to link an island to the main shore. Several glittering recesses of crystalline rocks are hollowed out within the main tufa structure. The Hon. Charles Hamilton created the two-mile park circuit between 1738 and 1773.

a bath house, all commanding ingenious views of the terrain walked earlier. Painshill is the cleverest of all Rococo gardens as Hamilton began with so few natural advantages. His waters had to be raised by a wheel and the slight rises of ground dramatised by tactical planting.[13]

Pococke's own favourite improvement, where his prose, always clumsy, becomes positively incoherent, was Hagley in Worcestershire, the creation of Lord Lyttelton who had been a close friend and supporter of Frederick, Prince of Wales.

Frederick's own Rococo improvements at Kew had been interrupted by his death in 1751, but in 1749 the Prince had set the country a notable example of Chinese garden building with a House of Confucius, delicately geometric in its latticing, its eaves bell-hung, its roof topped with a winged dragon. Faithful to her dead husband's intentions, the Prince's widow, Augusta, went on to stuff the level grounds of Kew with an absurd multiplicity of eclectic structures. An Alhambra, a Gothick Cathedral, a Chinese Menagerie, the great and surviving nine-storey Pagoda, a Turkish Mosque, a Ruined Arch and any number of classical temples all went up in the 1750s and 1760s, and this very visible royal favour for the eclectic must have done more than anything to spread the garden fashion among loyal subjects.[14]

'Butcher' Cumberland, the Prince's brother, was a less popular figure but his Rococo grounds at Virginia Water in Windsor Great Park seem to have been far more poetic in their conception, more interactive in their exoticism than Kew; also curiously feminine in their detail. Pococke

Sir Thomas Lyttelton's house at Hagley is situated near the western foot of a hill, which rises greatly and is improved into a park, round which there is a plantation of trees, and a shady walk; in the middle is wood and lawn, and on the south side a wood called the Hermitage . . . To the south are some pools round a hill, which appear from the heigth like a serpentine river . . . Entering the vale, at the end of it is an alcove seat, covered with pebbles curiously figured, in which are represented a cross, beads, and ornaments of pots and flowers. On the left is a walk half way up the hill, and another by the water, in which there is another alcove seat, and going up at the end of the vale, it passes by the hermit's fountain, cover'd with an old trunk of a tree, and so leads to the Hermitage at the south-east corner made with roots of trees, with a seat round it cover'd with matting, a rail and gate before it made of rude stakes. There is another walk back from this . . . up the hill to the summit of it, on which is built a ruined castle, with a turret at each corner; that to the south-east is entire, the others as well as the walls of the castle are made as ruinous, and the Gothick windows rising above the ruins have a beautiful effect. The castle is seen in different views from many parts of the lawns and wood . . . Ascending up the valley there is a walk on each side, one winds up to the prospect and also along the side of the hanging ground . . . on this is a rustick seat of bricks

opening to the water above it in the form of a Venetian window; a large piece of water comes up to this seat and a beautiful cascade falls down the rocks into it, by which it is divided into two parts, all finely adorned with wood. From the rustick building the rotondo above terminates the view, which is seen through a fine visto which in some places meets at top, and forms a sort of Gothick arch . . . we at length came to a grand lawn to the left, which is a rising ground to the north and west, and in the middle on an eminence is a half octagon open building, and a tent at the further end to the east; from this half octagon there is a view of the castle as in a woody vale between the hills, which rise over it, also of the Prince's [Frederick, Prince of Wales] pillar and another building on a heigth over the Prince's lawn. . . . Then you come to a rock-work of rough materials of the glass-house and quarries, which supports the hanging ground above . . . Below this to the right is a grotto where the water runs, and there is a statue of a Venus of Medici as coming up out of a fountain.

Bishop Pococke at Hagley Park, Worcestershire, June 1751

was greatly taken with the Duke's improvements: the lakes, cascades, 'great stones', 'an ostrich walking in the lawn', and on the serpentine:

a small yacht, which has sailed on the sea, a Chinese ship, the middle of which is high, covered and glazed, a Venetian gondola and five or six other different kinds of boats; at the other end is a wooden bridge of one arch, which, if I mistake not, I was informed is one hundred and ten feet wide.[15]

For his relaxed and intimate moments Cumberland had built 'a triangular tower, which is hexagon within, with a hexagon tower at each corner, which are round within'. It had shelves for books, 'china for tea and coffee' while the walls 'are adorned with festoons and flowers and fruits . . . in stucco, and painted in their natural colours'.[16] Mrs Lybbe Powys, who visited the hexagon tower a few years later and admired 'a chandelier of Chelsea china, the first of that manufacture, and cost £500', also enjoyed the Duke's 'Chinese Island, on which is a small house quite in the taste of that nation, the outside of which is white tiles set in red lead, decorated with bells and Chinese ornaments'.[17] This was large enough to include:

two state rooms, a drawing-room, and bed-chamber, in miniature each, but corresponds with the outside appearance; the chamber hung with painted satin, the couch-bed in the recess the same; in a drawing-room was a sort of Dresden tea-china, most curious indeed, every piece a different landscape, painted inimitably.[18]

With Cumberland Lodge, the Duke's seat, a mile distant, this description conveys vividly the extent to which, in this light-hearted period, the garden was becoming an extension of the main

This bell-hung and dragon-painted Chinese junk was only one of eight picturesque foreign craft gathered for the Duke of Cumberland's pleasure on Virginia Water in Windsor Great Park. It was devised upon the shell of a commercial Thames boat and owed more to pagoda roofs than to authentic sea-going junks.

house with the architecture far more important than tree planting or flower beds. This evidently was the Duke's *maison de plaisance* and it explains, at least in part, Talleyrand's celebrated nostalgia for the pre-Revolutionary '*douceur de la vie*', which only those who had been members of the eighteenth century's international élite could ever have experienced. On the other hand, the reverse side to that effete Rococo sophistication of park usage is the innocent sense of fun captured in a 1776 letter, which Henry Hoare, the rich banker turned country squire, wrote to Lord Bruce when Stourhead's grounds, Hoare's hobby over a lifetime, were in their eclectic prime and he was enjoying them with his grandchildren:

> Thank God they are all fine and well, and now make nothing of walking round the gardens; and I mounted the Tower Thursday with the dear children. The Temple of the Nymph is all enchantment to them, and the Cross new painted fills them with rapture.[19]

But then Stourhead, in the minds of most garden fanciers, must represent the epitome of English eighteenth-century garden design. Many others, besides those two grandchildren, have found the grotto of the Stourhead nymph to be 'all enchantment'. Mrs Lybbe Powys had, however, reservations about the 'red, blue, and gilt clothing', the paint which Hoare had laid over the figures on the Bristol High Cross once it had been re-erected at one entrance to his grounds. No raptures for her, she found it 'strikingly gaudy'.[20] It is an interesting side light on the aesthetic taste of this Rococo period that a medieval civic cross should have been brightly painted and that the garlands of stucco fruit and flowers in the Duke's hexagon, which twentieth-century purists would insist on painting stone on white or even white on white, were, in 1754, 'painted in their natural colours'.

When he came to transform Stourhead after his mother's death in 1741, Henry Hoare (1705–85) had three major advantages: his wealth, his maturity (he had just completed a thorough three year Grand Tour) and the topography of his grounds – a steep-sided Wiltshire valley watered by the six head-springs of the infant Stour. The evolution of his taste over the next forty years is worth consideration in some detail; partly because he had such a faultless eye for siting and for vistas, and partly because he and his grounds passed through in clear sequence most of the garden styles of the century.

His first phase, rarely noticed by visitors on the present admirably re-created circuit, was formal, virtually London and Wise: a straight avenue of firs (now replanted with deciduous trees) on level ground near the house, set apart from the valley pleasure grounds and focused on the 1746 Obelisk. From the end of this avenue a zig-zag path leads down through the woods. At chosen points little stone markers, the equivalent of those wooden signs in Shenstone's Leasowes, point enthusiasts of the Picturesque to various choice vistas; and at Stourhead 'choice' is an understatement. Sometimes the village church tower is framed by branches, at others the great scalloped cornice and rising dome of the Temple of Apollo appears between beech trees, almost two miles before the visitor will actually be able to reach it. Then there are glimpses of the Pantheon's larger but more sober dome across the lake with a mysterious huddle of rocks marking the Temple of the Nymph among darker trees.

While Hoare was not, like Switzer, Petre and Spence, a fanatical tree planter, Joseph Spence records that Hoare did toe the orthodox Pope line on colour contrasts, urging that: 'The greens should be ranged in large masses as the shades are in painting, to contrast the *dark* masses with the *light* ones, and to relieve each dark mass itself with little sprinklings of lighter greens here and there'.[21] Inevitably, however, most of the present planting of Stourhead is nineteenth or twentieth century in date, probably rather thicker and more be-laurelled in its under planting than it was in the eighteenth century. Another great difference, notably on the zig-zags of the descent we are following, is the loss of the eclectic fantasy buildings of the post-1757 phase in the garden. They were quite thickly clustered on this introductory slope and the visitor would have reached the valley floor bemused or delighted by, in roughly their order: a Venetian Seat, a Chinese 'Umbrella', a Chinese Pavilion and a Gothick Greenhouse, dismissed by the ever critical Horace Walpole as 'of false Gothic'.[22] All these and the Turkish Tent were swept away by Henry Hoare's successor, his grandson Richard Colt Hoare, in the post-1785 neo-classical purge previously mentioned.

In the event their loss makes any explanation of the several building campaigns of the garden simpler because they belonged to the third phase and if they had survived they would have been out of sequence here between phase one, the Formal, and phase two, the Virgilian-Palladian. Also, it has to be admitted, sudden excursions to China, Turkey and the medieval period could have come as a discordant distraction to the exquisitely unfolding scenes of an English Arcadia which can be enjoyed now that Colt Hoare has censored those exotics out of existence. It was the Irish visitor to Wooburn Farm, John Parnell, who wrote, after experiencing the eclectic switch-back laid out by Southcote:

Nothing prevents the eye from taking in all the buildings at one view, or at least the greater part, which, though pleasing to the last degree in themselves, as they are of different orders, or rather the orders of different nations, is an amazing absurdity. Where different nations are thus introduced into an improvement they should at least be hid from one another by an hill, wood or clump of trees . . . to exhibit a Grecian Temple within an hundred yards of a Gothic which comes again as near a Chinese is as irreconcilable to Fancy as to Nature or Reason.[23]

Buildings of four 'nations' would have jostled each other on this slope in Stourhead immediately before the visitor had to prepare for the garden's Virgilian solemnities around the lake, so Parnell's criticism is a serious one.

The lake at Stourhead directs the inner circuit of the garden and pulls the whole composition together. It is largely artificial and the dam, or head, which creates it was not in place until 1754. Round its shores are set the temples of the original Virgilian iconography: that of Ceres/Flora (1744–6) at the foot of the descent, the Temple or Grotto of the Nymph on the further shore, built in three stages of increasing theatrical potency (1748, 1751 and 1776), finally the great Pantheon or Temple of Hercules (1753–4). All three were, in their original form, designed by the Palladian architect, Henry Flitcroft (1697–1769), who was trained by Lord

In the Virgilian iconography of Stourhead's garden buildings Henry Hoare intended this miniature Pantheon as the home of heroic Hercules, a reward to Aeneas for threading the dark caverns and following the path of virtue. Henry Flitcroft completed it in 1754. It has a centrally heated interior of an unexpected, ruddy gloom where a statue of Hercules, middle-aged and nobly nude, stands among an odd assortment of Olympian gods and Christian saints.

Burlington. Henry Hoare was influenced equally by his reading and by his collection of paintings. Virgil's *Aeneid* gave him the theme for these temples of the garden's second phase, an attractive copy of a Claude Lorrain painting, still in Stourhead house, gave him the idea for the Pantheon, seen domed and porticoed across water with trees behind it. Later another book, Richard Wood's *The ruins of Balbec* (1757), would give him the design of the Temple of Apollo, and Voltaire's eulogy on King Alfred in his *L'Histoire Générale* inspired Hoare to raise the triangular 160 foot King Alfred's Tower on Kingsettle Hill, part of the park's seven mile outer circuit.

The theme taken from the *Aeneid*: Aeneas' visits to a Sibyl in the Underworld where she urged him on to noble virtue and the foundation of Rome, would have been nothing without Hoare's astonishing sense of visual theatre and the excellence of Flitcroft's designs. The Temple of Flora with its gloriously élitist '*Procul O Procul Este Profane*' ('Begone, you who are uninitiated! Begone!') is fine but unremarkable. It is the Grotto of the Nymph which is the marvel of Stourhead, one hard to equal anywhere in Italy and one deliberately evolved over twenty-eight years to thrill the visitor by twists and turns, light and darkness, sounds and unexpected sights. This, more than anything else, brought 'crowds of country people' flocking and so much carriage trade of gentry that Hoare had to enlarge the village inn to an hotel to accommodate them.[24] Even so, when

' A Landscape, with magnificent Buildings, and a View of the Sea' (Aeneas at Delos) from Claude's Liber Veritatis *suggests the real visual inspiration for Stourhead's Pantheon. It also mirrors Henry Hoare's painterly composition of the pleasure grounds as seen from Stourton village, with the Palladian Bridge in the foreground, the lake in the middle distance and the Temple of Flora to the right. A painting of the same subject attributed to Claude still hangs in Stourhead House.*

Mrs Lybbe Powys arrived in 1776, every room was taken and she had difficulty finding rooms in the next village, where Horace Walpole and Robert Adam had secured the best rooms before her.

That makes the essential point about Rococo Gardens: they were popular. They really gave pleasure. They were the Alton Towers and the Disneylands of their time offering harmless, interactive, psychic thrills. Stourhead, even stripped of some of its thrills, draws more visitors now than it ever did. The National Trust has to exercise ingenuity to cope with them. Few visitors forget their first experience of the Grotto of the Nymph – the descent between dark holm oaks and yews into gloom, a twist in the passage (the stagey addition of 1776), the sound of falling water and then the triple assault under the impending rocky roof. To the right the statue of the Nymph sleeps vulnerably above the tumbling waters. Below her lies the most exotic and Romantic cold bath in Britain. Henry Hoare declared that 'a souse in that delicious bath and grot, fill'd with fresh magic, is Asiatick luxury, and too much for mortals'.[25] But that is only one element of the 'fresh magic'. To the left, framed dramatically by rocks and viewing at apparently the water level of the lake, the eye is drawn directly to the contrived composition of village church tower, Bristol High Cross and the Palladian Bridge, the lake seeming to wind away into a river. Lastly, straight ahead, out of the darkness the silvery figure of a river god, John Cheere's masterpiece, beckons eerily, urging the traveller on into further darkness, but eventually up into

John Cheere's brilliantly theatrical statue of a river god, Baroque rather than Palladian in atmosphere, beckons a fearful visitor to pass through the shadows, climb up into light and so arrive at the Pantheon as a reward for courage. The statue was added to the Grotto of the Nymph in 1751.

light and the Pantheon of heroic virtue. This last statue was added in 1751 completing a composition Palladian in detail, Baroque in feeling and Rococo in its twisting route.

The Pantheon is another visual prodigy. A curious warm light, best described as a subdued aubergine, fills the domed hall and all around the gods stand high. It is one of the few places left where the Olympians (even though one is the Christian Saint Susanna) can still raise a frisson of awe. Hercules in the centre, by Rysbrack, is nude and elderly, but by 1754, when the Pantheon was built, Henry Hoare was himself middle-aged and might have empathised.

With the completion of the Pantheon and the raising of the gods the second phase of Hoare's garden buildings had been achieved, and in June 1757 James Hannaway, writing in the *London Chronicle*, boasted unwisely that at Stourhead there were 'no Chinese works, no monsters of imagination, no deviations from nature, under the fond notions of fashion or taste'.[26] In fact when Bishop Pococke had made an appreciative visit in 1754, Hoare was already planning to set islands in the lake, on 'one of which is to be a Mosque with a Minaret'.[27] The mosque did not materialise but, encouraged perhaps by royal examples, Hoare was amusing himself, his family and his visitors by the early 1760s with the Gothick, Chinese and Turkish ventures previously mentioned.

It is not always appreciated that, in addition to these, there was also, until it was dismantled in 1814, a second full-scale Rococo grotto, that of the Hermit or Druid's Cell, as complex and twisting as the Grotto of the Nymph.[28] Just as modern theme parks have, every other year, to add a new frightening roller-coaster ride to draw visitors back again, so in 1771 Henry Hoare opened his Hermit's Cell, leading off from the Rock-work Bridge of 1762–5. A gloomy double dog-leg of passage led into the three-chambered cell, its vault supported on five rugged pillars; and here again a carefully sited window offered a surprise view down over the lake. Tables and lamps supplied a Gothick glimmer in the middle chamber.

There remained the Temple of Apollo in its inspired neo-classicism, the Palladian Bridge and then the High Cross before the village, refreshment and the hotel. Nothing in Stourhead was an anticlimax. For those with a day to spend there was the outer circuit, with St Peter's Pump (1768), a conduit head rescued, like the High Cross, after a Bristol street-widening scheme, King Alfred's Tower with its 225 stone steps, and the Convent in the Wood, which claimed 'two very ancient pictures found in the ruins of Glastonbury Abbey' and 'very pretty Gothic elbow-chairs'.[29] Walpole's *The Castle of Otranto* of 1764 could have inspired that. But what had inspired Henry Hoare to this whole delightful pleasure garden? Prestige in the county perhaps, and a genial determination to cheer up his family after a tragic sequence of early deaths of wives, a son and daughters. One thing is clear. The gardens at Stourhead were neither inspired nor even laid out by professional gardeners. Like most of the other mid-century Rococo gardens which have been mentioned they were an educated gentleman's hobby. Amateurs like Hoare, Hamilton, Anson, Princess Augusta at Kew, Cumberland at Virginia Water, Shenstone and Southcote, were leading the way. They might call in professional architects like Henry Flitcroft and William Chambers, but it was the patron who decided the exotic subjects. During her visit to Stourhead Mrs Lybbe Powys was emphatic on this point:

> All the buildings and plantations are the present owner's doing, without any assistance but common workmen to plan or lay out the whole seven miles' extent, nor could Brown [Capability] have executed it with more taste and elegance.[30]

What Stourhead helps to explain is the enduring popularity of England's ruling classes and their avoidance of any insular equivalent of the French Revolution. The Rococo Garden was a potent instrument of social cohesion.

CHAPTER TWELVE

CAPABILITY BROWN – THE PROFESSIONAL AND HIS IDEAL ENGLISH PARKSCAPE

With contemporaries hailing him as 'immortal' before he was fifty and with his landscaping consultancy handling more than 170 major commissions between 1751 and 1783, it is hard to deny that Lancelot Brown (1716–83) was a significant figure in English garden history. The question is, significant for what? Did he offer any new aesthetic perspective to park and garden design or was he rather an efficient businessman who responded alertly to the social pressures of the landed gentry at a time when their rent rolls were rising and they had money to spend? He certainly devised a park formula; he took a limited number of elements – the belt of trees on an estate's limits, a semi-natural clumping of trees on wide, smooth lawns and a serpentine lake – and made them a standard park layout, one to be found not only on the estates his firm had handled, but on literally several thousand estates across the country reshaped by men he had trained or by his imitators: Adam Mickle, William Emes, Francis Richardson, Nathaniel Richmond and Richard Woods.[1]

Confident, quizzical and persuasive, this engraving after a portrait of Lancelot Brown by Nathaniel Dance goes some way to explain Brown's remarkable ability to bridge the class gap and become, though only a farmer's son, the confidant of a king, a prime minister and many of the peers.

But these elements had all been current for many years before Brown picked upon them. That account of Hagley Park by Bishop Pococke, given as the text for the previous chapter, mentions them as standard features of a Rococo park, and Pococke was writing in 1751, the year when Brown first set up as an independent consultant. So Brown was not, in the usual sense, an innovator. But could a drive towards landscape minimalism, a reduction of parks to their bare functional forms, a stripped down elegance, be innovation of a kind? It is no accident that Brown's reputation has risen since the mid-twentieth century, another period when minimalism and a simplification of design forms was at a premium.

Viewed retrospectively Brown comes across as George London reborn. London died in 1714, Brown launched out as a consultant in 1751. Between those two dates lie the golden years of the great amateurs, poets, peers and artistic adventurers like William Kent. They were not men who turned out a hundred roughly similar gardens in a lifetime but creators of just a few, or even one, celebrated, original and much visited garden. Before them and after them are the professionals, the Londons and the Browns: nursery magnates selling their plants and trees, drainage and hydraulics experts, leaders of small teams of technicians but able to control a hundred or more temporary labourers when the harvest was gathered and seasonal unemployment had set in. Brown was adept in all the necessary technical fields – dam building, land drainage, trenching, planting – and in addition he was a competent, though never an inspired, architect. He could take in the potential of an estate, its 'capabilities', after an hour on horseback and then have it staked out by his team within a day. His efficiency was never in doubt and for all his multiple projects (in one particularly profitable year he coined £34,000 and his average intake was £15,000) he was conscientious. Most of his reshaping schemes involved work over anything up to four or five years, but he visited regularly to assess progress and left detailed instructions to his site managers. His 'minutes' or written instructions left after each inspection of the improvements at Burton Constable, Yorkshire have been preserved in all their precise and practical detail.

The interesting questions are whether this efficiency was all or was his real genius more one for handling clients, a social flair at a time when society was stratified and formal manners were an art in themselves?

As the middle-class, but far less socially successful, Humphry Repton put it: 'Neither Mr Brown nor his immediate followers were men of Liberal Education and therefore they have left no record in writing to explain their practice'.[2] Yet Brown, whose whole character is blank in contemporary records, not only achieved royal patronage, the key to success in his profession, but became a friend of the bluff, eccentric George III and something of an arbiter in political relationships entirely outside the range of gardening. He was the son of a Northumbrian farmer, educated until he was sixteen, a long period for someone of his class and circumstances, at the local school in Cambo, near Wallington. After a few years of intensive tree planting between 1732 and 1739 at the nearby Kirkharle Hall, he moved down south, manoeuvred himself into a Stowe connection at neighbouring Wotton in Buckinghamshire and a year later, 1740, was employed at Stowe itself by Lord Cobham. In the most remarkable leap of all he was appointed head gardener at Stowe, the most celebrated and experimental garden in England, in 1741 when he was still twenty-five years old. Brown needs to be seen in the perspective of Stowe's past garden designers. At only twenty-five he was employed by a landowner and a politician who had comparatively recently given Vanbrugh and Bridgeman a free hand and who was, in 1741, building classical temples to the designs of Kent and a Gothic Temple of Liberty to the design of James Gibbs. The concentration of talent was formidable and Lord Cobham himself had demonstrated a rare ability to move forwards in garden design, from George London-style formalism to Bridgeman's directive geometry of avenues and now, in the 1730s and 1740s, to the selective felling of avenue trees and the soft, irregular planting of Kent. If anyone should be called the Father of English Landscape Gardening it is Cobham.

4 sept. 1773 Hints from Mr Brown

1 West front – Plantation adjoining Miss Constable's Garden to be planted with Low Shrubs, that the Wood etc., may be seen over it.

2 Shrubbery in Miss C's Garden a piece to be taken off and laid to Grass – as far as Larch Tree.

3 Trees proper for planting at Burton – Oak, Elm and Beech.

4 Small Plantations, the bad Trees, and Trees grown too tall, to be cut off about 6 Inches from the ground & let them shoot again – Preserve the best Shoot, and cut away the rest – By this method they will make better Trees.

5 Foot Walk to the Garden as staked out – without Shrubbery. To be made of Gravel six Feet wide. – Walk or Ride to the old Bridge thro' Shrubbery 8 Feet wide – That adjg Drying Yard 7.

6 Gravel Walk in West Front to be made about half the width it is at present.

7 Wood Yard in Mr B's plan taken away – Fixd behind the Stables – Plantation there removed farther back.

8 End of Sunk Fence next Old Bridge to be made as wide as the remains of the Pond to humour the width of the old Pond, and save Earth leading.

9 Menagerie Avenues, both left as they are & not Clump'd. – Sproatley Avenue same except the intermediate Firs taken away.

10 Screed of Wood from Yard Wood to Clumps in Sproatley Avenue to be made as Mr Brown directed in 1772 & about 300 Feet wide – Part planted & part sown with Seeds Acorns etc – Mr B will send some Beech Mast.

11 Menagery Pond – Long Stanks & Muddy Stanks to be widened & thron into one piece of Water – Join Long Stanks & Muddy Stanks by two Arms or branches through the Hill & leave an Island covered with Thorns – make a Ford over it for Carriages & horses & a foot Bridge.

12 Carriage Road to Garden to lead off from the Marton Road on this side Ruth Jackson's to the Avenue in Bacchus Field & from thence up to the garden leading to the Orchard.

13 Hedge to be taken away & a Sunk Fence made from Clump nearest Pailey Field Gate northwards to Clump near Red Gate adjoining Mill Field. – Road Gate at either end or both as you will.

14 Avenue between Mill Field & Pailey Field to be taken away (except a small Clump or two reserved in order to add Mill Hill & Mill Field to the Lawn).

15 Mix the Trees promiscuously in the plantations & Clumps & don't plant them in patches.

16 Thin all the Plantations of two or three years growth – all much too thick.

17 Medallion – for the Pediment in the West Front.

18 Take away Park Pale dividing Bacchus Field from the Park. Remake a Sunk Fence about 40 or 50 Yards North of the Pale Fence; and lead this into the new Sunk Fence round the House.

Capability Brown's 1773 Minutes for the landscaping at Burton Constable

Was he deliberately grooming the young Lancelot Brown to be the next shaper of garden design? On his past record it seems probable.

Now Brown was privileged to work for the next seven years to the directions of the largely absentee William Kent, settling the grounds around the brand new temples of the Elysian Fields and trimming the Hawkwell Fields to frame Gibbs's Gothic prodigy. It was an intense apprenticeship in the creation of the most richly elaborate and wildly eclectic Rococo garden design: a three-in-hand of the classical, the Gothic and the Chinese. And yet Brown would emerge, after the death of Kent in 1748 and Lord Cobham in 1749, to become the advocate in the 1750s of elegant minimalism, first achieved in Stowe's Grecian Valley, just when the great wave of Rococo gardening seemed to be breaking over the whole country. Few of his contemporaries were in tune with Brown. In 1741 a pioneer of the Rococo like Shenstone had still not taken possession of The Leasowes, Southcote had only been working on his Wooburn Farm for eight years. Henry Hoare did not inherit Stourhead until 1742, and his Pantheon and Grotto of the Nymph would not be in place until the mid-1750s. Joseph Spence was a great tree planter and relatively cool on eclectic garden buildings, but he looked forward rather to the wild, Picturesque gardeners of the end of the century than to Brown's refined minimalism.

As head gardener at Stowe from 1741 to 1751 Lancelot Brown supervised the planting, digging and draining required to bring the absentee William Kent's directions as to the Elysian Fields into effect. Two and a half centuries later something of Brown's styling survives around the Temple of British Worthies – the artificially neat banks of the lake and the opening in the backcloth of trees to allow a vista of escape further into the landscape.

There is, therefore, more of a case than might at first appear to be made for seeing Brown as a bold innovator working against, not with, the tide of fashion. Lord Cobham had generously allowed him to advise on neighbouring garden projects to make himself known. This was to give him a head start in the quest for commissions as he disengaged himself from Stowe. To understand the way his mind was working and his ideas developing in the face of practical situations, the key schemes to follow are those which he undertook in the late 1740s and early 1750s. In these he applied to entire parks the technique of subtle, feathery planting of trees, which he had learnt under Cobham and Kent's tuition, and disassociated himself gradually from the Rococo profusions of garden buildings. The Temple of Concord and Victory at Stowe and the landscaping of the Grecian Valley as its setting began in 1747. Brown contrived to turn the merest fold of Buckinghamshire pasture into an Arcadian valley by planting:

> sometimes close covers, and sometimes open groves; the trees rise in one upon high stems and feather down to the bottom in another; and between them are short openings into the park or the gardens.[3]

What he had done at Stowe, with the visual prop of a grand Ionic temple, he then proceeded to do in the same year as a favour for a neighbouring landowner, the Duke of Grafton, at

The Temple of Concord and Victory at the head of the Grecian valley at Stowe exemplifies the whole splendid misconception of an English Arcadia. By subtle planting Lancelot Brown has given a very slight undulation in the fields something of a valley's profile, but the idea that a great Ionic temple in Greece should be set above such gentle contours and lush woodland betrays an insular ignorance of geographical realities. The valley was to have been flooded with a lake and this would have given the temple a more Claudeian setting.

Wakefield Lodge, four miles to the north-east, but this time without the support of a garden building. Wakefield Lodge was the clearest pointer to the future, probably because there he was dealing with a sporting estate and with a peer who was not anxious to overspend. Sport and economy were two constant concerns of the average landowner. All Brown offered the Duke was a serpentine lake to focus views from the Lodge and, beyond the lake, a great, smooth lawn extending to the fringes of the forest, which he manicured in the Grecian Valley style. Upkeep was minimal and the layout was just sufficiently distinguished from 'unimproved' countryside to suggest a gentleman's presence. What was most important was that the Duke was delighted and would employ Brown again at his principal seat, Euston Hall in Suffolk. The House of Lords was a club, word of mouth commendations went quickly around and they would explain those prestigious commissions which came Brown's way in the 1750s.

The sporting element to eighteenth-century parks had at least as much to do with Brown's future minimalist tendencies as any conscious drive towards aesthetic elegance.[4] Wakefield Lodge commanded a forest area which extended to the northern reaches of Stowe's own park; at that time it would still have offered deer hunting and there were open fields for fox hunting and hare coursing to the north. Shooting would have been less important because sporting guns were long in the barrel, heavy to carry and unreliable. It was still predominantly a sport for young men prepared to beat their way through thick undergrowth, blazing away at anything that moved. As Brown's career advanced certain spin-offs from the Industrial Revolution and various Acts of Parliament would bring about radical changes to the sporting world. The right to shoot over land became increasingly a matter of prestige and a valued private preserve. Only freeholders with at least £100 a year had the right to shoot. Game Acts of 1707 and 1723 increased the penalties for poaching to hanging if the poacher was armed and had blackened his face. Then came the Act of 1755, forbidding all buying and selling of partridge and pheasant. This put a premium on poaching as the only way for ordinary customers to get a bird. Its aim had been to make the gift of a bird the exclusive perk of the gentry, but if anything it effected the reverse.

Meanwhile guns were getting progressively shorter, lighter and more deadly. Barrels that had been 3 feet 6 inches in 1760 would have shrunk by 1799 to 2 feet 6 inches; lead shot was being produced by William Watts at the Bristol shot tower in 1782 and in 1787 the patent breech created a more powerful charge.[5] In 1770 a book called *The Art of Shooting Flying* was published, and this urged the highly suggestible legion of sportsmen that true gentlemen only shot birds flying high. Until that time partridges had provided the usual targets for small shooting parties, and they flew low out of the turnip fields. Now the fashion moved to pheasants which could be relied upon to go up like noisy rockets, offer a substantial target to the short-sighted and be seen as the proper prey for gentlemen who, firing a positive spray of lead shot, would be likely to hit at least one bird. Formerly pheasants had been kept in pheasantries as ornamental pets, destined only later in life for the pot. Now they began to be bred as semi-wild birds and it was soon realised that pheasants flourished, not in deep forests, but on the edge of woodland. The perfect breeding ground for them was a shelter belt of trees, a belt such as Brown was equally ready to plant for aesthetic reasons and to provide privacy for a park. Soon spectacular beats of these woodland belts would raise hundreds of birds to fall victim to large organised shooting parties. For the gentry and for the poachers, parks were becoming prestige larders. No shooting party wants to be impeded by Chinese pavilions or ruined Gothic abbeys, therefore minimalist planting would become both functional and fashionable and the Rococo would go into a natural decline.

Most of this was, in 1747–9, still for the future, but the park at Wakefield Lodge was a foreshadowing and Brown was a man to heed lessons. Warwick Castle's grounds, where he began work in 1749, were less rewarding: a half-hearted compromise scheme with some of the old avenues thinned down and a number of exactly circular clumps lined up like soldiers on parade. Horace Walpole dismissed the grounds in a letter of July 1751 to George Montagu as 'well laid out by one Brown who has set up on a few ideas of Kent and Mr. Southcote. One sees what the prevalence of taste does; little Brook who would have chuckled to have been born in an age of clipt hedges and cockle-shell avenues, has submitted to let his garden and park be natural'.[6]

Croome d'Abitot and Great Packington were far more interesting. They were both begun in 1751, by which time Brown had moved with his growing family from Stowe to Hammersmith, close to London and within the nursery garden sector of Middlesex. It was with these two parks that Brown must have seen two distinct design paths diverging, and demanding that he should choose one way or another. Croome, laid out for the 6th Earl of Coventry, began as the kind of Rococo layout that might have been predicted from the ex-head gardener at Stowe, but then evolved into what was to become the characteristic Brownian minimalism. At Great Packington in Warwickshire, devised for Lord Guernsey, heir to the Earl of Aylesbury, an original Rococo design was rejected in favour of that minimalist treatment. Furthermore it was rejected by a young lord who had just become rich by

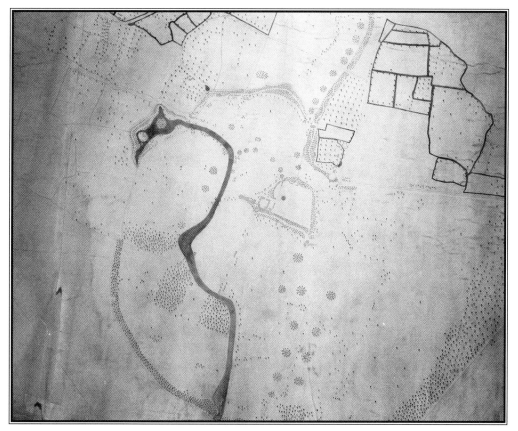

The park at Croome d'Abitot in Worcestershire, seen here in John Broome's map of 1768, was one of Brown's earliest and most defining commissions. He began work there in 1751, dividing the park with a bold serpentine terminating in a lake of casual outline with islands and a grotto. Tree belts define Croome's early boundaries to the west and north. Behind the house to the east lies a marl ridge. Brown dramatised this by plantings and by a new, Gothick towered, church.

marrying a daughter of the Duke of Somerset and who could, therefore, easily have afforded the eclectic buildings which Brown was hoping to raise; so its sleek minimalism was a deliberate choice.

It may appear unkind to concentrate on a Brown park at Croome which has been severed in the twentieth century by a motorway, but the M5 has been sunk tactfully into a trench and it actually divides the inner Rococo park of Brown's first creation from the outer extensions of later years, made to satisfy a growing fashion for the Picturesque. Croome was not a park designed to impress an approaching visitor; it is house-centred and works outward from Croome Court, Brown's first major architectural commission, a blockish neo-Palladian building with low-roof pavilions and an Ionic portico on its more welcoming, south front facing the Home Shrubbery. If he had been intent upon vistas Brown would have insisted on moving the house half a mile to the west where it would have enjoyed splendid views of the Severn valley with the whole range of the Malverns humped dramatically beyond. Thinking initially in Rococo terms, however, not Picturesque, he worked upon an intimate inscape. Set low in a marshy valley, with a marl ridge to the north and east and limited vistas in all other directions, Croome Court desperately needed visual relief. Remembering how he had converted a shallow fold of Buckinghamshire farmland at Stowe into a

With characteristic confidence Brown ordered the demolition of the old church at Croome, which had stood close to the house, and had a new St Mary Magdalene built, probably to his own design, up on the marl ridge where it could catch the eye as a picturesque termination to views from the house.

Grecian Valley by planting trees along its modest ridges, Brown heightened the marl ridge with a long belt of mixed deciduous trees and conifers. To draw the eye to this he demolished the old church near the house and rebuilt it, with a bold Gothic tower, up on the ridge. All other relics of Croome village were destroyed in his first ruthless clearing operation; the peasants were rehoused out of sight in High Green estate village. It was a stroke Brown was to repeat more famously and gracefully at Milton Abbey, in Dorset, in the 1770s. While this was not the first of such socio-aesthetic clearances of entire communities, Brown certainly made them common practice.

The ridge rose steeply immediately behind the house so now only the west and north-west views required enrichment. A long S-curved serpentine river replaced the marsh. It was crossed by a Chinese Bridge and backed in all its north–south length by a belt of trees hiding the lacklustre landscape beyond. At its northern tip the river was expanded into a lake to take a romantic three-arched grotto and an island, which would later be given a temple. This still left one gap to the north-west; this was filled by the Manley Grove clump and, in the 1760s, by Robert Adam's Temple Greenhouse. Various urns and terms and seats enriched the ridge. A 'pretty' rather than a 'beautiful' garden, one mile long and half a mile wide, had been created, split in half by the serpentine, with fine tree-dotted lawns. An interesting second stage was to follow. To escape the claustrophobia Adam designed a tall Rotunda circled by terms on the ridge behind the house. Over the years an outer ring of vistas would have to be created to serve this. These included a ruin, Dunstall Castle, to view which a gap was cut in Brown's southern tree belt, a Panorama Tower to command the Malverns in the west, and Pirton Castle on the edge of the old deer park to draw the eye much further north.[7]

All, in their way, were a response to and an enhancement of Brown's first concept.

At Great Packington, Brown followed up more confidently the lessons he was learning at Croome. Lord Guernsey had swept aside his proposals for 'My Lady's Lodge', a cut-down version of Inigo Jones's Queen's House at Greenwich, which would have dominated the eastern half of a twin-lobed park. He also rejected a nine-bay Palladian screen with twin lodges which would have struck a decisive classical note to the entry.[8] What survived was Brown at his boldest. The existing Great Pond was extended by a long curling serpentine that cut the entire park in half, east–west. Just one relic of Rococo thinking, a Chinese grotto and cascade, was to link the two lakes. Generous curving sweeps of woodland belted the northern limits of the park but, as at Stowe, the southern limits were left open. At the point of the cascade the woods swept down from the north, crossing the lakes to create two quite separate visual areas of broad lawns clumped irregularly. Almost all the formal gardens of *c.* 1700 were destroyed and an old right-of-way was ruthlessly severed by the narrow serpentine. The new layout had a great potential for shooting and two separate enclosures had been created without recourse to anything so demeaning as a hedge. Either of these areas could be grazed alternately by sheep or cattle,

Robert Adam's Rotunda, with its unassuming dome and elegant garlanded plaques, stands on the marl ridge immediately behind Croome Court. It was built in the 1760s as part of a scheme to widen the limited 'Rococo' vistas of the park to include modishly Picturesque landscape features like the Malvern Hills to the west and a large Gothick folly tower, Dunstall Castle, to the south.

while the lakes provided boating and fishing. At its eastern tip the serpentine curled away out of sight beyond a carriage bridge to suggest the continuing flow of a broad river, soon to become a standard Brownian device. The whole ensemble was elegantly uncluttered, it excluded the outside world, was unmarked by hedges, was multi-functional and Rococo only in the natural-seeming curvaceousness of its woodland lines. This was to be the future. Commissions in the same easy style at Kirtlington, Belhus, Burghley, Sherborne, Burton Constable, Longleat, Moor Park and Ragley would soon follow.

In his *Philosophical Enquiry* of 1757 Edmund Burke had virtually equated beauty with smoothness and commentators usually remark upon the overall smoothness of a typical Brown park.[9] There was always provision for carriages and those huge expanses of turf were also ideal for horse riding. It was the mark of a gentleman that he enjoyed a daily gallop and Brown supplied ample ridings. Farms and cottages were no longer considered desirable landscape features, but the gentry were usually enthusiastic for livestock breeding, so it was no badge of shame to have herds and flocks to crop the grass closely and to be admired by visitors. But in this, possibly the most

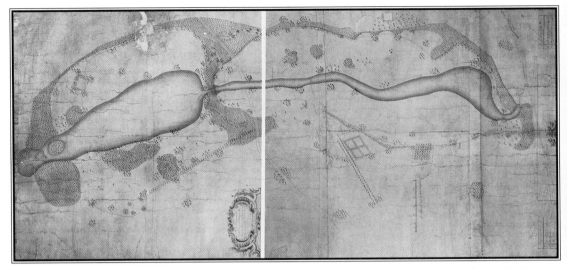

In its broad outlines of a dividing central serpentine, with belts of trees to define the park's limits and provide cover for the rearing of pheasants, Great Packington, Warwickshire, resembles Brown's layout at Croome. Both parks feature wide lawns or ridings with an irregular, graceful clumping of trees. But here at Packington, with two lakes, the scale is grander and Brown had the prototype for a sporting estate where profitable forestry and farming could be pursued unobtrusively.

heartless age of rural Britain, the actual farm buildings had to be concealed behind tree belts. It was the time of Oliver Goldsmith's *Deserted Village* when the old intimacy between landowner and peasant could no longer be taken for granted:

> Sweet smiling village, loveliest of the lawn,
> Thy sports are fled and all thy charms withdrawn;
> Amidst thy bowers the tyrant's hand is seen,
> And desolation saddens all thy green.[10]

As the peasantry multiplied they grew poorer and the landed gentry richer. Organised poaching was one manifestation of class warfare as were the counter measures: park walls, keeper's cottages and lodges at guarded entry points.

These were social pressures to which Brown responded eagerly. His, it could be argued, was 'the tyrant's hand' of the poem, imposing obsessive, tidying measures that ruined Goldsmith's 'Sweet Auburn, loveliest village of the plain,/Where health and plenty cheered the labouring swain'.[11] For Auburn read Croome d'Abitot, Great Packington, Milton Abbas or Stowe. Lancelot Brown, together with the 170 patrons of his industrious working career, can be identified as the villains of a country 'Where wealth accumulates and men decay'.[12] Goldsmith's angriest passage is aimed accurately at Brown's clearances:

> . . . The man of wealth and pride
> Takes up a space that many poor supplied;
> Space for his lake, his park's extended bounds,
> Space for his horses, equipage and hounds;
> The robe that wraps his limbs in silken sloth

Has robbed the neighbouring field of half their growth;
His seat, where solitary sports are seen,
Indignant spurns the cottage from the green;
Around the world each needful product flies,
For all the luxuries the world supplies:
While thus the land, adorned for pleasure all,
In barren splendour feebly waits the fall.[13]

Those were his lakes, his park's 'extended bounds', where cattle might be seen but not farms or cottages, and his shelter belts for the 'solitary sports' of the marksman in estates 'adorned for pleasure all'.

It could be urged that Brown was himself a victim of the system, obliged by an arrogant and indifferent aristocracy to tidy the poor out of sight like so much litter. But that would be to ignore the flexibility of the British class system and the extraordinary position which Brown carved out for himself as a mover, a shaper and an authority figure. This Northumbrian farmer's son was, in 1777, by private conversation and by letter, acting as a conciliator to heal a political breach between the King, George III, and one of his ex-prime ministers, the great Earl of Chatham. As Chatham himself wrote admiringly when recommending Brown to yet another rich client, 'he shares the private hours of the King, dines familiarly with his neighbour of Sion [the Duke of Northumberland] and sits down at the tables of all the House of Lords'.[14]

The portraits of Brown, both of which seem to have been painted at one sitting and taking him from his favourite angle, capture his cleverness and much more – a coy, sidelong self-confidence, a mouth on the edge of humour, large, knowing eyes which could flatter a listener by an impression of alert attention.[15] It is the face of a warm, approachable charmer who will ease his way through any barrier of rank. 'Now sir', said Chatham, after Brown had helped the crippled earl into his carriage, 'go and adorn your country'. 'Go you, my Lord', came back the glib reply, 'and save it';[16] it was an exchange between two living legends, both industriously perpetuating themselves. Brown was absolutely an Establishment man and for several decades was able to impose an Establishment aesthetic on country estates, working as a favour rather than as an employment. When Lord Bruce dared to quiz Brown for his failure to give a fixed scale of his fees for services at Tottenham Park in Wiltshire, Brown wrote back, more in sorrow than in anger:

All I can say upon it is that I should be very sorry to diminish my friends, and very sorry to increase my business, for I have so much to do that it neither answers for profit nor pleasure, for when I am galloping in one part of the world my men are making blunders and neglects which [make] it very unplesant . . . as to money matters your Lordship will satisfy me when your Lordship is pleas'd'.[17]

A short while before, Lord Bruce's agent, Mr Bill, had reported on one of Brown's regular and apparently rather frightening visits of inspection to check on the 'blunders and neglects' of his workforce:

He allowed lining out and finally settled the serpentine walk, all round the garden, marked such trees as were proposed to be taken away and gave general directions to Winckles upon everything that occur'd . . . In general he approves of what has been done except the taking away [of] a few large trees in one or two places. If the high bank and trees had been taken down, great would have been the fall indeed, Brown would have excommunicated us all.[18]

Abashed by the show of self-assurance, Lord Bruce continued to employ this untamed autocrat for another eight years: 1764–72. From the detailed contracts and annual 'minutes' of advice on progress, which Brown made as a result of all his 'galloping', it appears that when Chatham urged him to 'go and adorn your country', what he really meant was 'go and tidy it up'. Most periods of history have their particular ideal of beauty. What tends to be thought of as a Regency elegance actually dates back three or four decades earlier and is, more accurately, a George III tidiness: that stripped down purity of line, common to a group of mares in a Stubbs painting, to the younger John Wood's Royal Crescent at Bath or to the springing and line of a carriage. That snatch of Brown's conversation, always quoted, when he was explaining his method of landscaping to Hannah More in 1782, is strangely unrelated to the visuals of landscape painting. Instead Brown saw himself as if he were working in black and white, a punctuator or grammarian:

Now *there* I make a comma, and there, where a more decided turn is proper, I make a colon; at another part, where an interruption is desirable to break the view, a parenthesis; now a full stop, and then I begin another subject.[19]

It is a bloodless analysis of an often bloodless vista, but memorable, and one that would have flattered the wit of his listener.

Christopher Hussey, who did so much to revive Brown's reputation after the long and predictable nineteenth-century silence, responded eagerly to this streamlined element of Brown's landscapes. He recalled Edmund Burke and Dr Johnson's definitions of, respectively, Beauty and Happiness. Burke in his *Philosophical Enquiry* believed that 'being swiftly drawn in an easy coach, on a smooth turf, with gradual ascents and declivities' gave the best idea, not only of Beauty, but of its 'probable cause'.[20] Johnson's idea of Happiness was 'being swiftly drawn in a chaise over undulating turf in the company of a beautiful and witty woman'.[21] Brown's parks would have supplied exactly that experience to all his patrons; and there was a real craft behind what he offered.

Brown did not invent either the method of producing a soft, velvety turf or the technique for transplanting trees already half-grown. A letter of January 1748 from Lord Dacre of Belhus Hall, Essex, soon to become a patron of Brown, to Sanderson Miller the Agony Aunt and adviser to would-be park improvers and Gothicisers, relates how:

I have planted above 200 elms, the least of them above 20ft. high and many of them 30. These I have put in the grove behind my house where there were any spots of thin trees . . . Another thing I have done and a great piece of work it is, I have ploughed up all the ground round about my House (above 60 acres) which I do in order to clean it thoroughly and lay it down quite smooth and fine.[22]

Brown was only inheriting and offering, in a smooth commercial operation, the advances of the agricultural revolution.

That exhaustive round of checking on detail was largely aimed, as Lord Dacre's ploughing and cleaning had been, at neatness, the avoidance of angularities and the resilience of the turf over which his clients would ride or over which their carriages would roll. Clause 8 of his 1757 Contract with the 3rd Viscount Weymouth at Longleat lays down the most meticulous quality control:

> To drain and level all Ground circumscribed by the Stakes put in for the Boundary of this undertaking – Brown to dig the Stones at his Expence, Lord Weymouth to find Brush-Wood to lay upon the Stones. It is further understood in this Article, that the whole ground shou'd have a natural easy correspondent Level in all its Parts, that the whole shou'd be made smooth & Dry etc. as also to lay some of the sharp Sand, of the Hill on the clayey Parts of it by way of Dressing; And to sow with Dutch Clover & Grass seeds or turff all such parts as shall be broke up.[23]

It was typical of Brown that his next, 1762, Contract for Longleat involved moving the kitchen garden a mile away from the house but provided a scenic 'Ride or drive . . . of a sufficient width for Carriages' from Longleat to the banished garden.

A lowly vegetable garden had to be removed far away from the house, but then that distance had to be turned into the pleasurable experience of a smooth carriage ride. A Rococo layout was designed primarily to be walked around; a Capability Brown park was designed to be driven around. Mid-century improvements in coach and carriage design had much the same impact on society that the motor car was to have in the twentieth century. They both changed the way scenery was viewed. As for eclectic garden buildings, he did not personally dislike them because their construction meant good money to him. He supplied Burghley with a Jacobean-style bath house and a Gothic greenhouse and Wynnstay with a Greek Doric dairy. For the park at Blenheim he Gothicised High Lodge and proposed a lively Gothic setting for Rosamond's Well.[24] His Gothic cascade for Doddington Park is pure poetry and there was that Chinese grotto for Packington. But the high society, the very high society, in which he moved had tired of the Rococo Garden. The new mood was for rolling swiftly across broad, green generalisations of landscape and Brown satisfied this fashion at Chatsworth, Holkham, Syon, Wilton, Alnwick, Clandon and Heveningham to name just a few.

Keats asked that his epitaph should read 'Here lies one whose name was writ in water', but taking it in its literal sense it would have been appropriate for Brown. The parkscapes now commonly ascribed to him are second or third hand as far as their trees go. Their replantings are in a slightly different order and often of different species; but the lakes, the Brownian serpentines, are relatively authentic. His true landscape greats must be the lake at Blenheim and the combe at Prior Park. The first was a brilliant stroke of ruthless common sense which treated Vanbrugh's habitable viaduct as it deserved, drowning half of it but responding to its awesome scale. At Prior Park he simply but shrewdly swept away the Rococo confusions leaving the Palladian Bridge and its lake without distractions, funnelled at the foot of a steep, smooth lawn.[25] These were two clever corrections of other men's errors; Brown had a true eye for the genius of a place, though little time for the delights of discovery or any intimacy of scale. A park can make an impact without garden buildings but not without water. He took great pains on his inspection visits to get his lake levels exactly right, eight inches up or six down, though even with lakes he erred on the side of neatness: 'Make the sides sloping & keep the edges a neat Turf', he minuted on 21 September 1771 at Burton Constable; 'Lay the Earth at the nearest advantage making the adjacent Grounds slope gradually to the edge of the Lake'.[26]

In 1770, when Brown's career was at its peak and the advance of his style apparently irreversible, Thomas Whately published his *Observations on Modern Gardening*, running by 1771 into its third edition. As might be expected, this included an encomium on Brown, but also urged the study of Dove Dale, Matlock, Tintern Abbey, Middleton Dale and Piercefield. The smooth regularity of Beauty was being challenged by the roughness of the Sublime.

By 1780 Brown's autocracy was being challenged and there is a malicious anecdote, the source inevitably is Horace Walpole, in which the story goes that, when George III, the sharer with Brown of so many 'private hours', heard that the Royal gardener had suffered a fatal collapse from asthma on his own doorstep, the King hurried over 'to Richmond gardens and, in a tone of great satisfaction, said to the under-gardener, "Brown is dead! Now Mellicant, *you* and I can do *here* what we please"'.[27] Brown died in 1783, obliging as ever, at the right time, just before his enemies began to win the war of words against him. Already in 1776 Mrs Lybbe Powys, on a visit to Hardwick in Hampshire, may have been expressing a general sentiment when she remarked:

> Hardwick's merits is all its own, never has been indebted to modern improvements, and in this age may, for that reason, be thought more uncommon, as the rage for laying out grounds makes every nobleman and gentleman a copier of their neighbour, till every fine place throughout England is comparatively, at least, alike![28]

It is certainly possible to see Brown as the purveyor of a heartless, even philistine, topographical elegance to a sporting aristocracy unconcerned with the social needs of their tenants or the textured charm of their lands. Within a few years of Brown's death Humphry Repton would set himself up as Brown's natural successor, only to turn into a persuasive salesman for the bourgeois clutter and maximum expenditure of the Gardenesque, a complete reversal of the entire Brownian aesthetic.

CHAPTER THIRTEEN

THE WILD MEN OF THE WELSH BORDER – RICHARD PAYNE KNIGHT AND UVEDALE PRICE

P arks in the Capability Brown manner would remain in fashion as the acceptable setting for a large country house throughout the next two centuries; and they will probably still be maintained, elegantly dull, carefully clipped and drained, well into the twenty-first century. Like black tie evening wear for men of a certain class, they raise no comment and require no thought. But during the thirty years when Brown was establishing his pattern, two other developments in gardening were taking shape. On the Continent, in France and Germany, the so-called *Jardin Anglais* was becoming fashionable, while in England, as Whately had hinted as early as 1770, the Picturesque park style was finding a niche, though a very limited one. Both of these developments were related to the Rococo Garden and not to the Brownian style at all. It is an error to associate Brown with the continental *Jardin Anglais*. What French and German connoisseurs in park design enjoyed was to emulate Kew, Stowe and Stourhead, littering their layouts with buildings of eclectic fantasy: Chinese tea houses, ruined octagonal towers, Tahitian huts, even on occasion an artificial volcano which could stage eruptions. Brown's gracious vacancies had no appeal. The relationship between the earlier Rococo and the new Picturesque gardens in England was not so direct, but more one of topographical accident. A dramatic natural terrain tempted landowners into enhancing it with park buildings.

In its purest form, as advocated by Sir Uvedale Price (1747–1829) and practised by him on his estate at Foxley in mid-Herefordshire, a Picturesque park has no eclectic garden buildings at all. The Gainsborough painting of Foxley used to illustrate most accounts of Price's activities shows a lane running through attractive woodland with a very small church tower in the distance. There is nothing conventionally park-like about it, just an unspoilt, unkempt corner of Herefordshire woodland. And that was exactly Uvedale Price's aim. He owned a shallow valley, bought up land around it to form a compact whole and planted trees, beeches for preference, on the low hill crests to enclose his own ideal seclusion. There was one ride for visitors out to a minor viewing point, the Ladylift, but artists were not attracted to it in shoals as they were to other, more dramatic, Picturesque sites like Piercefield, Downton and Hawkstone. Gainsborough only visited it as a friend of the family.

There is a paradox here that, although a Picturesque park should, by its name, have painterly qualities, Foxley had very few. The truth is that, despite being politically a Whig, Price was emotionally a conservative and a paternalist, devoted to the preservation of the old order of countryside care. For all his highly plausible journalistic argument about the way Claude Lorrain, Jacob van Ruisdael and Salvator Rosa could and should influence park design, Price was more intent upon ecological conservation than on learning from landscape painters. He never accepted the contradictions in his argument that if Claude was really to be a park designer's model, then that park would have to be strewn with ruined Gothic towers, broken Roman aqueducts and forlorn classical temples. If he had been strictly honest, Price should have urged the imitation only of Claude's beautiful mature trees and his delicately complex foreground studies of undergrowth, rocks, ferns and pools. It was Nature unadorned that Price aimed to preserve and copy and that, in the late eighteenth century, was not a general enthusiasm, though it was one that Wordsworth would soon make fashionable in poetry. In that sense then the Picturesque movement was not closely related to park design at all, but more to conservation.

Where the earlier Rococo parks did link up with the Picturesque was in a shared response to a lively, rugged topography. Rococo layouts like Painshill were cleverly shaped to suggest hills, valleys and lakes where none naturally existed. At Stourhead it was the steep-sided valley which flattered Henry Hoare's temples. A flat Rococo park like Kew never takes fire for all its eclectic extravagance of buildings. So when Price's neighbour and disciple, Richard Payne Knight (1750–1824) came of age, with the naturally rugged gorge of the river Teme on the doorstep, almost literally, of his Downton house, he was unable to restrict himself to Price's refined ecological response. Typical Rococo park features like a hermit's cave and a Gothic cold bath were soon sited among the trees. Price never attempted to alter the ugly brick classical house he had inherited at Foxley; Payne Knight, on the other hand, indulged himself in Downton Castle, a fascinating and highly eclectic complex, half Gothic castle and half Romano-Greek villa in its exterior, conventionally classical and contemporary in its interiors.

Hawkstone, further up the Welsh border in north Shropshire, was blessed with an even more rugged topography than Downton; it had no river but an abrupt ridge of sandstone hills and the Claudeian wreck of a genuine Gothic castle tottering on the edge of a steep ravine. Its owners, the Hill family, father and son, Sir Rowland (1705–83) and Sir Richard (1732–1809), found their terrain irresistible; it favoured a Picturesque and a Rococo treatment so, over the years, they gave it both. For the average, lively-minded eighteenth-century park owner a Picturesque terrain cried out for a Rococo treatment. What else, in essence, was Hagley, Worcestershire, as Bishop Pococke had described it in 1751 and 1755, but Picturesque and Rococo? How could the Hills ever have given their sandstone ridge at Hawkstone the smooth conventional Brownian treatment even if they had wanted to?

If anyone can be described as the Father of the Picturesque in park design it has to be William Gilpin (1724–1804), who never owned or designed a park but was the intensely precious author of travel books, also a clergyman and an enlightened headmaster who never beat his pupils. Nothing in English park design falls into a neat sequence of cause and effect. In 1768 Gilpin published *An Essay on Prints*, airing his own views on art and landscape, but his first influential travel book, *Observations on the River Wye and several parts of South Wales*, did not come out until 1782, though it was based on a tour he had made in 1770. Meanwhile at least three other men had written similar travel books on the English countryside before him – Thomas Gray, Arthur Young and Dr John Brown – all in print by 1768 and often, as at Piercefield in Monmouthshire, anticipating Gilpin's actual park visits. To push the chronology of the Picturesque back even further, Piercefield's grounds had been handled with a conscious awareness of their Picturesque potential for the Sublime ever since 1752, when Valentine Morris inherited the estate from his father, a slave owner and sugar planter of Antigua. Edmund Burke's actual formulation of the Sublime came five years later in 1757; so the fashion had preceded the formula.

For all these precedents and anticipatory confusions, Gilpin's was to be the defining voice. His perceptions, definitions and directions on the truly Picturesque were to be the theoretical substructure for both Uvedale Price and Payne Knight. When in 1770 Gilpin and his party cast off to row down the Wye from Ross to Chepstow he was following an already well established tourist trail and the equally well established practice of recording, in that pre-photographic age, picture-worthy or picturesque sites by sketches and water-colours. To assist the amateur artist a Claude Glass, named after the artist, had become almost as essential as a picnic basket, and these little instruments, by their function and their effect, explain much of the perverse preciosity of the Picturesque movement. These glasses, which folded back into a neat travelling case, were small, convex mirrors, oval in shape and backed with black foil. Turning his or her back on a landscape the owner held the Claude Glass up and viewed the scene in a darkened oval miniature. Gilpin claimed that this brought composition, forms and colours close together in one complex view, though how it brought out, as he claimed, '*the beauty of the tints*', is hard to envisage.[1] A few of these once popular instruments have survived in science museums, and if replicas were made they would give modern garden historians a visual time machine restoring a lost angle of appreciation. Lacking them, anyone with access to a Gilpin first edition, like his *Observations on the River Wye*, can experience the Claude Glass image at second hand. The book is profusely illustrated with oval landscapes in colour tones of black, ochre and washed-out yellow. These concentrate upon the basic forms of hills, woodlands and rocks, not on a detail or on authentic colour. Green, for instance, has no place in a Gilpin water-colour. When he wrote of 'tints' he must have meant contrasts of light and shade.

Armed with such a glass the aficionado of the Picturesque could focus upon the composition of a landscape and on the correct or, in Gilpin's opinion, more commonly the incorrect, shape of a hill, undistracted by mere superficial beauties of leaf, flower or light reflected from water. Like most experts and pedants Gilpin loved to turn his art and his expertise into a pseudo-science cloaked in jargon. His introduction to the Wye began:

> Every view on a river is composed of four grand parts; the *area* which is the river itself; the *two side-screens*, which are the opposite banks and mark the perspective; and the *front-screen*, which points out the winding of the river . . . The ornaments of the Wye may be ranged under four heads – *ground* – *woods* – *rocks* – and *buildings*.[2]

Those last two 'ornaments', the rocks and the buildings, differentiate a Gilpin view from a Brownian park. Smoothness was the essence of a Brown landscape, roughness, particularly roughness in the foreground, was Gilpin's pleasure. For an artist with such a limited range of colours he was unexpectedly sensitive to the subtle textures of a view. That day on the Wye, in pouring rain, he noted 'sometimes so trifling a cause, as the rubbing of sheep against the sides of little banks or hillocs, will often occasion very beautiful breaks'.[3] Industry could enhance a scene. At Tintern's cannon foundry, 'Many of the furnaces on the banks of the river, consume charcoal, which is manufactured on the spot; and the smoke, which is frequently seen issuing from the sides of the hills; and spreading its thin veil over a part of them, beautifully breaks their sides, and unites them with the sky'.[4] That was written in 1770. Twenty-eight years later Wordsworth would write about exactly the same scene with Gilpin's feeling for the unity of all things, but he would romanticise the smoke trails of the charcoal burners into:

Thomas Hearne's 'Hermitage at Warkworth', from his 1786 Antiquities of Great Britain, *exemplifies the contemporary enthusiasm for sites of rocky grandeur with a numinous air of monkish associations – this was Salvator Rosa in England instead of the Apennines. John Beale's sincere Christian interest in hermits has become an historicist game.*

At one exact point in his boat trip down the Wye in 1770 William Gilpin decided that the ruins of Goodrich Castle were poised in a perfect Picturesque composition. He painted them in blacks, whites and yellows in an oval frame, as if seen through a Claude Glass, and published the view in his influential Observations on the River Wye *of 1782.*

. . . some Hermit's cave, where by his fire
The Hermit sits alone.[5]

The same Gothicising process went on at Hawkstone with towers and a hermit's cell. Gilpin would tolerate no such flight from realism.

On his wet day down the Wye only Goodrich Castle, taken from one precise angle, passed as 'correctly picturesque':

After sailing four miles from Ross, we came to *Goodrich-castle*; where a grand view presented itself; and we rested on our oars to examine it. A reach of the river, forming a noble bay, is spread before the eye. The bank, on the right, is steep, and covered with wood; beyond which a bold promontory shoots out, crowned with a castle, rising amongst trees.

This view, which is one of the grandest on the river, I should not scruple to call *correctly picturesque*; which is seldom the character of a purely natural scene.

Nature is always great in design. She is an admirable colourist also; and harmonizes tints with infinite variety and beauty: but she is seldom so correct in composition, as to produce an harmonious whole. Either the foreground or the background is disproportioned; or some awkward line runs across the piece; or a tree is ill-placed; or a bank is formal; or something or other is not exactly what it should be. The case is, the immensity of nature is beyond human comprehension. She works on a *vast scale*; and, no doubt, harmoniously, if her schemes could be comprehended. The artist, in the mean time, is confined to a *span*; and lays down his little rules, which he calls the *principles of picturesque beauty*, merely to adapt such diminutive parts of nature's surfaces to his own eye as come within its scope. – Hence, therefore, the painter who adheres strictly to the *composition* of nature, will rarely make a good picture. His picture must contain *a whole*; his archetype is but *a part*. In general, however, he may obtain views of such parts of nature, as with the addition of a few trees or a little alteration in the foreground, (which is a liberty that must always be allowed,) may be adapted to his rules; though he is rarely so fortunate as to find a landscape so completely satisfactory to him. In the scenery indeed at Goodrich-castle the parts are few; and the whole is a simple exhibition. The complex scenes of nature are generally those which the artist finds most refractory to his rules of composition.

In following the course of the Wye, which makes here one of its boldest sweeps, we were carried almost round the castle, surveying it in a variety of forms. Some of these retrospects are good; but, in general, the castle loses, on this side, both its own dignity and the dignity of its situation.

The views *from* the castle were mentioned to us as worth examining; but the rain was now set in, and would not permit us to land.

As we leave *Goodrich-castle*, the banks on the left, which had hitherto contributed less to entertain us, began now principally to attract our attention, rearing themselves gradually into grand sweeps; sometimes covered with thick woods, and sometimes forming vast concave slopes of mere verdure; unadorned, except here and there by a straggling tree: while the sheep which hang browzing upon them, seen from the bottom, were diminished into white specks.

William Gilpin, *Observations on the River Wye*, 1782

'Nature', he complained peevishly, 'is always great in design; but unequal in composition'.[6] Drifting, rejecting, sketching and appraising, Gilpin proceeded downstream, anticipating all the landscape concerns that Price and Payne Knight would identify twenty years later as essential tests of the true Picturesque. To him a bare stretch of river bank was an offence: 'The chief deficiency', he complained 'in point of wood, is of large trees on the edge of the water'. If the foreground was rocky then those rocks had to be delicately overgrown:

Tint it with mosses, and lychens of various hues, and you give it a degree of beauty. Adorn it with shrubs, and hanging herbage, and you still make it more picturesque. Connect it with wood, and water, and broken ground; and you make it in the highest degree interesting.[7]

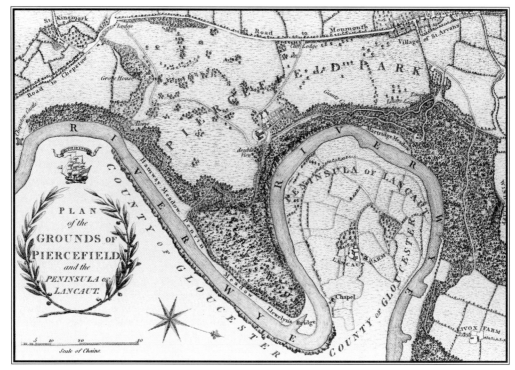

This map of the grounds of Valentine Morris's Piercefield, from William Coxe's 1801 Historical Tour in Monmouthshire, *explains the visits of Gilpin, Arthur Young, Uvedale Price and Humphry Repton. The drama of the winding river, with high wooded cliffs all along its western banks, was irresistible to the generation of Picturesque enthusiasts. It was usual for trippers down the Wye to land on Martridge Meadow and walk the course to Chepstow Castle.*

Payne Knight would follow every word of this stipulation when he commissioned Thomas Hearne to draw the ideal Picturesque park to illustrate his 1794 poem *The Landscape*.

Towards the end of a damp but memorable day Gilpin's boat swung round a bend of the now tidal river to reveal Piercefield and its precipices, the last grand climax to a Wye river trip. Squelching through red tidal ooze, a feature most visitors remarked upon, Gilpin landed on the narrow Martridge Meadow to climb the 300 foot limestone cliffs 'by an easy, regular, zig zag'.[8] Half way up he should have reacted to a stone giant, poised to hurl a boulder down on his head as he passed through the artificial Giant's Cave. But either he took another route or, more likely, ignored it as an intrusion on Nature.[9] It was Gilpin who gave Uvedale Price his dislike of imposed garden features. At the top of the cliff, with a glorious example of Edmund Burke's Sublime all around him, a frightening drop down to the Wye coiling through steep wooded hills and the Wyndcliff towering up to his right, Gilpin began characteristically to find fault. Then, and for the next thirty years, a Picturesque park seems to have been, for the addict, not so much a pleasure as a stiff test for the refined sensibility. The Lancaut peninsula, Piercefield's very own *ferme ornée*, was spread out below him, its every field, cottage, farmhouse and chapel ravishingly visible. But Gilpin insisted:

> We cannot however call these views picturesque. They are either presented from too high a point, or they have little to mark them as characteristic, or they do not fall into such composition, as would appear to advantage on canvas.[10]

When Jane Austen came to write *Northanger Abbey* (written in 1798–9, but published posthumously in 1818), Gilpin's hyper-critical visual sensibility was still modish. She mocked it and made Henry Tilney lecture Catherine Morland on the Picturesque jargon: 'fore-grounds, distances and second distances, side-screens and perspectives, lights and shades', then insisted that Catherine rejected the view of Bath from the top of the Beechen Cliff, 'as unworthy to make part of a landscape'.[11]

The next feature of Piercefield to upset Gilpin was Valentine Morris's underplanting of his woods with laurel:

> It is not the shrub which offends: it is the *formal introduction* of it. Wild underwood may be an appendage of the grandest scene. It is a beautiful appendage. A bed of violets, or lilies may enamel the ground, with propriety, at the root of an oak: but if you introduce them artificially as a border, you introduce a trifling formality; and disgrace the noble object, you wish to adorn.[12]

Even his punctuation is precious, but finally, faced with three miles of vertiginous vistas from the Wyndcliff to Chepstow Castle, he did relent allowing 'they are extremely romantic; and give a loose to the most pleasing riot of imagination'. He did not, however, particularise on this.[13]

Almost every visual treat open to Gilpin, Arthur Young and Thomas Whately can still be enjoyed. Roads have hardly intruded upon Piercefield's Picturesque route, though Chepstow racecourse has taken over the remainder of the park. The sequence of viewpoints from north to south, slightly overgrown at times, remains five-star in rating, only the Wyndcliff, with the widest views, has been cut off from the others by a main road. First comes the Temple, then the Lover's Leap, most suicidal of all, and the Giant's Cave down a side path to a ledge where, in the eighteenth century, a cannon would be fired to raise a distinct, five-fold echo from the cliffs. At the Apostle Rocks is the 'Double View' of the tortuous river. Arthur Young, who reached Piercefield two years before the dyspeptic Gilpin, hailed this as a view, 'at the very idea of which, my pen drops from my hand: The eyes of your imagination are not keen enough to take in this point, which the united talents of *Claud*, and a *Poussin*, would scarcely be able to sketch'.[14] His backwards glance, an attempt to see a view through the eyes of two dead artists, was characteristic of the period, a time as obsessed with the vision of Claude and Poussin as the early twentieth century was by the perceptions of the nineteenth-century French Impressionists.

Young complained at the Apostle Rocks that the Beautiful qualities of the view were overwhelmed by the Sublime: 'those views at *Persfield* which *are* beautiful, are all intermixed with the sublime; the farm beneath you [Lancaut] is superlatively so; the precipice you look down from, the hanging woods, and the rocks, are totally different'.[15] Whately, on the other hand, found beauty quite unadulterated by sublimity simply by looking west into Monmouthshire: 'a pleasant, fertile and beautiful country, divided into enclosures, not covered with woods, nor broken by rocks and precipices, but only varied by easy swells and gentle declivities'.[16]

After the Double View the visual tensions relax for a while as the path crosses the Pierce Wood peninsula, where a grotto has been hollowed out of the bank of a hill fort. Then comes the climax of the transformation: an entirely new view with the ruins of Chepstow Castle hanging on a low cliff over the river, the roofs of the little walled town, and beyond that a great reach of the Severn estuary with all its shifting sands and muds, widening to the Bristol Channel and dimly seen islands. Until the racecourse was imposed Piercefield must have presented the perfect Burkean duo: a 'Sublime' precipice walk lying beside the smooth 'Beauty' of a Brown-style park of clumped and belted lawns.

Uvedale Price would not have been happy with such a clear definition of, or division between, the Sublime and the Beautiful. One of the chief pegs on which he hung his spiteful, lively and eminently readable 1794 polemic, *An Essay on the Picturesque*, was his insistence that 'picturesqueness' (an abstract noun he claimed to have coined personally) was an aesthetic quality midway between Burke's Sublime and Beautiful and distinct from either. Price was a tabloid journalist *manqué* who has earned his place in garden history not by his own plantings at Foxley, but by the violence of his attacks on Lancelot Brown, Horace Walpole, William Kent and Humphry Repton. Those and his intermittent friendship and polemical partnership with Richard Payne Knight, his near neighbour at Downton Castle, have made him impossible to ignore. It can, however, be argued that he had more to do with the creation of an appreciative awareness of the natural landscape of rural England than with park or garden design. He was a romantic, a 'Green' before his time, a figure in that chain of writers – John Beale, Stephen Switzer, Joseph Spence – that leads, not to a new park style, but to Wordsworth's *Prelude*, which was written in its first brilliant state, unedited and fresh, in 1799, five years after Price's *Essay*.[17]

There are passages of advice in the *Essay* which can be described as relevant to park design, and they will be considered later. But first, it is Price writing as a sensitive conservationist who merits attention. He is, as usual, attacking Brown's 'improvements', the worst of which he judges to be:

> smoothing and levelling the ground: the moment this mechanical common place operation (by which Mr Brown and his followers have gained so much credit) is begun, adieu to all that the painter admires – to all intricacies – to all the beautiful varieties of form, tint, light and shade, every deep recess – every bold projection – the fantastic roots of trees – the winding paths of sheep – all must go; in a few hours the rash hand of false taste completely demolishes what time only, and a thousand lucky accidents, can mature, so as to become the admiration and study of a Ruysdale or a Gainsborough.[18]

It reads like some modern conservationist's protest against golf courses and there is both real feeling and truth in his anger. Price saw beech tree roots 'fasten on the earth with their dragon claws'; for him beauty lay not in parks but in country lanes and hedges 'and in old neglected quarries, and in chalk and gravel pits'.[19] His most practical suggestion for correctly improving a park was directed against Brown's clumps. These were Price's particular aversion: 'whose name, if the first letter was taken away, would most accurately describe its form and effect'.[20] Like Gilpin, Price loved undergrowth, so his proposal was that firs (not his favourite tree but quick growing) should be planted eight, twelve or even more feet apart and the spaces between them planted with lower evergreens. When the resultant tangle had matured for some years it could then be cut into groves and amphitheatres of thicket and loosely scattered trees. These would form, so he claimed, 'a gradation from the highest firs to the lowest undergrowth'.[21] It is easy to see why Foxley park was not on any well-beaten trail of estate visitations.

Price's elaborate page summaries, included with his chapter headings, give a fair survey of his views on the Picturesque landscape:

> Objects of reflection peculiarly suited to still water.
> Mr Brown's rivers have no objects of reflection.
> Verdure and smoothness, which are the characteristic beauties of a lawn, are in
>   their nature allied to monotony.
> Accident and neglect the sources of variety in unimproved parks and forests.

The established trees of the country ought to prevail in the new plantations.

Fir plantation improper for boundaries.

A common hedge often a more effectual boundary, and some highly beautiful.

This points out the necessity of a mixture of thorns, hollies, and the lower growth in all screens.

which read like the truisms of modern writings on ecology.

Much of Uvedale Price's reputation in the twentieth century stems from Christopher Hussey's pioneering *The Picturesque, Studies in a Point of View* (1927), and from a series of articles which Nikolaus Pevsner contributed to the *Architectural Review* over the months of 1944, including, 'The Genesis of the Picturesque' and 'Exterior Furnishings in Sharawaggi: the Art of Urban Landscape'. Pevsner believed that Price's critical analysis of the monotonous horizontals of the terraces in Bath and his diagnosis of that city's need for counteracting vertical structures and more trees, would save the planners of post-war housing estates from making the same mistakes. Very little came of this, but it did draw attention to Price's visual alertness and to the fact that here was a man born, in an ecological sense, two centuries too soon.

Richard Payne Knight was an altogether more formidable figure, with much wider interests than mere garden design. Price had been educated at Eton and Queen's College, Oxford. Knight was brought up at home by a repressive clergyman father who had married his housemaid, yet his son emerged as a man of questing scholarship in the fields of classical architecture, numismatology, religious philosophy and sexual anthropology. Aware that his friend Uvedale was slowly preparing a book on the Picturesque, Knight absorbed his ideas and redefined the Picturesque, not as a distinct quality in its own right, but more as an informed state of mind, a way of looking at scenes. In his usual arrogant and competitve style he then quickly wrote a poem on the subject, *The Landscape*, in three books, loading it heavily with his contempt for orthodox Christianity, and published it in 1794, pre-empting Price's tardy *Essay on the Picturesque*.

For much of its length *The Landscape* faithfully repeats Price's views on the malign influence of Lancelot Brown, 'Spreading o'er all its unprolific spawn/In never-ending sheets of vapid lawn'.[22] But a bracing, even ruthless realism enlivens his observations, most of all the vast footnotes added to the poem's second edition of 1795. How practical, he demanded, was it to try to imitate painters?

Scarcely any parts of our island are capable of affording the compositions of Salvator Rosa, Claude and the Poussins; and only the most picturesque parts those of Ruysdael, Berghem and Pynaker; but those of Hobbema, Waterloo and Adrian Vandervelde (which have also their beauties) are to be obtained everywhere.[23]

While thus consigning most English parks to such humble visuals of the Low Countries, Knight had his own Downton, inherited in 1764 from a rich iron-master grandfather, and this included the wooded gorge of the Teme. It was less dramatic than the lower Wye but more manageable and boasted its own industrial forge to add a Gilpinesque veil of coal dust and smoke to an already sinister stretch of river, where deep, brown pools alternated with noisy rapids. In landscape Knight's aim was:

. . . Nature's common works, by genius dress'd
With art selected and with taste express'd.[24]

To span the fast-flowing Teme and link up the circuit walk in the grounds of Downton Castle, Payne Knight had an Alpine Bridge of a curious rough fragility constructed and then, to advertise his Picturesque stylistic preferences, paid Thomas Hearne to paint it. Floods have long since swept the bridge away.

Less of an ecological puritan than Price, he believed, being himself the 'genius' in question, that he had the right and the duty: 'by carefully collecting and cherishing the accidental beauties of wild nature; by judiciously arranging them and skilfully combining them with each other, and the embellishments of art' to 'produce complete and faultless compositions in nature'.[25] This is what he maintained he had done with his Teme gorge.

This true garden of the wild Picturesque, 'judiciously arranged', survives like Piercefield, though it is far less accessible, as those delicately ricketty 'Alpine' bridges of Thomas Hearne's paintings, set on tottering wooden legs, were washed away long ago by floodwater, breaking the circuit walk. As mentioned at the opening of this chapter the Hermit's Cave and the wreck of that homo-erotic Gothic Cold Bath, with its provision for icy nudity in the heart of wild woodland, are still there and the river preserves its oddly threatening quality, overshadowed throughout its length with the trees that Gilpin and Price required on any river bank. To experience Payne Knight's sensitivity to mood and his need to control a visitor, it is rewarding to walk that stretch of path on its south bank where a low wall rises, gradually cutting off the river

Payne Knight's Alpine Bridge across the Teme led to this spartan Cold Bath in the woods where Knight could strip down in a rugged artificial cave before retiring to a snug little hovel at the side. The artist, William Owen, has shown a section of the Alpine Bridge in the bottom left of the picture. Knight was a confirmed bachelor.

in one of its dark, still reaches. The wall turns into a tunnel, then suddenly, through an aperture to the right, the river is revealed again but now in altered state as an angry torrent: a perfect example of Knight dramatising and 'cherishing the accidental beauties of wild nature'.[26]

Knight brought Humphry Repton, the rising star of garden design, to see Downton in 1789, largely to assert his own superior sensibility to landscape. Repton was impressed by the river's varying moods, sometimes 'roaring in the dark abyss below', sometimes 'a calm, glassy mirror, that reflects the surrounding foliage'.[27] He found the carefully prepared route for visitors 'enriched by caves and cells, hovels, and covered seats, or other buildings, in perfect harmony with the wild but pleasing horrors of the scene', quoting Payne Knight's own poem with approval: 'Tis *just congruity* of parts combin'd/Must please the sense, and satisfy the mind'.[28]

The Landscape is not often read today, but most garden books feature the two etchings which Thomas Hearne prepared for it to illustrate Knight's attack on Brown. One shows the ideal Picturesque park: in the foreground is a dense tangle of rocks and ferns, richly detailed with Gilpinesque 'breaks'; the river beyond is almost lost under overhanging bushes and flood debris. A frail 'Alpine' bridge crosses it and, almost lost in trees, is an Elizabethan house, irregular, bow-windowed and gabled, fronted by a terrace garden. The second is 'A landscape in the manner of "Capability" Brown'. It has the same planting of trees yet it is entirely different in impact. Its river has shorn banks, it describes a perfect S-curve of Hogarthian beauty and a dainty Chinese bridge

In a master stroke of persuasion, Richard Payne Knight commissioned from Thomas Hearne two illustrations for his long topographical poem, The Landscape, of 1794. This, the first, shows a dull modern country house in a park made tedious and bare by a conventional Capability Brown treatment of shaven lawns, manicured tree clumps, neat river banks and a foolish Chinese bridge.

In his second illustration Thomas Hearne demonstrated Payne Knight's ideal setting for a large Picturesque Elizabethan mansion of gables, bow windows, irregular rooflines and a terraced front. The grounds are wild, unkempt and richly textured with rocks, bushes, ferns and natural growth. There are far more trees and the stream wanders, half obscured by fallen tree trunks, under a rickety trestle bridge.

struts across it. All the park is bare lawn neatly clumped and sweeping to the walls of a plain box-like house; the foreground is entirely bare. Payne Knight and Hearne have made their point with admirable clarity. But show these two pictures today to a fair selection of the average intelligent public, asking them which version they prefer, and a good half of them will choose the bemocked Capability Brown parody. Knight was fighting against the grain of the English taste in landscape.

Hawkstone makes an appropriately compromising and confusing end to this chapter of stylistic indecision and refined uncertainty. There at least, Rowland and Richard Hill, who created the park, saw no contradiction between the extrovert Rococo and the intellectual Picturesque. If Stourhead is the perfection of Arcadian Rococo, then Hawkstone robustly rams the Rococo and the Picturesque together. After years of neglect its dizzying shelf walks and claustrophobic grotto tunnels have been cleared and the visitors have returned to restore the park to its essential populist gusto. It offered the Sublime at a level acceptable to the mid-eighteenth century. Downton Gorge, like Knight its 'cherisher', has something of the dark side about it. Even its near-atheist owner half believed that wood spirits haunted the place. Hawkstone is entirely of the day: its warm red sandstone softens all its horrors and it is so packed full with eclectic incidents and gentle terrors that it carries visitors along its routes at a cracking pace, ticking off items on their guide books, eager for the next cave, tower or precipice. This is a true pleasure garden, set well away from the Baroque house and the main park with its river-like Hawk Lake, which was laid out in 1784–90 by William Emes, one of Brown's ablest followers.

The pleasure ground was elaborated by the Hills themselves and from its inception they intended to make visitors welcome. Following the example of Castle Howard and Stourhead, they had an hotel built and Hawkstone soon became a favoured honeymoon venue for couples from Liverpool and the Potteries. With its Swiss Bridge, a 'Scene in Otaheite' to recall the voyages of Captain Cook, an Indian Rock and St Francis' Cave in addition to all the regular Rococo features – Hermitage, Gingerbread Hall, Grotto, White Tower, Vineyard and Menagerie – Hawkstone must be the most eclectic of all surviving parks. To represent the fashionable Picturesque it had the Red Castle, an Awful Precipice, a Cleft, a Rock Arch, the Fox's Knob, the Raven's Shelf, the Gulph, Reynard's Walk and a broad, conventional viewing terrace. With these it offered and still offers at active first-hand, an eighteenth-century equivalent of the harmless thrills that blockbuster films like 'Raiders of the Lost Ark' provide at passive second-hand two centuries later.

The Grotto is Hawkstone's most impressive experience. To reach it a narrow natural cleft in the sandstone cliff must be threaded. Then, bent over and in single file, visitors edge up a twisting tunnel with occasional glimpses of daylight through holes that were once windowed with stained glass. After an interminable climb the passageway opens into a broad chamber, the Labyrinth. Its artificial, though apparently natural, roof is supported on rough columns and here again the Claude Glass experience has been recreated, this time by oval apertures in the rock walls to focus the eye on features of the park. The exit leads out onto a high viewing terrace with a Gothic arch to frame the views again; the whole impressive complex was under construction in 1765.

The return route is anything but an anticlimax. First comes an arch high above the drive to the house; then, after the Hermitage (originally with its resident hermit gazing at a skull) comes the quite un-English experience of emerging from a tunnel under the Fox's Knob onto a ledge walk, the Raven's Shelf, half-way up the cliff. This winds and turns around projecting spurs, revealing at each twist some new aspect of the Grand Valley, the Elysian Hill and the Citadel, a symmetrical Regency dower house, more Gothick than Gothic. The tour ends where it began, at the Greenhouse, which is Gothick again. Uvedale Price would not have approved the

The Picturesque circuit, laid out over the last decades of the eighteenth century by Rowland and Richard Hill in the rugged sandstone hills of their park at Hawkstone, Shropshire, has survived almost entire to illustrate the kind of visual pleasures which Payne Knight was urging in his The Landscape. Here the Swiss Bridge crosses a gorge on the route to the gentle terrors of the Grotto.

Nature has met the Hills half-way at Hawkstone by sculpting out the soft sandstone into attractive shapes and what Dr Johnson called 'the horrors of its precipices'. Here at Reynard's Walk the visitors' circuit passes underneath an overhanging cliff face. Round the corner is the Fox's Knob, a Hermitage, a Cleft, a Rock Arch and similar Picturesque pleasures.

showmanship, Payne Knight and Repton might have found it unthematic. But this is the moment to recall Dr Johnson's exact words after he had toured Hawkstone:

> Though it wants water it excells Dovedale, by the extent of its prospects, the awfulness of its shades, the horrors of its precipices, the verdure of its hollows and the loftiness of its rocks. The ideas which it forces upon the mind, are the sublime, the dreadful, and the vast. Above is inaccessible altitude, below, is horrible profundity.[29]

When eighteenth-century writers discussed the concept of the Sublime they were not thinking in terms of the Alps or of Niagara, a waterfall indeed which Payne Knight dismissed scornfully as merely vast, though he had never set eyes on it. They were thinking in terms of Hawkstone's subtle terrors. What Dr Johnson called 'Sublime' we might describe as merely exciting or entertaining. Words have shifted treacherously in meaning, confusing our understanding of the Picturesque movement. Burke's treatise has become almost inaccessible by etymological change.

CHAPTER FOURTEEN
HUMPHRY REPTON – PUBLIC RELATIONS AND THE GARDENESQUE

H umphry Repton (1752–1818) is more elusive of definition than any other English landscape gardener of the eighteenth century because his heart and his instincts were in the nineteenth.[1] Before Victoria was even born, Repton was a Victorian, but of that same early Victorian, half Regency generation as Charles Dickens. He was grossly sentimental, stylistically open to whatever fashion a patron might prefer, a superb salesman, an indifferent businessman and a snob worthy of a whole chapter in Thackeray's *Book of Snobs*. Having failed in everything else he had tried, Repton decided to become a landscape gardener in 1788, when he was already 36 years old and the father of four children, three boys and a girl. His own father had been a Norwich-based excise officer and Repton would retain, throughout his life, a preference for the mild contours of East Anglian scenery. In 1812 he wrote, 'I can with truth pronounce that Sheringham possesses more natural beauty and local advantages than any place I have ever seen', and even allowing for the unctuous flattery which pervades all his 'Red Books' he probably meant this praise for Norfolk's gentle seaside undulations.[2]

Gentle, snobbish and sensitive, a mildly talented artist and a businessman forever being taken advantage of by potential clients, Humphry Repton has had himself drawn here in his own preferred image to illustrate his Fragments on the Theory and Practice of Landscape Gardening *of 1816.*

He was sent to Holland for his education, which gave him fluent Dutch but no obvious keys to social distinction, and his first venture as a textiles merchant working between the two countries got nowhere. Holland did, however, give him a taste for flowers and their technical production. There followed five happy years as a gentleman farmer at Sustead in Norfolk, raising a family, practising his talent as a topographical artist and helping his neighbours by staking out improvements on their grounds: new drives, groves and prospects. After a brief spell in Dublin as private secretary to

177

William Windham, the Viceroy's Chief Secretary, he came to Bath where he dabbled in journalism and sketching, losing money in a business venture over mail deliveries in which his partner, John Palmer, managed to profit considerably. Running short of funds he settled in a *cottage ornée*, thatched and bargeboarded, at Hare Street, near Romford, Essex, wrote a not very successful play and then decided that he might, with his political connections, do well as a landscape gardener. Lancelot Brown had been five years in the grave; now Humphry Repton would fill the void.

In a circular letter of 26 August that year, 1788, he named his guiding heroes or, as he called them, his 'breviary'.[3] These were Gilpin and Whately who have been quoted earlier, the French writer Rene Louis Gérardin, and the Revd William Mason, poet, painter and landscape adviser whose flower garden at Nuneham Courtenay, Oxfordshire, laid out for the 2nd Lord Harcourt in 1777, was just then gaining a national reputation. These four men, together with Brown, bracket accurately the range of Repton's stylistic preferences as he launched himself out onto a career for which he had virtually none of Brown's practical training in arboriculture, draining or the even more important field of man management and the complexities of contracting out work to builders and nursery gardeners. He had, however, one great sales gimmick: his Red Books. Already a reasonably competent artist, he had taken in Gérardin's advice in his *De la composition des paysages* of 1777, that no scene in nature should be attempted until it had first been painted.[4]

Vanbrugh and Kent have left their mark chiefly in garden buildings, Brown in his lakes. A Picturesque layout survives today by that particular natural feature, a sheer cliff or river gorge, which landowners like Payne Knight and the Hills had the vision to seize upon. Repton has left his mark principally on paper, not in groves, carriage-drives and plantings, though some of these survive, but in those seductively charming Red Books which he and his four children turned out industriously to capture the imagination of prospective clients. As a sales device and for Repton's posthumous reputation they were a stroke of genius. In good years, like 1791, he would produce twelve or more of these fascinating toys bound in red Moroccan leather. They varied in length according to the importance of the client. The Duke of Portland, for instance, would receive three for Welbeck, none of which resulted in any worthwhile additions to that least inspiring of ducal parks; but they remain, like the other Red Books, as treasures in museums, libraries and private collections, to be quarried eagerly by garden historians.

Their texts were handwritten in prose of cloying sweetness, often directed as if to coax infirm and carriage-bound old ladies. They invariably flatter the possibilities of an estate however unpromising the terrain. If a satisfying landscape could be contrived in Norfolk, as were Repton's earliest ventures of 1788, it could be contrived anywhere, except perhaps in the Fens.[5] But what has made the Red Books so celebrated is their trick of the overlays. Each book has several of these. With the overlay in place on a coloured illustration the house or its park is shown in its unimproved state, made by various unscrupulous touches of detail – a loitering tramp or a crumbling bank of ugly raw earth – to look even more unprepossessing than it was in reality.[6] But then, fold back the overlay and a new Elysium appears: the grounds as they will look if Repton's suggestions are accepted and the improvement is carried through. A lake will glitter where before there was only a marshy valley bottom, hedges will disappear and an aristocratic sweep of useless but beautiful lawn will take their place. Groves will expand or contract to reveal new vistas, happy peasants will labour and expensive carriages will bowl merrily along the drive towards a fine house embowered now among tastefully sited trees.

These illustrations with overlays were in essence miniature time machines, 'now' and 'then' captured at the flick of a piece of paper. They proved so popular that Repton reproduced them in three sumptuous volumes at various points in his career when the landscape business was flagging.

The view from Repton's own house on to the highway running through Hare Street village, Essex, before Repton's 'improvements' have been made. Passengers on the stagecoach can peer into his garden; the coarse geometry of the fence, the joints of meat hanging outside the butcher's, the bare tree-trunks, the ducks and the broad grass verge are all objects on Repton's blacklist.

When the overlay has been pulled back a typical Repton transformation is effected and Hare Street resembles a preview of Port Sunlight, the ideal suburb of Edwardian social manipulation. The garden has taken over the verge, banishing ducks and beggar man. Roses scramble up cottage trellises and tree-trunks, another on a tripod hides the joints of meat, flowering bushes give the new garden some privacy from the road and a herbaceous border, soon to be the staple of Victorian gardens, flourishes. Repton has, however, retained the animation of the street; he loves people.

Even now to handle them is a pleasure; there was *Sketches and Hints on Landscape Gardening* in 1795, *Observations on the Theory and Practice of Landscape Gardening* in 1803, and *Fragments on the Theory and Practice of Landscape Gardening* in 1816, just two years before his death. A Red Book was likely to remain in private possession but these, together with all his other lesser publications, made the Repton method and Repton's changing aesthetic opinions available to a much wider public. Before film was invented there could hardly have been a more effective way of giving the educated classes a sophisticated awareness of the possibilities of any given topography.

The one danger to these Red Books is that today they give the impression of wider landscape achievements than Repton actually attained. As a result of them his reputation stands at least as high as that of Brown; they seduce now as effectively as when they first came out. Stephen Daniels' definitive 1999 study, *Humphry Repton: Landscape Gardening and the Geography of Georgian England*, was lavishly illustrated to the usual high standards of Yale University Press, but not one of its 248 illustrations is a photograph of a Repton park in its present state. Far and away the majority are beautiful reproductions from Red Books, though not with the original moveable overlays. All the others are from contemporary paintings, maps and plans. As a result a mellow sepia haze hangs over the book, giving the impression of tremendous improvements across Britain. Only when the incisive and scholarly text is read in detail does the real picture emerge: that more often than not the client simply took the Red Book and then either left it as an entertainment for the ladies on a drawing-room table or carried through with his own team of labourers those alterations in the book which happened to take his fancy, or for which he had funds.

Where Brown, whom Repton claimed to succeed, would ride briskly around a park for a day, staking it out and then sending his own team of skilled labourers under a foreman to do exactly what he had ordered, Repton saw the whole process as a social treat where he and one of the gentry could gauge each other's sensibilities. 'The chief benefit I have derived from it', he wrote of his new profession, 'has been the society of those to whose notice I could not otherwise have aspired'.[7] He aimed to serve the will of a client rather than to impose his own will in its entirety. To be treated as a near social equal was the reward he coveted most. Some patrons obliged. At Harewood House he was in heaven for a fortnight, playing his flute each evening in a consort of members of Lord Harewood's family. The Duke of Portland, who was Home Secretary at the time, allowed Repton to sit working next to him in his study, hearing occasional Cabinet gossip. With the Duke of Bedford it was different. Repton had been hired, he was told:

> to freely give me your opinion, as to what alterations or improvements suggest themselves to your judgement, leaving the execution of them to my own direction or leisure.[8]

Portland enjoyed Repton's mild companionship, Bedford brusquely avoided it, but the results in each case were much the same: a yawning gap between a Red Book and a completed improvement. When he presented the Duke of Bedford with a Red Book for Endsleigh, the ducal holiday home in Devon, Repton apprehensively expressed the hope 'that my plans for Endsleigh, will not (as I have too often experienced) be a waste of Time, Thought and Contrivance'.[9] But that was exactly what they proved to be. The vast conservatory, terraced flower beds, treillage smothered in roses and grotto which, in Gardenesque mood, he had planned next to the Duke's *cottage ornée* never materialised; while for the middle distance the weir, cottage, mill and temple were also rejected. 'The occasional traffic and busy motion of persons crossing the Tamar', which Repton had projected in his usual populist, Gérardinesque confidence, was not in accord with Bedford's idea of holiday tranquillity.

In fact the Duke described him as 'a coxcombe' and George III used much the same term, 'coxcombery' to describe Repton's writings, though whether he had read a word of them is questionable. When garden designers become too eager to please, their employers begin to wonder what they are paying them for; and Repton charged high fees: five guineas a day once he had arrived, and then there was a rising scale from twenty to seventy guineas to cover the cost of his travel out from Romford in a hired post chaise. Lancelot Brown, who had been notoriously vague about fees because he could make so much more out of contracting labour, ended up as Sheriff of Huntingdonshire and the owner of a 13,000 acre estate. Repton, a mere gentleman adviser, continued to live in his large cottage on the main road of Hare Street in nervous terror of a bullying local landowner's attempt to legally subvert the terms of his lease.

It was his earthy lower-class competence which allowed Brown to become a friend to the King, to many lords and to at least one prime minister. Between the upper and lower classes there was usually an easy bonding as both knew their places; neither tried to assume the skills and functions of the other. Poor Repton, being middle class, well educated and an over-eager cultural prig, was more threatening. The cachet to employing Brown had been his known and easy familiarity with the monarch. Repton never managed to pull the same social trick with the King and he was far too dull and straight-laced to amuse the Prince Regent.

It was Repton's bad luck that the French Revolution broke out in 1789 and that war was declared in 1793 just a year after his commissions had peaked with twenty-eight new consultations in 1792. But the controversy which caused his consultations to drop like a stone to four in 1794 had its roots in a projected scheme and a Red Book of 1789 for Ferney Hall in south Shropshire. This had brought him up against Payne Knight and Uvedale Price, who were both spoiling for a fight with anyone they suspected of carrying on a Brownian tradition of smooth, wide lawns.

Ferney proved to be an absolute minefield as it was close to Payne Knight's Downton Castle. Always anxious to be liked, Repton made conciliatory approaches to Payne Knight and even sailed down the Wye with Uvedale Price, hoping that he was making the correct Picturesque responses. Gilpin had been, after all, one of his 'breviary' four. But both Price and Payne Knight, as self-appointed guardians of the Picturesque mysteries, remained critical and suspicious. Desperate to please, Repton asked Knight to show him around Ferney and advise him what to do. He was so unsure of himself that he even made a second visit to sit at the feet of the master; all to no avail; the owner Samuel Phipps dropped dead. But the damage was done; Price and Payne Knight had been alerted to the rise of a false prophet, a potential heir to Lancelot Brown. When Repton came back to Herefordshire again in 1792 and began behaving at Stoke Edith, like Brown at his most arrogant, attempting to move an entire village, a vicarage and a church spire simply to improve the view from the house, they would soon be ready with two pre-emptive strikes: Price's *Essay* and Payne Knight's *The Landscape*. Both were published in 1794 and not unconnected therefore with Repton's record low rate of consultations in the same year. They were right to mistrust him. Half the illustrations in his later, 1803, *Observations* show, under their overlays, ruthless Brownian impositions upon attractive existing landscapes.

Another very early commission, at Welbeck in Nottinghamshire for the Duke of Portland, may have settled Repton into patterns of ingratiating servility and a consequent directional impotence from which he never completely rallied. Socially and financially Welbeck was far more rewarding than Ferney, but it was still very thin on landscape achievements. Delighted to have a duke as a client, Repton grovelled assiduously in the manner of the times. In his unpublished 'Memoir', he recorded how by merely strolling the park with the Duke, 'I learnt more as a painter than if I had studied and copied the works of the best masters'.[10] Portland was a connoisseur of genre peasant detail and Repton marvelled at how,

> he would cautiously approach the spot where a group of men and children were resting or taking their noon day's meal, and pointing out some beautiful contrast in their attitude, or cheerful smile or countenance, he would stop in fear of destroying the magic of the picture by our intrusion.[11]

As for the 1790 Red Book, the first of the Welbeck three, Repton's protestation says it all:

> The great stile of improvement which Your Grace has with so much good taste & on so bold a scale adopted all round Welbeck leaves me with no other opportunity of displaying my skill than that of entering into the more minute detail of carrying your Grace's own ideas into execution.[12]

Portland was obsessed with a ridiculous scheme for piling up earth around the ground floor of Welbeck Abbey house. Repton did, however, suggest a dressed walk with grass verges, flowering shrubs and openings to views of the lake to make a new approach to the 'Dutchesses Garden', where he urged the cutting of more views in order to focus on some old oak trees. One wood should be given 'a concave line not only as a contrast to the plantation opposite which is convex, but to show a small esplanade of grass where the light will catch in the general view down the lake'.[13] For such subtleties of perception the Duke was ready to pay Repton a retainer of £100 a year and give him lodging at Welbeck for ten days each Easter. A second Red Book of 1793 picked up Gérardin's favourite theme: that parks should be made interesting by human activity. It illustrated a number of Gothic lodges, cottages and boat-houses, none of which were ever built as the Duke had run short of money. Repton used the text to stake out a claim to be sympathetic to the Picturesque doctrines of Price, trying to distance himself from Brown's dehumanised parkscapes:

> we ought never to forget that a park is a habitation of men, and not devoted to beasts of the forest . . . Woods enriched by buildings, water enlivened by a number of pleasure boats, alike contribute to mark a visible difference betwixt the magnificent scenery of a park, and that of a sequestered forest.[14]

A third Red Book of 1803 urged the complete rebuilding of Welbeck on a different site. Handsomely illustrated as usual, it was completely ignored. The Duke's favourite seat was not Welbeck but Bulstrode in the Chilterns. There Repton was permitted to make himself more useful by mapping out a superior new carriage circuit with forty-four viewing points. This was standard Brownian practice, however Repton managed to distance himself from Brown's old workforce which, he claimed, had lowered every hillock and filled in every declivity. But it was the Duke, not Repton, who supervised in person the restoration of tree roots to the light of day. Repton comments admiringly on this return of the ground to its original and natural shape in his *Observations* of 1803.[15] It was something for which Uvedale Price had campaigned persuasively in his *Essay* of 1794,[16] and another instance of Repton trying to ingratiate himself with the school of gardening which he felt to be in the ascendent.

Occasionally Fortune was kind. Not all the Red Books were wasted and not all Repton's parkscapes have been overlaid by later developments. In 1795 he was asked to prepare a Red Book solution to an unusually challenging estate at Blaise Castle, four miles north of Bristol. A rich Quaker banker, John Scandrett Harford, was building a dull classical house close to the road on the outskirts of Henbury, a gentrified village with a number of other villa retreats of Bristol merchants. Behind Harford's new house was a large, awkwardly shaped parkland of steep, forested, limestone hills divided by a deep, gloomy ravine which a previous owner had tried to turn into a lake, housing a steam powered pump for that purpose in a tri-lobed Gothick castle on the hill above.[17]

Repton's response was bold, imaginative and, because Harford had money and employed his own workforce to blast away to Repton's designs, completely successful. In July 1799 Harford was able, for the first time, to drive a friend around Repton's daringly engineered carriage-ways in a four-wheeled coach. That same day in the afternoon he whirled his wife around the same hairpin bends and giddy prospects in a phaeton. Later he may have walked Repton's poetical Precipice Walk to appreciate the Cavern and a view 'impossible to represent: it consists of a winding valley of wood and rock terminated by a smooth hill, and this is enlivened by frequent groups of carriages and company who visit the spot, and produce an astonishing contrast to the solemn dignity of this awful scene'.[18] It was typical of Repton that he should blandly assume that everyone shared his delight in company. Harford had, in fact, been trying for years to exclude visitors and close down all the rights of way across his park.

The trees have grown up and not all Repton's carefully prepared viewpoints can be enjoyed today, but at Blaise, better probably than anywhere else, his tightrope walk between the Brownian carriage park and the Picturesque wilderness can be evaluated. He created two carriage-drives. One ingeniously suggests to a newcomer that the house is set in the midst of a large, mountainous estate worthy of Mrs Radcliffe's *Mysteries of Udolpho*. A second was designed to give guests a thrilling Gothic drive beset with dramatic vistas of Wales, Piercefield and the Severn estuary with its busy shipping, all within the quite limited compass of the grounds. The first drive, coloured orange on the map in the Red Book, enters the park at the extremity of an outlying arm of woodland, thus providing a lonely, one-mile drive to a house which is actually sited a few yards from the main road. The carriage-way rises up to the arch of Repton's mood-setter – a Gothic tower lodge, blockish and quite formidable – then plunges downhill on a ledge which has been blasted out with gunpowder from a steep wooded hillside. 'I have made a road', Repton boasted, 'where Nature never intended the foot of man to tread, much less that he should be conveyed in the vehicles of modern luxury, but where man resides, Nature must be conquered by Art'. Remembering Uvedale Price he added the nervous proviso, 'without committing great violence on the Genius of the Place'; though the bore holes of the gunpowder charges are still visible on the rocks today.

During the descent into the ravine the Timber Lodge, an enchanting thatched cottage designed as if for geriatric gnomes, is passed on the left. Repton makes no mention of this as it would appear to be an outlier of Blaise Hamlet, that idyllic refuge for estate retirees which John Nash designed in 1811 for Harford on the other side of Henbury.[19] Repton's brief and financially barren partnership with Nash was not a time he ever wished to recall. But on one unusually steep, sharp bend a Woodman's Cottage, which Repton himself designed, is passed on the right. Compared with Nash's Hamlet cottages, which are full of coy spatial inventions, it is dull, but its function will be revealed when the drive reaches the house. At the bottom of the ravine stands a mill building but this, again, Repton does not mention as it must pre-date his consultation. The drive climbs up steeply, still through woodland, passes a flight of steps leading to the Cavern, the Precipice and Lover's Leap then, in a surprise view, bursts unexpectedly out of the trees by a left-hand bend to reveal the house, backed by trees on the edge of a broad green lawn.

When the overlay in this illustration for Repton's Red Book of Blaise Castle, Bristol, has been pulled back a staring white fence has been removed and, up the hill, an open grassy glade has been cut out of the woods. Above this relieving feature sits the new Woodman's Cottage. The smoke rising from its chimney produces 'that kind of vapoury repose over the opposite woods which painters often attempt to describe'.

The Red Book shows the view from the house, before the overlays are pulled back, as simply two dull wooded hills beyond a staring white fence. With the overlays taken back the fence is gone (Repton hated white objects of any kind) and the fringes of the woods have been thinned and broken by clumping. Up on the left Repton's Woodman's Cottage is plainly visible on its relieving patch of greensward, balancing the towers of the Castle on the right. In a touch stolen directly from Gilpin, Repton's prose drifts mellifluously on explaining the function of the cottage:

> The occasional smoke from the chimney will not only produce that cheerful and varying motion which painting cannot express, but it will frequently happen in a summer's evening that the smoke from this cottage will spread a thin veil along the glen, and produce that kind of vapoury repose over the opposite wood which painters often attempt to describe.

As an exasperated Daniel Malthus, Gérardin's English translator, remarked, 'I have been often so much disgusted by the affected and technical language of connoisseurship that I have been sick of pictures for a month, and almost of Nature, when the same jargon was applied to her'.[20]

The second carriage-drive, coloured green on the map, sets off from the house, enters the Castle woods and then, along two parallel climbing reaches, offers first on the right, then on the left, ever wider views across the Bristol Channel. Repton disapproved of a single focus, such as an obelisk or a tower, to any prospect. He believed that the viewer should be kept alert and, until

On the opposite page of the Blaise Red Book to the previous image Repton, the painter manqué, has enriched the view from the house by softening the line of the woods and bringing one clump of trees forward, a Brownian device. A herd of cows enlivens the meadow and one of the castle's three turrets has been elevated above the other two to 'give it more the character of a real castle'.

the trees grew up, a lively appreciation is what the carriage-way encouraged. Finally the drive opens, or opened, into 'a small lawn which surprizes by its unexpected contrast with the other wild part of this thickly wooded precipice', then swings into the pure theatre of a hilltop field entirely surrounded by wood and centred upon the triangular Castle which seems to cry out for tournaments and trumpets. This delightful fake is the same building, 'the oldest in the kingdom', which the dreadful Thorpe was taking Catherine Morland to visit on that disastrous expedition in Jane Austen's *Northanger Abbey*. Because he had not designed it himself, Repton felt that it needed 'more the character of a real castle' and offered a design to heighten one of the towers which Harford did not take up, nor was he tempted by the Ionic portico which Repton suggested as an addition to the Quaker proprieties of the main house.

Ideological consistency was not a feature of Repton's writings or of his practice. To the end of his career he was still trying to flatter Payne Knight, who despised him, and distance himself from Brown, his original master.

In his *Observations* of 1803 he piously deplored the current Regency fashion for building box-like single-room park gate lodges: 'very often the most squalid misery is found in the person thus banished from society, who inhabits a dirty room of a few square feet'.[21] Yet in his *Fragments* of 1816 he flaunted an overlay of a plain gated entrance arch which, when pulled back, revealed the 'improved' Repton entrance with tall gate piers and a neat, very small, single-room gate lodge.[22] This was for Wingerworth in Derbyshire, the seat of an old county family of the kind Repton loved and respected. At all times he deplored *nouveau riche* landowners for their supposed indifference to their tenants, but then shamelessly revelled in their wealthy company; he derided foolish chasing after novel styles of architecture, then in 1805 urged the Muslim and the Hindu for

SITUATION

When I compare the picturesque scenery of Downton Vale with the meagre efforts of art, which are attributed to the school of Brown, I cannot wonder at the enthusiastic abhorrence which the author of *The Landscape* expresses for modern Gardening: especially as few parts of the kingdom present more specimens of bad taste than the road from Ludlow to Worcester, in passing over which I wrote the contents of this small volume. And while I was writing, surrounded by plantations of firs and larches and Lombardy poplars, I saw new red houses, with all the fanciful apertures of Venetian and pseudo-Gothic windows, which disgust the traveller, who looks in vain for the picturesque shapes and harmonious tints of former times.

THE HOUSE

After the literary controversy between Mr. Knight and me, I should be sorry to be misunderstood as casting any reflection on the Castle Character of Downton; for although perhaps some may think that its outline was directed by the eye of a Painter, rather than that of an Antiquary, yet its general effect must gratify the good taste of both: and I should have been happy to have shewn my assent of that style, in adopting the Castle Character for the House at Stanage; but this would exceed my prescribed limitation; and since we cannot imitate the ancient Baronial Castle, let us endeavour to restore that sort of importance, which formerly belonged to the old Manor House; where the proprietor resided among his tenants, not only to collect the rents, but to share the produce of his estate with his humble dependents; and where plenteous hospitality was not sacrificed to ostentatious refinements of luxury.

GROUND ABOUT THE HOUSE

It may perhaps be observed by the trim imitators of Brown's defects, that the stables, barns, gardens, and other appendages, ought to be removed to a distance. I have, in my former volume, endeavoured to shew the folly of expecting importance in buildings without extent of appendages; and the absurdity of banishing to a distance those objects which are necessary to the comfort of a country residence. There is one point on which I believe my opinion may differ from the theory of the ingenious Author of *The Landscape*; at least so far as I have been told he has endeavoured to reduce it to practice near the house at Downton. I fully agree with him in condemning that bald and insipid custom, introduced by Brown, of surrounding a house by a naked grass field: but to remedy this by slovenly neglect, or by studied and affected rudeness, seems to be an opposite extreme not less offensive. A house is an artificial object, and the ground immediately contiguous may partake of the same artificial character. In this place, therefore, straight lines of garden walls and walks are advisable, together with such management, as may form the greatest possible contrast with that rude character, which should every where else prevail at Stanage.

Gothic Outline in Repton's Red Book for Stanage Park, from his *Fragments* of 1816

---

the Pavilion at Brighton with imaginative brilliance.[23] After attacking inordinate reliance upon pictures when designing a landscape he swung around to urge it as good practice; and although he had launched his career in the high-handed Capability Brown manner at Stoke Edith, he ended it writing sugary poems about bourgeois cottage gardens with pergolas and climbing roses.

There is probably no garden style of the past with which it is more difficult to empathise at the present day than with the Gardenesque. Pergolas, trellises, urns on pedestals in balustraded walls, formal stone terraces, shrubberies with gravel paths, formal beds geometrical with coloured ranks of bright flowers, fountains, specimen trees with metal name tags and supportive rows of greenhouses, all smack now of municipal parks, which were for the most part set up when the Gardenesque reigned unchallenged in the mid-nineteenth century. It was not until 1832 that the actual term 'Gardenesque' was coined by John Claudius Loudon (1783–1843). But as an almost subversive movement it had been a garden constant ever since the distant days of George London and Henry Wise.

The part played by flower planting in eighteenth-century landscape gardens has been the subject of a number of scholarly articles tracing its deployment from Richard Bateman at Old

Windsor in the 1720s and '30s, through William Kent at Carlton House in 1734 and Philip Southcote at Wooburn after 1735, to Thomas Wright at Becket Hall, Berkshire, in the 1740s and William Chambers's new formal gardens at Kew for Princess Augusta after 1756.[24] These studies mark the first retreat of the formal flower planters and then their stealthy advance and sudden victory in 1777 with William Mason's garden at Nuneham Courtenay. In old prints that garden may look like a cheap twentieth-century birthday card, complete with everything except love birds billing on the perch of a little wooden bird house, but that was the essential Gardenesque and Mason was not one of the four heroes of Repton's 'breviary' for nothing. Mason had even written 'Gardenesque' poetry about the greenhouse in his 1777 *The English Garden*:

> . . . All within was day,
> Was genial Summer's day, for secret stoves
> Through all the pile solstitial warmth convey'd.
> These led through isles of fragrance to the dome,
> Each way in circling quadrant.[25]

The concepts of the rich formal garden had even invaded Picturesque theory. Payne Knight felt strongly that a house needed a complex foreground. He achieved that at Downton by hurling rocks about and encouraging undergrowth, but in *The Landscape*, he was openly yearning after Elizabethan terracing:

> Just round the house, in formal angles traced
> It moved responsive to the builder's taste.
> Walls answer'd walls, and alleys, long and thin,
> Mimick'd the endless passages within.[26]

Payne Knight was writing in the stiff restraint of the heroic couplets which had been the poetic accompaniment to the parallel restraint of the Arcadian garden-park; but now he, and Repton with him, would live on into the lush imagery and sensuous versification of Keats and Shelley. Christopher Ricks has written sympathetically on *The Embarrassment of Keats*,[27] the over-ripe Cockney vulgarity of the odes to a *Nightingale, Psyche* and *Autumn*. With their lines that alternate between the exquisite and the excruciating they are the poetic equivalent of the Gardenesque. No-one has written yet on 'The Embarrassment of Repton' a man who, driven to design increasingly for suburban villas, where neither the Brownian nor the Picturesque would have been appropriate, revelled in a rich, sentimental lushness and wrote it up accordingly:

> In SPRING the garden begins to excite interest with the first blossoms of the crocus and snowdrop: and though its delights are seldom enjoyed in the more magnificent country residences of the Nobility, yet the garden of the Villa should be profusely supplied with all the fragrance and the beauty of blossom belonging to 'il gioventu del anno'.[28]

This quotation is from Repton's 1816 *Fragments*, his stylistic last will and testament, published two years before his death. The book is one long, persuasive argument for the Gardenesque, full of enjoyable hyperbole and harmless deceit. To damn Brown forever he illustrated the White Lodge in Richmond Park, first with a Brownian lawn up to its front door: 'the uncleanly,

For Lord Sidmouth at the White Lodge, Richmond, Repton swept away the casual Brownian deer park which ran right up to the house walls. In its place, as this view with its overlay pulled back shows, he proposed a broad gravel path flanked with a grand treillage for roses, a typical Gardenesque enrichment. Unfortunately, Sidmouth accepted only the straight path.

pathless grass of a forest, filled with troublesome animals of every kind, and some occasionally dangerous'.[29] With the overlay pulled back the Lodge is revealed with a straight gravel path centred on its door and hoop upon hoop of treillage ranged on each side, all enlivened with the inevitable roses. The text reads proudly: 'The Improvement has been executed in every respect by the present noble Inhabitant', who was Lord Sidmouth. But if we read a little further the truth comes out: 'with the exception of the Treillage Ornaments which may at any time be added'.[30] So in effect all Repton had done was to add a straight path. The Gardenesque ornaments that dominate the revealed illustration were wishful thinking; Sidmouth was not yet converted to the Gardenesque, but in the emotive, salesman's writing of his *Fragments* Repton was effectively consigning the parks and layouts of Lancelot Brown to history:

A large extent of ground without moving objects, however neatly kept, is but a melancholy scene. If solitude delights, we seek it rather in the covert of a wood, or the sequestered alcove of a flower garden, than in the open lawn of an extensive pleasure ground.[31]

In their place he projected the gardens of maximum commercial consumption, the ideal territories of the nurserymen's catalogues and the gardening manuals of the future. There, 'beds of bog earth should be prepared for the American plants', and 'the numerous class of rock plants should have beds of rugged straw prepared for their reception . . . but above all, there should be poles or hoops

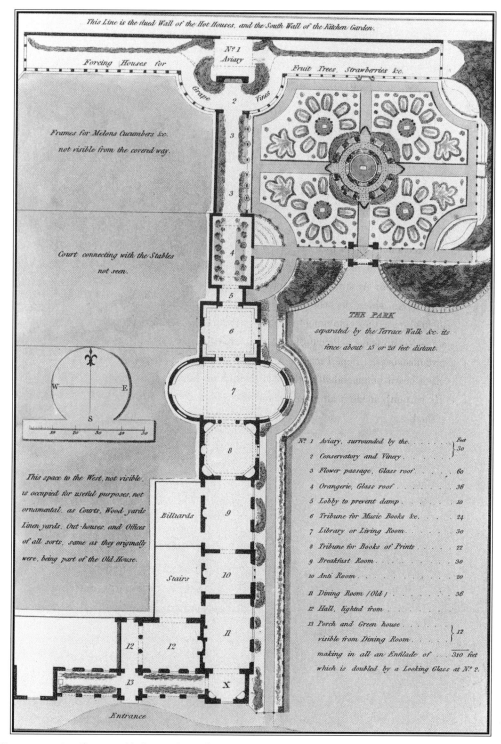

Repton was primarily responsible for introducing the concept of garden rooms, the drawing room linking up with the conservatory. In this proposal from his Fragments *a whole chain of linear rooms banishes the distinction between house and garden but demands an asymmetrical, Picturesque house plan.*

for those kind of creeping plants which spontaneously form themselves into graceful festoons, when encouraged and supported by art'.[32] These would demand a new relationship, intimate, even clinging, between the reception rooms of a house and its grounds, a complete rejection of Brown's bare lawns. 'No', Repton protested, 'rather let us go back to former times, when the lofty terraces of the *privy garden* gave protection and seclusion to the noble persons'.[33]

Fragment 25, 'To Lady ★★★★' demonstrates how logically Repton had followed through the architectural implications of his Gardenesque revolution. His plan has the Library leading via a Tribune for Music Books into a 'Lobby to Prevent Damp', an 'Orangerie' with a glass roof, a 'Flower Passage', also with a glass roof, 'Conservatory and Vinery', gloriously illustrated in full colour, domed and trellised, an 'Aviary' and lastly a long 'Forcing House' for grapes, peaches and strawberries.[34] Repton had seen all these offices built at Wooburn back in 1805, but away out in the park. Now he was shrewdly proposing them as physical extensions to the house itself, positioning William Mason's 'isles of fragrance' next door to the drawing-room.

In the early years of the eighteenth century the garden had shrunk and the park had grown. Now, in the early years of the nineteenth the reverse was happening and the garden was growing again. Classical restraint, which had allowed a severe Arcadia of grass and trees to develop, was weakening. In his last years Repton was using the Picturesque process of copying artists to rifle ornate foregrounds from Boucher and Fragonard, not wild woodland from Claude or temples from Poussin. As far back as his 1802 Red Book for Hooton Park, Cheshire, he had slipped a flowering urn on its pedestal into a foreground. In his 1816 Fragment 20 'Concerning Contracts' the foreground had become the whole.[35] A Keatsian rainbow arches over his colour plate of a conservatory with rambler roses, treillage where melons and lemons dangle, urns and goldfish bowls. Outside a straight path between flower beds, where tulips and hollyhocks are improbably both flowering at the same time, leads to the tall jet of a fountain. Here again, is the prototype for the tasteless birthday card, the kitsch garden, a composition to make Gertrude Jekyll despair, and the prose beside the picture is of matching quality. After a summer shower,

all nature seems revived; the ground and the plants send forth new and delightful odours, the flowers, the birds, the insects, all join to express their pleasure; and even the gold fish in a globe, by their frolic motion shew that they partake in the general joy, splashing the water, and sometimes leaping out of it to meet the welcome drops.[36]

The sun was setting and 'every spray was bespangled with drops hanging like diamonds, and each changing to all the colours of the rainbow, from whence they appeared to have fallen'.[37] In that same mood of tranquil appreciation Repton was preparing for his own personal sunset. His 'Memoir' closes with: 'My own profession like myself was becoming extinct. The ship was sinking, and it was time to quit it',[38] an emotional and factual inaccuracy for which Loudon, his up-and-coming young Scots rival, would not have thanked him. Repton had prepared his grave cosily against the south wall of Aylsham church in Norfolk. He was a gardener to the last and with a final turn of phrase that Keats might have envied, he had written to the vicar:

After twenty years of War which abridged me of many comforts I am now happy that I shall depart in Peace to sleep near the Ashes of my Parents, and have desired that mine may be so slightly enclosed as soon to dissolve and form part of the Garden mold of my warm, snug corner where I will soon be converted into the pabulum of Roses.[39]

NOTES

INTRODUCTION

1. Lilian Dickins & Mary Stanton (eds), *An Eighteenth-Century Correspondence* (1910), p. 416.

CHAPTER ONE

1. Scribbled in his Italian sketchbook and dated January 1615; quoted in Timothy Mowl & Brian Earnshaw, *Architecture Without Kings: The Rise of Puritan Classicism under Cromwell* (Manchester, 1995), p. 81.

2. For a full account of Jones's life and career see John Summerson, *Inigo Jones* (1966); a comprehensive bibliography is given in H.M. Colvin, *A Biographical Dictionary of British Architects 1600–1840* (1995), pp. 554–61.

3. Noted on f. 125; see the facsimile edition edited by Bruce Allsopp, *Inigo Jones on Palladio*, 2 vols (1970).

4. For Salomon and Isaac de Caus see Colvin, *Biographical Dictionary*, pp. 298–30; Roy Strong, *The Renaissance Garden in England* (1979), pp.73–5.

5. For the Richmond garden see Strong, *Renaissance Garden*, pp. 97–101.

6. For the Arundel house garden see Strong, *Renaissance Garden*, plates 111–13.

7. Quoted in John Charlton, *The Banqueting House, Whitehall* (HMSO, 1983), p. 6.

8. The Grotto is illustrated in Strong, *Renaissance Garden*, pl. 86.

9. For an oblique view of the Bedford garden and the newly laid out Piazza see John Harris, *The Artist and the Country House* (1979), pl. 34.

10. It was fashionable for a time after Howard Colvin's article, 'The South Front of Wilton House' (*Archaeological Journal*, **CXI** (1954), pp. 181–90), to attribute this front of Wilton and several seventeenth-century drawings related to its genesis to Isaac de Caus. The present author fought against this unsupported attribution, see *Architecture Without Kings*, pp. 31–47 and 'Inigo Jones Restored', *Country Life*, 30 January 1992. Eventually in 1999, Sir Howard, as he had become, abandoned the theory in his *Essays in English Architectural History* (New Haven, CT, & London, 1999), where he admits that 'those who . . . have in the past attributed this icon of English Palladianism to Inigo Jones were perhaps not far wrong' (p. 154), they were in fact right all the time. Authorities like Sir Nikolaus Pevsner and Sir John Summerson were never impressed by the Isaac de Caus attribution. The de Caus role in the rebuilding of Wilton and the creation of the garden must now be substantially down-graded to that of clerk of the works at the house and hydraulics engineer for Nicholas Stone's carved work at the Grotto.

11. E.S. de Beer (ed.), *The Diary of John Evelyn*, 6 vols (Oxford, 1955), **2**, pp. 109–10; for Rueil see Kenneth Woodbridge, 'The Picturesque Image of Richelieu's Garden at Rueil', *Garden History*, **9**, 1 (1981), pp. 1–22.

12. John Aubrey, *Memoires of Natural Remarques in the County of Wiltshire* (1847, ed. John Britton), pp. 83–4.

13. A small facsimile copy has been published: John Dixon Hunt (ed.), *Wilton Garden; New and Rare Inventions of Waterworks* (New York, 1982).

14. Lieutenant Hammond, 'Description of a Journey made into Westerne Counties', *The Camden Miscellany*, XVI (1936), pp. 66–7.

15. Christopher Morris (ed.), *The Illustrated Journeys of Celia Fiennes c. 1682–c. 1712* (1982), pp. 38–9.

16. For the design see John Harris, Stephen Orgel & Roy Strong (eds), *The King's Arcadia: Inigo Jones and the Stuart Court* (Arts Council, 1973), pl. 325.

17. Howard Colvin believes that Hammond was shown around, not by de Caus, but by Dominick Pile. But Pile was in charge of the Kitchen Garden at Wilton, not the Grotto (PRO, LC5/133, f. 53).

18. A wooden triumphal arch on the hill top with a lead equestrian statue of Marcus Aurelius was a late seventeenth-century addition to the park. The statue of the emperor was brought down from his hill top and now rides on Sir William Chambers's archway into the north forecourt of the house. Flora and Bacchus stand on the parapet of a nineteenth-century bridge across the Nadder. Of the four female statues now in the north forecourt, only Susanna is a Nicholas Stone original, but superb bass reliefs by the same artist: Europa, Venus and Tritons, which once ornamented de Caus's Grotto, now decorate a loggia in a later Italian garden. Elements of the grotesque interior stonework from the Grotto have been built into the façade of Park School House in the grounds. Le Sueur's bronze Gladiator was given to Sir Robert Walpole and now commands the entrance hall of Houghton House, Norfolk.

19. H.M. Colvin (gen. ed.), *The History of the King's Works Vol. IV 1485–1660 (Part II)*, (1982), pp. 268–70; see also Geoffrey Fisher & John Newman, 'A Fountain Design by Inigo Jones', *Burlington Magazine*, August 1985, pp. 531–2.
20. Quoted in Colvin, *Essays*, p. 139.
21. Quoted in Antony Griffiths & Gabriela Kesnerová, *Wenceslaus Hollar: Prints and Drawings* (1983), p. 84; see also pl. 96b.
22. Douglas Chambers, 'The tomb in the landscape: John Evelyn's garden at Albury', *Journal of Garden History*, **1**, 2 (1981), pp. 37–54; p. 38.
23. Subsequent quotations are taken from Sir Henry Wotton, *The Elements of Architecture* (1624; facsimile edition, ed. F. Hard, Charlottesville, VA, 1968), pp. 109–10.

CHAPTER TWO

1. The Hartlib manuscripts have been fully catalogued by the Hartlib Papers Project at the University of Sheffield. There is also a Royal Commission on Historical Manuscripts 'Report on the Correspondence and Papers of Samuel Hartlib (*c.* 1600–62), educationalist and natural philosopher' (1980).
2. *Samuel Hartlib his Legacie or an Enlargement of the Discourse on HUSBANDRY used in Brabant and Flaunders. Wherein are bequeathed to the Common-Wealth of England, more outlandish and Domestick Experiments & Secrets in reference to Universall HUSBANDRY* (1652), p. iv.
3. Quotation given forms part of the title of this pamphlet.
4. Hartlib, *A Discoverie for Division or Setting out of Land as to the Best Form* (1653), p. 10.
5. Quotation given forms part of the title page of this pamphlet.
6. Hartlib, *Enlargement of the Discourse on HUSBANDRY*, p. 63.
7. John Parkinson, *Paradisi in Sole, Paradisus Terrestris* (1628), see chapter 7: 'The severall times of the flowering of these Out-landish flowers'.
8. Hartlib, *Discoverie for Division*, p. 3.
9. Hartlib, *Discourse on Husbandrie* (2nd edition of 1652), p. 22.
10. Samuel Hartlib, *An Essay for the Advancement of Husbandry and learning or Propositions for the Erecting a Colledge of Husbandry and in order thereunto, for the taking in of Pupills or Apprentices AND ALSO Friends or Fellowes of the Same Colledge or Society* (1651), p. i.
11. Ibid., p. ii.
12. For the Balls Park layout see Timothy Mowl, 'New Science, Old Order: the Gardens of the Great Rebellion', *Journal of Garden History*, **13** (1993), pp. 16–35.
13. Hartlib, *Discoverie for Division*, p. 10.
14. Hartlib, *The Reformed Spirituall Husbandman* (1652), p. 21.
15. Hartlib, *Discoverie for Division*, p. iii.

CHAPTER THREE

1. Letter of 30 September 1659 from Beale to John Evelyn, quoted from Sheffield University Library, Hartlib MSS. 67/22, pp. 2–3, by Peter Goodchild, '"No Phantasticall Utopia, but a Reall Place". John Evelyn, John Beale and Backbury Hill, Herefordshire', *Garden History*, **19**, 2 (1991), pp. 105–27; p. 117.
2. Hartlib MSS. 25/6/3 & 4; see also Sir Henry Wotton, *The Elements of Architecture* (1624; facsimile edition), p. 109.
3. Hartlib MSS. 25/6/5.
4. John Beale, *Herefordshire Orchards, a Pattern for all England Written in an Epistolary Address to Samuel Hartlib Esq. By I.B. 1657*, p. 27.
5. Ibid., p. 58.
6. Ibid., p. 48.
7. Ibid., p. 47.
8. Ibid., p. 48.
9. Ibid., p. 49.
10. Goodchild, '"No Phantasticall Utopia"', p. 118.
11. Sir Thomas Hanmer, *The Garden Book of Sir Thomas Hanmer Bart*, printed from the MS. Volume of 1659 (Mold, 1993), p. 67.
12. E.S. de Beer (ed.), *The Diary of John Evelyn*, 6 vols (Oxford, 1955), **3**, pp. 114–15.
13. John Evelyn, 'Elysium Britannicum', Christ Church College Library, Oxford, MS. 45, f. 56.
14. Ibid., f. 56.
15. Ibid., f. 57.
16. Ibid., f. 57.
17. Ibid., f. 58.
18. Ibid., f. 58.
19. Ibid., f. 58.
20. Goodchild, '"No Phantasticall Utopia"', p. 119.
21. For Southcote's Wooburn see Chapter Ten of this study.

CHAPTER FOUR

1. E.S. de Beer (ed.), *The Diary of John Evelyn*, 6 vols, (Oxford, 1955), **2**, p. 551.
2. 'De Vita Propria Pars Prima' is included in vol. **1** of *The Diary of John Evelyn*, hereafter referred to as *Evelyn's Diary*; p. 6.
3. Ibid., **1**, p. 5.
4. Ibid., **4**, p. 413.
5. Ibid., **2**, p. 60; p. 46; p. 56.
6. Ibid., **1**, p. 55.
7. Ibid., **2**, p. 81.
8. Ibid., **3**, p. 61.
9. Ibid., **3**, p. 115.

10. Ibid., **2**, p. 392.
11. Ibid., **2**, p. 106.
12. Ibid., **2**, p. 107.
13. Ibid., **3**, pp. 60–1.
14. Ibid., **1**, p. 55.
15. Ibid., **2**, p. 133
16. From Evelyn's plan of the garden.
17. *Evelyn's Diary*, **3**, p. 110
18. From Evelyn's plan of the garden.
19. *Evelyn's Diary*, **1**, p. 38
20. Ibid., **4**, p. 116
21. Ibid., **4**, pp. 117–18.
22. Ibid., **3**, p.154.
23. Ibid., **3**, p. 573.
24. Ibid., **3**, p. 154.
25. Ibid., **3**, p. 561.
26. Ibid., **3**, p. 496.

CHAPTER FIVE

1. E.S. de Beer (ed.), *The Diary of John Evelyn*, 6 vols (Oxford, 1955), **3**, p. 324.
2. For Longleat see Michael McGarvie & John Harvey, 'The Revd George Harbin and his Memoirs of Gardening 1716–1723', *Garden History*, **11**, 1 (1983), pp. 6–36.
3. Stephen Switzer, *The Nobleman, Gentleman, and Gardener's Recreation*, 1715; quoted in David Jacques & Arend Jan van der Horst, *The Gardens of William and Mary* (Bromley, 1988), p. 30.
4. For more information on Wise's Grant of Arms see David Green, *Gardener to Queen Anne: Henry Wise (1653–1738) and the Formal Garden* (1956), appendix I, pp. 207–8.
5. The 1707 edition of *Britannia Illustrata* has been published in facsimile by John Harris & Gervase Jackson-Stops (eds), *Britannia Illustrata or Views of Several of the Queens Palaces also of the Principal Seats of the Nobility and Gentry of Great Britain* (1984).
6. Green, *Henry Wise*, p. 79.
7. F.L. Colville, *The Worthies of Warwickshire* (1869) attributes these lines to a labourer employed at Wise's garden at Brompton. Stephen Switzer seems the most likely versifier. Quoted in Green, *Henry Wise*, p. 12.
8. Green, *Henry Wise*, pp. 74–5.
9. For analytical illustrations of Rea's frets see Peter Goodchild, 'John Rea's Gardens of Delight: Introduction and the Construction of the Flower Garden', *Garden History*, **9**, 2 (1981), pp. 99–109.
10. George London & Henry Wise, *The Retir'd Gardener*, 1706, Chapter III: 'Of the different sorts of Parterres, and single Knots, with their Rise, and the Manner of Bordering and Planting them with Box'; p. 129.
11. Ibid., p.132.
12. Ibid., p.132.
13. Ibid., p.130.
14. Quoted in Green, *Henry Wise*, p. 126.
15. Christopher Morris (ed.), *The Illustrated Journeys of Celia Fiennes c. 1682– c. 1712* (1982).
16. *Westbury Court Garden* (National Trust), 1997, p. 34.
17. Ibid., p. 33.
18. Wise's layout is illustrated in Green, *Henry Wise*, pl. 21.
19. For Pontchartrain see Catherine Healey, 'The gardens of Pontchartrain: embellishment of an Ile de France estate in the 1690s', *Studies in the History of Gardens & Designed Landscapes*, **18**, 1 (1998), pp. 52–65.
20. Quoted in the current guide to Melbourne Hall Gardens (Derby, 1984), p. 2.
21. From Marvell's 'The Garden', lines 47–8.

CHAPTER SIX

1. See Timothy Mowl, 'Antiquaries, Theatre and Early Medievalism', in Christopher Ridgway & Robert Williams (eds), *Sir John Vanbrugh and Landscape Architecture in Baroque England 1690–1730* (2000), pp. 71–92.
2. For a full account of Bridgeman's life and work see Peter Willis, *Charles Bridgeman and the English Landscape Garden* (1977).
3. David Green, *Gardener to Queen Anne: Henry Wise (1653–1738) and the Formal Garden* (1956), pp. 148–50.
4. For a full account of Vanbrugh's life and work see Kerry Downes, *Vanbrugh* (1977).
5. Vanbrugh's time at Surat was discovered by Robert Williams and elucidated in his paper to the 'Sir John Vanbrugh & Landscape Architecture in Baroque England 1690–1730' conference held in York, 15–17 July 1999; subsequently published in Ridgway & Williams (eds), *Sir John Vanbrugh and Landscape Architecture*.
6. Stephen Switzer, *Ichnographia Rustica*, 1718; quoted in John Dixon Hunt & Peter Willis (eds), *The Genius of the Place: The English Landscape Garden 1620–1820* (1988), p. 158.
7. 'An Account of a Tour' by a Cambridge undergraduate, Bath Public Reference Library, MS. 38: 43, pp. 43–6; quoted in Charles Saumarez Smith, *The Building of Castle Howard* (1990), p. 126.
8. Sir William Temple, *Upon the Gardens of Epicurus: or, Of Gardnening, in the Year 1685*, first published in 1692 and quoted in Hunt & Willis (eds), *The Genius of the Place*, pp. 96–9; p. 99.
9. Ibid., p. 99. For a discussion of the term 'Sharawadgi' see Ciaran Murray, '*Sharawadgi* Resolved', *Garden History*, **26**, 2 (1998), pp. 208–13.
10. See the illustration of Moor Park given in Hunt & Willis (eds), *The Genius of the Place*, pl. 52. Another precedent for serpentine paths was the recently designed Bosquet de Louveciennes at Marly by J.H.

Mansart, which was studied by George London in 1699.

11. Stephen Switzer, *Ichnographia Rustica*, 2 vols, 1718, **1**, p. 87.

12. For this 'Architectural Parterre' see Saumarez Smith, *Castle Howard*, pp.137–41.

13. For the Villa Ludovisi see David Coffin, *Gardens and Gardening in Papal Rome* (Princeton, New Jersey, 1991), pp. 150–3.

14. Susan Gordon, 'The Iconography and Mythology of the Eighteenth-Century English Landscape Garden', PhD thesis (University of Bristol, 1999).

15. The Vanbrugh and Wise plan for Blenheim Park is illustrated in James Bond & Kate Tiller (eds), *Blenheim: Landscape for a Palace* (1987), pl. 57.

16. Bonamy Dobrée & Geoffrey Webb (eds), *The Complete Works of Sir John Vanbrugh*, 4 vols (1928), **4**, p. 30; the full text of Vanbrugh's 'Reasons Offer'd for Preserving some Part of the Old Manor' at Blenheim (11 June 1709) is given in Hunt & Willis (eds), *The Genius of the Place*, pp. 120–1.

17. For the Eaton landscape see Ian C. Laurie, 'Landscape Gardeners at Eaton Park, Chester: 1', *Garden History*, **12**, 1 (1984), pp. 39–57.

18. The plan is in the Bodleian Library, MS Gough Drawings, and illustrated in John Harris, 'The Beginnings of Claremont: Sir John Vanbrugh's Garden at Chargate in Surrey', *Apollo*, April 1993, fig. 5.

19. The house at Duncombe was built by the local architect William Wakefield in 1713–18. The open Ionic rotunda is set at the nothern end of a grass terrace which extends for half a mile in an arc above the narrow Rye valley. At the other end is a circular Tuscan Doric temple, similar to that at the neighbouring Rievaulx Terrace. A date of *c.* 1729 has been suggested for the Doric temple, but the Ionic rotunda could well be contemporary with Vanbrugh's Rotunda at Stowe. See David Watkin, *The English Vision: The Picturesque in Architecture, Landscape & Garden Design* (1982), p.10.

20. In a letter of 7 January 1724 to Lord Carlisle; quoted in Saumarez Smith, *Castle Howard*, p. 144

21. In a letter of 11 February 1724 to Lord Carlisle; quoted in Saumarez Smith, *Castle Howard*, p. 144..

22. Ibid., p.144.

23. Bridgeman's plans for Hackwood are in the Bodleian Library, Oxford and are illustrated in Willis, *Bridgeman*, pl. 52 (wrongly captioned Farley) and in *Country Life*, 10 December 1987.

CHAPTER SEVEN

1. Stephen Switzer, *The Nobleman, Gentleman, and Gardener's Recreation*, 1715; revised and enlarged to three volumes, published as *Ichnographia Rustica, or, The Nobleman, Gentleman, and Gardener's Recreation* in 1718; revised with a preface in 1742. Excerpts from the 1718 and 1742 editions are given in John Dixon Hunt & Peter Willis (eds), *The Genius of the Place: The English Landscape Garden 1620–1820 (1975)*, pp. 151–63.

2. Hunt & Willis (eds), *The Genius of the Place*, pp. 122–3.

3. Ibid., p. 122.

4. Ibid., p. 124.

5. Horace Walpole, *The History of the Modern Taste in Gardening* (1780; facsimile edition, ed. John Dixon Hunt, 1995), p. 28.

6. Ibid., p. 30.

7. Joseph Spence, *Observations, Anecdotes & Characters of Books & Men*, 2 vols (1966), **1**, p. 80. Spence quotes Pope as saying: 'Addison and Steele were a couple of H....S, I am sorry to say so, and there are not twelve people in the world that I would say it to at all'.

8. The *Spectator* essay is given in Hunt & Willis (eds), *The Genius of the Place*, pp. 141–3.

9. Ibid., p. 141.

10. Ibid., p. 142.

11. Ibid., pp. 142–3.

12. Ibid., p. 141.

13. Quoted in Peter Goodchild, '"No Phantasticall Utopia but a Reall Place". John Evelyn, John Beale and Backbury Hill, Herefordshire', *Garden History*, **19**, 2 (1991), p. 118.

14. Hunt & Willis (eds), *The Genius of the Place*, p. 143.

15. Ibid., pp. 204–8.

16. *Ichnographia*, **1**, p. 9.

17. Hunt & Willis (eds), *The Genius of the Place*, p. 163: 'I was always a Promoter of this Farm-like Way of Gardening, before it was used by any body in any place in *Great-Britain*'.

18. Ibid., p. 146.

19. Ibid., p. 145.

20. Ibid., p. 145.

21. Switzer, *Ichnographia*, **3**, p. 5.

22. Berkshire Record Office, D/EX 258/9. I am grateful to Dr Tom Williamson for bringing this to my attention.

23. Switzer, *Ichnographia*, **3**, p. 5.

24. Ibid., **3**, p. 3.

25. Ibid., **3**, p. 3.

26. Ibid., **3**, p. 3.

27. Ibid., **1**, p. 190.

28. Ibid., **2**, p. 115.

29. Quoted by James Sambrook, 'Pope and the Visual Arts' in Peter Dixon (ed.), *Alexander Pope, Writers and their Background* (1972), p. 162.

30. Switzer, *Ichnographia*, **3**, p. 44.

31. Ibid., **3**, p. 88.

32. The authorship of the Leeswood gates is uncertain, both Robert Bakewell and the Davies brothers of nearby Bersham have been suggested; see Ifor Edwards, *Davies Brothers: Gatesmiths* (1977), pp. 71–7.

33. Switzer, *Ichnographia*, **1**, p. 338.

34. See *Country Life*, 30 July 1943.

35. Walpole, *History*, p. 55.
36. Hunt & Willis (eds), *The Genius of the Place*, p. 162.
37. Ibid., p. 153.
38. Ibid., p. 141.
39. Switzer, *Ichnographia*, **3**, p. vi.

CHAPTER EIGHT

1. George Sherburn (ed.), *The Correspondence of Alexander Pope*, 5 vols (Oxford, 1956), **2**, p. 47: Digby to Pope, 21 May 1720.
2. Watteau was in London in 1719; see Marianne Roland Michel, 'Watteau and England', in Charles Hind (ed.) *The Rococo in England: A Symposium* (Victoria & Albert Museum, 1986).
3. For plans and views of the Grotto see Anthony Beckles Willson, *Alexander Pope's Grotto in Twickenham* (1998).
4. From an anonymous visitor's 'An Epistolary Description of the Late Mr. Pope's House and Gardens at Twickenham' (1747) given in John Dixon Hunt & Peter Willis (eds), *The Genius of the Place: The English Landscape Garden 1620–1820* (1975), pp. 247–53; p. 249.
5. Ibid., p. 250.
6. *Correspondence*, **2**, p. 296: Pope to Edward Blount, 2 June 1725.
7. Ovid, *Metamorphoses*, III, lines 157–60; quoted in Maynard Mack, *The Garden and the City: Retirement and Politics in the Later Poetry of Pope 1713–1743* (1969), p. 58.
8. Quoted in Mack, *The Garden and the City*, appendix A, p. 238.
9. Joseph Spence, *Observations, Anecdotes and Characters of Books and Men*, 2 vols (1966); **1**, Obs. 604.
10. Mavis Batey, *Alexander Pope: The Poet and the Landscape* (1999), illustration on p. 62.
11. *Correspondence*, **2**, p. 372: Pope to the Earl of Oxford, 22 March 1726.
12. Hunt & Willis (eds), *The Genius of the Place*, p. 252.
13. Spence, *Observations*, **1**, Obs. 610.
14. Ibid., **1**, Obs. 611.
15. Pope, *Windsor Forest*, lines 17–18; 21–2.
16. From his *Epistle to Lord Burlington*, 1731, line 57.
17. W.S. Lewis (ed.), *The Yale Edition of Horace Walpole's Correspondence*, 48 vols (1937–83); **21**, p. 417: Walpole to Mann, 20 June 1760.
18. Ibid., **21**, p. 417.
19. *Correspondence*, **3**, p. 134: Lord Bathurst to Pope, 19 September 1730.
20. Maynard Mack (ed.), *The Poems of Alexander Pope*, 11 vols (1967); **7**, lines 144–5.
21. Ibid., **7**, lines 167–70.
22. Switzer, *Ichnographia*, **1**, p. xxxviii.
23. Ibid., **1**, p. xxxviii.
24. Ibid., **1**, p. xl.
25. Ibid., **1**, p. xxxix.
26. Ibid., **1**, p. xxxviii.

27. Hunt & Willis (eds), *The Genius of the Place*, p. 247.
28. Nikolaus Pevsner, 'The Genius of the Picturesque', *Architectural Review*, June 1944, pp. 139–45.
29. The term 'artinatural' was first used by Batty Langley in his 1728 *New Principles of Gardening or The Laying Out and Planting Parterres, Groves, Wildernesses, Labyrinths, Avenues . . . After a More Grand and Rural Manner than has Been Done Before* (1728); see John Harris, 'The Artinatural Style', in Hind (ed.) *The Rococo in England*, pp. 8–20.
30. Quoted by Christopher Hussey in *Country Life*, 23 June 1950.
31. Ibid.
32. A Gothick Ivy Lodge and Round Tower were later added to Cirencester Park.
33. Hunt & Willis (eds), *The Genius of the Place*, p. 210.
34. *Correspondence*, **2**, p. 513: Pope to Martha Blount, 4 September 1728.
35. For Pope's work at Prior Park see Gillian Clarke, *Prior Park: A Compleat Landscape* (Bath, 1987).
36. *Correspondence*, **4**, p. 239.
37. *Epistle to Lord Burlington*, lines 108–10, 116–17.
38. *Correspondence*, **3**, p. 217.
39. *Epistle to Lord Burlington*, lines 25–6, 35–8.
40. Ibid., lines 57–64.

CHAPTER NINE

1. Walpole's text was printed by the Strawberry Hill Press in 1771, but not published until 1780; see Walpole, *The History of the Modern Taste in Gardening* (facsimile edition based on the 1782 edition of the text, ed. John Dixon Hunt, 1995).
2. For a fuller discussion of Walpole's relationship with Lincoln and his biased memoirs of the two Georges see Timothy Mowl, *Horace Walpole: The Great Outsider* (1996).
3. Walpole, *History*, p. 43.
4. Ibid., p. 43.
5. Ibid., pp. 43–4.
6. For Walpole's Strawberry Hill layout see Mowl, *Horace Walpole*, pl. 27.
7. W.S. Lewis (ed.), *The Yale Edition of Horace Walpole's Correspondence*, 48 vols (1937–83); **20**, p. 380: Walpole to Horace Mann, 12 June 1753.
8. Ibid., p. 380.
9. For an eighteenth-century view of Badminton park see Michael Liversidge & Jane Farrington (eds), *Canaletto & England* (1994), fig. 5.
10. Walpole, *History*, pp. 47–8.
11. See John Dixon Hunt, *William Kent: Landscape Garden Designer* (1987), pl. 106.
12. Walpole, *History*, p. 48.
13. Robert Castell, *The Villas of the Ancients Illustrated* (1982 facsimile edition), p. 9.
14. Ibid., pp. 80–1.
15. Ibid., p. 83.

16. Ibid., p. 116.
17. Ibid., p. 117.
18. Ibid., pp. 116–17.
19. Ibid., p. 116.
20. Norfolk Record Office, MC 184/10/1.
21. Langley, *New Principles of Gardening*, p. iii.
22. Ibid., p. viii.
23. Ibid., p. x.
24. Ibid., p. x.
25. See Hunt, *William Kent*, pls. 34–7.
26. Joseph Spence, *Observations, Anecdotes and Characters of Books and Men,* 2 vols (1966), **1**, Obs. 616.
27. For a complete list of the trees see David Coombs, 'The Garden at Carlton House of Frederick Prince of Wales and Augusta Princess and Dowager of Wales', *Garden History*, **25**, 2 (1997), 153–77.
28. For Kent's state barge see Michael I. Wilson, *William Kent: Architect, Designer, Painter, Gardener, 1685–1748* (1984), pp. 130–3.
29. For Rokeby see Giles Worsley, *Classical Architecture in Britain: The Heroic Age* (New Haven, CT, & London, 1995), pp. 138–9; also the same author in *Country Life*, 19 March 1987.
30. Quoted in John Harris, *The Palladian Revival: Lord Burlington, his Villa and Garden in Chsiwick* (New Haven, CT, & London, 1994), pp. 196–7.
31. Spence, *Observations*, **1**, Obs.
32. For Kent's drawings of all these buildings see Hunt, *William Kent*, plates section.
33. Batty Langley, *A Sure Method of Improving Estates by Plantations* (1728), p. 85.
34. George Clarke, 'Heresy in Stowe's Elysium', in Peter Willis (ed.), *Furor Hortensis: Essays on the History of the English Landscape Garden in Memory of H.F. Clark* (1974), pp. 49–56.
35. Walpole, *History*, pp. 49–50.
36. See Ulrich Müller, 'Rousham: A Transcription of the Steward's Letters, 1738–42', *Garden History*, **25**, 2 (1997), pp. 178–88.
37. Ibid., p. 186: letter of 6 December 1740 from White to Dormer: 'He [MacClary] has now fully determined in the first place to remove ye two Seats six foot nearer the House, and raise ye ground about three foot where they are to fix't; so that you are to goe from ye Terras upon a levell to ye Seats, from whence a better prospect will be had than heretofore'.
38. Mavis Batey & David Lambert, *The English Garden Tour: A View into the Past* (1990), pp. 156–61.
39. Mavis Batey, 'The Way to View Rousham by Kent's Gardener', *Garden History*, **11**, 2 (1983), pp. 125–32; p. 128.

CHAPTER TEN

1. George Sherburn (ed.), *The Correspondence of Alexander Pope*, 5 vols (Oxford, 1956), **2**, p. 503.
2. Joseph Spence, *Observations, Anecdotes and Characters of Books and Men*, 2 vols (1966), **2**, Obs. 1125.
3. Ibid., **1**, Obs. 603.
4. Batty Langley, *New Principles of Gardening or The Laying Out and Planting Parterres, Groves, Wildernesses, Labyrinths, Avenues . . . After a More Grand and Rural Manner than has Been Done Before* (1728), pp. x–xi.
5. For Petre see Douglas Chambers, *The Planters of the English Landscape Garden* (1993), pp. 103–19.
6. Ibid., p. 112.
7. Quoted in John Riely, 'Shenstone's Walks: The Genesis of The Leasowes', *Apollo*, **110**, September 1979, pp. 202–9; p. 203.
8. Paget Toynbee (ed.), *Satirical Poems published anonymously by William Mason with Notes by Horace Walpole* (1926), pp. 39–40.
9. Quoted in James Sambrook, 'Wooburn Farm in the 1760s', *Garden History*, **7**, 2 (1979), pp. 82–101; p. 100.
10. Ibid., p. 86.
11. Spence, *Observations*, **2**, Obs. 1131.
12. Ibid., **2**, Obs. 1127.
13. Ibid., **2**, Obs. 1128.
14. Ibid., **2**, Obs. 1132.
15. Ibid., **2**, Obs. 1133.
16. Ibid., **2**, Obs. 1144.
17. Ibid., **2**, Obs. 1139.
18. Ibid., **2**, Obs. 1138.
19. Ibid., **2**, Obs. 1143.
20. Ibid., **1**, Obs. 615.
21. Ibid., **2**, pl. opposite p. 424.
22. J. Cartwright (ed.), *The Travels through England of Dr Richard Pococke (1750–57)* 2 vols (Camden Society, 1888–9), **2**, p. 260.
23. Sambrook, 'Wooburn Farm', p. 85.
24. Quoted (under Shenstone) in *Dictionary of National Biography*.
25. Ibid.
26. Quoted in Christopher Gallagher, 'The Leasowes: A History of the Landscape', *Garden History*, **24**, 2 (1996), pp. 201–20; p. 206.
27. Quoted in Riely, 'Shenstone's Walks', p. 203.
28. From Shenstone's *Unconnected Thoughts on Gardening*; quoted in Hunt & Willis (eds), *The Genius of the Place*, p. 289.
29. Ibid., p. 290.
30. Ibid.
31. Quoted in Mavis Batey & David Lambert, *The English Garden Tour: A View into the Past* (1990), p. 182.
32. Gallagher, 'The Leasowes', p. 204.
33. Ibid.
34. Riely, 'Shenstone's Walks', pp. 203–4.
35. Gallagher, 'The Leasowes', p. 204.
36. Ibid., p. 208.
37. Riely, 'Shenstone's Walks', p. 206.
38. Gallagher, 'The Leasowes', p. 210.
39. Hunt & Willis (eds), *The Genius of the Place*, p. 290.
40. Riely, 'Shenstone's Walks', p. 207.
41. Hunt & Willis (eds), *The Genius of the Place*, pp. 294–6.

42. Gallagher, 'The Leasowes', p. 211.
43. Ibid., p. 210.

CHAPTER ELEVEN

1. Nikolaus Pevsner, 'The Genius of the Picturesque', *Architectural Review*, November 1944, pp. 139–45.
2. John Harris, 'Painter of Rococo Gardens: Thomas Robins the Elder', *Country Life*, 7 September 1972; Eileen Harris, 'The Wizard of Durham: The Architecture of Thomas Wright', *Country Life*, 26 August and 2, 9 September 1971; see also John Harris & Martin Rix, *Gardens of Delight: The Rococo English Landscape of Thomas Robins the Elder*, 2 vols (1978).
3. For an analysis of Dublin and Bristol Rococo interiors see Timothy Mowl & Brian Earnshaw, *An Insular Rococo: Architecture, Politics and Society in Ireland and England, 1710–1770* (1999).
4. Apart from a modest Gothic remodelling at Hampton Court of 1732, Kent's first major essays in both Chinese and Gothic appear to have been for Esher Place, Surrey where he was working in the early 1730s for Henry Pelham: see John Harris, *William Kent 1685–1748: A Poet on Paper* (Soane Gallery Exhibition Catalogue, 1998), pls 9, 10 & 15. Plate 15 is a drawing of an octagonal Chinoiserie kiosk with lattice-work panels, tiled roof and dragons holding bells in their mouths.
5. For Ripa see Patrick Conner, *Oriental Architecture in the West* (1979), pp. 26–8; pl. 15.
6. See Patrick Conner, 'Britain's First Chinese Pavilion?', *Country Life*, 25 January 1979.
7. For Anson's work see John Martin Robinson, *Shugborough* (National Trust, 1989)
8. The best record of these ephemeral Chinoiserie structures is given in Conner, *Oriental Architecture*.
9. For Pococke see Mowl & Earnshaw, *An Insular Rococo*, Chapter 4; also Michael McCarthy, '"The dullest man that ever travelled"? A Re-assessment of Richard Pococke and of his Portrait by J.E. Liotard', *Apollo*, May 1996, pp. 25–9.
10. J. Cartwright (ed.), *The Travels through England of Dr Richard Pococke*, 2 vols (Camden Society, 1888–9), **1**, p. 68.
11. Ibid., **2**, pp. 137–8.
12. For Hyett and Painswick see Timothy Mowl, 'In the Realm of the Great God Pan', *Country Life*, 17 October 1996; also Roger White & Timothy Mowl, 'Thomas Robins at Painswick', *Journal of Garden History*, **4**, 2 (1994), pp. 163–78.
13. For Painshill see Mavis Batey & David Lambert, *The English Garden Tour: A View into the Past* (1990), pp. 186–90.
14. For views of Kew see Conner, *Oriental Architecture*, pp. 80–1; also John Harris, *Sir William Chambers: Knight of the Polar Star* (1970), pls 22–40.
15. Cartwright (ed.), *Pococke*, **2**, p. 63
16. Ibid., **2**, p. 62.

17. Emily J. Cleminson (ed.), *Passages from the Diaries of Mrs Philip Lybbe Powys of Hardwick House, Oxon. A.D. 1756 to 1808* (1899), p. 114.
18. Ibid., pp. 114–15.
19. Quoted in Kenneth Woodbridge, *The Stourhead Landscape* (National Trust, 1982), p. 28.
20. Cleminson (ed.), *Lybbe Powys*, p. 169.
21. Quoted in Woodbridge, *Stourhead Landscape*, p. 61.
22. Ibid., p. 31.
23. James Sambrook, 'Wooburn Farm in the 1760s', *Garden History*, **7**, 2 (1979), pp. 82–101; p. 94.
24. Woodbridge, *Stourhead Landscape*, p. 27.
25. Ibid., p. 23.
26. Ibid., p. 21.
27. Cartwright (ed.), *Pococke*, **2**, p. 43.
28. For a 1779 plan and section of this by F.M. Piper see Woodbridge, *Stourhead Landscape*, p. 54.
29. Cleminson (ed.), *Lybbe Powys*, p. 171.
30. Ibid., p. 169.

CHAPTER TWELVE

1. Articles on Richard Woods and William Emes are given in the bibliography under this chapter heading. The most authoritative work on Brown is by Dorothy Stroud, *Capability Brown* (1950).
2. From the Red Book for Hewell (1812); quoted in Stephen Daniels, *Humphry Repton: Landscape Gardening and the Geography of Georgian England* (New Haven, CT, & London, 1999), p. 103.
3. Quoted from Thomas Whately's *Observations on Modern Gardening* in *Stowe Landscape Gardens* (National Trust, 1997), pp. 45–6.
4. The more practical, utilitarian side to mid-eighteenth-century landscaping is discussed in Tom Williamson, *Polite Landscapes: Gardens and Society in Eighteenth-Century England* (Stroud, 1995), Chapter Six: 'Beauty and Utility', pp. 119–40.
5. For a fuller account see Williamson, *Polite Landscapes*, pp. 130–40.
6. Quoted in Stroud, *Capability Brown*, p. 33.
7. Dunstall Castle, by Adam, dates from 1766; the Panorama Tower was conceived by Adam in the 1760s, but not built until the 1790s to designs by James Wyatt; Pirton Castle is also by Wyatt and dates from 1797. My thanks to Tom Oliver for this information.
8. For these structures see Marcus Binney, 'Packington Hall, Warwickshire', *Country Life*, 9 July 1970.
9. Edmund Burke, *A Philosophical Enquiry into the Origin of Our Ideas of the Sublime and Beautiful* (1759; facsimile edition, Scolar Press, Menston, 1970).
10. Oliver Goldsmith, *The Deserted Village* (1770), lines 35–8.
11. Ibid., lines 1–2.
12. Ibid., line 52.
13. Ibid., lines 275–86.
14. Stroud, *Capability Brown*, p. 125.

15. For portraits of Brown by Nathaniel Dance-Holland and Richard Cosway see Stroud, *Capability Brown*, pp. 35 and 133 respectively.
16. Ibid., p. 177.
17. Ibid., p. 101.
18. Ibid., p. 101.
19. Ibid., p. 199.
20. Burke, *Enquiry*, p. 300.
21. Quoted by Christopher Hussey in Stroud, *Capability Brown*, p. 17.
22. Lilian Dickins & Mary Stanton (eds), *An Eighteenth-Century Correspondence* (1910), pp. 135–6.
23. Brown made four contract visits to Longleat in 1757, 1758, 1759 and 1763: Longleat Archives, Thynne Papers Box XXX (vol. LXXVII), ff. 280–9. This reference is made with the permission of the Marquess of Bath.
24. For Brown's Classical and Gothic buildings see Stroud, *Capability Brown*, pp. 208–9.
25. For Prior Park see Gillian Clarke, *Prior Park: A Compleat Landscape* (Bath, 1987); Timothy Mowl, *Palladian Bridges: Prior Park and the Whig Connection* (Bath, 1993).
26. Elisabeth Hall, '"Mr Brown's Directions": Capability Brown's Landscaping at Burton Constable (1767–82)', *Garden History*, **23**, 2 (1995), p. 157.
27. W.S. Lewis (ed.), *The Yale Edition of Horace Walpole's Correspondence*, 48 vols (1937–83); **29**, p. 304: Walpole to William Mason, 19 May 1783.
28. Emily J. Cleminson (ed.), *Passages from the Diaries of Mrs Philip Lybbe Powys of Hardwick House, Oxon. A.D. 1756 to 1808* (1899), pp. 174–5.

CHAPTER THIRTEEN

1. Malcolm Andrews, *The Search for the Picturesque: Landscape Aesthetics and Tourism in Britain, 1760–1800* (1989), p. 69.
2. William Gilpin, *Observations on the River Wye and Several Parts of South Wales, etc., Relative Chiefly to Picturesque Beauty* (1782), pp. 8–9.
3. Ibid., p. 9. A 'break' was Picturesque jargon for a glimpse or snatch of perception. Arthur Young employed the term more frequently even than Gilpin.
4. Ibid., p. 12. Whately's *Observations* describes industrial scenes on the Wye with the same appreciation for heaps of cinders and the beat of forge hammers mingling with the roar of the weir.
5. William Wordsworth, 'Lines composed a few miles above Tintern Abbey, on revisiting the banks of the Wye during a tour. July 13, 1798', lines 21–2.
6. Gilpin, *Observations on the River Wye*, p. 19.
7. Ibid., p. 14.
8. Ibid., p. 39.
9. The several features on the route are discussed in Elisabeth Whittle, '"All these inchanting scenes":

Piercefield in the Wye Valley', *Garden History*, **24**, 1 (1996), pp. 148–61. The artificial cave was there in 1770, but the giant was possibly a later addition.
10. Gilpin, *Observations on the River Wye*, p. 40.
11. Jane Austen, *Northanger Abbey* (1818), Chapter 14.
12. Gilpin, *Observations on the River Wye*, p. 41.
13. Ibid., p. 40.
14. Arthur Young, *A Six Weeks Tour through the Southern Counties of England and Wales* (Dublin, 1768), p. 119.
15. Ibid., p. 125.
16. Whately, *Observations*, p. 241.
17. The first version of *The Prelude* was written in the winter of 1798/9, but not published until 1850.
18. Sir Uvedale Price, *An Essay on the Picturesque* (1794), p. 28.
19. Ibid., pp. 28–30.
20. Ibid., p. 190.
21. Ibid., p. 231.
22. Richard Payne Knight, *The Landscape* (1795), Book II, p. 34.
23. Ibid., p. 45.
24. Ibid., p. 38.
25. Ibid., pp. 47–8.
26. For the Downton landscape and Thomas Hearne's paintings see Andrew Ballantyne, *Architecture, Landscape and Liberty: Richard Payne Knight and the Picturesque* (Cambridge, 1997); especially pp. 276–80.
27. Ibid., p. 276.
28. Ibid., p. 276.
29. Quoted in *Hawkstone: A Short History and Guide* (Hawkstone Park Leisure, 1993), p. 10.

CHAPTER FOURTEEN

1. The most definitive account of Repton's life and work to date is Stephen Daniels, *Humphry Repton: Landscape Gardening and the Geography of Georgian England* (New Haven, CT, & London, 1999).
2. Ibid., p. 93.
3. Repton to Norton Nicholls, 26 August 1788, Bristol University Library, 180/1.
4. Translated by Daniel Malthus in 1783 as *An Essay on Landscape*.
5. Catton, outside Norwich, for Jeremiah Ives, was his first consultation and, allowing for the difference in terrain, was handled exactly like Blaise Castle of 1795.
6. In the *Monthly Review* for January 1796, William Marshall noted that an unimproved view 'is represented as a scene without spirit or animation, while to the other every master-stroke of Mr R's pencil is given'.
7. Letter from Repton to Lord Sheffield, 22 December 1805; quoted in Daniels, *Repton*, p. 150.
8. Daniels, *Repton*, p. 173.
9. From Repton's Red Book for Endsleigh; quoted in Daniels, *Repton*, p. 189.

10. The 'Memoir' is in the British Library, Add. MS. 62112; quotation from Daniels, *Repton*, p. 158.

11. Ibid., p. 157.

12. Ibid., p. 158

13. Ibid.

14. Ibid., p. 164.

15. Humphry Repton, *Observations on the Theory and Practice of Landscape Gardening* (1803), p. 13.

16. Sir Uvedale Price, *An Essay on the Picturesque* (1794), p. 30.

17. The castle was built for Thomas Farr by the architect Robert Milne in 1766.

18. The Friends of Blaise Castle Museum, where the original is deposited, have produced an abridged copy of the 1796 Red Book from which this and subsequent quotations are taken. It is available in the Museum Shop.

19. This cottage could just conceivably be by Thomas Wright and of 1750s date; Wright was working for the 4th Duke of Beaufort at Badminton, Gloucestershire and Norborne Berkeley at Stoke Park in Bristol at this time.

20. Daniels, *Repton*, p. 118.

21. Repton, *Observations*, p. 142.

22. Humphry Repton & John Adey Repton, *Fragments on the Theory and Practice of Landscape Gardening* (1816), p. 64.

23. For Repton's rejected designs for the Pavilion and its gardens see Daniels, *Repton*, pp. 192–205.

24. Most notably by John Harris (see Bibliography). However, a major study was just about to appear as this book was in proof stage: Mark Laird, *The Flowering of the Landscape Garden: English Pleasure Grounds 1720–1800* (Philadelphia, PA, 1999).

25. William Mason, *The English Garden* (1783); passage taken from Book IV.

26. Richard Payne Knight, *The Landscape* (1795), Book II, p. 32 (lines 25–8).

27. Christopher Ricks, *Keats and Embarrassment* (Oxford, 1974).

28. Concerning Lord Coventry's villa at Streatham; from Repton, *Fragments*, p. 73.

29. Ibid., p. 85.

30. Ibid.

31. Ibid., p. 99.

32. Ibid., p. 101.

33. Ibid., p. 48.

34. Ibid., p. 129.

35. Ibid., p. 101.

36. Ibid., p. 100.

37. Ibid.

38. Quoted in Daniels, *Repton*, p. 21.

39. A letter of January 1815; quoted in Ibid., p. 101.

SELECT
BIBLIOGRAPHY

The bibliography is arranged according to chapters with primary printed sources given first, then secondary printed sources and lastly seminal articles relating to the topic under discussion; other articles will be found in the notes and are not repeated here. 'Standard Texts and General Surveys' gives a broad background to the stylistic periods and there will be other relevant articles in the three scholarly journals concerned with garden history. These are: *Studies in the History of Gardens & Designed Landscapes*, formerly *Journal of Garden History: An International Quarterly*, *Garden History: The Journal of the Garden History Society* and the *New Arcadian Journal*. There are also articles on specific gardens in *Country Life*, for which there is a 'Cumulative Index' held by the reference departments of most public libraries. Further references to specific articles on gardens and landscapes can be found in Ray Desmond's *Bibliography of British Gardens*, 1988. Place of publication is London unless otherwise specified.

STANDARD TEXTS AND GENERAL SURVEYS

William Howard Adams, *The French Garden 1500–1800* (1979)

B. Sprague Allen, *Tides in English Taste* (Cambridge, MA, 1937)

Mavis Batey, *Regency Gardens* (1995)

Mavis Batey & David Lambert, *The English Garden Tour: A View into the Past* (1990)

Julia Berrall, *The Garden* (1978)

Ann Bermingham, *Landscape and Ideology: the English Rustic Tradition 1740–1860* (1986)

James Bond, *Somerset Parks and Gardens; A Landscape History* (Tiverton, 1998)

Jane Brown, *The Pursuit of Paradise: A Social History of Gardens and Gardening* (1999)

Edmund Burke, *A Philosophical Enquiry into the Origin of Our Ideas of the Sublime and Beautiful* (1759; facsimile edition, Scolar Press, Menston, 1970)

Michael Charlesworth, *The English Garden: Literary Sources & Documents*, 3 vols (Mountfield, 1993)

Judith Chatfield, *A Tour of Italian Gardens* (1988)

H.F. Clark, *The English Landscape Garden* (1948)

Kenneth Clark, *The Gothic Revival: An Essay in the History of Taste* (1928)

David Coffin (ed.), *The Italian Garden* (Dumbarton Oaks, Washington DC, 1972)

——, *The English Garden: Meditation and Memorial* (Princeton, NJ, 1994)

Terry Comito, *The Idea of the Garden in the Renaissance* (1978)

Miles Hadfield, *A History of British Gardening* (1985)

——, *British Gardeners: a Biographical Dictionary* (1980)

Stewart Harding & David Lambert, *Parks and Gardens of Avon* (Bristol, 1994)

John Harris, *The Artist and the Country House* (1979)

Gwyn Headley & Wim Meulenkamp, *Follies: A Guide to Rogue Architecture in England, Scotland and Wales* (1986)

Robert Hewison, *The Heritage Industry: Britain in a Climate of Decline* (1987)

James Howley, *The Follies and Garden Buildings of Ireland* (New Haven, CT, & London, 1993)

John Dixon Hunt & Peter Willis (eds), *The Genius of the Place: The English Landscape Garden 1620–1820* (1988)

——, *The Figure in the Landscape: Poetry, Painting, and Gardening During the Eighteenth Century* (1977)

John Dixon Hunt & Peter Willis (eds), *Gardens and the Picturesque: Studies in the History of Landscape Architecture* (1992)

Christopher Hussey, *English Gardens and Landscapes 1700–1750* (1967)

Gervase Jackson-Stops, *The Country House Garden* (1987)

——, *An English Arcadia 1600–1990: Designs for Gardens and Garden Buildings in the Care of the National Trust* (1991)

David Jacques, *Georgian Gardens: The Reign of Nature* (1983)

Barbara Jones, *Follies and Grottoes* (1953)

M.R. Lagerlof, *Ideal Landscape: Annibale Carracci, Nicolas Poussin and Claude Lorrain* (1990)

Mark Laird, *The Flowering of the Landscape Garden: English Pleasure Grounds 1720–1800* (Philadelphia, PA, 1999)

Claudia Lazzaro, *The Italian Renaissance Garden* (New Haven, CT, & London, 1990)

James Lees-Milne, *The Earls of Creation: Five Great Patrons of Eighteenth-Century Art* (1962)

Karin Lindegren (ed.), *Fredrik Magnus Piper and the Landscape Garden* (Katrineholm, 1981)

Edward Malins, *English Landscaping and Literature, 1660–1840* (1966)

Elizabeth Wheeler Manwaring, *Italian Landscape in Eighteenth-Century England: A Study Chiefly of the Influence of Claude Lorrain and Salvator Rosa on English Taste 1700–1800* (New York, 1925)

Georgina Masson, *Italian Gardens* (1961)

Sheila McTighe, *Nicolas Poussin's Landscape Allegories* (1996)

Monique Mosser & G. Teyssot (eds), *The History of Garden Design: the Western Tradition from the Renaissance to the Present Day* (1991)

Timothy Mowl & Brian Earnshaw, *Trumpet at a Distant Gate: The Lodge as Prelude to the Country House* (1985)

David Neave & Deborah Turnbull, *Landscaped Parks and Gardens of East Yorkshire* (1992)

Ian Ousby, *The Englishman's England: Taste, Travel and the Rise of Tourism* (1990)

Douglas Ellory Pett, *The Parks and Gardens of Cornwall* (1998)

Nikolaus Pevsner, *The Picturesque Garden and its Influence Outside the British Isles* (1974)

——, *Studies in Art, Architecture and Design*, 2 vols (1968)

John Martin Robinson, *The English Country Estate* (1988)

Paul Stamper, *Historic Parks & Gardens of Shropshire* (Shrewsbury, 1996)

David Stuart, *Georgian Gardens* (1979)

John Summerson, *Architecture in Britain: 1530–1830* (Harmondsworth, 1977)

Christopher Taylor, *Parks and Gardens of Britain: A Landscape History from the Air* (1998)

Christopher Thacker, *The History of Gardens* (1979)

——, *The Genius of Gardening: The History of Gardens in Britain and Ireland* (1994)

Tom Turner, *English Garden Design: History and Styles since 1650* (1986)

Robin Whalley & Anne Jennings, *Knot Gardens and Parterres* (1998)

Roger White, (ed.), *Georgian Arcadia: Architecture for the Park and Garden* (1987)

Elisabeth Whittle, *The Historic Gardens of Wales* (1992)

Tom Williamson, *Polite Landscapes: Gardens and Society in Eighteenth-Century England* (Stroud, 1995)

Tom Williamson & Liz Bellamy, *Property and Landscape* (1987)

Peter Willis (ed.), *Furor Hortensis: Essays on the History of the English Landscape Garden in Memory of H.F. Clark* (Edinburgh, 1974)

Humphrey Wine, *Claude: The Poetic Landscape* (1994)

CHAPTER ONE

Primary Printed Sources

John Aubrey, *Memoires of Natural Remarques in the County of Wiltshire* (1847, ed. John Britton)

Isaac de Caus, *Wilton Garden; New and Rare Inventions of Waterworks*, 1640 (facsimile, ed. John Dixon Hunt, New York, 1982)

——, *Nouvelle Invention de lever L'eau plus hault que sa source* (1644)

——, *New and Rare Inventions of Water Works* (1659)

Solomon de Caus, *Les Raisons de Forces Mouvantes* (Frankfurt, 1615)

——, *Les Raisons de Forces Mouvantes* (1624)

Lieutenant Hammond, 'Description of a Journey made into Westerne Counties', *The Camden Miscellany*, XVI (1936)

Christopher Morris (ed.), *The Illustrated Journeys of Celia Fiennes c. 1682 – c. 1712*, (1982)

Henry Wotton, *The Elements of Architecture* (1624; facsimile edition, ed. F. Hard, Charlottesville, VA, 1968)

Secondary Printed Sources

John Bold, *Wilton House and English Palladianism* (1988)

Howard Colvin, *Essays in English Architectural History* (New Haven, CT, & London, 1999)

John Harris, Stephen Orgel & Roy Strong (eds), *The King's Arcadia: Inigo Jones and the Stuart Court* (Arts Council, 1973)

John Harris & A.A. Tait, *Catalogue of the Drawings by Inigo Jones, John Webb and Isaac de Caus at Worcester College, Oxford* (1979)

John Harris & Gordon Higgott, *Inigo Jones: Complete Architectural Drawings* (1989)

John Dixon Hunt, *Garden and Grove – The Italian Renaissance Garden in the English Imagination: 1600–1750* (Princeton, NJ, 1986)

Timothy Mowl & Brian Earnshaw, *Architecture Without Kings: The Rise of Puritan Classicism under Cromwell* (Manchester, 1995)

Roy Strong, *The Renaissance Garden in England* (1979)

John Summerson, *Inigo Jones* (1966)

Articles

J.K. Burras, 'Britain's Oldest Botanic Garden', *Country Life*, 15 July 1971

Timothy Mowl & Brian Earnshaw, 'Inigo Jones Restored', *Country Life*, 30 January 1992

CHAPTER TWO

Primary Printed Sources

Walter Blith, *The English Improver Improved, or the Survey of Husbandry Surveyed* (1652)

Samuel Hartlib, *A Discourse of Husbandrie used in Brabant and Flanders, shewing the Wonderfull Improvement of Land there* (1650)

——, *Samuel Hartlib his Legacie or an Enlargement of the Discourse on HUSBANDRY used in Brabant and Flaunders* (1652)

——, *Cornu Copia, a Miscellaneum of Luciferous and most Fructerous Experiments, Observations, and Discoveries Immethodically Distributed*, 1652

——, *The Reformed Spirituall Husbandman* (1652)

——, *A Discoverie for Division, or Setting out of Land as to the Best Form* (1653)

——, *Discourse of the whole Art of Husbandry, both Foreign and Domestick* (1659)

Gervase Markham, *Farewell to Husbandry* (1631)

John Ogilby, *The Works of Publius Virgilius Maro* (1654)

John Parkinson, *Paradisi in Sole, Paradisus Terrestris* (1628)

John Worlidge, *Systema Agriculturae, Being The Mystery of Husbandry Discovered and layd Open* (1668)

Secondary Printed Sources

G.H. Turnbull, *Hartlib, Dury and Comenius: Gleanings from Hartlib's Papers* (Liverpool, 1947)

Charles Webster, *The Great Insturation: Science, Medicine and Reform, 1626–1660* (1975)

R.E. Young, *Comenius in England* (Oxford & London, 1932)

Articles

Timothy Mowl, 'New Science, Old Order: the Gardens of the Great Rebellion', *Journal of Garden History*, **13** (1993), pp. 16–35

Giles Worsley, 'Snitterton Hall, Derbyshire', *Country Life*, 5 March 1992

CHAPTER THREE

Primary Printed Sources

John Beale, *Herefordshire Orchards, a Pattern for all England Written in an Epistolary Address to Samuel Hartlib Esq.*, (1657)

Thomas Hanmer, *The Garden Book of Sir Thomas Hanmer Bart* (1659) (Mold, Clwyd, 1993 printing from the original MS volume)

Sir Henry Wotton, *The Elements of Architecture* (1624)

Articles

Peter Goodchild, '"No Phantastical Utopia but a Reall Place". John Evelyn, John Beale and Backbury Hill, Herefordshire', *Garden History*, **19**, 2 (1991), pp. 105–27

Timothy Mowl, 'New Science, Old Order: the Gardens of the Great Rebellion', *Journal of Garden History*, **13** (1993), pp. 16–35

CHAPTER FOUR

Primary Printed Sources

E.S. De Beer (ed.), *The Diary of John Evelyn*, 6 vols (Oxford, 1955)

Moses Cook, *The Manner of Raising, Ordering, and Improving Forest and Fruit Trees* (1676)

John Evelyn, *The French Gardener* (translated from Nicholas de Bonnefois) (1658)

——, *Sylva, or a Discourse of Forest-Trees and the Propogation of Timber* (1664)

——, *Directions for The Gardiner at Says-Court*, ed. Geoffrey Keynes (Nonesuch Press edition, 1932)

Secondary Printed Sources

Mavis Batey, *Oxford Gardens* (1982)

Therese O'Malley & Joachim Wolschke-Bulmahn (eds), *John Evelyn's 'Elysium Britannicum' and European Gardening* (Dumbarton Oaks, Washington DC, 1998)

Articles

Douglas Chambers, 'The Tomb in the Landscape: John Evelyn's Garden at Albury', *Journal of Garden History*, **1**, 1 (1981), pp. 37–54

Peter Goodchild, 'John Smith's Paradise and Theatre of Nature', *Garden History*, **24**, 1 (1996), pp. 19–23

——, 'John Smith's Paradise and Theatre of Nature: The Plans', *Garden History*, **25**, 1 (1997), pp. 28–44

Frances Harris, 'The Manuscripts of John Evelyn's "Elysium Britannicum"', *Garden History*, **25**, 2 (1997), pp. 131–7

Prudence Leith-Ross, 'A Seventeenth-Century Paris Garden', *Garden History*, **21**, 2 (1993), pp. 151–57

——, 'The Garden of John Evelyn at Deptford', *Garden History*, **25**, 2 (1997), pp. 138–52

Timothy Mowl, 'New Science, Old Order: the Gardens of the Great Rebellion', *Journal of Garden History*, **13** (1993), pp. 16–35

CHAPTER FIVE

Primary Printed Sources

John Harris & Gervase Jackson-Stops (eds), *Britannia Illustrata or Views of Several of the Queens Palaces also of the Principal Seats of the Nobility and Gentry of Great Britain*, 1707 (facsimile edition, 1984)

George London & Henry Wise, *The Compleat Gard'ner: or, Directions for Cultivating and Right Ordering of Fruit-Gardens, and Kitchen-Gardens* (1699)

——, *The Retir'd Gardener* (1706)

Secondary Printed Sources

Mavis Batey & Jan Woudstra, *The Story of the Privy Garden at Hampton Court* (1995)

Reginald Blomfield, *The Formal Garden in England* (1901)

Helen M. Fox, *André Le Nôtre* (no date)

David Green, *Gardener to Queen Anne: Henry Wise (1653–1738) and the Formal Garden* (1956)

John Harris, *William Talman: Maverick Architect* (1982)

John Dixon Hunt, *Garden and Grove – The Italian Renaissance Garden in the English Imagination: 1600–1750* (Princeton, NJ, 1986)

David Jacques & Arend Jan van der Horst, *The Gardens of William and Mary* (Bromley, 1988)

E. Macdougall & F.H. Hazelhurst, *Dumbarton Oaks Colloquium: The French Formal Garden* (Dumbarton Oaks, Washington DC, 1974)

G. & L. Madder, *The English Formal Garden* (1997)

Anthony Mitchell, *The Park and Garden at Dyrham* (National Trust, 1977)

Christopher Morris (ed.), *The Illustrated Journeys of Celia Fiennes c. 1682 – c. 1712* (1982)

Articles

Ruth Duthie, 'The Planting Plans of some Seventeenth-Century Flower Gardens', *Garden History*, **18**, 2 (1990), pp. 77–102

Peter Goodchild, 'John Rea's Gardens of Delight: Introduction and the Construction of the Flower Garden', *Garden History*, **9**, 2 (1981), pp. 99–109

Laurence Pattacini, 'André Mollet, Royal Gardener in St James's Park, London', *Garden History*, **26**, 1 (1998), pp. 3–18

Susan Taylor-Leduc (ed.), 'Seventeenth Century French Garden History', *Studies in the History of Gardens & Designed Landscapes*, **18**, 1 (1998)

Simon Thurley, 'William and Mary's Privy Garden at Hampton Court Palace', *Apollo*, September 1995, pp. 3–22

CHAPTER SIX

Primary Printed Sources

Bonamy Dobrée & Geoffrey Webb, *The Complete Works of Sir John Vanbrugh*, 4 vols (1928)

Secondary Printed Sources

James Bond & Kate Tiller (eds), *Blenheim: Landscape for a Palace* (Gloucester, 1987)

Kerry Downes, *Vanbrugh* (1977)

David Green, *Blenheim Palace* (1956)

Christopher Ridgway & Robert Williams (eds), *Sir John Vanbrugh and Landscape Architecture in Baroque England 1690–1730* (Stroud, 2000)

Peter Willis, *Charles Bridgeman and the English Landscape Garden* (1977)

Laurence Whistler, *The Imagination of Vanbrugh and his Fellow Artists* (1954)

Articles

Howard Colvin & Alistair Rowan, 'The Grand Bridge in Blenheim Park', in John Bold & Edward Chaney (eds), *English Architecture Public and Private: Essays for Kerry Downes* (1993), pp. 159–75

Miles Hadfield, 'Climax of England's Formal Gardens', *Country Life*, 21 June 1973

Frances Harris, 'Charles Bridgeman at Blenheim?', *Garden History*, **13**, 1 (1985), pp. 1–3

John Harris, 'Diverting Labyrinths', *Country Life*, 11 January 1990

——, 'The Beginnings of Claremont: Sir John Vanbrugh's Garden at Chargate in Surrey', *Apollo*, April 1993

Peter Willis, 'Charles Bridgeman and the English Landscape Garden: New Documents and Attributions', in John Bold & Edward Chaney (eds), *English Architecture Public and Private: Essays for Kerry Downes* (1993)

CHAPTER SEVEN

Primary Printed Sources

3rd Earl of Shaftesbury, *Letter Concerning the Art or Science of Design* (1712)

Stephen Switzer, *The Nobleman, Gentleman, and Gardener's Recreation*, 1715; revised and enlarged as *Ichnographia Rustica, or, The Nobleman, Gentleman, and Gardener's Recreation* (1718)

——, *The Practical Kitchen Gardiner* (1727)

Horace Walpole, *The History of the Modern Taste in Gardening* (1780; facsimile edition, ed. John Dixon Hunt, 1995)

Secondary Printed Sources

Douglas Chambers, *The Planters of the English Landscape Garden: Botany, Trees, and the Georgics* (1993) (Chapter 5: 'Rural and Extensive Landscape: Switzer and *Ingentia Rura*')

CHAPTER EIGHT

Primary Printed Sources

George Sherburn (ed.), *The Correspondence of Alexander Pope*, 5 vols (Oxford, 1956)

Maynard Mack (ed.), *The Poems of Alexander Pope*, 11 vols (1967)

Joseph Warton, *An Essay on the Genius and Writings of Pope* (1782)

Secondary Printed Sources

Mavis Batey, *Alexander Pope: The Poet and the Landscape* (1999)

Benjamin Boyce, *The Benevolent Man: A Life of Ralph Allen of Bath* (1967)

Morris Brownell, *Alexander Pope & the Arts of Georgian England* (Oxford, 1978)

——, *Alexander Pope's Villa: a View of Pope's Villa, Grotto and Garden: a Microcosm of English Landscape* 1980

Gillian Clarke, *Prior Park: A Compleat Landscape* (Bath, 1987)

Peter Dixon, *Alexander Pope, Writers and their Background* (1972)

James Lees-Milne, The Earls of Creation (1986)

Peter Martin, *Pursuing Innocent Pleasure, The Gardening World of Alexander Pope* (1984)

Timothy Mowl, *Palladian Bridges* (Bath, 1993)

Anthony Beckles Willson, *Alexander Pope's Grotto in Twickenham* (Twickenham, 1998)

Articles

Morris Brownell, 'The Gardens of Horatio and Pope's Twickenham: An Unnoticed Parallel', *Garden History*, **5**, 2 (1977), pp. 9–23

Anthony Beckles Willson, 'Alexander Pope's Grotto in Twickenham', *Garden History*, **26**, 1 (1998), pp. 31–59

CHAPTER NINE

Primary Printed Sources

Robert Castell, *Villas of the Ancients Illustrated*, 1728 (facsimile edition,1982)

Batty Langley, *New Principles of Gardening or The Laying Out and Planting Parterres, Groves, Wildernesses, Labyrinths, Avenues . . . After a More Grand and Rural Manner than has Been Done Before* (1728)

——, *A Sure Method of Improving Estates by Plantations* (1728)

Horace Walpole, *The History of the Modern Taste in Gardening*, 1780 (facsimile edition ed. by John Dixon Hunt, 1995)

Secondary Printed Sources

Douglas Chambers, *The Planters of the English Landscape Garden* (1993) (Chapter 2: 'The Translation of Antiquity: Pliny and Virgil')

George Clarke, *Descriptions of Lord Cobham's Garden's at Stowe (1700–1750)* (1990)

Terry Friedman, *James Gibbs* (New Haven, CT, & London, 1984)

John Harris, *The Palladian Revival: Lord Burlington, his Villa and Garden at Chiswick* (New Haven, CT, & London, 1994)

John Dixon Hunt, *William Kent: Landscape Garden Designer* (1987)

——, *William Gilpin – A Dialogue upon the Gardens . . . at Stow* (1976)

David Jacques, *Georgian Gardens: The Reign of Nature* (1983)

John Martin Robinson, *Temples of Delight: Stowe Landscape Gardens* (1990)

Kimberley Rorschach, *The Early Georgian Landscape Garden* (1983)

Michael I. Wilson, *William Kent: Architect, Designer, Painter, Gardener, 1685–1748* (1984)

Giles Worsley, *Classical Architecture in Britain: The Heroic Age* (New Haven, CT, & London, 1995)

Articles

Mavis Batey, 'The Way to View Rousham by Kent's Gardener', *Garden History*, **11**, 2 (1983), pp. 125–32

H.F. Clark, 'Eighteenth-Century Elysiums: The Role of "Association" in the Landscape Movement', *Journal of Warburg and Courtauld Institutes*, **VI**, (1943), pp. 165–89

George Clarke, 'Military Gardening at Stowe', *Country Life*, 18 May 1972

——, 'Grecian Taste and Gothic Virtue', *Apollo*, **92** (1973), pp. 566–77

——, 'Heresy in Stowe's Elysium', in Peter Willis (ed.), *Furor Hortensis: Essays on the History of the English Landscape Garden in Memory of H.F. Clark* (1974), pp. 49–56

David Coombs, 'The Garden at Carlton House of Frederick Prince of Wales and Augusta Princess and Dowager of Wales', *Garden History*, **25**, 2 (1997), pp. 153–77

John Harris, 'Serendipity and the Architect Earl', *Country Life*, 28 May 1987

John Hayes, 'English Patrons and Landscape Painting', *Apollo*, March 1966, pp. 188–97; June 1966, pp. 444–51; April 1967, pp. 254–9

Hal Moggeridge, 'Kent's Garden at Rousham', *Journal of Garden History*, **VI** (1984), pp. 187–266

Ulrich Müller, 'Rousham: A Transcription of the Steward's Letters, 1738–42', *Garden History*, **25**, 2 (1997), pp. 178–88

Cinzia Maria Sicca, 'Lord Burlington at Chiswick: Architecture and Landscape', *Garden History*, **10**, 1 (1982), pp. 36–69.

'The Political Temples of Stowe', *New Arcadian Journal*, no. 43/44 (1997)

Laurence Whistler, 'The Authorship of the Stowe Temples', *Country Life*, 29 September 1950

Giles Worsley, 'Rokeby Park, Yorkshire', *Country Life*, 19 March 1987

CHAPTER TEN

Primary Printed Sources

James M. Osborn (ed.), *Joseph Spence, Observations, Anecdotes, and Characters of Books and Men*, 2 vols (1966)

Slava Klima (ed.), *Joseph Spence: Letters from the Grand Tour* (1975)

William Shenstone, *Works in Verse and Prose*, 2 vols (1764)

Marjorie Williams (ed.), *The Letters of William Shenstone* (Oxford, 1939)

Secondary Printed Sources

Mavis Batey & David Lambert, *The English Garden Tour* (1990)

Douglas Chambers, *The Planters of the English Landscape Garden: Botany, Trees, and the Georgics*, (1993) (Chapter 10: 'Nature's still Improv'd but never Lost: Philip Southcote and Wooburn Farm'; Chapter 11: 'Prospects and the natural beauties of Places: Joseph Spence'; Chapter 12: 'Smoothing or Brushing the Robe of Nature: William Shenstone and The Leasowes')

Articles

Christopher Gallagher, 'The Leasowes: A History of the Landscape', *Garden History*, **24**, 2 (1996), pp. 201–20

R.W. King, 'Joseph Spence of Byfleet (Part 1)', *Garden History*, **6**, 3 (1978), pp. 38–64

Peter Martin, 'Joseph Spence's Garden in Byfleet: Some New Descriptions', *Journal of Garden History*, **3**, 2 (1983), pp. 121–29

E. Charles Nelson, 'Joseph Spence's Plan for an Irish Garden', *Garden History*, **15**, 1 (1987), pp. 12–18

John Riely, 'Shenstone's Walks: The Genesis of The Leasowes', *Apollo*, **110**, September 1979, pp. 202–9

James Sambrook, 'Wooburn Farm in the 1760s', *Garden History*, **7**, 2 (1979), pp. 82–101

Michael Symes, 'New Light on Oatlands Park in the Eighteenth Century', *Garden History*, **9**, 2 (1981), pp. 136–56

CHAPTER ELEVEN

Primary Printed Sources

J. Cartwright (ed.), *The Travels through England of Dr Richard Pococke 1750–57*, 2 vols (Camden Society, 1888–9)

Emily J. Cleminson (ed.), *Passages from the Diaries of Mrs Philip Lybbe Powys of Hardwick House, Oxon. A.D. 1756 to 1808* (1899)

Paul Decker, *Gothic Architecture Decorated* (1759)

Lilian Dickins & Mary Stanton (eds), *An Eighteenth-Century Correspondence . . . Sanderson Miller* (1910)

William & John Halfpenny, *Chinese and Gothic Architecture Properly Ornamented* (1752)

Eileen Harris, *Thomas Wright Arbours and Grottos, a Facsimile . . . with a catalogue of Wright's Work in Architecture and Garden Design* (1979)

William Hogarth, *The Analysis of Beauty*, 1753 (1997 edition)

Batty Langley, *Ancient Architecture Restored and Improved* (1742)

W.S. Lewis (ed.), *The Yale Edition of Horace Walpole's Correspondence*, 48 vols (1937–83)

Horace Walpole, *The History of the Modern Taste in Gardening* (1780; facsimile edition, ed. John Dixon Hunt, 1995)

William Wrighte, *Grotesque Architecture, or Rural Amusement* (1767)

Secondary Printed Sources

Isabel Wakeling Chase, *Horace Walpole: Gardenist. An Edition of Walpole's 'The History of the Modern Taste in Gardening', with an Estimate of Walpole's Contribution to Landscape Architecture* (Princeton, NJ, 1943)

Patrick Conner, *Oriental Architecture in the West* (1979)

John Harris, *Sir William Chambers: Knight of the Polar Star* (1970)

——, *William Kent 1685–1748: A Poet on Paper* (Sloane Gallery Exhibition Catalogue, 1998)

John Harris & Martin Rix, *Gardens of Delight: The Rococo English Landscape of Thomas Robins the Elder* (1978)

Gervase Jackson-Stops, *An English Arcadia, 1600–1990* (1991)

Timothy Mowl, *Palladian Bridges* (Bath, 1993)

——, *Horace Walpole: The Great Outsider* (1996)

Timothy Mowl & Brian Earnshaw, *An Insular Rococo: Architecture, Politics and Society in Ireland and England 1710–1770* (1999)

John Martin Robinson, *Shugborough* (National Trust, 1989)

Alistair Rowan, *Garden Buildings* (no date)

Michael Snodin (ed.), *Rococo – Art and Design in Hogarth's England* (1984)

Michael Symes, *The English Rococo Garden* (Princes Risborough 1991)

Roger White, *Georgian Arcadia: Architecture for Park and Garden* (Georgian Group, 1987)

Kenneth Woodbridge, *The Stourhead Landscape* (National Trust, 1982)

Articles

Robert D. Bell, 'Archaeology and the Rococo Garden: The Restoration at Painswick House, Gloucestershire', *Garden History*, **21**, 1 (1993), pp. 24–45

Mavis Collier & David Wrightson, 'The Re-Creation of the Turkish Tent at Painshill', *Garden History*, **21**, 1 (1993), pp. 46–59

John Cornforth, 'In Pursuit of Thomas Robins', *Country Life*, 25 December 1975

Eileen Harris, 'The Wizard of Durham: The Architecture of Thomas Wright', *Country Life*, 26 August, and 2, 9 September 1971

——, 'So Rare, So Elegant: The Restored Grotto at Hampton Court House', *Country Life*, 18 December 1986

John Harris, 'Painter of Rococo Gardens: Thomas Robins the Elder', *Country Life*, 7 September 1972

John Harris, 'The Artinatural Style', in Charles Hind (ed.), *The Rococo in England* (1986), pp. 8–20

——, 'A Pioneer in Gardening: Dickie Bateman Re-assessed', *Apollo*, October 1993

Richard Haslam, 'Studley Royal, North Yorkshire', *Country Life*, 27 March 1986

Alison Hodges, 'Painshill Park, Cobham, Surrey (1700–1800)', *Garden History*, **2**, 1 (1973), pp. 39–68

Gervase Jackson-Stops, 'The West Wycombe Landscape, *Country Life*, 20 June 1974

——, 'The Orient and the Antique: The Shugborough Landscape', *Country Life*, 11 July 1991

David Jacques, 'On the Supposed Chineseness of the English Landscape Garden', *Garden History*, **18**, 2 (1990), pp. 180–91

Malcolm Kelsall, 'The Iconography of Stourhead', *Journal of the Warburg and Courtauld Institutes*, **XLVI** (1983), pp. 133–43

Michael McCarthy, 'Thomas Wright's "Designs for Temples" and related Drawings for Garden Buildings', *Journal of Garden History*, **1**, 2 (1981), pp. 55–66

——, 'Thomas Wright's Designs for Gothic Garden Buildings', *Journal of Garden History*, **1**, 3 (1981), pp. 239–52.

——, '"The dullest man that ever travelled"?: A Re-assessment of Richard Pococke and of his Portrait by J.E. Liotard', *Apollo*, May 1996, pp. 25–9

Jennifer Meir, 'Sanderson Miller and the Landscaping of Wroxton Abbey, Farnborough Hall and Honington Hall', *Garden History*, **25**, 1 (1997), pp. 81–106

Timothy Mowl, 'Rococo and Later Landscaping at Longleat', *Garden History*, **23**, 1 (1995), pp. 56–66

——, 'In the Realm of the Great God Pan', *Country Life*, 17 October 1996

Ciaran Murray, '*Sharawadgi* Resolved', *Garden History*, **26**, 2 (1998), pp. 208–13

Michael Symes, 'Charles Hamilton's Plantings at Painshill', *Garden History*, **11**, 2 (1983), pp. 112–24

——, 'Preparation of a Landscape Garden: Charles Hamilton's Sowing of Grass at Painshill', *Garden History*, **13**, 1 (1985), pp. 4–8

Roger White & Timothy Mowl, 'Thomas Robins at Painswick', *Journal of Garden History*, **4**, 2 (1984), pp. 163–78

Kenneth Woodbridge (ed.), 'Stourhead in 1768: Extracts from an unpublished journal by Sir John Parnell', *Journal of Garden History*, **2**, 1 (1982), pp .59–70.

CHAPTER TWELVE

Primary Printed Sources

Thomas Hinde, *Capability Brown* (1986)

Edward Hyams, *Humphry Repton and Capability Brown* (1971)

Dorothy Stroud, *Capability Brown* (1950)

Roger Turner, *Capability Brown* (1985)

Articles

David W. Booth, 'Blenheim Park on the Eve of "Mr Brown's Improvements"', *Journal of Garden History*, **15**, 2 (1995), pp. 107–25

Fiona Cowell, 'Richard Woods (?1716–93): A Preliminary Account', *Garden History*, **14**, 2 (1982), pp. 85–119

——, 'Richard Woods (?1716–93): A Preliminary Account, Part II', *Garden History*, **15**, 1 (1987), pp. 19–54

——, 'Richard Woods (?1716–93): A Preliminary Account, Part III', Garden History, **15**, 2 (1987), pp.115–35

Elisabeth Hall, '"Mr Brown's Directions": Capability Brown's Landscaping at Burton Constable (1767–82)', *Garden History*, **23**, 2 (1995), pp. 145–74

Timothy Mowl, 'Air of Irregularity', *Country Life*, 11 January 1990

John Phibbs, 'Groves and Belts', *Garden History*, **19**, 2 (1991), pp. 175–86

Walter Wilde, 'Not Just a Pupil of Brown's: The Work of William Emes', *Country Life*, 15 October 1987

Peter Willis, 'Capability Brown in Northumberland', *Garden History*, **9**, 2 (1981), pp. 157–83

CHAPTER THIRTEEN

Primary Printed Sources

W. Combe, *The Tour of Dr Syntax in Search of the Picturesque, a Poem* (1812)

William Gilpin, *Observations on the River Wye and Several Parts of South Wales, etc., Relative Chiefly to Picturesque Beauty* (1782)

——, *Three Essays: on Picturesque Beauty; on Picturesque Travel; and on Sketching Landscape. To which is added a Poem on Landscape Painting* (1792)

Richard Payne Knight, *The Landscape, a Didactic Poem* (1795)

Richard Payne Knight, *An Analytical Inquiry into the Principles of Taste* (1805)

Uvedale Price, *An Essay on the Picturesque* (1794; expanded as *Three Essays on the Picturesque*, 3 vols, 1810)

Thomas Whately, *Observations on Modern Gardening Illustrated by Descriptions* (Dublin,1770)

Arthur Young, *A Six Weeks Tour through the Southern Counties of England and Wales* (Dublin, 1768)

Secondary Printed Sources

Malcolm Andrews, *The Search for the Picturesque: Landscape Aesthetics and Tourism in Britain, 1760–1800* (1989)

——, *Landscape and Western Art* (1999)

Andrew Ballantyne, *Architecture, Landscape and Liberty: Richard Payne Knight and the Picturesque* (Cambridge, 1997)

C.P. Barbier, *William Gilpin: his Drawings, Teaching and Theory of the Picturesque* (Oxford, 1963)

Mavis Batey, *Jane Austen and the English Landscape* (1998)

Peter Bicknell (ed.), *Beauty, Honour and Immensity: Picturesque Landscape in Britain 1755–1850* (1981)

Michael Clarke & Nicholas Penny, *The Arrogant Connoisseur: Richard Payne Knight 1751–1824* (Manchester, 1982)

Gina Crandell, *Nature Pictorialized; "The View" in Landscape History* (1993)

Stephen Daniels & Charles Watkins, *The Picturesque Landscape: Visions of Georgian Herefordshire* (Nottingham, 1994)

Frank Hessman, *Richard Payne Knight: Twilight of Virtuosity* (1974)

John Walter Hipple, *The Beautiful, the Sublime and the Picturesque in Eighteenth-Century British Aesthetic Theory* (Carbondale, 1957)

Christopher Hussey, *The Picturesque, Studies in a Point of View* (1927)

E.W. Mainwaring, *Italian Landscape in Eighteenth-Century England* (New York, 1925)

Timothy Mowl, *William Beckford: Composing for Mozart* (1998)

Ian Ousby, *The Englishman's England: Taste, Travel and the Rise of Tourism* (1990)

Michael Symes, *William Gilpin at Painshill: The Gardens in 1772* (1994)

David Watkin, *The English Vision: The Picturesque in Architecture, Landscape and Garden Design* (1982)

Articles

Mavis Batey, 'The Picturesque: An Overview', *Garden History*, **22**, 2 (1994), pp. 121–32

David Lambert, '"The Poet's Feeling": Aspects of the Picturesque in Contemporary Literature, 1794–1816', *Garden History*, **24**, 1 (1996), pp. 82–99

Nikolaus Pevsner, 'The Genius of the Picturesque', *Architectural Review*, June 1944

Sophieke Piebenga, 'William Swarey Gilpin (1762–1843): Picturesque Improver', *Garden History*, **22**, 2 (1994), pp. 175–96

Elisabeth Whittle, '"All these inchanting scenes": Piercefield in the Wye Valley', *Garden History*, **24**, 1 (1996), pp. 148–61

CHAPTER FOURTEEN

Primary Printed Sources

William Mason, *The English Garden* (1783)

Humphry Repton, *Sketches and Hints on Landscape Gardening* (1794)

——, *Observations on the Theory and Practice of Landscape Gardening* (1803)

——, *An Enquiry into the Changes of Taste in Landscape Gardening* (1806)

Humphry Repton & John Adey Repton, *Fragments on the Theory and Practice of Landscape Gardening* (1816)

Secondary Printed Sources

George Carter (ed.), *Humphry Repton, Landscape Gardener 1752–1818* (1982)

Stephen Daniels, *Humphry Repton: Landscape Gardening and the Geography of Georgian England* (New Haven, CT, & London, 1999)

Edward Hyams, *Humphry Repton and Capability Brown* (1971)

Mark Laird, *The Flowering of the Landscape Garden: English Pleasure Grounds 1720–1800* (Philadelphia, PA, 1999)

Edward Malins (ed.), *The Red Books of Humphry Repton* (1976)

Dorothy Stroud, *Humphry Repton* (1975)

Nigel Temple, *John Nash and the Village Picturesque* (Gloucester, 1979)

Articles

Hazel Fryer, 'Humphry Repton's Commissions in Herefordshire: Picturesque Landscape Aesthetics', *Garden History*, **22**, 2 (1994), pp. 162–74

John Harris, '"Gardenesque": the Case of Charles Greville's Garden at Gloucester', *Journal of Garden History*, **1**, 2 (1981), pp. 167–78

——, 'Garden of the Mason School: Stoke Park, Buckinghamshire', *Country Life*, 3 October 1985

John Dixon Hunt (ed.), 'Humphry Repton', *Journal of Garden History*, **16**, 3 (1996)

John Phibbs, 'A Reconsideration of Repton's Contribution to the Improvements at Felbrigg, Norfolk, 1778–84', *Garden History*, **13,** 1 (1985), pp. 33–44

Nigel Temple, 'Humphry Repton, Illustrator, and William Peacock's *Polite Repository*, 1790–1811', *Garden History*, **16**, 2 (1988), pp. 161–73

INDEX

Page numbers in *italic* indicate illustrations and captions